Ownership and Nurture

Ownership and Nurture
Studies in Native Amazonian Property Relations

Edited by
Marc Brightman, Carlos Fausto
and Vanessa Grotti

berghahn
NEW YORK · OXFORD
www.berghahnbooks.com

First published in 2016 by
Berghahn Books
www.berghahnbooks.com

© 2016, 2020 Marc Brightman, Carlos Fausto and Vanessa Grotti
First paperback edition published in 2020

All rights reserved. Except for the quotation of short passages for the purposes of criticism and review, no part of this book may be reproduced in any form or by any means, electronic or mechanical, including photocopying, recording, or any information storage and retrieval system now known or to be invented, without written permission of the publisher.

Library of Congress Cataloging-in-Publication Data

Names: Brightman, Marc, editor. | Fausto, Carlos, editor. | Grotti, Vanessa Elisa, editor.
Title: Ownership and nurture : studies in native Amazonian property relations / edited by Marc Brightman, Carlos Fausto and Vanessa Grotti.
Description: New York : Berghahn Books, 2016. | Includes bibliographical references and index.
Identifiers: LCCN 2015045877| ISBN 9781785330834 (hardback : alk. paper) | ISBN 9781785330841 (ebook)
Subjects: LCSH: Indians of South America—Material culture—Amazon River Region. | Indians of South America—Land tenure—Amazon River Region. | Material culture—Amazon River Region. | Land tenure—Amazon River Region.
Classification: LCC F2230.1.M34 O86 2016 | DDC 981/.13—dc23
LC record available at hjp://lccn.loc.gov/2015045877

British Library Cataloguing in Publication Data

A catalogue record for this book is available from the British Library

ISBN 978-1-78533-083-4 hardback
ISBN 978-1-78920-754-5 paperback
ISBN 978-1-78533-084-1 ebook

Contents

List of Figures vii

Foreword by James Leach ix

Acknowledgements xiii

Introduction. Altering Ownership in Amazonia 1
Marc Brightman, Carlos Fausto and Vanessa Grotti

1. Masters, Slaves and Real People: Native Understandings of Ownership and Humanness in Tropical American Capturing Societies 36
Fernando Santos-Granero

2. First Contacts, Slavery and Kinship in North-Eastern Amazonia 63
Vanessa Grotti and Marc Brightman

3. Fabricating Necessity: Feeding and Commensality in Western Amazonia 81
Luiz Costa

4. Parasitism and Subjection: Modes of Paumari Predation 110
Oiara Bonilla

5. How Much for a Song? The Culture of Calculation and the Calculation of Culture 133
Carlos Fausto

6. The Forgotten Pattern and the Stolen Design: Contract, Exchange and Creativity Among the Kĩsêdjê 156
Marcela Stockler Coelho de Souza

7. Doubles and Owners: Relations of Knowledge, Property and Authorship among the Marubo 186
Pedro de Niemeyer Cesarino

8. Ownership and Wellbeing among the Mebêngôkre-Xikrin:
   Differentiation and Ritual Crisis   209
   Cesar Gordon

9. Temporalities of Ownership: Land Possession and its
   Transformations among the Tupinambá (Bahia, Brazil)   232
   Susana de Matos Viegas

Index   257

Figures

5.1 Aluminium pans received by the owners of the *Takwaga* festival. Kuikuro village of Ipatse, Xingu Indigenous Park, Brazil, 1998. Photo: Carlos Fausto. 136

5.2 A young woman with chiefly status leading an internal *luki*. Kuikuro Village of Ipatse, Xingu Indigenous Park, Brazil, 2013. Photo: Carlos Fausto. 138

5.3 Matü confects the *akunga,* the shamanic doll. Kuikuro Village of Ipatse, Xingu Indigenous Park, Brazil, 2002. Photo: Carlos Fausto. 140

5.4 Kanu sings during a Jamugikumalu festival. Kuikuro Village of Ipatse, Xingu Indigenous Park, Brazil, 2010. Photo: Carlos Fausto. 146

6.1 A Kĩsêdjê couple in full regalia. *Kĩsêdjê Kapẽrẽ: alfabetização na língua suyá.* São Paulo: ISA/Fafo, 1999. 159

6.2 *Anhi ro kütêmtêm,* 'a spiral on me.' Drawing: Wetanti Suyá, 2006. 161

6.3 *Tepsók nhõ sókó,* 'wooden lip plug design.' Drawing: Wetamtxi Suyá, 2006. 161

6.4 *Anhi ro roptxi,* 'a jaguar on me.' Drawing: Wetantxi Suyá, 2006. 161

6.5 Recreating the *Pyj* design: the *si* pattern. Ngôjhwêrê village, Xingu Indigenous Park, Brazil, 2006. Photo: M.S. Coelho de Souza. 164

6.6 Recreating the *Pyj* design: filling in the *si* with the *kango* pattern. Ngôjhwêrê village, Xingu Indigenous Park, Brazil, 2006. Photo: M.S. Coelho de Souza. 164

6.7	The *sīpê* and *kajngōrō* design patterns. Ngôjhwêrê village, Xingu Indigenous Park, Brazil, 2006. Photo: M.S. Coelho de Souza.	165
6.8	Formal transformations of the *Pyj* pattern. Drawing: M.S. Coelho de Souza, 2009.	166
6.9	The chief Kuiussi painted with the *anhi ro kũntêmtêm* and the *ndo sôkô* patterns. Ngôjhwêrê village, Xingu Indigenous Park, Brazil, 2007. Photo: M.S. Coelho de Souza.	176
6.10	The facial pattern *ndo sôkô*. Drawing produced during the Grendene workshop, Ngôjhwêrê village, Xingu Indigenous Park, Brazil, 2006. Photo: M.S. Coelho de Souza.	176
6.11	The lip plug design painted on the Wadubati's back. Ngôjhwêrê village, Xingu Indigenous Park, Brazil, 2007. Photo: M.S. Coelho de Souza.	177
7.1	Paulino Joaquim Memãpa, 'Earth Planting Spirits.' Coloured pencil, graphite and watercolour on paper, 210 x 297 mm, 2005. Collection of Pedro Cesarino.	190
7.2	Paulino Memãpa, 'The Emergence of Kana Voã.' Coloured pencil, graphite and felt tip pen on paper, 210 x 297 mm, 2005. Collection of Pedro Cesarino.	191
9.1	A dwelling place. Diagram by Susana Matos Viegas.	237
9.2	Genealogical diagram showing distant places of residence in the territory. Diagram by Susana Matos Viegas.	242
9.3	A non-plastered *casa de sopapo* or *casa de taipa de mão*. Bahia, Brazil, 1998. Photo: Susana Matos Viegas.	243
9.4	The hole from which clay was extracted for a home in a kin-based dwelling. Acuípe, Bahia, Brazil, 2004. Photo: Susana Matos Viegas.	244

Foreword

Ownership and nurture.
What if we begin here, rather than with the Lockean assumption of nature, commonly given to be appropriated by human labour? What if ownership did not take for its template a world of human subjects in rightful control over inanimate objects, but the nurture of kin, or of animals? What if nurture also implied superiority, or even capture? Or it implied mutual dependence: an externalized capacity for self-definition? These are questions this volume suggests we should ask. And then, what happens when ownership over other persons linked to nurture is absolute and institutionalized? Or objects directly constitute human persons through their ability to inscribe human qualities? Or when owning comes in many different forms? When in fact 'the form and nature of transactions defines the relationships between the objects and transactors involved'?[1] Well, for a start we will need to think again about what property, ownership and *belonging* implies, how it is achieved, and under what circumstances.

Just for a moment, imagine that all that you are, your very flesh and blood, your body and all that you know, arise and have their origins in specific other people. (Is this so far-fetched?). Those other people have laboured to produce you, have dedicated their capacities and efforts to the production of your existence. The substance that makes and sustains your body, the foods that give it solidity and have grown it, the knowledge that allows you to do anything: *this* is what connects you to those other people. Your status as a human being is dependent upon the recognition of this reality. There is nothing exclusive about your body because it is always the outcome and interest of others. In turn, what you do with your body is not only influenced by the ongoing history of your emergence in relation to other people (and powers) but actually *only possible* because of those relations. Close family take different roles in constituting the very body you operate. More distant kin provide other elements appropriate to their relation and interest in you. Your body is always their interest, and whatever you can produce has to be thought about in terms of how you can acknowledge and reciprocate their involvement. This reciprocation may occur through your own nurture of distant others. In this scenario, knowing and acting on recognition of other people's difference, their capacity for nurture or action, is what it *is* to be a human being. And just as you are owned and owed to others, all those whom you yourself – in your extended form of already being many other people – nurture, feed, advise, offer company or land or labour to, are parts of you.

Now think of how 'ownership' looks under these conditions. A complex system of overlapping and intertwined interests results in nothing like private property, common property or communal ownership. The complexity in the abstract is boggling, but this lived, 'ownership' manifests in daily motivations and caregiving, in long-term projects to make public displays or reciprocations, in positive obligations and positive enmities, in the give and take and morality of kinship that is also 'economy', 'politics' and 'creativity'. We are forced to rethink the most fundamental assumptions about our own lives and our anthropology. And all this is (only) one imagined rendering of a possible foundation for 'ownership', one made possible (in this case) through ethnographic analysis in a contemporary small language group on the north coast of Papua New Guinea.

The expert analysis of South American societies, contextualized within a comparative anthropological frame as happens in the chapters to follow, fosters just such a generative exposure of complex conceptual and social relations. Relations where responsibility, multiplicity and belonging, ownership and nurture, are key. They allow us to rethink what it is to be human.

In the volume you are about to read, we find different versions of belonging and its rationale in South America. They are eloquently rendered. Reading these chapters is a matter of conceptualizing the coming into being of different social forms. We are offered analysis of the principles that shape the emergence of persons and art forms, hierarchy, and conviviality. Acts of nurture, morality, obligation, dependence, control; practices of self and other: all figure in distinctly Amazonian ways. They are examples that help us rethink bodies and personhood. They help us reconceptualize the *cosmological* basis of different forms of ownership. The chapters offer detailed and sophisticated studies that allow insight into many different versions of ownership. They have the kind of depth that invites fundamental questions.

If we can suspend our usual assumptions, it is possible to approach ownership as the general, inclusive category *to be defined* with close attention to the ethnographic material at hand. The excitement and interest of doing so lie in the depth to which one must delve into a social form to reveal and make present the possibilities of conceiving of human beings in diverse and vital ways. For me, 'property' is not the general term for analysis, as property is already part of the particular histories of several modes of conceptualizing, institutionalizing, and practising ownership over both people and things. To clearly define a version of property as a particular historically situated form of ownership makes it possible to compare, for example, a Roman notion of the person, the state, and responsibility, with forms of control over the person, or the power of disposal over persons, in Amazonian societies. In each case, this 'property' is a specific case of power and control over a special category of person. In the latter, it seems clear that this was not a matter of 'economic' gain, but the production of kin and the incorporation of the life force of the 'other'. That makes it a distinct form of ownership. It might have correspondence to Roman property but cannot be simply said to 'be' 'property'.[2]

In turn, to realize the specificity of 'private property' as a particular form incorporating possessive individualism and a construction of a particular subject/object distinction, is also to locate it within a specific history – that is, not to propose it as a universal form, but rather to be specific about elements such as spirit's distinction from matter, the role of the state as guarantor, or the reliance on the notion of 'nature'. All these have effects on people's relations with respect to 'things'. This volume offers insight into many other forms of ownership. Private property is clearly an inadequate conceptual tool with which to approach them. That is not to deny that possession, appropriation, inequality, objects, subjects, *or any other factor an analyst might choose to isolate* can or does exist in other forms of ownership. But it offers a healthy corrective to the dominant view of private property as a universally practised institution. To put it simply, the choice of *ownership and nurture* as the key references throws many other modes of being human into relief, making them apparent. A focus on these terms helps to distinguish property from other modes of ownership. As Melanesianists theorizing the person have often argued, what is of interest is the specific configuration of factors produced by and producing the social, political, and economic organizations they partake of, not advancement or refutation of the validity of one or another universal mode of human organisation.

To be specific about one form of ownership and its historical situation is also to open the genuine possibility of comparison across forms, times and regions, and to invite considered explication of the composition of particular social forms. Possessive individualism is not an inevitable outcome of humans' interactions with their environment, or with each other. For all Locke's argument for the rationality of property, of its appearing to be a natural consequence of the need for survival (and therefore appropriation) – that very sense of its fitness, its 'naturalness' – emerged from a series of assumptions about origins, a cosmological imagination that could only ever be one version of human possibility. The chapters collected here present other cases, other origin points and therefore specific cosmological imaginations with their own obvious (to those involved) ramifications for the right and natural connection between persons and between persons and things.

The authors eschew conventional notions of property through an attention to a wider category of ownership. They reveal how ownership is embedded in assumptions about the person, the political, growth and support, and the subject. These assumptions are made visible through ethnographic analysis that confounds simple binary oppositions between subjects and objects, or labour and nature. What follows is a further possibility. That is, the realization that distinctions between common and private property, collective and individual ownership, property in persons and property in things, are also inadequately narrow for the lived realities of ownership. In these chapters, who one is, how that is calculated, and what forms connections to others (and the powers of the world) take, have inseparable, form-generating presence in the practice and conceptualization of being human. The chapters suggest intelligent and imaginative engagement with complex ethnographic realities of 'ownership' as a multifaceted and almost primal factor in different modes of being human. Of course! Power, concern, care, agency, action, responsibility and creativity flow from the organization of people in relation to one another, and in relation to things. This inevitably involves connection and attempts at control. Whether one owns or is owned by spirits, the connection is undeniable and fundamental. The variability of connection and the effects of these modes are part of the variety and diversity of human being. In these engrossing chapters, a profound truth is made visible in superbly generative ways. They offer both multiple possibilities for understanding an 'ownership relation in the Amazonian sense of the word'[3] and an irresistible ground for further comparative effort.

James Leach
Perth, July 2015

Notes

1. Editors' introduction, this volume. See also Hirsch and Strathern 2004.
2. It remains to be seen whether projecting Amerindian captivity onto the category of slavery does or does not eclipse the originality of the indigenous relational structures of dependency.
3. Fausto, this volume.

Acknowledgements

This book has been a long time in the making, and many people have helped us along the way. The project was originally conceived by Marc Brightman and Vanessa Grotti as a panel for the American Anthropological Association's annual meeting in Philadephia in 2009, but when this was abandoned due to lack of travel funding, Carlos Fausto suggested holding a workshop together the following April at his own institution, the Museu Nacional in Rio de Janeiro. The workshop was entitled 'Relações (im)próprias: propriedade e bem-viver na Amazônia', and everyone who participated contributed a chapter to this book. The successful organization of 'Relações (im)próprias' was made possible by the dynamism and devotion of Luana Almeida and Caco Xavier. We also wish to thank all who took part in the exceptionally rich discussion at the workshop. The workshop was funded by PPGAS-MN/UFRJ and FINEP, and Marc Brightman and Vanessa Grotti received travel funding from the ESRC and the British Academy.

INTRODUCTION

Altering Ownership in Amazonia

Marc Brightman, Carlos Fausto and Vanessa Grotti

> What if there were other possible forms of rights between people concerning things ... besides the ones we have built in the last three centuries? What if there is no boolean logic to be expected here, not just a yes or no possibility?
> —Carneiro da Cunha, *'Culture' and Culture*

This book revolves around two concepts: ownership and nurture. The objective is twofold. On one hand, it is an attempt to bring these concepts, as they appear in the anthropological literature and as they are expressed in indigenous practices and concepts, into dialogue (and into tension). On the other hand, it is to articulate them, investigating the practical and emotional nexus that exists between ownership and nurture in native Amazonia. Since the end of the 1980s, certain aspects of what is expressed by the idea of nurture have been explored in the regional ethnography in processual studies of kinship, especially with regard to intimate relations within the so-called 'domestic sphere'. A rich literature has grown around notions such as care, feeding and commensality, focusing on the processes through which identity and kinship are constituted (e.g. Gow 1991; McCallum 2001; Vilaça 2002). However, such notions do not reveal the full sociological implications of processes of nurture in Amazonia, which frequently also articulate asymmetrical relations of ownership or mastery.

Until recently indigenous Amazonia appeared refractory to the idea of ownership. This image results as much from the theoretical options available as from empirical phenomena with their own historicity. A substantial part of the ethnographic record of Amazonia coincides with the indigenous peoples' demographic nadir since the beginning of the Conquest. This was reached between the 1940s and the 1960s. Only in the 1970s did the downward trend begin to reverse itself. A large number of the studies written towards the end of the twentieth century strongly reflect this historical moment, during which indigenous Amazonia was characterized by small, mutually isolated populations in the wake of the breakdown of native social networks through the process of colonization

(Fausto and Heckenberger 2007). At the time, this historical situation was seen as corresponding to an original state expressing an essential characteristic of Amazonian societies: their aversion to power, to hierarchy and, of course, to property.[1] It was this conjuncture between a historical situation and an anthropological imaginary that made Amazonia seem a *terra nullius* for the concepts of ownership and mastery.

Towards the end of the 1980s, this imaginary began to change. The first impulses came from the 'historical turn' in anthropology (Ortner 1984) and from the criticisms of 'ethnographic projection' in archaeology (Roosevelt 1989). The past came knocking on the door once again, and the comfortable illusion that we were studying something like an essence of indigenous sociality was progressively abandoned.[2] To a large extent, the historicist wave that heated up anthropological temporality was the product of a global sociohistorical warming that was also felt in the indigenous realities of the time. For those who began their research in Amazonia in the 1980s (as one of us did), the comparison with the present is surprising. Not only have indigenous populations grown since then, but they have extended their networks of interconnection at broadband-like speed (literally, given that the Internet has reached some Amazonian villages in the twenty-first century). A new rhythm of transformation has been imposed upon, and at the same time actively sought by, native Amazonians, giving rise to what some Amerindians call the 'time of projects', which has succeeded the 'time of slavery', the 'time of rubber' and the 'time of FUNAI'.[3] In this new time, 'project' and 'culture' have become keywords.

The 'time of projects' is linked to the virtualization of value and knowledge in postindustrial capitalism – that is, to the growing predominance of intangible goods over manufactured items – and to its correlative tendency, the 'becoming-property' of the immaterial. In the wake of this process, the Western notion of ownership came to have growing practical impact in the villages, especially in the guise of 'intangible heritage' or 'cultural property'.[4] Many projects of NGOs and anthropologists today revolve around these concepts, which are the object of negotiation, tension and invention, as we shall see in some chapters of this book (Coelho de Souza, Fausto). More broadly, property became a theme of the most acute importance for indigenous peoples in general. Whether it be a matter of de jure ownership or de facto possession of objects tangible (e.g. land) or intangible (e.g. knowledge), indigenous peoples are almost by definition engaged in a struggle for ownership and control of resources. Many claims to indigenous identity themselves are claims to prior habitation and, by implication, prior possession of territory in relation to colonizing peoples and states. Moreover, claims to property are in this context also often highly emotive claims to identity (Harrison 1999; Rowlands

2004), perhaps because of Western legal frameworks' 'tendency to flatten difference in the interests of procedural uniformity' (Brown 2004: 60).[5]

In this book, we aim not only to understand these contemporary negotiations around the notion of heritage and property, but also to analyse the indigenous concepts and practices that pre-date (and predate upon) them and form the basis from which new translational and creative processes are established. If the notion of ownership gained visibility in Amazonia largely through this new interethnic dynamic, our hypothesis is that it was always fundamental in the constitution of these societies, and that it is bound up with processes of nurture (Brightman 2010; Fausto 2008, 2012a). Ethnographic accounts of Amazonia have often bypassed or ignored the question of property or ownership, appearing to confirm early anthropologists' and early modern political theorists' assumptions that property was absent in 'primitive' societies. But what do we make of native social systems in which a different relation of ownership is pervasive and plays a structuring role?

Ownership in Perspective

Western regimes of ownership have specific and well-documented histories. What Maine presents as a universal progression from 'status' to 'contract' stands as a rough guide to the Western history of property relations. His critical narrative begins with the Roman legal theory of 'natural modes of acquisition', focusing on one of these, *Occupatio* (occupancy), which he defines as 'the advisedly taking possession of that which at the moment is the property of no man, with the view ... of acquiring property in it for yourself' (1912 [1861]: 259). He further notes that this informs the theory of the Origin of Property, which is at once a popular theory and the one most accepted by jurists. According to such ideas, occupancy would be 'the process by which the "no man's goods" of the primitive world became the private property of individuals in the world of history' (264), a definition that illustrates well the assumption on which the colonial (and postcolonial) acquisition of indigenous land was based. However, as Maine argues, occupancy is grounded on two assumptions: first, that it must have been a 'growth of a refined jurisprudence and of a settled condition of the laws', because it is based on an established assumption that 'all things are presumed to be somebody's property' (269); and second, that the actors involved are individuals. In fact, he asserts, 'there is a strong *à priori* [sic] improbability of our obtaining any clue to the early history of property, if we confine our notice to the proprietary rights of individuals' (271).

The presence of the individual as the basic unit of property relations becomes more thoroughly embedded with the rise of capitalism, and much writing about ownership, both legal and sociological, continues to take this for granted. To facilitate our comparative aim, let us take the image of property in capitalism suggested by MacPherson, who coined one of the most influential expressions to refer to this regime: 'possessive individualism'. MacPherson (1962: 3) argues that the central difficulty of modern liberal-democratic theory is its 'possessive quality', which 'is found in its conception of the individual as essentially the proprietor of his own person or capacities, owing nothing to society for them'.[6]

In liberal states, something approaching this view of the individual is at the heart of common-sense and modern legal assumptions about the nature of ownership, with reference to both material and immaterial objects. It underlies the concepts of authorship and creativity expressed in intellectual property law (Cesarino this volume), and through the Lockean process of 'mixing' part of oneself with the land through labour, it underpins property law – particularly in those regimes in which land is appropriated through enclosure and cultivation (Viegas this volume). When Locke, in his second Treatise (1988 [1689]), laid out his definition of the ownership and individuation of property, he was giving lucid expression to a practice that existed in both the wave of land enclosures taking place in England at the time, and the creation of colonial plantations.[7] Indeed, the conquest of the Americas played a significant role in the emergence of modern European modes of thought on the subject of ownership and appropriation. Tully (1993: 166) argues that 'Locke's concepts of political society and property are, among other things, a sophisticated theoretical expression of the basic arguments of early colonial writers.' Sixteenth-century intellectuals tried hard to fit the native American peoples into their existing cosmological categories. This story is less simple than usually depicted. Sometimes Amerindians were characterized as nonhumans or 'natural' slaves (both of which were unfit to own property; see Pagden 1982), but at other times they were granted fully human status (though not the same rights).[8]

When Locke (1988: II, 5, §49) wrote that 'in the beginning all the world was *America*', Amerindian humanity was not at stake any more, but the relation to property was. Amerindians were taken as living in the state of nature, before the individuation of property through labour. God gave the world to men in common, but, says Locke, 'it cannot be supposed that He meant it should always remain common and uncultivated. He gave it to the use of the *Industrious* and *Rational* (and *Labour* was to be his *Title* to it) ...' (II, 5, §34). If Amerindians do not labour on individual parcels, they own nothing – the land remains vacant and can rightfully be appropriated. The denial of different forms of ownership over land was necessary to impose the idea of property as private and exclusive. This idea would have a long-term consequence for indigenous people and is still today a matter of intense conflict in Latin America.[9]

Among all types of property, immovable, 'real' property is what has been paradigmatic in Western thought, the transformation and enclosure of land being foundational events for Locke's and Rousseau's accounts of inequality and the State. Territorial rights are fiercely contested in the Amazon and elsewhere. Such disputes are fought on the terms of mainstream notions of ownership of land. Indeed, the very notion of land ownership and the need for it are held to arise only through the consequences of a market economy. From the point of view of monetized, market society, land that falls under a different regime of ownership is not owned at all, but wasted. The kinds of disputes that affect indigenous peoples in Amazonia hinge on the encounter between, on one hand, the imperatives of market society (whether they take the form of small-scale peasant, agro-industrial frontier, logging or mining interests), and on the other hand, something else more heterogeneous and less easy to define: a way of inhabiting a place that cannot be simply defined as an extension of land, for it is constituted by multiple relations of ownership between humans and nonhumans.

What Hann (1998: 1) calls the 'dominant liberal paradigm', which emphasizes 'free individuals, competitive markets, pluralistic civil societies and the "rule of law",' has been actively promoted through international diplomacy and development aid, and exported from the United States and Europe with something approaching missionary zeal (Rist 2008). In many disciplines discussions of property are limited in application to 'mature Western societies and in particular to the United States', and emphasize 'control, privacy and individuality ... pos[ing] hazards for cross-cultural application' (Munzer 1990: 8). But private property and liberal ideology remain less widely accepted than it would appear from the debates between their proponents and detractors (Hann 1998: 2). The discipline of legal pluralism, for instance, has produced an important body of work on the differences and relationships between property regimes in established national legal systems. Beyond this, it has brought recognition that property rights are dynamic rather than stable, and that they cannot always be neatly separated into categories such as public and private, collective and individual (Geisler and Daneker 2000).[10]

Recent approaches to property have explored systemic interdependencies through empirical studies that show the role of kinship, document and examine concrete examples of legal pluralism, and problematize the State as the holder of privileged rights in all property.[11] Building on this work, von Benda Beckmann, von Benda Beckmann and Wiber (2006: 14) provide the following definition of property: 'Property in the most general sense concerns the ways in which the relations between society's members with respect to valuables are given form and significance'.[12] In these terms, property should be understood as a 'general analytical category', like 'economy, marriage, religion, household and law' (32, fn. 14). These authors regard it as having three main elements: social units that can hold property rights and obligations (individuals, groups, lineages, corporations, states); the construction of valuables as property objects; and sets of rights and obligations that social units can have with respect to such objects (15). Thus property serves as a cover term for different arrangements in diverse social and historical settings. They argue that property's nature differs at distinct 'layers of social organisation': the 'legal/institutional', the 'concrete' (social relationships), and the 'ideological', and that these layers must be kept analytically separate. While we agree that their methodology improves on the dominant view of property-by-numbers and believe it can provide a comparative framework, the ethnographic material presented in this volume exposes its limitations, for it shows that 'layers of social organisation' cannot always be separated out and undermines any claims of the universal validity of categories such as property, economy or law. In lowland South America, as in Melanesia for example (Leach 2011), it may be preferable to distinguish between 'ownership' as a general area of inquiry implying the investigation of conceptions of (and) rights in things, persons and so forth, and 'private property' as a specific mode of ownership with implications of possessive individualism and a particular construction of the subject/object distinction.[13]

If the heyday of globalization theory saw some anthropologists get caught up in the seductive imagery of capital flows arising from the consequences of neoliberal deregulation, other strands of anthropology offered a way of attaining the conceptual friction needed to understand concrete changes. Strathern's (1996) work on property did precisely this: she advocated trying to understand social networks through the ways in which they were 'cut' by property relations, which give them form and definition. Ownership emerges from the anthropological analysis as above all a relational phenomenon. On one level property rights are relations between persons with regard to things (or other persons), but on another level they are produced and transformed by relationships between indigenous groups and the State, and between property regimes, even as they play an important role in articulating intercultural relations themselves. As Hirsch and Strathern (2004: 7) put it, at this conjuncture 'for the social scientist, property has become a dangerously interesting term to use'.

It has likewise become 'dangerously interesting' for Amerindians in the wake of new uses (and abuses) introduced by intellectual property rights and cultural heritage policies. In relation to states and nonindigenous society, 'indigenous culture' itself has been transformed into a form of property as 'heritage' (Brown 1998), leading to its commodification and to states picking and choosing aspects of 'heritage' they consider worth protecting (Engle 2010: 141ff.).[14] Carneiro da Cunha's (2009) essay on culture and 'culture' illustrates some of the perils of such a relational strategy. As she notes, the Convention for Biological Diversity in 1992 marked a decisive moment in the history of the emergence of indigenous claims to ownership over traditional knowledge. Although it referred to 'holders' rather than 'proprietors' of traditional knowledge, 'transactions over traditional knowledge, whether they involve informed consent for research or contracts for benefit sharing, actually produce a relation approaching ownership' (Carneiro da Cunha 2009: 9). The terms of subsequent debates and political and legal struggles remained set by Euro-American conceptual frameworks and 'metropolitan ideas', which greatly influenced the notion of indigenous rights; thus, '[s]imply put, indigenous knowledge is conceptualized as the negative of mainstream prevailing ideas. As such, indigenous people seem inextricably destined to impersonate the obverse of capitalism's possessive individualistic assumptions' (27). Reasoning as if 'the obverse of the individual were everywhere the collective', the mainstream conceptualization of indigenous knowledge offers indigenous peoples 'one of two choices: collective intellectual property rights or a commons regime', leading indigenous peoples to argue pragmatically for the former (28).

Within the movement to protect traditional knowledge, which emerged from the 1980s, some tried to address the fact that indigenous peoples had different concepts of property. This led to the term 'property' being dropped, although issues of ownership and control were still being discussed in practical terms. In the early 1990s, for example, the Global Coalition for Bio-Cultural Diversity created a Working Group on Intellectual Property Rights, but its name soon changed to the Working Group on Traditional, Cultural and Scientific Resource Rights. As Posey and Dutfield (1996: 3) explain, '[t]he term "property" in IPR was dropped, because property for indigenous peoples frequently has intangible, spiritual manifestations, and, although worthy of protection, is *inalienable* or can belong to no human being. Instead, the term "traditional resource rights" (TRR) was adopted to reflect the necessity of rethinking the limited and limiting concept of IPR' (original emphasis).

Read in the light of the material presented in this book, this passage illustrates how even the most sensitive and best informed attempts to reconcile indigenous culture with the categories of international law suffer from the inescapable rigidity of these categories and their assumptions about temporality: namely, that institutions and relationships do not – or should not – change over time; or else that they should retain a particular status for a fixed period at the end of which they abruptly expire, rather than transforming dynamically.[15] It may be true that some forms of indigenous Amazonian property are indeed alienable, but this is sometimes negotiable in terms that are opaque or invisible to Euro-American observers because what is owned is not so much things themselves as relations. In other words, intangible property relations are less relations between people with regard to things than they are rights over relationships (Coelho da Souza, Cesarino, this volume).

Property in Amazonia

Before the rise of 'modern' ethnology in Amazonia, the *Handbook of South American Indians* included in its comparative volume a chapter on 'Property among Tropical Forest and Marginal Tribes', by Robert Lowie (1949: 351), organized 'under the familiar categories of Real Estate, Chattels, Incorporeal Property, and Inheritance'. Despite using only data from the first half of the century, it shows surprising analytical sophistication. Of particular relevance is Lowie's discussion of the third category, in which he analyses ownership relations in regard to songs, spells, names and ritual prerogatives.[16]

It is possible to argue that the subsequent neglect of indigenous forms of ownership in Amazonian ethnology derives, at least in part, from the low tangibility of property in the region, which led it to pass almost unnoticed until the recent dawn of global concern with intellectual and cultural property (Hann 1998: 5). This would not have been the case, however, if we had paid attention to Lowie's much earlier article, 'Incorporeal Property in Primitive Societies', originally published in the *Yale Law Journal* in 1928, in which he starts by challenging Morgan's statement that property rights were weakly developed in primitive societies, contesting the 'dogma of general primitive communism' by affirming the 'wide prevalence of individually owned forms of incorporeal property' (1960: 228). Lowie then focuses on examples of ceremonial prerogatives among North American indigenous peoples, showing how different this form of ownership is from what he calls 'absolute ownership'. Discussing the case of the Blackfoot sacred bundles (evocative, of course, of Maine's 'bundles of rights'), he observes:

> Only by this quasi-apostolic succession can the rapport with the supernatural world be maintained; hence an invasion of copyright would not help insure the blessings – longevity, health, and happiness – linked with authorized ownership. On the other hand, the genuine proprietor cannot lose the benefits connected with a bundle: 'the bundle may be lost or destroyed without seriously damaging the owner, since he owns the ritual which is immaterial. (1960: 231–32)

The transference of the 'sacred bundles' implies a double relationship (between two persons and with a supernatural source), which authorizes ownership but does not make it absolute. In the same vein, Lowie states that 'Dr. Malinowski demonstrates conclusively that the *toli-waga* or 'canoe-owner', to use the nearest English equivalent, is not an absolute owner' (236), since his maternal kinsmen have a strong claim on the object. The owner cannot cut his canoe from his kinship network in order to own it as her exclusive private property. Contrary to Locke's proprietory model, the individual here does not even exclusively own her or his (own) body.

Lowie lays the groundwork for discussion on both 'incorporeal' and 'corporeal' property in Amazonia, which often cannot be clearly differentiated within a given ethnographic context. In very contemporary language, he writes in an article in the *Handbook* that '[t]he stock in trade of a medicine man can be classed under the head of chattels when viewed as tangible objects or as incorporeal property insofar as a vision or other supernatural sanction copyrights their use' (1949: 360). There are thus different 'things' owned, but not necessarily different regimes of ownership according to each category. Fausto's (2008, 2012a) general model of ownership relations in Amazonia is meant to apply to societies both 'object-poor', like the Parakanã (2001, 2012b), and 'object-rich', like the Wauja of the Upper Xingu (Barcelos Neto 2008).[17]

At this level of our investigations, then, we are not concerned with identifying or classifying different regimes of ownership (or 'property') in Amazonia. We agree with Hugh-Jones's critique (2013) of the overgeneralization of a single social formation for the whole region. He is certainly correct in affirming that the characterization of Amazonia as devoid of objects mediating social relationships does not apply across space or through time. Indeed, there are areas, such as the Upper Xingu and North-West Amazonia, in which the 'principle of substitution' (Godelier 1982; Lemonnier 1990) between persons and things operates on many levels. In these areas, objects have transcontextual value, serving for the acquisition of other artefacts or services, and for compensation for marriage and offences, thus multiplying the modes of generating and maintaining social ties. Although these cases may seem different from the current standard model of Amazonian societies, we believe that at this point they must be treated together, so this book dedicates three chapters to them (Coelho de Souza, Fausto, Gordon).

The absence of property as a subject of Amazonian ethnology also derives from a number of theoretical choices and the feeble influence of Marxism in the region's anthropology. A good illustration of this is the attack that Pierre Clastres launched on Maurice Godelier, in which he argued that it was absurd to analyse societies such as those of Amazonia or Melanesia through a framework deriving from the study of the history of Western industrial capitalism. In so doing he correctly criticized the Marxist assumption of a universal history, but he implicitly denied the possibility that some sort of ownership might play a key role in non-Western societies (and histories) (Clastres 1977). Clastres' main *combat* was political, aiming at the pervasive idea that 'the State is the destiny of every society' (1977: 159). He inverted the terms of evolutionary theories of State formation so that 'primitive society' could *not* be said to lack a centralized power, but to positively conjure it in order to avoid the division of society into rulers and ruled. Clastres was right to criticize the depiction of 'primitive society' in negative terms. However, his 'against-ology' was too centred upon the State and left little space for conceptualizing the kind of power relations that pervaded these societies. Property was perforce absent from Clastres' picture – rightly so, were we to limit it to a model of exclusive property rights (or 'absolute ownership', to use Lowie's expression). But once we set out to investigate alternative regimes of ownership, different ways of establishing relations between persons and things surface.[18]

Whatever the reasons for the exclusion of ownership from the majority of works relating to Amazonia, the resurgence of anthropological interest in property through the late 1990s and early 2000s spurred certain Amazonia specialists to explore the regional case more thoroughly. Fausto's interest in ownership emerged out of his study of predation as a moment in a movement of appropriation and familiarization (1999, 2007), and as is likewise true for Costa (2007) and Cesarino (this volume), out of the empirical observation of the importance of indigenous concepts of ownership as they express themselves in proliferating fractal relationships of mastery. Like these authors, Brightman (2010) approached property in Amazonia by letting go of the concept's theoretical baggage and exploring an ethnographically grounded theory of property in the manner of Rivière's (1993) seminal exhortation to 'Amerindianise' kinship concepts. He thus proposed that property is a structuring feature of these societies, but in a very different way from what we have come to expect from Euro-American practices, ideologies and norms (Brightman 2010). This difference lies partly in the relationship to time. That property relations must be constantly renewed and reiterated is arguably a feature of all property systems, but in Amazonia it is more explicitly articulated. Property itself appears as a process (Viegas this volume), that is, a way of establishing relations between persons by provisionally cutting relations between people and things. Moreover, here we cannot rely on the clear distinctions between persons and things (or places) that we might look for if we adopted one of the 'big 4' templates for theorizing property.[19]

In Amazonia, the transformation of space to make gardens, for example, involves cutting a network of living beings and extending networks of domesticated plants; thus, the ownership of nonhuman persons is part of the process of place-making. Creativity begets ownership, and the making of artefacts may create new persons (cf. Van Velthem 2003) who may be in turn become owners themselves. Such processes of creative appropriation are, as we shall see, very close to familiarizing processes of nurture.

The characteristic Amazonian feature of ownership as a process should be set against a longer standing theoretical interest in the ethnography of the region, in the subject of wealth and value. As the ecological evidence started to weigh against the ecofunctionalist assumption that material scarcity, particularly of high-quality protein, was the key driver of social processes, Rivière (1984), taking a political economy approach, argued that the significant scarce resource was people, implying that human beings themselves were the most highly valued economic good. He had in mind the control over people exercised through bride service but does not appear to have suspected how important more general modes of dependency are throughout the area, or what implications these have for local conceptions of ownership and mastery.

Meanwhile, various specialists in the more structurally differentiated societies of Central Brazil, the Xingu and North-West Amazonia called attention to the role of ceremonial valuables (especially body ornaments, aerophones and names) as property or prerogatives of collective and individual persons (Barcelos Neto 2008; Hugh-Jones 2009: 54; Lea 2012; Turner 2009: 156ff.). This renewed interest in artefacts did not remain restricted to the 'object-rich' societies of Amazonia, however. A growing concern with materiality opened a fresh venue of inquiry for an old anthropological question: the relation between persons and things. In Amazonia, the debates on animism and perspectivism offered an initial framework within which artefacts were reconsidered in a general way (Viveiros de Castro 2004; Santos-Granero 2009); that is, beyond the classic fields of material culture and indigenous art studies. The main issue at stake was the conceptualization of artefacts in a world in which the subject-object distinction is by definition fuzzy (and even inapplicable). What is the place of artefacts in a universe where personhood extends far beyond the human? Questions about the agency, life and subjectivity of artefacts are at the forefront of this growing literature (Fausto 2011; Fausto and Severi 2014; Lagrou 2011; Lagrou and Severi 2014).

In this book, what interests us most is the ownership of artefacts whose 'thingness' is always open to questioning. Their object-condition is an ambiguous one, since artefacts can prove to have, to use Santos-Granero's apt expression, an occult life. This fact reinforces the close link between the ownership of objects (especially ceremonial ones) and the mastery that shamans exert over their auxiliary spirits, warriors over their captives, killers over the victim's spirit, and so on. These relations of adoptive filiation between a master and a wild pet – wild because never completely tamed (Fausto 1999: 949) – appears to be highly pertinent in regard to artefacts. A closer look at the role of objects in native Amazonian societies reveals that appropriating and nurturing acts of 'domestication' are often necessary to maintain their status – even in the case of utilitarian objects such as carrying baskets. To give one example, among the Mamaindê, a carrying basket abandoned in the forest can 'become a jaguar and return to attack its owner'. Such objects 'must be constantly "domesticated" lest they turn into animals' (Miller 2009: 67). As Erikson (2009: 188) suggests, in Amazonia '"things", rather than being conceived as *independent subjects,* seem to be considered as semi-autonomous *subordinates.* In other words, "things" seem to be less perceived as full subjects than as fully subjected. Apart from leading an "occult life" of their own, they are also submitted to an "overt life" of dependency as "obedient things"' in much the same way as children, captives, clients and pets are.

Yet this intimate relation between people and artefacts does not imply that most 'movable property' in Amazonia is inalienable. The regimes of circulation vary widely depending on the object, its use and the people involved. Shamanic objects are rarely transmitted but can circulate between master and novice in the process of apprenticeship; ceremonial artefacts may be attached to individual persons or social segments and be the object of exclusive display; the use and production of body ornaments may be generalized or restricted to some individuals or entire groups. Within this range of variation, there seems to be a distinction between regimes of ownership in which tangible and intangible wealth is the object of collective segmentary appropriation, organizing a regime of circulation and transmission, and another kind of regime in which appropriation is open to all but is individually attained, and ownership is seldom transmissable.[20] The literature on trade complexifies this distinction and demonstrates that in many parts of Amazonia, objects circulated widely within more or less extensive networks articulated through individual trading partnerships or 'formal friendships' that transcended consanguineal and affinal categories (Brightman 2007; Santos-Granero 2007). In addition to these traditional interethnic forms of trade, trade with Europeans took place from the very start of the colonial period (Grotti 2013), including also the exchange of people for things (Karadimas 2001; Santos-Granero this volume).

Objects acquired through trade have more than a utilitarian value: displayed in domestic spaces, they represent narratives of 'their owner's past exploits and travels to distant spheres of alterity' (Grotti 2011; 2013: 17), thus becoming a focus of prestige and the magnification of personhood

(Hugh-Jones 2013). This display of wealth approaches paroxysm in the more recent inflationary acquisitiveness, as in the case of the Xikrin, analysed by Gordon (2006). This urge to acquire, however, should not be mistaken for the emergence of a form of possessive individualism in Amazonia; rather, it is an expression of a powerful cultural desire to engage with alterity, the sine qua non of Amerindian social reproduction, which is in several cases manifested in ritual celebrations of excess (Grotti 2007, forthcoming; Nahum-Claudel 2012).

In sum, the various forms of attachment of things to people in Amazonia have still to be ethnographically accounted for. As the following chapters show, these distinct cases are pervaded by a common language of ownership that defines a general mode of relation between not only persons and things, but also persons and parts of persons.

Nurture and Relations of Dependence

This book also explores how notions of ownership articulate with kinship, particularly with two relational modes that are normally deemed to characterize consanguine relations: commensality and feeding – or, more broadly, nurture. This move became possible thanks to new approaches in kinship studies that stem from a critique advanced in the late 1960s and early 1970s (Needham 1971; Schneider 1968). This critique represented a turning point in anthropology, largely anticipating the destabilization of the nature/culture dichotomy that marked subsequent decades. Having initially impacted on gender studies, this destabilization spread until it reached the ontological foundations of naturalism, putting into question the opposition between the given and the made. Concurrent with the appearance of Marilyn Strathern's (1980) 'No Nature, No Culture: The Hagen Case', there began in Amazonian studies a period whose slogan could be 'No nature, all nurture: the Amazonian case'. The 'alimentary forms of social life', to paraphrase Viveiros de Castro (1992), came to be seen as the fundamental operators of Amerindian sociality. Based neither on an idiom of substance nor on the membership of stable social groups, the ties of kinship were produced ('constructed', 'fabricated') by means of alimentary relations (e.g. Gow 1991; Vilaça 1992; McCallum 2001). Beyond this, relations of dependence were held to be created through practices and discourses of care and teaching; here, there is a form of metaphysical nurture that transforms and appropriates the other via the performance of knowledge transmission (Grotti 2007).

The phrase 'alimentary relations' must here be understood broadly, for it includes not only feeding or sharing *with* someone, but also eating or being eaten *by* someone (Fausto 2007). In other words, it includes both the idiom of cannibalism and that of commensality. These idioms marked the difference between two schools of Amazonian studies in the 1980s and 1990s, whose leading figures were Viveiros de Castro (1993) and Joanna Overing (1989). Both schools focused on 'eating', although in different ways: the approach privileging the idiom of predation looks at the Amerindian social world from the outside in, taking relations independently of any ethico-moral content (Taylor 1985; Vilaça 2000; Viveiros de Castro 1993), whereas the approach privileging the idiom of sharing took as its object everyday relations founded on an ethic of care, which constituted an ideal of peaceful sociability (Overing 1989, 2003; Overing and Passes 2000).[21]

If both lines of study took 'eating' as the fundamental idiom of social relations, it was because this is indeed an Amazonian fact, and only secondarily an anthropological artefact. Despite the epistemological hypochondria that we inherited from postmodernism, the truth is that acts of ethnographic fabrication frequently allow themselves to be contaminated by native acts of creativity. Yet the boundary between these lines of study proved more porous in the subsequent decades as new ethnographic studies explored aspects of the alimentary relations of social life, experimenting with both structurally and phenomenologically oriented approaches (Gow 2001; Lima 2005).

In this book, we take a fresh look at the subject of appropriation, not only by articulating the idiom of nurture and ownership, but also by revisiting both through more recent ethnography. Although Amazonianist literature has concentrated on 'eating with' as a mechanism for the production of identity, some authors (especially McCallum 2001), have devoted attention to acts of 'giving food', especially in relations between mothers and daughters. In some cases, the act of giving food may imply asymmetrical relations between non-kin or between 'becoming-kin': Vilaça (2002) observed that Wari' parental feeding is an act of 'making kin out of others', in such a way that feeding a baby is also a case of 'nurturing the Other' (Grotti 2007, 2010). More recently, Fausto and Costa (2013) proposed an articulation between feeding and ownership, maintaining that if this alimentary form is a hallmark of parent-child relations constituting consanguine kinship, then it is also a key operator in the constitution of relations of meta-consanguinity, that is, relations of adoptive filiation characteristic of relations of mastery and idioms of dependence in Amazonia. Luiz Costa comes back to this argument in his chapter here, offering a detailed description of pet-keeping among the Kanamari, showing how nurturance – the provision of love and care, especially in the form of food – is the central mechanism for producing mastery relations. While the 'other' in Costa's text is an animal captured young and transformed into a pet, it is not unusual for Amazonian pets to be addressed as 'my son' or 'my daughter', or for child-rearing to be described as a process of 'undoing' animality (Grotti 2007; Gow 1997). Costa thus brings his understanding into line with Grotti's broader concept of nurture as a process of control and appropriation through a heterogeneous set of caring actions.

These approaches may help us come closer to understanding the viewpoint of the 'victim' or 'subjected subject', who may actively seek relations of dependence. How should we conceptualize this agency of the patient? This question is the focus of Bonilla's chapter. She describes an 'alimentary form' hitherto little explored in the study of mastery: parasitism. Rival (1998) was probably the first to put 'the prey at the center' in her study of the Huaorani. She suggested that the position of prey was not entirely negative and could be actively sought in some historical circumstances. Bonilla developed this argument in a series of texts on the Paumari, an Arawá-speaking people of the Western Amazonia region (Bonilla 2005, 2007), where evidence of the cosmopolitical centrality of dependent relations abounds (e.g. Walker (2012, 2013).[22] This phenomenon appears to be historically related to debt peonage, and thus particularly associated with Western Amazonia; yet it is consistent with the broader pattern in which ownership and dynamic asymmetry are at the heart of Amerindian social relations.

Despite the overall predominance of predation as a relational structure mediating Self and Other in Amazonia, new ethnographic data indicates that in certain societies of the region (especially the Juruá-Purus river system), parasitism can also serve as a model for social relations both among humans and between humans and nonhumans.[23] In her chapter, Bonilla argues that the Paumari of the middle Purus construct their relationship with their nonindigenous bosses from the perspective of the parasite, thus inverting the sense of capture and mastery: in accepting the condition of prey they seek to convert themselves into parasites, making their bosses into unwitting providers. For Bonilla, this is not merely a case of the general instability of relations between master and pet, but rather an outcome of a specific positive perspective of the subjected subject.

Bonilla connects this idea to the fact that, from a parasitical point of view, the directional ideal is not to live among one's own, as the safe conviviality of kinship would not ensure well-being: a parasite among parasites would die of starvation. This critique is directed towards authors such as Overing and Passes (2000) and Belaunde (2001), who unambiguously associate the Amerindian horizon of well-being with domestic sociality, kinship and identity, that is, the pleasures of the daily round.

Gordon's discussion of well-being among the Xikrin-Kayapó resonates with Bonilla's critique and carries it forward. As he shows in his contribution, the very definition of well-being among this Ge-speaking people necessarily implies continuous production of a certain 'coefficient of differentiation', without which society would fall into a state of indifferentiation, a sort of generalized incest. It is not without reason that Ge people expend so much energy on the production of superimposed differences in the form of moieties, age classes, hierarchies of 'beauty' and so on. This is above all about producing an interior Other, an external interiority, whereas in the Paumari case well-being depends on an exterior Other, an exteriority to be internalized in the form of a parasitic relation. Difference, rather than sameness, is at the heart of Xikrin and Paumari notions of well-being. The weight of evidence in this book, as elsewhere, tells us that even the least formally structured societies of the region, such as those of the Guianas and of Western Amazonia, share – though in different proportions and modalities – the idea that a world of sameness is sterile, and that life cannot thrive without the risky desire for difference, a proposition originally articulated by Overing Kaplan (1981; also Overing 1983–84), that would be developed in different directions in the following decades.

Initially the divergence took the form of an opposition between theoretical styles and analytic emphasis on either internal peaceful sociability or external predatory relations, which corresponded to different conceptions of what constitutes the ontological foundations of Amerindian socialities: identity or alterity. However, both approaches tended to agree on one aspect: the privileging of symmetrical relations, with a correspondingly low thematization of power and dependence. This book explores Amerindian asymmetrical relations, in particular those constituted through a practice of care and protection. As Grotti (2007, 2009a, 2009b, 2010, 2012, forthcoming) has pointed out, the ethics of care are by no means confined to the domestic or the everyday; nor are they necessarily instruments of egalitarianism – on the contrary, care is closely connected to control and is the means by which relations of dependence are created.

Some studies of pets and adoption of enemies have also drawn attention to the fundamental point that to nurture and domesticate others is also to assert a form of ownership over them. Pets and children, like captured enemies, are dependents that need looking after. The asymmetrical nature of, for example, parent-child and captor-captive relations of dependence is sometimes more clearly appaarent in contexts of contact and change, when cross-cultural encounters reveal the creative use of words or projects that can be relevant to all parties involved. Anthropological studies from the past twenty years document an eagerness to extend 'civilization', education, and above all Evangelical Christianity to neighbouring groups (Howard 2001). It is time to address the role of recent historical changes in articulating commensality and nurture as expressions of egalitarianism and brotherhood in Amazonia (Vilaça 1997; Xavier 2013) to the same extent that ethnohistory has effectively adressed the impact of European conquest and slavery on the instigation of indigenous practices of warfare and capture (Ferguson and Whitehead 1992). We do not want to imply that the centrality of care and nurture results directly from exposure to Christianity, or that Amazonian warfare is a product of the Conquest, as Brian Ferguson (1995) has argued; instead we contend that there is an 'equivocal compatibility' (Pina-Cabral 2001) between indigenous and nonindigenous understandings of these alimentary forms that generates a number of working misunderstandings deserving closer attention. For instance, as Grotti (forthcoming) argues, the expansion of intertribal and interethnic relations of Christian brotherhood may represent a creative form of strategic regional expansion reminiscent of sixteenth-century Amerindian capturing societies.

The literature on the indigenous slave trade in South America previously focused upon European slaving and its moral justification based on the distinction between *caribes*, cannibal/Carib Indians that were captured for the Europeans by the *guatiaos* or *aruacas* (Whitehead 2011: 14). Amerindians were thus portrayed mostly as victims of slavery, which was assumed to be an originally European phenomenon (Overing Kaplan 1975: 20). Santos-Granero's (2009) history of native forms of captive slavery, which he summarizes and develops in his contribution to this volume, assembled evidence that the appropriation of human Others was in fact a widespread practice in Amazonia for centuries and had an influential cosmopolitical role, one that is compatible with our understanding of indigenous forms of social and ritual production.

Brightman (2007) and Grotti (2007) have both documented the recent history of the capture and incorporation of a group of Akuriyo hunter-gatherers by Trio horticulturalists, and the continued subjection of the former by the latter. As these authors show in this volume, although the events took place at the instigation of Protestant missionaries, indigenous categories shared by both Trio and Akuriyo provided the cultural conditions for the appropriation of human persons. Indeed, ideals of human equality, together with individualism, were part of the cultural package that the missionaries sought – and in this respect failed – to transmit to the Amerindians.[24]

By situating these different cases historically, we can better understand the ways in which the incorporation of human persons within an asymmetric relational scheme can oscillate between forms of visible inequality and weaker expressions, such as bride service. Full-fledged egalitarianism seems to be restricted mainly to very mobile, small groups, but even in these cases the cultural categories for relations of dependence tend to be present. Like the Akuriyo, the Western Parakanã studied by Fausto (2001) are quite egalitarian, despite highly operative relations of mastery. Here it is important to distinguish between asymmetry and inequality. The conflation of these two ideas has resulted in a widespread failure to recognize asymmetric relations that do not express themselves in terms of social inequality. Thus, though the Western Parakanã are a striking example of an egalitarian society, Fausto developed his ideas on mastery and familiarizing predation from data on shamanism and warfare among this people. In other words, an asymmetric relational mode that Santos-Granero finds operative in highly unequal sociopolitical contexts of the past is remarkably productive among an overall egalitarian society in the present. This shows that a structure of long duration, allowing connection between the past and the present, is being actualized independent of the degree of violence and inequality, which varies according to the peoples involved and the historical circumstances. Unlike Santos-Granero, though, we prefer to privilege the cosmopolitical lenses of Amerindian mastery over the juridico-economic categories of Western slavery as a way of understanding the relational structure of dependency in Amazonia.[25]

In harbouring relatively different views on the subject of asymmetric relations in Amazonia, this volume aims to instigate both theoretical debate and new empirical analysis on the subject. On the one hand, one cannot simply project the present onto the past, ignoring the profound historical changes due to the European conquest and colonization. On the other, indigenous systems of dependence are not extinct phenomena. In some cases, like that of the Arawak-speaking Kinikinau presently living among the Kadiwéu, it remains to be documented ethnographically whether this is effectively a case of collective servitude similar to that described for other Chané (Arawak) people in the past (and one might also mention the Akuriyo or the Makú). It is interesting to note that the Kadiwéu (Mbaya-Guaykuru) are among the few indigenous peoples to have effectively adopted horses and cattle, whose hides today are marked with the same graphic signs used to mark their captives in the past.[26] In any case, the study of 'declarations of dependence' from beyond Amazonia suggests that it may in fact be the liberal ideals of equality and self-ownership that are the exception to the general rule (Cohen 1995; Dumont 1977). As James Ferguson (2013: 237) puts it, such declarations 'are a challenge to liberal common sense', presenting as they do 'the theoretical and political challenge of a form of agency that seeks its own submission'. As Bonilla (2013: 247) comments, such cases show 'that subjection, far from being only the result of the domination of the state, constitutes its own logic, founded on kinship and a relational conception of the person that is at the base of a social and cosmopolitical dynamic which exceeds our ideals of social well-being and autonomy'. How this image of care and protection binding people in asymmetric relationships in Amazonia relates to the literature on contemporary moral theory, in which care is a key virtue in articulating an alternative to the liberal justice-oriented ethics (Baier 1994; Held 2006), remains an open question. This literature was highly inspirational for Overing, particularly in its initial focus on intimate relations and its articulation with feminist theory (Gilligan 1982; Larrabee 1993). We can only hope that this book will help keep the conversation going by opening a new area for debate.

Ownership, Authorship and the Self

Earlier assumptions about Amazonia, whether of a Hobbesian or a Rousseauian hue, were brought into question by the political economy style of analysis epitomized by Rivière and Terence Turner. Rivière posits an Amerindian social contract based on kinship, noting that '[t]he advantages that can be obtained from living with others can only be obtained if individuals are willing to give up some of their personal freedom ... the people of Guiana are no freer from the general constraints of social life than anyone else' (1984: 95). Yet, self-ownership and equality could not be said to be at the heart of social systems that were organized around the control of persons. Focusing on consanguine ties, Joanna Overing and Alan Passes challenged this view by emphasizing their affective nature, thus suggesting that, to put it in terms of property relations, this was if anything a case of mutual belonging (Overing and Passes 2000).

Although mutual belonging appears to characterize a number of relations among Amerindian peoples, we conceive of it as neither necessarily symmetrical nor reciprocal. That is why we prefer to focus, as does Strathern (1988, 2005), on the claims that persons can make on other persons. As we saw in the quotation of Lowie on the Trobriand canoe: the owner is not an 'absolute owner', because people have claims on him. He does not own himself. Self-ownership is an absent concept, one that Locke had to affirm explicitly against the religious understanding of God's (and by extension the King's) ownership of people.[27] In Amazonia, however, the owner is neither an individual self nor a unitary god but a magnified person composed of multiple relationships. The crucial distinction, as Fausto (2012a: 36) suggests, is that here 'the founding relation is not self-identity: the Self and the Same do not merge in the construction of the Amerindian person. The multiplicity and fractality of ownership relations imply internally composite subjects, "self-different" persons (Viveiros de Castro 2002: 377)'. Instead of ownership, we would better qualify the Amazonian case as one of *altership*, since what connects a person to an object is not exclusive of what connects that person to other human and non-human persons. Actually, in some cases, objects are precisely what make such connections possible, as is the case of the Nambikwara Mamaindê personal adornments studied by Miller (2009), which are, as she argues, a sort of 'alterity card' permitting the passage between different relational contexts (Miller 2012, 2015).

This is not merely a play on words, as becomes clear in contexts where Western conceptions of ownership and Amazonian conceptions of altership come into contact. Music provides a case in point. Anthony Seeger, after explaining how different actors (composer, author, performer, music publisher, record label, etc.) own different rights to songs and performances in Western ownership regimes, refers to the Ge-speaking Suyá (Kĩsêdjê) of Mato Grosso, among whom he carried out fieldwork. For them,

> there is no such thing as a human 'composer.' All songs are either 'revealed' through direct contact between human spirits and animals, from whom the human spirits learn new songs, or through appropriation from another human ... community. One of the songs they sing today was originally sung by a jaguar. It was overheard and remembered by a man whose spirit was living with the jaguars, and he taught it to the rest of the community.

And this is not all, for in historical time, he continues,

> the 'master' (*kandé*, which I have also translated as 'owner/controller') of the song is the moiety whose members sang it for the first time. The other moiety must ask the controlling moiety's permission in order for the whole community to sing it.

These convoluted ownership rights over the 'jaguar song' become even more complex nowadays

> when you add a researcher with a tape recorder, an archive, an ethnographic recording, and requests to license songs from that recording for feature films. By Brazilian law this song was 'traditional' and difficult to protect. How does one defend the rights of a collectivity? How does one define a jaguar as an individual author? What is the lifetime of a jaguar (does it matter)? [US law for example protects creative works for the author's lifetime plus 70 years] And since a song is revealed and ultimately religious, what is the lifetime of a God? (Seeger 2004: 75–76).

The Tupi-speaking Parakanã provide another example: they employ a language of mastery to talk about the chain of asymmetric relations through which songs are appropriated from the outside and executed inside. Songs are given by enemies in dreams to men and are generically called 'jaguar'. A dreamer is said to be a 'master of jaguar' (*jawajara*), meaning that he is the owner of both songs and the dreamt enemy, conceived as his pet. Owners never kill their pets, so the ritual act of dancing and singing is considered a killing: the dreamer cannot perform his own song in the ritual but must give it to a third person who will be the jaguar-song executioner (Fausto 1999, 2012b). Who, in this case, would then be the author of the song? The most probable answer is the dreamt enemy, whereas the dreamer would be its owner-controller. However, even the dreamt enemy is not conceived as a composer, since song is his person qua music. It is a sort of quantum of predatory capacity that circulates among the living – a jaguar-part of an enemy that becomes part of the dreamer's and the executioner's person (Fausto 2004, 2007). Tainted by altership, humans do not themselves become authors, but *alterers* capable of othering themselves and switching perspectives in order to appropriate new songs and new names.

In the Parakanã case, in contrast to the Kĩsêdjê one, the owner/controller is an individual, not a group. He has no right to sing the jaguar-song and has to alienate it to another person who will ritually execute it. Once dead, this jaguar-song cannot be sung again in a ritual, nor can it be inherited. The contrast outlined here marks different sociocosmic regimes in Amazonia, the ones described above as centripetal and centrifugal. Songs among Kĩsêdjê, once appropriated from the outside, become part of a lore owned by and transmitted within a social group; among the Parakanã, songs must on the contrary be continuously appropriated to move the ritual machinery. There is no lore or tradition to be remembered and transmitted. One has to learn a generative scheme, not a more or less fixed repertoire as occurs among Ge-speaking people or in the Upper Xingu (Fausto, Franchetto and Montagnani 2011; Fausto this volume).

In his chapter, Cesarino addresses some of these issues from the perspective of the Marubo, a Panoan people from the Javari Valley, particularly with regard to shamanic verbal arts. As he points out, a common thread runs through all the different regimes of 'authorship' in Amazonia: the absence of the free, autarchic, Solar author. Creativity is not the action of a sovereign individual who owns his[28] own ideas, but the condensation of multiple relations with alterity. What Cesarino calls 'the decentralization of the author-function' is itself a function of a different regime of personhood, one that does not resolve into a simple opposition between individual versus collective ownership.

The translation of Amazonian mastery relations into a Western proprietary language becomes even more problematic when we note that these multiple relational chains apply not only to 'intangible property' such as songs, names or spells, but also to ritual objects like masks and musical instruments. As items of material culture, musical instruments may be owned by their makers, but their music may be owned by clans or moieties, and be created by nonhuman agents. In some cases, 'sacred' flutes are kept hidden from certain members of society (i.e., women and children) and exchanged only under exceptional circumstances, if at all. Some are 'copies' of water spirits or other nonhuman beings yet maintain the agentive potential of the original (Menezes Bastos 2011). The ideas of heritage and cultural property provide at best a placeholder for the complex sets of rights and obligations that are embedded in such objects, but they are a poor substitute. Even as copies, their sacred aspects may remain after they have been transformed into commodities (Augustat 2011).

Coelho de Souza's contribution to this volume is a theoretically challenging analysis of the (re)lease of Kĩsêdjê designs for payment to a fashion company. The designs, despite being items of material culture, are nonetheless part of the immaterial, or intangible, heritage of the Kĩsêdjê. They are produced through a particular creative process and perceived in different ways by different actors, in terms of what the author calls models of 'exchange' and 'contract'. As she writes, 'when rights are at stake – cultural or knowledge rights, for instance – these never arise as collective rights unequivocally ascribable to peoples or groups, but as a vast network of heterogeneous prerogatives, entitlements and obligations that does not fit easily in the moulds of legal representation required by the form of contracts'. Coelho de Souza argues that, in contrast to Western property forms, in Amerindian appropriations 'objects are less passive registers of a subject's capacities than personified objectifications of their relationships, appearing not as simple *things,* but as *persons,*' thus bringing our understanding of exchange in Amazonia closer to the *locus classicus* of exchange, Melanesia.

Land, Territory and Property

Even 'land', or in Lowie's terms, 'real estate', is no mere 'thing' for native Amazonians. With indigenous territories constantly under threat from the agro-industrial and mineral frontier, it is materially and practically urgent to find a way of talking about land in the Amazonian case. Land rights activists evoke generic images of 'mother earth', 'sacred groves' and 'ancestral lands'. Although those who are familiar with the relevant ethnographic facts may regard these as simplistic images, they can be read as placeholders for a desire to preserve a way of life, a space for traditional culture to thrive – in short, 'culture as land' (Engle 2010: 162ff.). In fact, rather than humans merely holding preferential rights over tracts of land understood as a natural object, ownership proliferates and binds places together through relations between nonhuman persons, with whom humans must interact in a variety of ways, including hunting, gardening and shamanism.

Butt Colson (2009), in her monograph on the Akawaio, has tried to translate indigenous relationships to land into terms intelligible to state or international law, on the premise that claims to land need to be based on richly detailed documentation of local indigenous practices over long time periods. In language intended for nonspecialist readers, she outlines

> three basic principles underlying Akawaio and Arekuna property rights: that of collective, communal rights to land and resources; the right of families and individuals to acquire and use these resources for themselves within the community lands of their own river area or portion of river area; the obligation to share with kin and affines a generous part of that which has been acquired and made available. Abandonment of land entails its return to the community for other families and members to use in the future. Those outside a local community, wishing to use certain resources in that community's lands, have to obtain permission from the leader and his followers. (349)

In general, it seems that land is not owned as such except when it is cultivated as a swidden (Brightman 2010; Viegas this volume). As Gow (1991: 80) writes, the 'owners' of crops in gardens are the married couple who plant them. As Viegas shows in this volume, time is important here, for ownership is subject to forgetting: just as the dead may need to be forgotten so that the living may reproduce and names may circulate once again (Taylor 1993), so must places in the landscape that have been 'somebody's' garden at last return to the forest to regenerate and recirculate, eventually to be appropriated once more (Brightman 2010). The temporality of land ownership here differs from that of Western property rights, with the exception of copyrights and patents, which are 'designed to expire' (Brown 2004).

Rights over land also include territorial rights, which are translations of the spheres of influence of particular sociopolitical units. In indigenous terms these are articulated in terms of ownership, but ownership takes the form of a network of relationships: '[e]ach category of space ... has the form of a community of beings related together as owners and owned' (Gow 1991: 80). Peter Gow gives a clear description of the pervasive kind of ownership that is common to many native Amazonian societies. For the Piro, *Sachamama*, 'forest mother', the land anaconda, is the 'source' of the forest; she 'lies curled up in a hole, and from her the forest and its plants emanate'. A related spirit entity, *Sacharuna*, 'forest person', also known as the 'boss' or 'chief' of the forest, patrols the forest, protecting areas especially rich in game from hunters.[29] As Gow writes,

> [i]n the 'high forest' live the most desirable game animals, like spider monkeys, macaws, tapirs, and white-lipped peccaries. These inhabitants of the forest are created and controlled by their *dueños*, 'owners', and by their *madres,* 'mothers'... the 'mother' is the source from which the species 'comes', and ... looks after her species. The 'owner' is often assimilated to the 'mother', but is easier to define. The 'owner' is often called the 'boss' (*patrón*) or 'chief' (*curaca*) of a territory in the forest, and the animals of that territory are his pets. (Gow 1991: 79)

Here, then, we have a hierarchy of owners or magnified persons, as described by Fausto (2008, 2012a) and Cesarino (this volume). What is particularly significant here is that the relationship of the species to its *dueño* or *madre* is the same as that of the forest to *Sachamama* and *Sacharuna* (Gow 1991: 79). The recursive logic of master-owner relations, described in Cesarino's chapter, thus permeates the landscape, which is under the regime of a cosmopolitical economy of persons both human and nonhuman.

Unlike ritual objects and intangible possessions, land is neither inherited nor exchanged (Viegas this volume). But care and nurture play a central role in ownership of places. As Viegas writes in this volume, '[p]ossession of a garden is thus associated with looking after or having the responsibility for a given thing'. Contemporary threats to territorial rights are such that places in the landscape that are not owned by human persons must be protected by other means. For example, Tukanoan peoples have campaigned for certain locations in the Upper Negro basin in North-West Amazonia – 'geographic features, such as islands, marsh areas, creek mouths, shallows, outcrops, rocks and ridges, as well as the sites of old malocas and the "transformation houses", stopover points on the journey of the giant anaconda who brought the ancestors of the current groups to the Uaupés' – to be recognized as their intangible cultural property, as 'sacred places' (Andrello 2010). As Andrello shows, the process of plotting mythical narratives into maps of the landscape raises considerable practical and epistemological difficulties. Inevitably, something is lost in translation between property regimes. Yet this process of translation is an urgent matter of justice: as David Hume (1975) has argued, it is when competition arises and people begin to perceive a threat to their possessions that a formalization of property relations becomes necessary.

Thus, equivocal and 'dangerous' though the concepts of property and ownership may be, they are also unavoidable. When native Amazonians enter into property relationships with outsiders and engage with the market-based economy, this is not an encounter between societies without property and a world society based upon property. Such relationships raise problems of translation, not problems due to presence or lack of relevant institutions or categories. The purpose of this book is to enhance our understanding of all of these things.

Marc Brightman is Professor of Anthropology at the University of Bologna, and author of *The Imbalance of Power: Leadership, Masculinity and Wealth in Amazonia* (2016). He co-edited (with V. Grotti and O. Ulturgasheva) *Shamanism in Rainforest and Tundra: Personhood in the Shamanic Ecologies of Contemporary Amazonia and Siberia* (2012) and *Rethinking the "Frontier" in Amazonia and Siberia: Extractive Economies, Indigenous Politics and Social Transformations* (2007).

Carlos Fausto is Associate Professor of Anthropology at the Museu Nacional, Federal University of Rio de Janeiro, and Senior Fellow of the National Council for the Development of Science and Technology (CNPq). He is the author of *Os Índios antes do Brasil* (2000), *Inimigos Fiéis: História, Guerra e Xamanismo* (2001) and *Warfare and Shamanism in Amazonia* (2012). He co-edited (with M. Heckenberger) *Time and Memory in Indigenous Amazonia* (2007) and (with C. Severi) *L'Image Rituelle* (2014).

Vanessa Grotti is Part-Time-Professor at the European University Institute in Florence. She is the co-editor, with Marc Brightman and Olga Ulturgasheva, of *Shamanism in Rainforest and Tundra: Personhood in the Shamanic Ecologies of Contemporary Amazonia and Siberia* (2012) and *Rethinking the "Frontier" in Amazonia and Siberia: Extractive Economies, Indigenous Politics and Social Transformations* (2007). Her monograph *Living with the Enemy: First Contacts and the Making of Christian Bodies in Amazonia* is due to be published by Berghahn Books.

Notes

1. However, some authors took care to underline their awareness of the historical circumstances of the phenomena they described: see Rivière et al. (2007); Lévi-Strauss (1955).
2. Notice the number of edited books concerning Amazonia's history that have appeared since then: Hill's *Rethinking History and Myth* (1984) and *History, Power and Identity* (1996); Carneiro da Cunha's *História dos Índios no Brasil* (1992) and (with Viveiros de Castro), *Amazônia: Etnologia e História* (1993); Whitehead's *Histories and Historicities in Amazonia* (2003); Fausto and Heckenberger's *Time and Memory in Indigenous Amazonia* (2007), and above all the two volumes of *The Cambridge History of the Native Peoples of the Americas* dedicated to South America (Salomon and Schwartz 1999).
3. FUNAI is the Fundação Nacional do Índio, the Brazilian national agency for the administration, protection and tutelage of native peoples. On this conception of history as a succession of times, common in Western Amazonia, see Gow (1991), Taylor (2007) and Costa (in press).
4. This occurred later in Amazonia than in other regions of the world, as is also the case for Melanesia and Polynesia. Not by chance, specialists in these ethnographic areas have dedicated important works to the theme (Geismar 2005; Harrison 1992, 2000; Hirsch and Strathern 2004; Leach 2003; Strathern 2005).
5. But see Carpenter, Katyal and Riley's (2009) defense of the use of property laws to protect indigenous cultural heritage. See also Brown's critique (2010) and their response (Carpenter et al. 2010).
6. Macpherson may have overstated his case: Munzer (1990: 41ff.) argues that persons 'do not own their bodies but ... they do have limited property rights in them'.

7. Yet, to be precise, Locke's ideas cannot be reduced to a justification of the appropriation of land. He conceived of an inextricable link between self-ownership, self-identity (the persistence of personal identity through time and space) and property rights. If Locke indeed advanced a model of the free agent, which would make property an index of agency (Fausto 2012a: 34), his main aim was not to found a model of the capitalist entrepreneur and his accumulative drive, but to enunciate, as Tully (1993: 117) puts it, a theory of popular sovereignty against absolutism.
8. As early as 1503, Queen Isabel of Castile distinguished 'Cannibal' peoples (*Caníbales*), who could be captured and enslaved, from those who, like the Taino, should be converted to civilization (Whitehead 1984). In 1530, Bartolome de las Casas obtained a royal decree from Charles I prohibiting indigenous slavery in Peru, and seven years later Pope Paul III promulgated the bull *Sublimus Dei*, which not only forbade the enslavement of Amerindians but also attributed a soul to them, meaning a human condition.
9. The practice of laying claim to ownership or dominion of a territory by the reading of a text was a common colonial practice rehearsed mostly in the English colonies. For the misunderstanding emerging from two different conceptions of propriety and ownership, see Viegas (this volume).
10. According to von Benda-Beckman et al. (2006), the dominant disciplines concerned with property (political science, economics and law) tend to emphasize normative approaches over accurate description, with the consequence that 'property models that purport to be universal are in fact largely based on Western legal categories', especially 'private legal ownership, often regarded as the apex of legal and economic evolution as well as a precondition for efficient market economies'.
11. Regimes of ownership concerning indigenous land rights are an apt example. In Brazil, where the majority of our examples come from, the Constitution defines indigenous lands as those that are permanently occupied by indigenous people, those that are necessary for their productive activities, those indispensable for the preservation of environmental resources necessary for their well-being, and those necessary to their physical and cultural reproduction in accord with their uses and traditions. These rights are classified as 'original rights', meaning that they predate the Conquest of the Americas. No private land title superposed on indigenous lands has any value, and the State has no obligation to pay any compensation. It is important to notice that the indigenous populations have the usufruct of these lands, but their possession remains with the nation (*União*).
12. Contrast with e.g. this definition by the economist Douglas North: 'the essence of property rights is the right to exclude, and an organisation which has a comparative advantage in violence [i.e. the State] is in the position to specify and enforce property rights' (in Geisler 2006: 42).
13. We are indebted to our first anonymous reviewer for this formulation.
14. According to Rowlands (2004: 207–8), cultural rights legislation was influenced by the evolutionary notion that the ownership of movable goods was encouraged by the development of market economies and the freeing of personal property from collective controls; thus cultural property was sometimes criticized as a 'backward' form of collective ownership and seen to restrict individual ownership and threaten the 'basic tools of international industry and trade'.

15. Intellectual property rights, such as patents and copyrights, are of course time limited, which has presented other sets of difficulties in relation to their possible application to traditional knowledge (Brown 2004; Seeger 2004).
16. 'Property' comes from the Latin *proprietatem*, which is the nominal form of the adjective *proprius*, meaning 'one's own', and although *propre* was used to refer to wealth or private property in Norman and Anglo French, *propreté* appears to have entered the English language primarily to denote *propriety*, correctness in dress or behavior. For its part, 'own' comes from the Proto-Germanic **aigana-*, of which the Old English *agen* is a cognate, meaning 'to have', and it tellingly shares this etymology with the verb 'owe'. The verb form 'own' becomes obsolete in later Middle English, except in the derivative noun form 'owner', until its revival in the late sixteenth century. Thus there is nothing particularly 'modern' about the association of ownership or property with personhood. In contrast to the fairly similar etymological associations of these terms, the verb 'possess' derives from the Latin *posse + sedere*, thus combining the notions of power and 'sitting' (*OED*).
17. It remains to be seen how this model applies to either the Upper Xingu or Upper Negro River, or to the Ge and Bororo, whose regimes of ownership are particularly intricate (see Lea 2012). In all these cases, it seems that a further sociological and ceremonial elaboration of this relational scheme may help to explain how chieftainship became institutionalized in some of these peoples.
18. Since Mauss (1990), the gift has offered an alternative model to think about these relations, one that contrasts with the commodity model. Nonetheless, the rich literature on exchange has often (though not always) taken the nature of ownership for granted, despite the fact that some form of ownership must always be implicit in exchanges of gifts or commodities (Ingold, Riches and Woodburn 1988: 6). In any case, as Hugh-Jones (2013) argues, if the gift was present in Amazonian models, it was mostly absent as an empirical fact.
19. In economics, property tends to be thought of in terms of what von Benda Beckmann et al. 2006: 9) call the 'big 4' universal types: open access, common, state and private.
20. See e.g. Fausto's (2012b: 301–4) distinction between centripetal and centrifugal systems in Amazonia: in the latter, the capture of agentive capacities in the outside predominates, and the circulation of wealth within the group is limited; in the former, the horizontal and vertical circulation of wealth occupies the place of its appropriation from the outside, so that internal differentiation and transmission become more productive than predation.
21. The differences between these two schools also reflected different takes on the central debates at the time, which revolved around such dichotomies as public/private, domestic/political, everyday time/ritual time, normative ethics/ethics of caring, which were the focus of an important literature inspired by feminist social theory (Baier 1994; Collier and Rosaldo 1981; Ortner and Whitehead 1981).
22. For further references on this topic, see Fausto's comments on Walker's article (2012c, 2013).
23. For an example outside this region, see Karadimas (2003) on the Miraña of the Caquetá River basin, in Colombia.
24. Here we see how contradictory the expansion of Christianity (both Catholic and Evangelical) can be: though directed towards an extension of universal brotherhood to all people under God's aegis, it simultaneously generates new relations of dependence and hierarchy – a paradox that has accompanied all Western co-

lonial projects since the beginning. In this sense, the working misunderstanding is established by the conflation of two different conversion systems: indigenous familiarizing predation, and Christian brother–becoming.
25. Fausto (1997, 1999) proposed the master–wild pet dialectic as a replacement for the master-slave one. Taking inspiration from Erikson (1987) and Descola (1994), he suggested that the way Amerindians manage asymmetric relations with other people, animals and plants does not imply the same level of control and reification as in husbandry and slavery.
26. According to Boggiani (1945 [1894]), these signs were marks of ownership derived from the famous Kadiwéu body graphic designs (see also Lévi-Strauss and Belmont 1963; Santos-Granero 2009: 122–23).
27. As St Paul writes in his first epistle to the Corinthians: '6:19 What? know ye not that your body is the temple of the Holy Ghost which is in you, which ye have of God, and ye are not your own? 6:20 For ye are bought with a price: therefore glorify God in your body, and in your spirit, which are God's.' (*Holy Bible*). According to Vilaça (in press) this verse of I Corinthians is quoted by the Wari' in their evangelical cults. The author relates this fact to the enduring concept of the multiple person intrinsic to their own Christian experience.
28. Such individuals tend to be conceived of as male persons.
29. This relationship between the notions of 'source' and 'owner' has echoes elsewhere: e.g. for the Trio, the term *entu* signifies owner, boss and 'source' (Brightman 2010). Among the Pano-speaking Sharanawa, the term *ifo* has also the semantic connotations of authority and originator (Déléage 2009).

References

Andrello, G. 2010. 'Origin Narratives, Transformation Routes: Heritage, Knowledge and (A)symmetries on the Uaupés River', *Vibrant* 10(1): 495–528.
Augustat, C. 2011. 'Sacred Musical Instruments in Museums: Are They Sacred?' in J. Hill and J.-P. Chaumeil (eds), *Burst of Breath: New Research on Indigenous Ritual Flutes in Lowland South America*. Lincoln: University of Nebraska Press, pp. 357–70.
Baier, A. 1994. *Moral Prejudices: Essays on Ethics*. Cambridge, MA: Harvard University Press.
Barcelos Neto, A. 2008. *Apapaatai: Rituais de Máscaras no Alto Xingu*. São Paulo: EDUSP.
Belaunde, L.E. 2001. *Viviendo Bien: Género y Fertilidad entre los Airo-Pai de la Amazonía Peruana*. Lima: Centro Amazónico de Antropología y Aplicación Práctica, Banco Central de Reserva del Peru.
Boggiani, G. 1945 [1894]. *Os Caduveos*. Belo Horizonte: Itatiaia.
Bonilla, O. 2005. 'O Bom Patrão e o Inimigo Voraz: Predação e Comércio na Cosmologia Paumari', *Mana: Estudos de Antropologia Social* 11(1): 41–66.
———. 2007. 'Des Proies si Désirables: Soumission et Prédation pour les Paumari d'Amazonie Brésilienne', Ph.D. dissertation. Paris: Ecole des Hautes Etudes en Sciences Sociales (EHESS).
———. 2013. "Be My Boss!' Comments on South African and Amerindian Forms of Subjection', *Journal of the Royal Anthropological Institute* 19(2): 246–47.

Brightman, M. 2007. 'Amerindian Leadership in Guianese Amazonia', Ph.D. dissertation. Cambridge: Cambridge University.
———. 2010. 'Creativity and Control: Property in Guianese Amazonia', *Journal de la Société des Américanistes* 96(1): 135–67.
Brown, M. 1998. 'Can Culture be Copyrighted?' *Current Anthropology* 39(2): 193–222.
———. 2004. 'Heritage as Property', in K. Verdery and C. Humphrey (eds), *Property in Question: Value Transformation in the Global Economy*. Oxford and New York: Berg, pp. 49–68.
———. 2010. 'Culture, Property, and Peoplehood: A Comment on Carpenter, Katyal, and Riley's "In Defense of Property"', *International Journal of Cultural Property* 17(3): 569–79.
Butt Colson, A. 1973. 'Inter-tribal Trade in the Guiana Highlands', *Antropológica* 34: 5–70.
———. 2009. *Land: its occupation, management, use and conceptualization. The case of the Akawaio and Arekuna of the Upper Mazaruni District, Guyana*. Panborough: Last Refuge.
Carneiro da Cunha, M. 1992. *História dos Índios no Brasil*. São Paulo: Fapesp/Companhia das Letras/SMC.
———. 2009. *Culture and Culture: Traditional Knowledge and Intellectual Rights*. Chicago: Prickly Paradigm Press.
Carpenter, K.A., S.K. Katyal and A.R. Riley. 2009. 'In Defense of Property', *Yale Law Journal* 118(6): 1022–125.
Clastres, P. 1977. *Society Against the State: The Leader as Servant and the Humane Uses of Power among the Indians of the Americas*. New York: Urizen Books.
Cohen, G. 1995. *Self-Ownership, Freedom and Equality*. Cambridge: Cambridge University Press.
Collier, J. and M. Rosaldo. 1981. 'Politics and Gender in Simple Societies', in S. Ortner and H. Whitehead (eds.), *Sexual Meanings*. Cambridge: Cambridge University Press, pp. 275–329.
Costa, L. 2007. 'As Faces Do Jaguar: Parentesco, História e Mitologia entre os Kanamari da Amazônia Ocidental', Ph.D. dissertation. Rio de Janeiro: PPGAS-Museu Nacional, Universidade Federal do Rio de Janeiro.
———. In press. 'Becoming Funai: a Kanamari Transformation', in H. Veber and P. Virtanen (eds.), *Creating Dialogues: Indigenous Perceptions and Forms of Leadership in Amazonia*. Boulder: University of Colorado Press.
Déléage. P. 2009. *Le Chant de l'Anaconda: L'Apprentissage du Chamanisme chez les Sharanahua*. Nanterre: Société d'Ethnologie.
Descola, P. 1994. 'Pourquoi les indiens d'Amazonie n'ont-ils pas domestiqué le pécari? Généalogie des objets et anthropologie de l'objectivation'. In B. Latour and P. Lemonnier (eds) *De la préhistoire aux missiles balistiques: l'intelligence sociale des techniques*. Paris: La Découverte, pp. 329–344.
Dumont, L. 1977. *Homo aequalis: genèse et épanouissement de l'idéologie économique*. Paris: Gallimard.
Engle, K. 2010. *The Elusive Promise of Indigenous Development: Rights, Culture, Strategy*. Durham: Duke.
Erikson, P. 1987. "De L'Apprivoisement à L'Approvisionnement: Chasse, Alliance et Familiarisation en Amazonie Amérindienne", *Techniques et Cultures* 9: 105–40.

———. 2009. 'Obedient Things: Reflections on the Matis Theory of Materiality', in F. Santos-Granero (ed.), *The Occult Life of Things: Native Amazonian Theories of Materiality and Personhood*. Tucson: University of Arizona Press, pp. 173–90.
Fausto, C. 1999. 'Of Enemies and Pets: Warfare and Shamanism in Amazonia', *American Ethnologist* 26(4): 933–56.
———. 2001. *Inimigos Fiéis: História, Guerra e Xamanismo na Amazônia*. São Paulo: EDUSP.
———. 2004. 'A Blend of Blood and Tobacco: Shamans and Jaguars among the Parakanã of Eastern Amazonia', in N. Whitehead and R. Wright (eds), *In Darkness and Secrecy: The Anthropology of Assault Sorcery and Witchcraft in Amazonia*. Chapel Hill, NC: Duke University Press, pp. 157–78.
———. 2007. 'Feasting on People: Eating Animals and Humans in Amazonia', *Current Anthropology* 48(4): 497–530.
———. 2008. 'Donos Demais: Propriedade e Maestria na Amazônia', *Mana: Estudos de Antropologia Social* 14(2): 329–66.
———. 2011. "Le Masque de l'Animiste: Chimères et Poupées Russes en Amérique Indigène". *Gradhiva* 13:49-67.
———. 2012a. 'Too Many Owners: Mastery and Ownership in Amazonia', in M. Brightman, V. Grotti and O. Ulturgasheva (eds), *Animism in Rainforest and Tundra: Personhood, Animals, Plants and Things in Contemporary Amazonia and Siberia*. London: Berghahn Books, pp. 85–105.
———. 2012b. *Warfare and Shamanism in Amazonia*. Cambridge: Cambridge University Press.
———. 2012c. 'Masters in Amazonia: Harry Walker's "Demonic Trade: Debt, Materiality and Agency in Amazonia"', *Journal of the Royal Anthropological Institute* 18(3): 684–86.
———. 2013. 'Feeding and Being Fed: Reply to Walker', *Journal of the Royal Anthropological Institute* 19(1): 170–78.
Fausto, C. and L. Costa. 2013. 'Feeding (and Eating): Reflections on Strathern's "Eating (and Feeding)"', *Cambridge Anthropology* 31(1): 156–62.
Fausto, C., B. Franchetto and T. Montagnani. 2011. 'Les formes de la mémoire: Art verbal et musique chez les Kuikuro du Haut Xingu (Brésil)'. *L'Homme* 197: 41–69.
Fausto, C. and M. Heckenberger. 2007. *Time and memory in indigenous Amazonia: anthropological perspectives*. Gainesville, University Press of Florida.
Fausto, C. and C. Severi 2014. 'L'Image rituelle: Agentivité et mémoire'. *Cahiers d'Anthropologie Sociale* 10. Paris: L'Herne.
Ferguson, B. 1995. *Yanomami Warfare: A Political History*. Sante Fe, NM: School of American Research Press.
Ferguson, R. B. and N. L. Whitehead. 1992. *War in the Tribal Zone: Expanding States and Indigenous Warfare*. Sante Fe, NM: School of American Research Press.
Ferguson, J. 2013. 'Declarations of Dependence: Labour, Personhood, and Welfare in Southern Africa', *Journal of the Royal Anthropological Institute* 19(2): 223–42.
Geisler, C. 2006. 'Ownership in Stateless Places', in F. von Benda Beckmann, K. von Benda Beckmann and M. Wiber (eds), *Changing Properties of Property*. Oxford: Berghahn Books, pp. 40–57.
Geisler, C. and G. Daneker. 2000. *Property and Values: Alternatives to Public and Private Ownership*. Washington DC: Island Press.

Geismar, H. 2005. 'Copyright in Context: Carvings, Carvers and Commodities in Vanuatu', *American Ethnologist* 32(3): 437–59.
Gilligan, C. 1982. *In A Different Voice*. Cambridge, MA: Harvard University Press.
Godelier, M. 1982. *La Production des Grands Hommes*. Paris: Fayard.
Gordon, C. 2006. *Economia Selvagem: Ritual e Mercadoria entre os Índios Xikrin-Mebêngôkre*. São Paulo: UNESP.
Gow, P. 1991. *Of Mixed Blood: Kinship and History in Peruvian Amazonia*. Oxford: Clarendon Press.
———. 1997. 'O Parentesco com Consciência Humana: O Caso Piro.' *Mana* 3(2): 39–65.
———. 2001. *An Amerindian Myth and its History*. Oxford: Oxford University Press.
Grotti, V. 2007. 'Nurturing the Other: Wellbeing, Social Body and Transformation in Northeastern Amazonia'. Ph.D. dissertation. Cambridge: Cambridge University.
———. 2009a. 'Protestant Evangelism and the Transformability of Amerindian Bodies in Northern Amazonia', in A. Vilaça and R. Wright (eds), *Native Christians: Modes and Effects of Christianity Among Indigenous Peoples of the Americas*. London: Ashgate, pp. 109–26.
———. 2009b. 'Un Corps en Mouvement: Parenté, "Diffusion de l'Influence" et Transformations Corporelles dans les Fêtes de Bière Tirio, Amazonie du Nord-est', *Journal de la Société des Américanistes* 91(1): 73–96.
———. 2010. 'Incorporating the Akuriyo: Contact Expeditions and Inter-ethnic Relations in Northeastern Amazonia', *OSO, Tijdschrift voor Surinamistiek en het Caraibisch Gebied* 29(2): 284–99.
———. 2011. 'Like Scars on the Body's Skin: The Display of Ancient Things in Trio Houses, Northeastern Amazonia', in P. Fortis and I. Praet (eds), *Exploring the Dangers and Virtues of Ancient Things*. St. Andrews: Journal of the Centre for Amerindian, Latin American and Caribbean Studies, pp. 236–62.
———. 2012. 'Happy with the Enemy: Kinship, Pacification and Corporeal Transformations in Trio Beer Feasts, Northeastern Amazonia'. *Anthropology and Humanism* 37(2): 191–200.
———. 2013. 'The Wealth of the Body: Trade Relations, Objects, and Personhood in Northeastern Amazonia'. *Journal of Latin American and Caribbean Anthropology* 18(1): 14–30.
———. (forthcoming). *Living with the Enemy: First Contacts and the Making of Christian Bodies in Amazonia*. Oxford: Berghahn Books.
Hann, C. 1998. *Property Relations: Renewing the Anthropological Tradition*. Cambridge: Cambridge University Press.
Harrison, S. 1992. 'Ritual as Intellectual Property', *Man* 27(2): 225–44.
———. 1999. 'Identity as a scarce resource'. *Social Anthropology*, 7(3): 239–251.
———. 2000. 'From Prestige Goods to Legacies: Property and the Objectification of Culture in Melanesia', *Comparative Studies in Society and History* 42(3): 662–79.
Held, V. 2006. *The Ethics of Care*. New York: Oxford University Press.
Hill, J. (ed). 1984. *Rethinking History and Myth: Indigenous South American Perspectives on the Past*. Chicago: University of Illinois Press.
———. 1996. *History, Power and Identity: Ethnogenesis in the Americas 1492-1992*. Iowa: University of Iowa Press.
Hirsch, E. and M. Strathern. 2004. *Transactions and Creations: Property Debates and the Stimulus of Melanesia*. New York: Berghahn Books.

Holy Bible, King James Version 1999[1611]. New York: American Bible Society.
Howard, C. 2001. 'Wrought Identities: The Waiwai Expeditions in Search of the "Unseen Tribes"'. Ph.D. dissertation. Chicago: University of Chicago.
Hugh-Jones, S. 2009. 'The Fabricated Body: Objects and Ancestors in Northwest Amazonia', in F. Santos-Granero (ed.), *The Occult Life of Things: Native Amazonian Theories of Materiality and Personhood*. Tucson: University of Arizona Press, pp. 33–59.
———. 2013. 'Bride-Service and the Absent Gift', *Journal of the Royal Anthropological Institute* 19(2): 356–77.
Hume, D. 1975. 'Of Justice', in L.A. Selby-Bigge (ed.), *An Enquiry Concerning Human Understanding and Concerning the Principles of Morals*. Oxford: Oxford University Press, pp. 183–204.
Ingold, T., D. Riches and J. Woodburn. 1988. *Hunters and Gatherers, vol. 2: Property, Power and Ideology*. Oxford: Berg.
Karadimas, D. 2001. 'Parenté en Esclavage: Pratiques Matrimoniales et Alliances Politiques chez les Miraña d'Amazonie Colombienne', *Droit et Cultures* 39: 81–100.
———. 2003. 'Dans le Corps de mon Ennemi: L'Hôte Parasité chez les Insectes Comme un Modèle de Reproduction chez les Miraña d'Amazonie Colombienne', in E. Motte-Florac and J. Thomas (eds), *Les 'Insectes' dans la Tradition Orale*. Leeuwen: Peeters, pp. 487–506.
Lagrou, E. 2011. 'Le graphisme sur les corps amérindiens: des chimères abstraites?' *Gradhiva* 13: 69–93.
Lagrou, Els and C. Severi (eds). 2014. *Quimeras em diálogo: grafismo e figuração nas artes indígenas*. Rio de Janeiro: 7Letras.
Larrabee, M.J. (ed.) 1993. *An Ethic of Care: Feminist and Interdisciplinary Perspectives*. New York: Routledge
Lea, V. 2012. *Riquezas Intangíveis de Pessoas Partíveis: Os Mẽbêngôkre (Kayapó) do Brasil Central*. São Paulo: EDUSP/FAPESP.
Leach, James. 2003. 'Owning Creativity: Cultural Property and the Efficacy of Custom on the Rai Coast of Papua New Guinea', *Journal of Material Culture* 8(2): 123–43.
———. 2011. 'The Problem of Property in Customary Tenure: An Example from Papua New Guinea'. Paper presented at 'The Value of Land', Lisbon, 9–10 September.
Lemonnier, Pierre. 1990. *Guerre et Festins: Paix, Échanges et Compétition dans les Highlands de Nouvelle-Guinée*. Paris: Maison des Sciences de L'Homme.
Lévi-Strauss, C. 1955. *Tristes Tropiques*. Paris: Plon.
———. 1958 [1952]. 'La Notion d'Archaïsme en Ethnologie', in *Anthropologie Structurale*. Paris: Plon, pp. 119–39.
Lévi-Strauss, C. and N. Belmont. 1963. "Marques de Propriété dans Deux Tribus Sud-Américaines". *L'Homme* 3: 102–8.
Lima, T. S. 2005. *Um Peixe Olhou para Mim : O Povo Yudjá e a Perspectiva*. São Paulo and Rio de Janeiro: Editora UNESP/ Instituto Socioambiental/ NuTI.
Locke, J. 1988 [1689]. *Two Treatises of Government*. Cambridge: Cambridge University Press.
Lowie, R. 1949. 'Property Among Tropical Forest and Marginal Tribes', in *The Handbook of South American Indians*, vol. 5. Washington DC: Smithsonian Institute. pp. 351–68.

———. 1960. *Selected Papers in Anthropology.* Berkeley: University of California Press.
Macpherson, C.B. 1962. *The Political Theory of Possessive Individualism: Hobbes to Locke.* Oxford: Oxford University Press.
Maine, H. 1912 [1861]. *Ancient Law, Its Connection with the Early History of Society and Its Relation to Modern Ideas.* London: John Murray.
Mauss, M. 1990 [1950]. *The Gift: The Form and Reason of Exchange in Archaic Societies.* London: Routledge.
McCallum, C. 2001. *Gender and Sociality in Amazonia: How Real People Are Made.* Oxford: Berg.
Menezes Bastos, R. 2011. 'Leonardo, the Flute: On the Sexual Life of Sacred Flutes among the Xinguano Indians', in J. Hill and J-P. Chaumeil (eds), *Burst of Breath: New Research on Indigenous Ritual Flutes in Lowland South America.* Lincoln: University of Nebraska Press, pp. 69–92.
Miller, J. 2009. 'Things as Persons: Body Ornaments and Alterity Among the Mamaindê (Nambikwara)', in F. Santos-Granero (ed.), *The Occult Life of Things: Native Amazonian Theories of Materiality and Personhood.* Tucson: University of Arizona Press, pp. 60–80.
———. 2012. 'Alterity Cards: Transformation and Identity Among the Mamaindê (Nambikwara) of Brazilian Amazonia'. Paper presented at 54th International Congress of Americanists, University of Vienna, 15–20 July.
———. 2015. 'Carteira de Alteridade: Transformações Mamaindê (Nambiquara)'. *Mana* 21(3): 553–585.
Munzer, S. 1990. *A Theory of Property.* Cambridge: Cambridge University Press.
Nahum-Claudel, C. 2012. 'Working Together for Yankwa: Vitalizing Cosmogony in Southern Amazonia (Enawene-nawe)', Ph.D. dissertation. Cambridge: Cambridge University.
Needham, R. (ed.). 1971. *Rethinking Kinship and Marriage.* London: Tavistock.
OED Online. Oxford University Press, December 2015. Web. 4 February 2016.
Ortner, S. 1984. 'Theory in Anthropology Since the Sixties.' *Comparative Studies in Society and History* 26(1): 126–166.
Ortner, S. and H. Whitehead. 1981. *Sexual Meanings.* New York: Cambridge University Press.
Overing, J. 1983–84. 'Elementary Structures of Reciprocity: A Comparative Note on Guianese, Central Brazilian, and North-West Amazon Socio-political Thought'. *Antropologica* 59–62: 331–48.
———. 1989. 'The Aesthetics of Production: The Sense of Community among the Cubeo and Piaroa', *Dialectical Anthropology* 14: 159–75.
———. 2003. 'In Praise of the Everyday: Trust and the Art of Social Living in an Amazonian Community'. *Ethnos* 68(3): 293–316.
Overing, J. and A. Passes (eds). 2000. *The Anthropology of Love and Anger: The Aesthetics of Conviviality in Native Amazonia.* London: Routledge.
Overing Kaplan, J. 1975. *The Piaroa: A People of the Orinoco Basin.* Oxford: Oxford University Press.
———. 1981. 'Review Article: Amazonian Anthropology.' *Journal of Latin American Studies* 13: 151–64.
Pagden, A. 1982. *The Fall of Natural Man: The American Indian and the Origins of Comparative Ethnology.* Cambridge: Cambridge University Press.
Pina-Cabral, J. de. 2001. *Between China and Europe: Person, Culture, and Emotion in Macao.* London: Continuum.

Posey, D. and G. Dutfield. 1996. *Beyond Intellectual Property: Toward Traditional Resource Rights for Indigenous Peoples and Local Communities.* Ottawa: International Development Research Centre.

Rist, G. 2008. *The History of Development from Western Origins to Global Faith.* London: Zed Books.

Rival, L. 1998. 'Prey at the Centre: Resistance and Marginality in Amazonia', in S. Day, E. Papataxiarchis and M. Stewart (eds), *Lilies of the Field: Marginal People Who Live for the Moment.* Boulder, CO: Westview, pp. 61–79.

Rivière, P. 1984. *Individual and Society in Guiana.* Oxford: Clarendon.

———. 1993. 'The Amerindianisation of Descent and Affinity', *L'Homme* 126–28: 507–16.

Rivière, P., D. Fajardo Grupioni, D. Tilkin Gallois, G. Barbosa, R. Sztutman and R. Duarte do Pateo. 2007. 'A Propósito de Redes de Relações nas Guianas', *Mana: Estudos de Antropologia Social* 13(1): 251–73.

Roosevelt, A. 1989. 'Resource Management in Amazonia before the Conquest: Beyond Ethnographic Projection', in D.A. Posey and W. Balée (eds), *Resource Management in Amazonia: Indigenous and Folk Strategies.* New York: The New York Botanical Garden, pp. 30–62.

Rowlands, M. 2004. 'Cultural Rights and Wrongs: Uses of the Concept of Property', in K. Verdery and C. Humphrey (eds), *Property in Question: Value Transformation in the Global Economy.* Oxford: Berg, pp. 207–26.

Salomon, F. and S. Schwartz. 1999. *Cambridge History of the Native Peoples of the Americas. Vol. 3: South America.* 2 vols. Cambridge: Cambridge University Press.

Santos-Granero, F. 2007. 'Of Fear and Friendship: Amazonian Sociality beyond Kinship and Affinity', *Journal of the Royal Anthropological Institute* 13(1): 1–18.

———. 2009. *Vital Enemies: Slavery, Predation and the Amerindian Political Economy of Life.* Austin: University of Texas Press.

Schneider, D.M. 1968. *American Kinship: A Cultural Account.* Englewood Cliffs, NJ: Prentice Hall.

Seeger, A. 2004. 'The Selective Protection of Musical Ideas: The "Creations" and the Dispossessed', in K. Verdery and C. Humphrey (eds), *Property in Question: Value Transformation in the Global Economy.* Oxford: Berg, pp. 69–84.

Strathern, M. 1980. 'No Nature, No Culture: The Hagen Case', in C. P. MacCormack and M. Strathern (eds), *Nature, Culture and Gender.* Cambridge: Cambridge University Press, pp. 174–222.

———. 1988. *The Gender of the Gift: Problems with Women and Problems with Society in Melanesia.* Berkeley: University of California Press.

———. 1996. 'Cutting the Network'. *Journal of the Royal Anthropological Institute* (N.S.) 2(3): 517–35.

———. 2005. *Kinship, Law and the Unexpected: Relatives Are Always a Surprise.* Cambridge: Cambridge University Press.

Taylor, A.-C. 1985. 'L'Art de la Réduction: La Guerre et les Mécanismes de la Différenciation Tribale dans la Culture Jivaro', *Journal de la Societé des Américanistes* 71(71): 159–73.

———. 1993. 'Remembering to Forget: Identity, Mourning and Memory Among the Jivaro', *Man* 28 (4): 653–78.

———. 2007. 'Sick of History: Contrasting Regimes of Historicity in the Upper Amazon', in C. Fausto and M. Heckenberger (eds.), *Time and Memory in*

Indigenous Amazonia: Anthropological Perspectives. Gainsville: University Press of Florida, pp. 133–68.
Tully, J. 1993. *An Approach to Political Philosophy: Locke in Contexts.* Cambridge: Cambridge University Press.
Turner, T. 2009. 'Valuables, Value, and Commodities Among the Kayapo of Central Brazil', in F. Santos-Granero (ed.), *The Occult Life of Things: Native Amazonian Theories of Materiality and Personhood.* Tucson: University of Arizona Press, pp. 152–72.
Van Velthem, L. 2003. *O Belo é a Fera: A Estética da Produção e da Predação entre os Wayana.* Lisbon: Museu Nacional de Etnologia/ Assírio e Alvim.
Vilaça, A. 1992. *Comendo Como Gente: Formas do Canibalismo Wari'.* Rio de Janeiro: Editora da UFRJ.
———. 1997. 'Christians without Faith: Some Aspects of the Conversion of the Wari (Pakaa Nova)'. *Ethnos* 62(1–2): 91–115.
———. 2000. 'Relations Between Funerary Cannibalism and Warfare Cannibalism: The Question of Predation', *Ethnos* 65(1): 83–106.
———. 2002. 'Making Kin Out of Others in Amazonia', *Journal of the Royal Anthropological Institute* 8(2): 347–65.
———. In press. *Praying and Preying: Christianity in Indigenous Amazonia.* Los Angeles, CA: University of California Press.
Viveiros de Castro, E. 1992. *From the Enemy's Point of View: Humanity and Divinity in an Amazonian Society.* Trans. C. Howard. Chicago: University of Chicago Press.
———. 1993. 'Alguns Aspectos da Afinidade no Dravidianato Amazônico', in E. Viveiros de Castro and M. Carneiro da Cunha (eds), *Amazônia: Etnologia e História Indígena.* São Paulo: NHII-USP/FAPESP, pp. 150–210.
———. 2002. *A Inconstância da Alma Selvagem.* São Paulo: Cosac and Naify.
———. 2004. 'Exchanging Perspectives: The Transformation of Objects into Subjects in Amerindian Ontologies'. *Common Knowledge* 10(3): 463–484
Viveiros de Castro, E. and M. Carneiro da Cunha (eds). 1993. *Amazônia: Etnologia e História Indígena.* São Paulo: Núcleo de História Indígena e do Indigenismo da USP/FAPESP.
von Benda Beckmann, F., K. von Benda Beckmann and M. Wiber. 2006. 'The Properties of Property', in F. Von Benda Beckmann, K. von Benda Beckmann and M. Wiber, *Changing Properties of Property.* Oxford: Berghahn Books, pp. 1–39.
Walker, H. 2012. 'Demonic Trade: Debt, Materiality and Agency in Amazonia', *Journal of the Royal Anthropological Institute* 18(1): 140–59.
———. 2013. *Under a Watchful Eye: Self, Power, and Intimacy in Amazonia.* Berkeley: University of California Press.
Whitehead, N. 1984. 'Carib Cannibalism: The Historical Evidence', *Journal de la Société des Américanistes* 70(1): 69–87.
———. 2003. *Histories and Historicities in Amazonia.* Lincoln: University of Nebraska Press.
———. 2011. 'Introduction', in N. Whitehead, *Of Cannibals and Kings: Primal Anthropology in the Americas.* University Park: Pennsylvania State University Press.
Xavier, C. 2013. 'Os Koripako do Alto Içana: etnografia de um grupo indígena evangélico', Ph.D. dissertation. Rio de Janeiro: PPGAS-Museu Nacional, Universidade Federal do Rio de Janeiro.

CHAPTER 1

Masters, Slaves and Real People
Native Understandings of Ownership and Humanness in Tropical American Capturing Societies

Fernando Santos-Granero

'Property' is a notion that has been only marginally addressed in tropical American anthropology. Both Fausto (2008) and Brightman (2010) have discussed the reasons for this indifference at length. Here I would only like to stress that the lengthy persistence of this state of things is to a great extent due to the widely accepted view that property plays an insignificant role in the region's highly egalitarian indigenous societies. In *La société contre l'Etat,* Pierre Clastres (1974: 174), the staunchest defender of this position, argued that 'primitive' societies such as those found in tropical America are 'a type of society in which property is unknown because it is rejected'. Clastres' equation of private property with accumulation, inequality, power and – at least implicitly – coercion and exploitation, is not new in Western philosophy. In his prizewinning essay, *Discours sur l'origine et les fondements de l'inégalité parmi les hommes* (1755), Jean-Jacques Rousseau resolutely condemned property as the origin of all social evils. Almost a hundred years later, in his work, *Qu'est-ce que la propriété? Recherche sur le principe du droit et du gouvernement* (2008), Pierre-Joseph Proudhon proclaimed no less intensely that property was a form of robbery and therefore the root of social inequality.

What is new in Clastres' essay is the idea that by rejecting the possibility of property, 'primitive' societies managed to stall the emergence of the State and with it its corollaries, inequality and coercion. Whereas it is true that private property over natural resources is largely absent in native tropical American societies – at least in the capitalist sense of the term – and that, at present, these societies show a remarkable degree of egalitarianism, this cannot be attributed to some intrinsically Amerindian metaphysical resistance to the notion of property, nor has it prevented indigenous societies from developing structures of inequality and coercion. The view that indigenous peoples have been forever engaged in a struggle against property is not supported by the historical record, which shows that at the time of contact with Europeans many native tropical American polities were engaged in large-scale processes of subjugating enemy peoples, whether as captive slaves, servant groups or tributary populations (Santos-Granero 2009a). None of these polities had the kinds of institutions that underpinned state formations like those of the Maya, Aztec, and Inca. But neither were they egalitarian societies, unyielding on questions of personal autonomy and averse to vertical forms of authority like characteristic present-day tropical American societies. All of them had developed, or were in the process of developing, supralocal forms of authority, often in the form of hereditary paramount or regional chiefs; and all showed signs of internal stratification, including, in some cases, the formation of a permanent body of full-time warriors. It should be clear, however, that whereas in both pre- and post-Columbian times most slaves were war captives or descendants of captives, not all war captives became necessarily slaves (see Erikson 1986; Fausto 2001).

In this chapter I contend that property in the Western sense of the term was not unknown in tropical America. I base my argument on analysis of the status of war captives in three different native regimes of capture and servitude at the time of contact with Europeans.[1] After elaborating on ideas first presented in a recent work on indigenous forms of slavery (Santos-Granero 2009a) and examining three cases from very different areas – the Tukano, Conibo and Chiriguaná – I suggest that captive slaves had the character of 'absolute and coalescent property' in the Roman-law sense of the concept, which is the foundation of present-day Western notions of property. Property in this sense is understood as being based on the rights of *usus* (the right to use or possess the property), *fructus* (the right to enjoy the fruits of property), and *abusus* (the right to abuse or alienate the property by transforming it, transferring it, or even destroying it). I maintain that it is precisely the case that in some contact-era tropical American societies, the rights masters had over the people they had captured in war justifies the use of the much discussed and semantically charged term 'slavery' to describe those people's condition. In effect I propose, following Testart (1998), that the crux of the slave condition is the total power that masters have over their slaves: power to be cruel or gentle, to be demanding or nurturing, to give life or take it away. In Testart's (1998: 32) words: 'No profession, no social role, no task, no way of life, is typical of the slave condition; that which is typical is neither what slaves do or how they live, because that depends on the goodwill of their masters; it is not what the master does to his slaves, but rather that he can do whatever he pleases, that he has the right to do whatever he pleases'. In this view, it is not slavery that defines a type of society but the society that defines a type of slavery; the corollary being, according to Testart (1998: 41), that 'there are as many forms of slavery as there are types of societies for which slavery exists'.

In this work I argue that Amerindian masters had total power over their war captives under the form of rights of *usus, fructus* and *abusus* – even if these rights were not conceived in such terms or encoded in a legal system. I hold that three conditions allows considering war captives as items of personal property: (1) the perception that enemy peoples were less than human and as such potential slaves; (2) the view that captives were forever indebted to their masters, who had spared their lives when they captured them; and above all (3) the idea that since captives were the product of their captor's efforts, they were as much their personal property as their houses, gardens or clothes. Ownership of war captives was, I argue, substantiated as much on indigenous notions of productive agency and ensoulment as on native taxonomies of humanness and conceptions of personal indebtedness.

At the same time, I propose that although indigenous forms of slavery were based on ideologies of predation/subordination and notions of property that resonate strongly with those found in Western slaveholding societies, they differed substantially from Western slavery insofar as they were informed by alternative notions of property and mastery based on caring, nurture, consubstantiality and well-being, such as those described by Grotti, Brightman and Fausto in this volume. It would therefore be a mistake, as Brightman (2010) has pointed out, to take the Western definition of property as a measure or referent against which to define Amerindian notions of property. In native tropical America, property relations are grounded as much in capture and predation as in nurturing and familiarization. In fact, it could be said that in this region these two elements are key components of all relations of ownership, albeit in different combinations: in some instances the predatory element dominates; in others, it is the nurturing element that prevails. The property relations involving the capture and enslavement of enemy people that are discussed in this chapter are thus not intrinsically opposed to similar notions examined in other chapters. Fluctuating between predation/capture and nurture/familiarization, indigenous notions of ownership can assume different forms. The predominance of the nurture/familiarization dimension in present-day indigenous notions of property and ownership is undoubtedly related to the fact that the social transformations involving increasing political centralization, greater internal stratification and larger polities that began in pre-Columbian times were abruptly interrupted due to colonial pressures, putting an end to the more extreme forms of dependence.

I suggest that the existence of these alternative but coexisting modes of envisioning property relations explains why, even in the most hierarchical native tropical American capturing societies, captive slaves' status as 'absolute and coalescent property' was not fixed. With the passage of time, growing intimacy and consubstantiality between masters and slaves – conditions facilitated by coresidence and commensality – meant that captive slaves, or their descendants in the first or second generations, came to be regarded as having achieved the status of 'real people'. From that point onwards they could no longer be treated as absolute property and were often incorporated into their captors' society through marriage or adoption. I therefore conclude that although ownership of human beings was not unknown in native tropical America, such a condition was never conceived of as more than a transitory state of affairs – an instance of the process that Kopytoff and Miers (1977), referring to African forms of slavery, have provocatively labelled the 'slavery-to-kinship continuum'. This suggests that in native tropical America, as elsewhere, notions of property were not homogeneous; that different notions of property could coexist within the same society; and that the status of a thing or being as an item of property was not fixed but relational, that is, subject to transformation in accordance to changes in the nature of the relation between possessor and possessed.

Taxonomies of Humanness and Alterity

In contrast with slavery as practised in other parts of the world, in tropical America slavery always assumed the form of exo-servitude, that is, the enslavement of people belonging to societies other than those of their captors (Lévy-Bruhl 1931: 9). This preference stemmed from a particular taxonomy of beinghood and alterity that distinguishes the condition of personhood from that of humanness. In such taxonomies most living beings – as well as a large range of natural objects and artefacts – are considered 'persons', but only some are regarded as 'real humans' or 'real people' (Santos-Granero 2011, 2012). Both these conditions are relative, with some persons regarded as being more persons than others in terms of their capacity for consciousness, agency and intentionality, and some humans being considered more human than others in terms of their capacity to lead a 'civil' life – that is, to observe those social requirements judged indispensable to attaining a correct and moral life. Members of capturing societies viewed themselves as 'real' or 'true' people, as opposed to other peoples whom they perceived as less human than themselves to different degrees and thus potentially enslavable. In such societies, those regarded as least human were the most prone to be enslaved.

The Tukano-speaking peoples of the Vaupés River basin (in Colombia and Brazil) – including the Tukano proper as well as the Cubeo, Desana, Barasana and Makuna, among others – refer to themselves as *mahsá*, a term that can be translated as 'true people' (Chernela 1993: 47). In contrast, they refer to the Makú, their interfluvial neighbours and enemies, whom they used to enslave starting in the late eighteenth century at the latest, as *pohsá* (Reichel-Dolmatoff 1996: 83; C. Hugh-Jones 1979: 57; Århem 1981: 121). Most authors translate this latter term as 'servants' or 'servant people'. Giacone (1965: 96) goes even further, rendering it as 'slave of others, one who works without remuneration'. According to Reichel-Dolmatoff (1971: 19), however, the term *poyá* – a variant of *pohsá* – derives from *poyári*, which denotes 'something incomplete or abnormal' or 'something that is almost-but-not-quite', in reference to the fact that Tukano regard Makú as 'not entirely people'.

From a Tukano point of view, the Makú are in effect the absolute Others or anti-Tukano (Jackson 1983: 158). They (purportedly) live deep into the forest instead of along the open riverbanks; they are nomads dwelling in fragile lean-tos instead of large, sturdy malocas; they subsist on hunting and gathering instead of fishing and agriculture; instead of being well provisioned they are incapable of feeding themselves; they are not tall, well built and clean but small, with ugly features and unclean habits; they go about unadorned instead of donning rich ornaments and especially the *uhtabu*, the white cylindrical quartz stone pendant used by all Tukano men; they speak an awful gibberish instead of the beautiful Tukanoan languages; they lack an elaborate ritual life; and – worst of all from a Tukano point of view – they are incestuous in that they marry within their language group instead of exogamously. These traits, according to the Tukano, characterize the Makú as not real people and thus potential slaves (Jackson 1991: 25; Reichel-Dolmatoff 1971: 18; Silverwood-Cope 1990: 129).

Among the Pano-speaking Conibo of the Ucayali River (Peru) we find a similar social taxonomy. Known as Lords of the Ucayali, the Conibo were depicted by seventeenth-century chroniclers as feared by their semi-riverine and interfluvial neighbours, against whom they undertook yearly raids to seize captives and loot. They called themselves *húnibo* – *húni* means 'people' and *bo* is a plural marker – in the sense of 'the people' or 'real people'. In turn they regarded all their neighbours as *nahua*, a term meaning both 'foreigner' and 'enemy' ('Diccionario cunibo-castellano y castellano-cunibo' 1927: 413). Conibo saw *nahua* people as representing a different form of humanity, one closer to animality, because they lacked one or more of the cultural practices Conibo people regarded as signs of a 'civilized' status: wearing cotton tunics, elongating the heads of male and female babies, and circumcising nubile girls (DeBoer 1986: 238).

In the Conibo taxonomy of alterity, their most savage neighbours were the Pano-speaking Uni (Cashibo), Amahuaca, Remo, Sensi, Mayoruna and Capanahua, who went around naked, had round heads, and except in the case of the Uni, did not practise female circumcision. These hinterland peoples were considered cannibalistic, dirty and savage. Slightly less savage were the Arawak-speaking Ashaninka, who wore cotton tunics but did not practise head elongation or female circumcision, and the Yine (Piro), who wore tunics and practised female circumcision but did not elongate their heads. The Pano-speaking Shipibo and Setebo, peoples who engaged in all these practices, were considered enemies but not savages. Most Conibo raids were directed at peoples with round heads, a situation reminiscent of that found in the Pacific North-West Coast of North America (MacLeod 1928: 645–47).

The Tupi-Guaraní-speaking ancestors of the Chiriguaná, as the present-day Chiriguano were called in early colonial sources – were newcomers to the Southern Andes of Bolivia at the time of contact, having arrived from the east in several waves in the fifteenth and early sixteenth centuries. In the process they displaced, or subjugated as servant groups or tributary populations, Inca colonists, highland frontier peoples, and the native Arawak-speaking Chané. Although there is evidence that the invaders brought some of their women with them, it is said that most took women from the native Chané population. This, it was claimed, was why they were called Chiriones, which in Tupi-Guaraní means 'mixed bloods, children of Chiriguaná men and women from other nations' (Suárez de Figueroa 1965: 404). As Combès and Lowrey (2006) suggest, however, in this process the Tupi-Guarani invaders were Arawakized as much as their Chané captives were Tupi-Guaranized. The people resulting from these unions retained the Tupi-Guarani language and called themselves *ava* or *aba*, a term meaning 'man', in the double sense of man as gender and man as condition. When used as a self-designation this term is usually associated with the intensifier *-eté*, which may be translated as 'true', signifying the Chiriguaná as 'true men'. In contrast, the Chiriguaná called their indigenous neighbours, and especially the Chané, *tapui* or *tapíi*. According to Ruiz de Montoya (1876: 355r, 376v), this term is composed of the nouns *tap*, 'purchased thing', and *teíi*, 'generation', in the sense of collectivity, whether of animals or people. Thus, the term *tapui* can be translated as 'purchased people' and, by extension, 'slave people'. This is what an early anonymous chronicler meant when he claimed in 1573 that: 'Their custom is to be constantly engaged in war against other peoples that do not speak their tongue, all of whom they call slaves' (Relación anónima en la que se hace referencia al descubrimiento hecho por Solís del Río de la Plata 1941: 66). On the basis of more recent research, Riester et al. (1979: 264) assert that *tapui* also connotes 'enemy' and as such is equivalent to the term *ñanaigua,* meaning 'forest people' or 'barbarians' – although one anonymous reviewer argues that this is erroneous and that *ñanaigua* is the term used by the Chiriguaná to refer to the Guaycuru- and Zamuco-speaking peoples of the Gran Chaco.

In all these examples members of capturing societies justified the enslavement of their enemies by referring to them by terms that evoked notions of backwardness, wildness and an inferior humanity. In some instances they regarded their preferred victims as marked with the stigma of servitude even before they were actually defeated and subjugated. Ushique, a late nineteenth-century Conibo chief, offered an interesting rationale for this particular conception: 'Cashibo are mostly our maroon servants who have taken to the woods; they speak our language, although badly, and we go from time to time to retrieve their offspring as they reproduce' (Stahl 1928: 150). Similar notions are present among the Tukano and the Chiriguaná, suggesting that tropical American capturing societies viewed their preferred enemies as slave-breeding or servant-breeding populations – in other words, as breeders of future property.

Captivity as a Gift of Life

Whereas classical slavery revolved around the capture of adult men and women to engage or sell them as labourers, raiders in native tropical America were interested in taking only children and young women. This is true of the three cases analysed here. In addition, some peoples, like the Tukano and Chiriguaná, used to subject entire collectivities to incorporate them as servant groups. In most slave raids, old men and women were often killed in revenge for past grievances, while fallen warriors were executed in order to obtain highly valued bodily trophies, or kept temporarily alive before being consumed in cannibalistic rituals. Captured children were often the only survivors of their natal villages. As such, they owed their lives to their captors' whim and for this reason were indebted to them and belonged to them for as long as their masters wished. In Patterson's (1982: 26) words, 'slaves entered the relationship as a substitute for death'. The gift of life bestowed by captors on their captives is thus an important component in turning the latter into property.

Tukano raids against Makú bands were quite frequent (Spruce 1908: I, 477; Wallace 1853: 288). As a result, Makú captive slaves, mostly young women and children, were found in almost every Tukano village. In addition, some villages also held sway over small Makú bands that had been subjected by force of arms to avenge alleged sorcery attacks or the pillaging of Tukano gardens, or that had surrendered voluntarily to escape famine or constant harassment by their Tukano neighbours (Coudreau 1887:

160–64, 179; Koch-Grünberg 1995: II, 236). According to Koch-Grünberg (1995: II, 236), members of attached servant groups did not act as 'domestic slaves', but rather as 'day labourers' only called upon to render certain services. Despite their subordinate status, Makú servant groups retained some autonomy and the right to live together and maintain their family links. They were not as alienated as captive slaves.

Both Makú captive slaves and attached Makú bands owed their lives to their Tukano masters, because the latter had either spared their lives at the time of capture or sheltered and fed them when they were starving. With the passage of time, some Makú captive slaves and servant groups managed to regain their autonomy. Even then they maintained links of attenuated servitude – best characterized as ties of clientship – with their former masters (Coudreau 1887: 179; Koch-Grünberg 1906: 881).

Conibo raided their round-headed neighbours even more intensely than the Tukano did the Makú. Their yearly expeditions gathered large numbers of warriors for long periods of time (Amich 1975: 297). Each year, hundreds of Conibo canoes departed from the Ucayali towards the Urubamba or Tambo rivers to raid their enemies (Samánez y Ocampo 1980: 82). Most authors suggest that the main objective of Conibo raids was the capture of women, attributing this practice to Conibo polygamy (Amich 1975: 298; Buenaventura 1906: 345–46). A careful reading of the sources[2] demonstrates, however, that the capture of children was as important as the abduction of women, if not more so (Biedma 1981: 95). In contrast, adult males were always killed in battle or tortured and killed after being captured. Conibo raiders took pride in taking the heads and hearts of killed enemy warriors (ibid.). They displayed these war trophies in their houses as signs of their courage but more probably – given the widespread Amerindian belief that heads and hearts are the seats of potent generative forces (Taylor 1993: 660; Goldman 2004: 348) – as sources of fertility, to be used to benefit the slayer and his family. Young women and children were therefore the only survivors of Conibo raids, owing their lives to those who captured them.

The Chiriguaná were described as 'unruly people' who raided the inhabitants of both the lowland and highland regions to take captives whom they either made them slaves or ritually ate. By the turn of the sixteenth century Chiriguaná had put an end to their exo-cannibalistic practices (Díaz de Guzmán 1979: 76). From then on, male enemies were either killed or sold as slaves to Spanish agents. Chiriguaná raids were fearsome affairs. The attackers killed the old, the sick and all others who could not flee. They took as many captives as possible, especially children but also young men and women (Giannecchini 1996: 328). In addition they took the heads of dead enemy warriors or, if this was not possible, their scalps. The earliest mention of this practice is from 1617, when a Chiriguaná band killed five Spanish traders and, after cutting their heads, 'made a great feast' (Díaz de Guzmán 1979: 80). It is not clear whether this ceremonial practice predated the colonial encounter, but since it is well attested in later sources in relation to indigenous enemies and as constituting a central feature of victory rituals, it most probably did (Corrado and Comajuncosa 1990: I, 46; Thouar 1991: 58–59; Giannecchini 1996: 324). In such rituals the head trophies of enemy warriors were paraded throughout the captors' village and over the pots of fermented *changüi*, presumably to disseminate the life-giving forces contained in them among all participants (Giannecchini 1996: 328). Not all Chiriguaná raids ended in the massacre of the enemy and the enslavement of those whose lives had been spared. Often, entire Chané groups chose to surrender, to avoid the loss of life and property entailed by waging war against their powerful enemies. Such people were generally resettled as servant groups in the environs of the conquering Chiriguaná settlements. The notion that war captives owe their lives to their captors' benevolence or caprice is an important element in the transformation of captives into property. By sparing their lives, captors forced their captives into a debt relation that ended only with death.

Productive Agency and Ensoulment

The most important element justifying the transformation of war captives into property was the common indigenous notion that the creative act grants the maker rights of ownership over that which he or she has made (Dumont 1976: 34; Jackson 1983: 57; Wright 1998: 296; McCallum 2001: 7; Brightman 2010). Creativity, or productive agency, can assume a variety of forms. It can refer to the production of material things with one's own hands, such as canoes (Wilbert 1993: 57), gardens (Murphy 1960: 63), curare (Erikson 2009: 176–77), or cassava bread (Belaúnde 2001: 177). But it can also refer to the production of extraordinary things made to appear through one's ritual activities, such as spirit helpers (Harner 1973: 118) or sacred songs (Smith 1977: 181). It involves all things that are obtained as the result of one's negotiating abilities to barter, purchase or engage in gift exchange of not only trade goods (Thomas 1982: 47) but also women (Rivière 1969: 41; Dumont 1976: 40; Murphy and Murphy 1985: 133). In addition, it concerns the social production of bodies, especially those of one's own children (Santos-Granero 1991: 211; McCallum 2001: 16). Lastly, it involves all collective initiatives originating from one's abilities as a leader and organizer, and sometimes the products thereof, such as fishing with *timbó* (Murphy and Murphy 1985: 94) or malocas (C. Hugh-Jones 1979: 46). This explains why in native tropical American societies one can own pots and weapons, houses and gardens, names and spirit familiars, children and prey, ritual ceremonies and fishing expeditions, but one cannot own the land, the rivers, the forests or the wild animals – none of which are of human creation.

In all these cases, ownership appears as an instance of incorporation, since the act of creation involves a transfer of soul substance from the creator to his or her creation. This process of ensoulment entails a kind of embodiment by which the ensouled objects become, as it were, an 'extension of their owners' bodies' (Santos-Granero 2009b: 14; Crocker 1985: 112). This is especially true in the context of the production of artefacts, which appear as the materialization of the subjective dimensions of their makers (McCallum 2001: 92; Erikson 2009: 176; S. Hugh-Jones 2009: 48; Lagrou 2009: 209). In such cases ensoulment assumes the form of a material embodiment of nonmaterial intentionalities (Viveiros de Castro 2004: 470). Artefacts, cooked food and beverages constitute the objective expression of the knowledge, skills and affects of their makers, and thus partake of the latter's subjectivity (Karsten 1923: 12; McCallum 2001: 93; Belaúnde 2001: 177). This agrees with the indigenous notion that views makers and their products as related in terms of filiation. As Lagrou (2009: 209) has suggested, artefacts are often described as the 'children' of their makers.

Members of native tropical American capturing societies, well aware that war captives were the result of their personal endeavours, often equated enemy peoples with animals of prey and the capture of enemies with the hunting of animals. The notion that captives belonged to those who seized them was reinforced by the idea that captives, like artefacts, are the 'children' of their makers. From an indigenous viewpoint, children are brought to life through the expenditure of their parents' bodily fluids and energies (Wagley and Galvão 1949: 69; McCallum 2001: 16). They are endowed with social identity through the ritual bodily practices their parents perform on their behalf, and they are kept alive through the productive activities their parents conduct so as to meet their daily needs for food and drink. For this reason, Amerindians often assert that children are 'owned' by their parents, whereas they regard orphans as 'without owner' (Rivière 1969: 243; Santos-Granero 1991: 211; Belaúnde 2001: 121). Similarly, captives came into being through the efforts of their captors, who expend energy and may even risk their lives to capture them. They were given a new social identity through rituals of enslavement organized on their behalf by their captors and their wives (cf. Santos-Granero 2005, 2009a: chapter 5). And they were nourished with food and drink nominally produced by their masters and mistresses. Captors and parents owned the people they captured, or gave birth to, because they were responsible for causing them to exist.

These two conceptions – the equation of enemies with prey and captives with children – were connected to a third notion: the conceptualization of captive-making as a civilizing project. In line with the idea that enemies were game and potential prey, Amerindians regarded war captives and especially captured children as pets, positioned midway between animality and humanity. Thus the assimilation of war captives was, as Fausto (1999, 2001) has compellingly argued, understood as a process of 'familiarization'. As quasi-animals, captives had to be tamed; as quasi-humans, they had to be civilized. This notion, expressed in native terms meaning simultaneously 'to make slaves, pets or friends' and 'to tame/pacify' is central to native tropical American forms of slavery. Hence, it could be said that indigenous slavery was as much about turning people into pets as about turning pets into people.

Some Tukanoan groups assert that Makú are not real people but rather 'children of the jaguar' (Giacone 1949: 88), thus placing them firmly in the animal sphere. Makú captives belonged to whoever had captured them. In contrast, members of subjugated Makú bands were nominally owned by the chief, or 'owner', of the maloca, who could distribute them among members of his or other malocas as he pleased (Koch-Grünberg 1995: II, 236). The Tukanoan noun 'master', *pekcace,* has the same root as the terms 'hunter', *pekcaieegue,* and 'hunting', *pekcaieecé* (Giacone 1949: 172, 174). These terms suggest that the Tukano generally viewed the Makú as game animals and Makú captives as hunted prey. More importantly, by equating masters with hunters Tukano underscored the warriors' agency in the process of turning captives into property.

Several sources suggest that the Tukano treated their Makú captives as pets (Koch-Grünberg 1995: I, 276) or 'as a particularly useful sort of dog' (McGovern 1927: 248), but there is no linguistic evidence that this is what the Tukano themselves had in mind. We do know, however, that the Tukano regarded their Makú captives as being even less than dogs, for it is said that whereas Tukano mothers allowed their children to play with dogs, they thought it very degrading if they played with Makú children (McGovern 1927: 248).

The Conibo used two terms to refer to war captives. The first term, *hiná,* has been translated as 'captive', 'slave', or 'live-in servant' (Marqués 1931: 143, 148, 155), but also as 'domestic animal', 'household servant', and 'adoptive child' ('Diccionario' 1927: 405, 457). The likening of captives to pets – both statuses resulting from Conibo warrior/hunters' custom of killing the progenitors of enemies and animals – is reinforced by the term *hináqui,* which the above sources render as 'to raise slaves and animals' (Marqués 1931: 148; 'Diccionario' 1927: 405). Since this term is made up of the root *hiná* – 'slave or domestic animal' – and the causative suffix *acqui,* meaning 'to cause to be', it would be better translated as 'to make slaves and pets'. Such a rendering reveals not only the importance that the Conibo attributed to the agency of warriors and hunters in the making of captives and pets, but also the significance they attributed to the act of 'causing to be' as the basis for property claims. The notion of *hináqui* is further associated to that of *rágue áqui*. Translated as 'to tame' or 'to domesticate' (Marqués 1931: 134), this expression can be actually broken down into the terms *rag* = 'friend', and *ácqui* = causative suffix, thus meaning 'to cause someone to be a friend'. Frank (1994: 182–85) translates a similar term, *raëati*, used by the Uni, the archenemies of the Conibo and Pano speakers like the latter, as 'to civilize or pacify'.

Early seventeenth-century dictionaries of the Tupi language, which shares 96 per cent of its lexemes with Chiriguaná (Dietrich 1986: 194), contain a rich vocabulary for master/slave relations that is steeped in images and metaphors of hunting. This vocabulary accords well with what we know of Chiriguaná warring practices, which included raiding for captives and the subjection of entire non-Chiriguaná settlements as servant groups. The term that designated actual captive slaves – as opposed to potential slave peoples or *tapui* – was *tembiau*. This term is related to both *tembiara*, which has the connotation of 'prey taken in hunting or war', and *mímbába*, meaning 'domestic animal' (*Vocabulario na lingua brasilica* 1938: 352, 146, 408). It is made up of the terms *tembiá*, which can be rendered as 'that which I seized while hunting, fishing or warring', and *haïhúbá*, 'to gain someone's goodwill through love' (Ruiz de Montoya 1876: 377v, 139r). These apparently contradictory expressions convey the paradoxical position in which war captives found themselves in Chiriguaná society. Initially forced violently into slavery through raiding and capture, they were eventually loved and taken care of as wives or adoptive children. This ambivalence was possibly more marked in the early days of the Tupi-Guarani invasion of eastern Bolivia, when the mostly male invaders were in search of wives, than in later times, when their society became more stable and raiding was no longer the main means of obtaining a spouse. Be that as it may, Chiriguaná warriors clearly ideologically equated the violent taking of war captives with the seduction and taming of reluctant women and children. Additionally, Chiriguaná conceived of the process of making captives as a civilizing act. Thus, the term *aimoauje*, 'to subject the enemy in war', has the same root as the terms *aimobiár*, meaning 'to tame an animal', and *aimonhirõ*, 'to pacify' (*Vocabulario* 1938: 371, 100, 324). These terms confirm that the Chiriguaná also equated enemies to animal prey, and war captives to wild animals domesticated and kept as pets. It also explains why war captives – the product of a warrior's productive agency – always remained the property of the warriors who had captured them (Thouar 1991: 59).

The above suggests, as Brightman (2010: 144) has put it, that in Amerindian thought 'creativity begets ownership'. This is so because, through their productive agency, creators instil part of their soul stuff, affects and skills into their creations, making them, as it were, a part of themselves. This suggests that in native tropical America property is tightly linked to processes of ensoulment and assumes the form of an extension – however tenuous – of the owner's body.

Mastery and Absolute Property Rights

If it is true that productive agency and ensoulment bestow on the creator rights of property over that which he or she has created, it is no less true that these rights are not always absolute. In other words, not everything that results from one's productive agency and is therefore 'owned' can be bartered or sold, let alone destroyed or killed. Though they may have the rights of *usus* and *fructus* over that which they own, indigenous owners do not always have the right of *abusus* (alienation) over everything they own – as also holds true in Western societies with respect, for instance, to items of property regarded as 'historical heritage' or 'national treasure'. Children and wives may be 'owned' in the sense of being the product of one's exertions or exchanges, but they are rarely bartered or sold, and only under very special circumstances can they be legitimately killed (Santos-Granero 2002, 2004, 2011). This is so because native moral imperatives place 'real people' – one's own people – and especially those to whom one is related, whether as kin or as affine, outside the sphere of absolute and coalescent property. In contrast, native tropical American warriors acquired full rights of property over the people they captured in war.

According to Giacone (1965: 114), the term the Tukano used to denote ownership – *viogue* – conflates the notions of 'master', 'owner' and 'chief'. Tukano masters had absolute and coalescent rights of property over their captive slaves and, to a lesser extent, over members of their servant groups. That they had rights of *usus* and *fructus* over their Makú slaves and attached servants is evidenced by the fact that the latter were forced to do all the heavy and unrewarding work for their masters' families (McGovern 1927: 209). They were used to carry out farming activities and do household chores (Koch-Grünberg 1906: 877). They provided their masters with game, fish and forest products (Koch-Grünberg 1995: II, 276). They also carried out other arduous tasks, for example serving as paddlers in long-distance fluvial trips (Koch-Grünberg 1995: II, 246). And they acted as personal attendants to their masters and mistresses (McGovern 1927: 249; Koch-Grünberg 1995: I, 310). Makú captive and servant children were used as babysitters for their masters' younger children (Biocca

1965: I, 481). And young, unattached Makú female captives were forced to provide their sexual favours to Tukano youngsters and occasionally even to older married men (Koch-Grünberg 1995: I, 277; McGovern 1927: 249).

Tukano masters also had rights of *abusus* over both their Makú captives and attached servant groups. Makú captive slaves were sold in intra- and intertribal trading networks in exchange for prestige goods, namely personal ornaments and ceremonial objects (Kok 1926: 922; Wallace 1853: 288, 300; Goldman 1963: 105–6). In later times, they were also traded to white people for industrial goods, especially rifles (Coudreau 1887: 179). Tukano men often traded the children they had begotten with their Makú slaves (Stradelli 1890: 433). In turn, Tukano chiefs had not only the right to distribute members of Makú servant groups among the different households that composed their malocas, but also the right to give them away as presents to allied chiefs (Koch-Grünberg 1995: II, 236; Goldman 1963: 105). In extreme cases, members of Makú servant groups could be traded as captive slaves to other Tukano malocas in exchange for ceremonial objects, a sign of the fine line that separated them from captive slaves (Goldman 1963: 105–6). More importantly, under certain circumstances Tukano masters had power over the life and limb of their Makú slaves and servants, for instance in cases in which the latter were accused of killing a member of the master's family through sorcery (Biocca 1965: I, 194).

The Conibo term for 'master', *hibo*, also has the meaning of 'owner' and 'chief' (Márques 1931: 134; 'Diccionario' 1927: 394, 404, 437, 455). Conibo masters and mistresses had rights of *usufructus* over their captive slaves. Adult captive women were expected to work under the direction of their mistress, planting, weeding, harvesting and carrying loads of agricultural produce (Amich 1975: 93). Captive women were also expected to weave mosquito nets and other textiles (Stahl 1928: 150). In addition, they were often taken as concubines or forced to provide sexual favours to their masters (Raimondi 1905: 217–18; Stahl 1928: 150). Captive children were charged with taking care of the older members of their masters' household (Stahl 1928: 150). When they grew older, they assumed more laborious, time-consuming tasks, being expected to clear gardens, carry large loads of firewood and build canoes (DeBoer 1986: 233; Amich 1975: 93; Stahl 1928: 150). Similarly, when Conibo men went on a trading or visiting trip, their male captives were expected to do all the heavy work, including paddling, loading and unloading cargo, and carrying the canoe on their shoulders whenever necessary (Stiglich 1905: 344; DeBoer 1986: 233).

Conibo masters also had the right of *abusus* over their captive slaves. Victorious raiders returning home with numerous captives kept some of them for their own service, trading the rest with fellow tribesmen or, in later times, Europeans. An early source reports that Conibo raiders preferred to keep all captive girls for themselves and traded only some of the boys (Raimondi 1905: 218). Intertribal commerce in war captives was quite extensive. Recent captives provided the bulk of the trade. But there is evidence that Conibo people sometimes traded captive children they had raised as their children and even captive women they had kept as concubines. Such captives, we are told, were exchanged with other Conibo men or sold to foreigners (Marcoy 1869: I, 629; Ordinaire 1887: 308). While all sources agree that Conibo people treated their captive slaves kindly (Girbal y Barceló 1924: 161), they also indicate that captive slaves who did not comply with their masters' wishes were publicly punished in yearly multi-village meetings in which disputes and cases of insubordinate or disrespectful servants were presented, discussed and dealt with (Stahl 1928: 159).

Like their Tukano and Conibo counterparts, Chiriguaná masters – *yara* (*Vocabulario* 1938: 195, 389; Gonçalves Dias 1858: 75) – used their captive slaves and servants to perform the heaviest domestic tasks, although this does not mean that masters were exempted or totally abstained from productive work. More importantly, the obligations of subordinates varied according to their status (captive slaves or members of servant groups), their seniority (newly taken or long-time captives) and the bonds they had established with their masters. The most important task assigned to Chané female captives and servants was farming, a task at which they excelled. In addition, captive women were charged with most household chores, including preparation of maize beer and care of their masters' children (Lizárraga 1968: 84; Combès and Saignes 1991: 80). They also did most of the spinning and weaving of cotton textiles, as Chiriguaná women were little inclined to perform these demanding tasks (Polo de Ondegardo 1991: 137). They furthermore served as their masters' concubines. Captive men and boys were expected to do the most arduous agricultural tasks. They also had menial obligations, such as kindling the fire during the night to keep their masters warm or serving as porters whenever their masters travelled (Arriaga 1974: 70). Additionally, slaves and servants trained in the arts of war by their Chiriguaná masters were expected to join them in their raids against their enemy – often their own people – and fight in the frontline (Polo de Ondegardo 1991: 136).

Historical sources indicate that Chiriguaná masters treated their slaves and servants well (Giannecchini 1996: 328). However, subordinates who refused to comply with their masters' wishes could be punished. This must have happened quite often, since it is said that captives used to prepare magical charms to keep their masters from thrashing them (*Vocabulario* 1938: 234). More importantly, Chiriguaná masters and mistresses held the power of life and death over their captives (Arriaga 1974: 63).

Captive women had to accede to their captors' sexual demands lest they be killed (Nino 1912: 279). Captive children, for their part, were considered the property of the wife of the man who captured them. As such, we are told, these wives 'were their absolute owners, they could sell them to whomever they pleased and, if necessary, also kill them' (Giannecchini 1996: 328). Captive slaves were bartered in intra- and intertribal networks (Nino 1912: 279) and could be inherited by the children of those who captured them (Susnik 1968: 35).

In brief, captive slaves could be exchanged at indigenous and colonial markets, given as gifts, physically punished and, under certain circumstances, even killed with total impunity. It is this right, the right of *abusus* that granted masters total power over their slaves, that constitutes, as Testart (1998: 32) has so lucidly argued, the crux of the slave condition.

Consubstantiality and the Unmaking of Slave Property

The status of native tropical American captive slaves as absolute and coalescent property of those who had captured them, or of those who had obtained them through trade, was not an everlasting condition. Slaves, but more often their descendants in the first or second generations, were eventually incorporated into their captors' society through marriage or adoption. This change of status seems to have resulted from the indigenous notion that commensality and coresidence generates a kind of consubstantiality between those who share food and live under the same roof, making them of the 'same kind'. This notion is widespread in native tropical America. Crocker (1985: 81) noted that the Bororo 'feel that persons who live together over the years come eventually to partake of a single organic identity'. Referring to the Yine (Piro), Gow (1991: 114) claims that commensality is crucial to the creation and maintenance of 'civilized' social life, insofar as the 'eating of "real food" creates kinship'. McCallum (2001: 104) asserts that among the Cashinahua the sharing of food generates 'a shared identity (both) as kin and as real human beings'. And Belaúnde (2001: 186) reports, in relation to the Airo pai, that '[b]y eating from the same plate people of both genders develop an intimate link between them insofar as it is thought that all kinds of physical and moral traits can be transmitted or "affixed" when sharing food from a plate'. Through conviviality and the sharing of 'real food', captive slaves and other subordinates were thought to gradually acquire the traits of 'real people', so they eventually came to be regarded as family members. With the passage of time, such fictive kinship links were often formalized when 'tamed' or 'civilized' captives were incorporated as either spouses or adoptive children.

The process of assimilation of Makú people into Tukano society differed, depending on whether they had been captured individually in war or subjected collectively as a servant group. In either case, Makú subordinates were not allowed to sleep in their masters' maloca or eat with them (McGovern 1927: 186, 248; Giacone 1949: 88; Biocca 1965: I, 472; Knobloch 1972: 105). This explains why the process of integration of subordinates was more prolonged in Tukanoan societies than among the Conibo and Chiriguaná, and why it was generally a collective rather than an individual affair. Given the almost universal Tukano refusal to marry Makú people, female Makú captives were rarely taken as concubines. As we have seen, however, they had to be sexually available to the men of the maloca (Koch-Grünberg 1995: I, 277; Goldman 1963: 96). If these furtive relationships led to pregnancies, the children of such unions were not recognized as legitimate Tukano (Stradelli 1890: 433; Silva 1962: 409). Makú captive men were even less likely to be assimilated through marriage, for no Tukano woman would accept marriage to a Makú. As a result, in most cases Makú captives married among themselves. Such captive couples, according to McGovern (1927: 248), 'were allowed to live a family life so that they could breed further slaves for their masters'.

Makú servant groups had a better chance of being assimilated into their masters' societies. Early on, Koch-Grünberg (1995: II, 91) pointed out that several low-ranking sibs among the Tukano-speaking Cubeo were known to descend from Makú servant groups forced to abandon their nomadic life and settle down. As a result of prolonged conviviality and coresidence, such groups had adopted the Cubeo language and cultural practices that, from a native point of view, constituted visible signs of their newly acquired 'civilized' status. Full assimilation was marked by intermarriage between the incorporated Makú and their former Tukano masters (Silverwood-Cope 1990: 74). Once such marriage exchanges took place, the Tukano often chose to forget the ancestry of their Makú forest affines. This affinal amnesia played a large role in the assimilation of Makú servant groups and long-time captive slaves as Tukano low-ranking or servant sibs, a process reported not only among the Cubeo but also among the Tukano proper (Reichel-Dolmatoff 1996: 42), the Desana (Coudreau 1887: 164; Koch-Grünberg 1995: I, 251), the Bará (Jackson 1983: 159), and the Makuna (Århem 1981: 13).

Among the Conibo, war captives had little chance of being fully assimilated during their lifetimes, even if they had been taken as children. All sources concur that, as the result of prolonged coresidence, captive children soon learned Conibo language, aesthetics and social etiquette (Girbal y Barceló 1964: 282). They nonetheless were not considered to be fully Conibo because they had not undergone head elongation and, in the case of captive women, had not been circumcised, signs of their 'wild' and 'uncivilized' condition. Lacking the marks of 'true' Conibo people, captive children were generally not allowed to marry Conibo men and women (Fry 1907: 477). Sources indicate that captive women could be taken by Conibo men as concubines for themselves or their sons, and meritorious captive men could sometimes be given a Conibo woman in marriage (Stiglich 1905: 344; Stahl 1928: 150). Nevertheless, the general tendency was for captives to marry other captives, preferably from their own society of origin (Fry 1907: 474). Captive couples continued to live together with their masters as members of their households.

The children born of such unions, however, were subjected to head elongation and raised as 'legitimate' Conibo (*legítimo Conibo*) (Stahl 1928: 164). They were taught Conibo language and cultural practices, and girls were circumcised after puberty (Fry 1907: 474). Only after having been marked as true Conibo, or 'real people', were these children allowed to take Conibo spouses. They were then entitled to all the rights enjoyed by the Conibo and led lives almost indistinguishable from Conibos'. This would explain why some authors assert that from a Conibo perspective, 'Conibos are those who are born in the tribe bearing that name' (Fry 1907: 474). It also explains why early sources report that the descendants of captive slaves became part of the general Conibo population in the lapse of two generations (Girbal y Barceló 1964: 282).

The manner in which Chiriguaná people integrated and assimilated their war captives varied over time. During the first stage, when the eastern slopes of the Bolivian Andes were conquered by the Chiriguaná's Tupi-Guarani ancestors – still not very numerous – they increased their numbers by taking captive Chané women as their wives, or by giving their daughters in marriage to captive Chané boys who had proven their courage as warriors (Polo de Ondegardo 1991: 138). The children of these mixed marriages were raised as Tupi-Guarani and were assimilated as fellow tribespeople, giving rise to the Chiriguaná ethnic group as it came to be known by the Spaniards in the early sixteenth century (Díaz de Guzmán 1979: 72–73). As the intensity of Chiriguaná attacks increased, and with it the number of Chané people taken as captives, it became increasingly difficult for these to become rapidly assimilated into Chiriguaná society.

In this second stage, captive children continued to be raised as Chiriguaná, but they were not immediately adopted by their captors. They were still considered to be captive slaves and as such were seldom allowed to take Chiriguaná spouses, being forced to marry among themselves. In such cases their children were considered to be 'the property of their master as long as they live under their dominion' (Giannecchini 1996: 328). Captive women continued to be taken by Chiriguaná men, but now as concubines rather than wives. The children of such mixed unions retained the stigma of their captive origin and were called and treated as *tapui*, 'real or potential captives' (Métraux 1930: 328). Mixed Chiriguaná-Chané children, however, stood a better chance of becoming assimilated than did the children of captive Chané couples. Thus, young captive men who stood out as brave warriors were rapidly recruited into Chiriguaná mainstream society as *queremba,* or 'warriors'.

Birth into Chiriguaná society, together with the consubstantiality favoured by conviviality, generated the conditions for the gradual transformation of Chané captives into *ava,* or real Chiriguaná. Such tamed captives were no longer treated as *tapui* or *tembiau,* but rather as 'grandchildren'. In turn, former captives stopped addressing masters or owners as *cheya,* 'my master', and began treating them as *chirámui,* 'my grandfather' or *chiyari,* 'my grandmother' (Susnik 1968: 32). With the passage of time, these former subordinates initially incorporated as 'quasi-kin' became assimilated as actual kin and affines, completing the transition from slavery to kinship typical of many African and native tropical American societies (see Kopytoff and Miers 1977).

Thus, from an indigenous perspective, captive slavery was a process rather than a fixed condition. Captive slaves were regarded as 'people in the making'. They began as less-than-human beings, but conviviality and consubstantiality caused them to undergo a double process of familiarization and incorporation through marriage and adoption, by which they finally achieved the status of civilized, true human beings, that is, of people with whom one can establish kinship ties.

Final Remarks

For native tropical American societies, the slave condition was less an opposition between freedom and lack of freedom than one between humanity and non-humanity, sociality and non-sociality. As Kopytoff and Miers (1977: 17) have argued in relation to African societies, 'the antithesis of "slavery" is not "freedom" qua autonomy but rather "belonging"'. Slaves in kin-based societies are foreigners – 'others' who do not belong because they are considered to be less than human – and are therefore believed to lack the arts of civility and social life (Lévy-Bruhl 1931: 14). In such societies, people 'like us' cannot be enslaved. They can be fought against and even captured, as we know was occasionally the case among the Tukano and the Chiriguaná, but they cannot be enslaved. Only Others 'different from us' can be assigned the status of captive slaves, which entails the condition of being absolute and coalescent property in the ancient Roman sense.

From this perspective, then, the slave condition of foreigners precedes their capture, seen only as a confirmation of their essential status. Capture and the rituals of enslavement that follow confirm this virtual status by uprooting and alienating captives, thereby depriving them of social ties, and depersonifying them, that is, depriving them of their original social personas (Patterson 1982). Such a process produces people who lack the basic rights accorded to full members of capturing societies – not only the right to have control over their own persons, but also the right of being a person. From a native viewpoint, then, foreigners are enemies and potential slaves who lack all rights and are entirely at the disposal of their virtual masters.

In addition, because they owed their lives to their captors, who had spared them, captives were understood to be totally indebted to their masters, who could dispense with their lives at their whim. Above all, however, captive slaves were conceived of as the property of their captors, for they were the outcome of the productive agency of their captors, who had 'caused them to be'. As their captors' property, captive slaves could be bartered, given as gifts or destroyed. This gave rise to an active trade in captive slaves and even created the conditions for the emergence of annual interethnic fairs, where captives from various societies were taken to be exchanged, as was the case in inland Guiana, the Darien Peninsula and the Venezuelan coast (Sparrey 1625: 1249; López de Gómara 1946: 199, 206). Historical evidence specifies indigenous rates of exchange for war captives, who were generally traded for other native prestige goods, indicating that this kind of commerce developed long before the arrival of Europeans. Among the Conibo a captive boy could be exchanged for a canoe (Marcoy 1869: I, 468). The price of a captive woman among the Tukano was an *uhtabu*, the valued quartz stones used as pendants by Tukano men (Kok 1926: 922). We do not have information on Chiriguaná exchange rates for captive slaves, but given what we know of other slaveholding indigenous societies it is more than probable that they also existed among them.

Captives were especially vulnerable to being traded immediately after their capture, before they were integrated into their captors' society through rituals of enslavement (Santos-Granero 2005). Once they were marked as alien subordinates and integrated as members of their captors' households, the chances of being traded diminished considerably. In no way did this situation mean that captives were no longer considered as property, however. Rather, as the result of prolonged conviviality and consubstantiality, some captives were 'singularized' as family members and thus set apart as non-tradable (Kopytoff 1986). Here, we find the reason why native tropical Americans were not always willing to sell their captive servants to European slave traders. Processes of 'singularization' were not definitive, however. As the historical evidence indicates, captives could be de-singularized and reintroduced into the sphere of trade for a number of reasons, the most important being a rebellious disposition.

In the logic of native tropical American slavery, however, the unmaking of slaves was as important, if not more so, than the making of slaves. Indigenous slavery was not about transforming people into property for economic purposes, as had been the case in Western societies since ancient times, but rather about appropriating as much life force from enemy Others as possible under the logic of what I have called the Amerindian 'political economy of life' (Santos-Granero 2009a: Chapter 9). This included, among other things, the taking of bodily trophies thought to contain the vitality of the executed enemies; the stealing of collective life-giving amulets, effigies and ritual paraphernalia; and the capturing of children and young women to augment the demographic base of the capturing society by increasing the numbers of warriors and mothers of future warriors. Indigenous forms of slavery entailed the capture, civilization and incorporation of enemy Others.

Such a process involved a continuum that progressed from predation to familiarization, to integration as outsiders, and finally to assimilation as insiders. It entailed equal doses of force and persuasion, coercion and seduction, predation and nurturing. Assimilation was achieved via adoptive filiation and gradual consanguinization (Descola 1994: 339; Menget 1988: 71, 1996: 141; Fausto 1999: 938) or, more often, through affinal consanguinity, that is, by the adoption of children as future in-laws (Taylor 2000: 324, 2001: 54; Cormier 2003: 93, 114; Halbmayer 2004: 161). In either case, the ultimate aim was the production of kin. Thus, native tropical American slavery was not only about civilizing the Other – that is, making people out of Others – but was above all about assimilating the Other, that is, making Others into kin (see Vilaça 2002). It is this trait that makes indigenous forms of slavery unique. Despite being based on ideologies of subordination and notions of property similar to those found in Western slaveholding societies, native tropical American peoples entertained alternative notions of ownership based on love, caring and nurturing that allowed them to transform what they considered uncivil, less-than-human people into civil close kin. In other words, they had the means to transform captives as objects of property into kin as subjects of property.

Fernando Santos-Granero is Senior Staff Scientist at the Smithsonian Tropical Research Institute. His many publications include *The Power of Love: The Moral Use of Knowledge amongst the Amuesha of Central Peru* (2001) and *Vital Enemies: Slavery, Predation, and the Amerindian Political Economy of Life* (2009). He also edited, among other works, *The Occult Life of Things: Native Amazonian Theories of Materiality and Personhood* (2009) and *Images of Public Wealth or the Anatomy of Well-being in Indigenous Amazonia* (2015).

Notes

1. This study is based not only on the earliest sources available for each case but also on those written throughout the time period in which the societies of the sample still retained their autonomy. This means that in some cases the sources consulted cover a period of two or even three centuries. To make the amount of literature I surveyed more manageable, I confined the documentary research to published documents, conferring priority to documents produced by persons who actually witnessed the events they recounted – conquistadors, missionaries and explorers reporting about their own experiences – or by lay and religious historians who relied on oral or written accounts obtained directly from eyewitnesses. I excluded most secondary sources – for example, the works of nineteenth- and twentieth-century historians – except when their accounts were based on materials no longer available to present-day scholars. To avoid using unconfirmed or dubious data, I discarded data that is not verified by at least two independent sources. The reliability of the most cited sources used in this work is discussed in Appendix 1 of my book *Vital Enemies* (Santos- Granero 2009a).

References

Amich, J. 1975. *Historia de las misiones del convento de Santa Rosa de Ocopa*. Lima: Editorial Milla Batres.
Århem, K. 1981. *Makuna Social Organization: A Study in Descent, Alliance and the Formation of Corporate Groups in the North-Western Amazon*. Stockholm: LiberTryck.
Arriaga, P.J. 1974. 'Carta annua del P. Pablo Joseph de Arriaga, por comisión al P. Claudio Aquaviva, Lima, 3 Abril, 1596', in A. de Egaña (ed.), *Monumenta Peruana*, vol. 6. Rome: Apud 'Institutum Historicum Societatis Iesu', pp. 12–81.
Belaúnde, L.E. 2001. *Viviendo bien. Género y fertilidad entre los Airo-Pai de la amazonía peruana*. Lima: Centro Amazónico de Antropología y Aplicación Práctica / Banco Central de Reserva del Perú.
Biedma, M. 1981. *La conquista franciscana del Alto Ucayali*. Lima: Milla Batres.
Biocca, E. 1965. *Viaggi tra gli Indi Alto Rio Negro-Alto Orinoco*, 3 vols. Rome: Consiglio Nazionale delle Ricerche.
Brightman, M. 2010. 'Creativity and Control: Property in Guianese Amazonia'. *Journal de la Société des Américanistes* 96(1): 135–67.
Buenaventura Bestard, J. 1906. 'Carta de ... acompañada de un mapa é informe de la misiones del río Ucayali ... 21 Noviembre, 1819'. In Víctor M. Maúrtua (comp.), *Juicio de límites entre el Perú y Bolivia*, vol. 12. Barcelona: Imprenta de Henrich y Comp., pp. 339–355. (12 vols.)
Chernela, J. 1993. *The Wanano Indians of the Brazilian Northwest Amazon: A Sense of Place*. Austin: University of Texas Press.
Clastres, P. 1974. *La société contre l'Etat*. Paris: Les Editions de Minuit.
Combès, I. and K. Lowrey. 2006. 'Slaves without Masters? Arawakan Dynasties among the Chiriguano (Bolivian Chaco, Sixteenth to Twentieth Centuries)'. *Ethnohistory* 53(4): 689–714.
Combès, I. and T. Saignes. 1991. *Alter ego: naissance de l'identité Chiriguano*. Paris: Editions de l'Ecole des Hautes Etudes en Sciences Sociales.

Cormier, L.A. 2003. *Kinship with Monkeys: The Guajá Foragers of Eastern Amazonia*. New York: Columbia University Press.
Corrado, A.M. and A. Comajuncosa. 1990. *El colegio franciscano de Tarija y sus misiones*, 2 vols. Tarija, Bolivia: Editorial Offset Franciscana.
Coudreau, H.A. 1887. *La France équinoxiale*, 2 vols. Paris: Challamel ainé.
Crocker, J.C. 1985. *Vital Souls: Bororo Cosmology, Natural Symbolism, and Shamanism*. Tucson: University of Arizona Press.
DeBoer, W.R. 1986. 'Pillage and Production in the Amazon: A View through the Conibo of the Ucayali Basin, Eastern Peru', *World Archaeology* 18(2): 231–46.
Descola, P. 1994. 'Pourquoi les Indiens d'Amazonie n'ont-ils pas domestiqué le pécari? Généalogie des objets et anthropologie de l'objectivation'. In B. Latour and P. Lemonnier (eds.), *De la préhistoire aux missiles balistiques. L'intelligence sociale des techniques*. Paris: Editions La Découverte, pp. 329–344.
Díaz de Guzmán, R. 1979. 'Relación breve y sumaria que haze el governador don Ruiz Díaz de Guzmán al Real Consejo de Su Majestad, y a su Visorey destos reynos del Piru, y a su Real Audiencia de la Plata, en razón de las crueldades, muertes, y robos que an hecho los Indios Chiriguanas desta provincia, donde al presente está en su conquista y pacificación', in R. Díaz de Guzmán, *Relación de la entrada a los Chiriguanos*. Santa Cruz de la Sierra: Fundación Cultural 'Ramón Darío Gutiérrez', pp. 71–80.
'Diccionario cunibo-castellano y castellano-cunibo'. 1927. In B. Izaguirre (ed.), *Historia de las misiones franciscanas y narración de los progresos de la geografía en el oriente del Perú*, vol. 13. Lima: Talleres Gráficos de la Penitenciaría, pp. 391–474.
Dietrich, W. 1986. *El idioma chiriguano*. Madrid: Instituto de Cooperación Iberoamericana.
Dumont, J.-P. 1976. *Under the Rainbow: Nature and Supernature among the Panare Indians*. Austin: University of Texas Press.
Erikson, P. 1986. 'Altérité, tatouage et anthropophagie chez les Pano: La belliqueuse quête du soi'. *Journal de la Société des Américanistes* 72: 185–209.
———. 2009. 'Obedient Things: Reflections on the Matis Theory of Materiality', in F. Santos-Granero (ed.), *The Occult Life of Things: Native Amazonian Theories of Materiality and Personhood*. Tucson: University of Arizona Press, pp. 173–91.
Fausto, C. 1999. 'Of Enemies and Pets: Warfare and Shamanism in Amazonia', *American Ethnologist* 26(4): 933–56.
———. 2001. *Inimigos fiéis. História, Guerra e xamanismo na Amazônia*. São Paulo: Editora da Universidade de São Paulo.
———. 2008. 'Donos demais: maestria e domínio na amazônia', *Mana* 14(2): 329–66.
Frank, E. 1994. 'Los Uni', in F. Santos and F. Barclay (eds), *Guía etnográfica de la alta amazonía*, vol. 2. Quito: Facultad Latinoamericana de Ciencias Sociales / Instituto Francés de Estudios Andinos, pp. 129–238.
Fry, C. 1907. 'Diario de los viajes y exploración de los ríos Urubamba, Ucayali, Amazonas, Pachitea y Palcazu, 1888', in C. Larrabure i Correa (comp.), *Colección de leyes, decretos, resoluciones y otros documentos oficiales referentes al Departamento de Loreto*, vol. 11 of 18 vols. Lima: Imprenta La Opinión Nacional, pp. 369–589.
Giacone, A. 1949. *Os Tucanos e outras tribus do rio Uaupés, afluente do Negro-Amazonas*. São Paulo: Imprensa Oficial do Estado São Paulo.
———. 1965. *Gramática, dicionários e fraseología da língua dahceié ou tucano*. Belém, Brazil: Universidade do Pará.

Giannecchini, D. 1996. *Historia natural, etnografía, geografía y lingüística del Chaco Boliviano (1898)*. Tarija, Bolivia: Fondo de Inversión Social / Centro Eclesial de Documentación.

Girbal y Barceló, N. 1924. 'Diario del viaje que yo Fr. ..., misionero apostólico del Colegio de Ocopa ... hice desde el pueblo de Laguna, capital de Mainas, por los famosos ríos Marañón y Ucayali, Año 1790', in B. Izaguirre (ed.), *Historia de las misiones franciscanas y narración de los progresos de la geografía en el Oriente del Perú*, vol. 8. Lima: Talleres Tipográficos de la Penitenciaría, pp. 101–84.

———. 1964. Prosiguen los viages del padre misionero Fray Narciso Girbal. *Mercurio Peruano* 11: 276–291.

Goldman, I. 1963. *The Cubeo: Indians of the Northwest Amazon*. Urbana: University of Illinois Press.

———. 2004. *Cubeo Hehénewa Religious Thought: Metaphysics of a Northwestern Amazonian People*. New York: Columbia University Press.

Gonçalves Dias, A. 1858. *Diccionario da lingua Tupy chamada lingua geral dos indigenas do Brazil*. Leipzig: F.A. Brockhaus.

Gow, P. 1991. *Of Mixed Blood: Kinship and History in Peruvian Amazonia*. Oxford: Clarendon Press.

Halbmayer, E. 2004. '"The One Who Feeds Has the Rights." Adoption and Fostering of Kin, Affines and Enemies Among the Yupka and Other Carib-speaking Indians of Lowland South America'. In F. Bowie (ed.), *Cross-Cultural Approaches to Adoption*. London and New York: Routledge, pp. 145–164.

Harner, M.J. 1973. *The Jivaro: People of the Sacred Waterfalls*. Garden City, NY: Anchor Press/Doubleday.

Hugh-Jones, C. 1979. *From the Milk River: Spatial and Temporal Processes in Northwest Amazonia*. Cambridge: Cambridge University Press.

Hugh-Jones, S. 1993. 'Clear Descent or Ambiguous Houses? A Re-examination of Tukanoan Social Organisation', *L'Homme* 33(2–4): 95–120.

———. 2009. 'The Fabricated Body: Objects and Ancestors in Northwest Amazonia', in F. Santos-Granero (ed.), *The Occult Life of Things: Native Amazonian Theories of Materiality and Personhood*. Tucson: University of Arizona Press, pp. 34–59.

Jackson, J.E. 1983. *The Fish People: Linguistic Exogamy and Tukanoan Identity in the Northwest Amazon*. Cambridge: Cambridge University Press.

———. 1991. 'Hostile Encounters between Nukak and Tukanoans: Changing Ethnic Identity in the Vaupés, Colombia', *The Journal of Ethnic Studies* 19(2): 17–39.

Karsten, R. 1923. *Blood Revenge, War, and Victory Feasts among the Jibaro Indians of Eastern Ecuador*. Bureau of American Ethnology, Bulletin 79. Washington, DC: Government Printing Office.

Knobloch, F.J. 1972. 'The Maku Indians and Racial Separation in the Valley of the Rio Negro', *Mankind Quarterly* 13(2): 100–109.

Koch-Grünberg, T. 1906. 'Die Makú', *Anthropos* 1(4): 877–99.

———. 1995. *Dos años entre los indios. Viajes por el noroeste brasileño, 1903–1905*, 2 vols. Bogotá: Editorial Universidad Nacional.

Kok, R.P. 1926. 'Quelques notices ethnographiques sur les Indiens du Rio Papuri', part 2, *Anthropos* 21(5–6): 921–37.

Kopytoff, I. 1986. 'The Cultural Biography of Things: Commoditization as Process', in Arjun Appadurai (ed.), *The Social Life of Things: Commodities in Cultural Perspective*. Cambridge: Cambridge University Press, pp. 64–94.

Kopytoff, I. and S. Miers. 1977. 'African "Slavery" as an Institution of Marginality', in S. Miers and I. Kopytoff (eds), *Slavery in Africa: Historical and Anthropological Perspectives*. Madison: University of Wisconsin Press, pp. 3–81.

Lagrou, E. 2009. 'The Crystallized Memory of Artifacts: A Reflection on Agency and Alterity in Cashinahua Image-Making', in F. Santos-Granero (ed.), *The Occult Life of Things: Native Amazonian Theories of Materiality and Personhood*. Tucson: University of Arizona Press, pp. 192–213.

Lévy-Bruhl, H. 1931. 'Théorie de l'esclavage', *Revue Générale du Droit* 55(1): 1–17.

Lizárraga, R. de. 1968. 'Descripción breve de toda la tierra del Perú, Tucumán, Río de la Plata y Chile', in *Biblioteca de Autores Españoles*, vol. 216. Madrid: Ediciones Atlas, pp. 1–213.

López de Gómara, F. 1946. 'Hispania Victrix. Primera y Segunda Parte de la Historia General de las Indias, con todo el descubrimiento, y cosas notables que han acaecido desde que se ganaron hasta el año 1551; con la conquista de Méjico y de la Nueva España', in *Biblioteca de Autores Españoles*, vol. 22. Madrid: Ediciones Atlas, pp. 155–455.

MacLeod, W.C. 1928. 'Economic Aspects of Indigenous American Slavery', *American Anthropologist* 30(4): 632–50.

Marcoy, P. 1869. *Voyage a travers l'Amérique du Sud de l'Océan Pacifique a l'Océan Atlantique*, 2 vols. Paris: Librairie de L. Hachette et Cie.

Marqués, B. 1931. 'Vocabulario de la lengua Cuniba', *Revista Histórica* 9(2–3): 117–95.

McCallum, C. 2001. *Gender and Sociality in Amazonia: How Real People are Made*. Oxford and New York: Berg.

McGovern, W.M. 1927. *Jungle Paths and Inca Ruins*. New York and London: The Century Co.

Menget, P. 1988. 'Notes sur l'adoption chez les Txicão du Brésil Central'. *Anthropologie et Sociétés* 12(2): 63–72.

Métraux, A. 1930. 'Etudes sur la civilisation des Indiens Chiriguano', *Revista del Instituto Etnológico de la Universidad Nacional de Tucumán* 1(3): 295–493.

Murphy, R.F. 1960. *Headhunters' Heritage: Social and Economic Change among the Mundurucú Indians*. Berkeley: University of California Press.

Murphy, Y. and R.F. Murphy. 1985. *Women of the Forest*. New York: Columbia University Press.

Nino, B. de. 1912. *Etnografía chiriguana*. La Paz: Tipografía Comercial de Ismael Argote.

Ordinaire, O. 1887. 'Les sauvages du Pérou', *Revue d'Ethnographie* 6: 265–322.

Patterson, O. 1982. *Slavery and Social Death: A Comparative Study*. Cambridge, MA: Harvard University Press.

Polo de Ondegardo, J. 1991. 'Relation du Licencié Polo au vice-roi Toledo sur les mœurs des Chiriguano et comment leur faire la guerre', in I. Combès and T. Saignes (eds), *Alter ego: naissance de l'identité Chiriguano*. Paris: Editions de l'Ecole des Hautes Etudes en Sciences Sociales, pp. 135–42.

Proudhon, P.-J. 2008. *What Is Property? Or, an Inquiry into the Principle of Right and Government*. Retrieved January 2010 from http://www.gutenberg.org/files/360/360-h/360-h.htm

Raimondi, A. 1905. 'Informe sobre la provincia litoral de Loreto por A. Raimondi', in C. Larrabure y Correa (comp.), *Colección de leyes, decretos, resoluciones y otros documentos oficiales referentes a Loreto*, vol. 7. Lima: Imprenta de 'La Opinión Nacional', pp. 118–278.

Relación anónima en la que se hace referencia al descubrimiento hecho por Solís del Río de la Plata. 1941. In *Documentos históricos y geográficos relativos a la conquista y colonización rioplatense,* vol. 1. Buenos Aires: Talleres S.A. Casa Jacobo Peuser Ltda., pp. 65–68.

Reichel-Dolmatoff, G. 1971. *Amazonian Cosmos: The Sexual and Religious Symbolism of the Tukano Indians.* Chicago: University of Chicago Press.

———. 1996. *Yuruparí: Studies of an Amazonian Foundation Myth.* Cambridge, MA: Harvard University Press.

Riester, B., J. Riester, B. Schuchard and B. Simon. 1979. 'Los Chiriguano', *Suplemento Antropológico* 14(1–2): 259–304.

Rivière, P. 1969. *Marriage Among the Trio: A Principle of Social Organisation.* Oxford: Clarendon Press.

Rousseau, J.-J. 1999 [1755]. *Discourse on Inequality.* Oxford: Oxford University Press.

Ruiz de Montoya, A. 1876. *Tesoro de la lengua Guaraní.* Leipzig: B.G. Teubner.

Samánez y Ocampo, J.B. 1980. *Exploración de los ríos peruanos, Apurímac, Eni, Tambo, Ucayali y Urubamba, hecho por José B. Samánez y Ocampo en 1883 y 1884.* Lima: SESATOR.

Santos-Granero, F. 1991. *The Power of Love: The Moral Use of Knowledge amongst the Amuesha of Central Peru.* London: Athlone Press.

———. 2002. 'St. Christopher in the Amazon: Child Sorcery, Colonialism, and Violence among the Southern Arawak', *Ethnohistory* 49(3): 507–43.

———. 2004. 'The Enemy Within: Child Sorcery, Revolution and the Evils of Modernization in Eastern Peru', in N.L. Whitehead and R.M. Wright (eds), *In Darkness and Secrecy: Witchcraft and Sorcery in Native South America.* Durham: Duke University Press, pp. 272–305.

———. 2005. 'Amerindian Torture Revisited: Rituals of Enslavement and Markers of Servitude in Tropical America', *Tipití. Journal of the Society for the Anthropology of Lowland South America* 3(2): 147–74.

———. 2009a. *Vital Enemies: Slavery, Predation, and the Amerindian Political Economy of Life.* Austin: University of Texas Press.

———. 2009b. 'Introduction: Amerindian Constructional Views of the World', in Fernando Santos-Granero (ed.), *The Occult Life of Things: Native Amazonian Theories of Materiality and Personhood.* Tucson: University of Arizona Press, pp. 1–29.

———. 2011. 'Hakani e a campanha contra o infanticídio indígena: percepções contrastantes de humanidade e pessoa na Amazônia brasileira'. *Mana* [online] 17(1): 131–59.

———. 2012. 'Beinghood and People-Making in Native Amazonia: A Constructional Approach with a Perspectival Coda', *HAU: Journal of Ethnographic Theory* 2(1): 181–211.

Silva, Alcionilio Brüzzi Alves da. 1962. *A civilização indígena do Uaupés.* São Paulo: Missão Salesiana do Rio Negro.

Silverwood-Cope, P. 1990. *Os Makú: povo caçador do noroeste da Amazônia.* Brasília: Editora Universidade de Brasília.

Smith, R.C. 1977. 'Deliverance from Chaos for a Song: Preliminary Discussion of Amuesha Music', PhD dissertation. Ithaca, NY: Cornell University.

Sparrey, F. 1625. 'The Description of the Ile of Trinidad, the Rich Countrie of Guiana, and the Mightie River of Orenoco, Written by ...', in S. Purchas (ed.), *Purchas, His Pilgrimages,* 4 vols. London: William Stansby for Henrie Fetherstone, 4: 1247–50.

Spruce, R. 1908. *Notes of a Botanist on the Amazon and Andes*, 2 vols. London: Macmillan.
Stahl, E.G. 1928. 'La tribu de los Cunibos en la región de los lagos del Ucayali', *Boletín de la Sociedad Geográfica de Lima* 45(2): 139–66.
Stiglich, G. 1905. 'La región peruana de los bosques, 1904', in C. Larrabure i Correa (ed.), *Colección de leyes, decretos, resoluciones y otros documentos oficiales referentes al Departamento de Loreto*, 18 vols. Lima: Imprenta La Opinión Nacional, 15: 308–495.
Stradelli, E. 1890. 'L'Uaupés e gli Uaupés', *Bolletino della Societá Geografica Italiana* 3(5): 425–53.
Suárez de Figueroa, L. 1965 [1586]. 'Relación de la ciudad de Santa Cruz de la Sierra, 1586'. In M. Jiménez de la Espada (ed.), *Relaciones Geográficas de Indias*. Biblioteca de Autores Españoles, vol. 183. Madrid: Ediciones Atlas, pp. 402–6.
Susnik, B. 1968. *Chiriguanos: dimensiones etnosociales*. Asunción: Museo Etnográfico Andrés Barbero.
Taylor, A.-C. 1993. 'Remembering to Forget: Identity, Mourning, and Memory among the Jivaro', *Man* 28(4): 653–78.
———. 2000. 'Le sexe de la proie. Représentations jivaro du lien de parenté', *L'Homme* 154–55: 309–34.
———. 2001. 'Wives, Pets, and Affines: Marriage among the Jíbaro'. In Laura M. Rival and Neil L. Whitehead (eds.), *Beyond the Visible and Material: The Amerindianization of Society in the Work of Peter Rivière*. Oxford: Oxford University Press, pp.45–56.
Testart, A. 1998. 'L'esclavage comme institution', *L'Homme* 145: 31–69.
Thomas, D.J. 1982. *Order without Government: The Society of the Pemon Indians of Venezuela*. Urbana: University of Illinois Press.
Thouar, E.A. 1991. *A travers le Gran Chaco. Chez les Indiens coupeurs de têtes, 1883–1887*. Paris: Phébus.
Vilaça, A. 2002. 'Making Kin Out of Others in Amazonia'. *Journal of the Royal Anthropological Institute* 8: 347–365.
Viveiros de Castro, E. 2004. 'Exchanging Perspectives: The Transformation of Objects into Subjects in Amerindian Ontologies', *Common Knowledge* 10(3): 463–84.
Vocabulario na lingua brasilica. Manuscrito português-tupí do seculo XVII, coordenado e prefaciado por Plinio Ayrosa. 1938. São Paulo: Departamento de Cultura.
Wagley, C. and E. Galvão. 1949. *The Tenetehara Indians of Brazil: A Culture in Transition*. New York: Columbia University Press.
Wallace, A.R. 1853. *A Narrative of the Travels on the Amazon and Rio Negro, with an Account of the Native Tribes, and Observations of the Climate, Geology, and Natural History of the Amazon Valley*. London: Reeve and Co.
Wilbert, J. 1993. *Mystic Endowment: Religious Ethnography of the Warao Indians*. Cambridge, MA: Harvard University Center for the Study of World Religions.
Wright, R.M. 1998. *Cosmos, Self, and History in Baniwa Religion: For Those Unborn*. Austin: University of Texas Press.

CHAPTER 2

First Contacts, Slavery and Kinship in North-Eastern Amazonia

Vanessa Grotti and Marc Brightman

The Trio, Wayana and Akuriyo are Carib-speaking Amerindians of the border regions of Brazil, southern Suriname and southern French Guiana.[1] We have carried out field research since 2003 in southern Suriname, in a predominantly Trio village shared with a number of Wayana and most of the surviving Akuriyo. A relationship of asymmetry has evolved between the Trio and Akuriyo since the late 1960s, although arguably from a native point of view these two populations have engaged in a relationship of mutual avoidance as far back as people can remember. Despite, or perhaps because of, the memory of prior encounters between them, the Trio and Akuriyo would probably have maintained their mutual avoidance longer, had it not been for the intervention of evangelical missionaries.

These missionaries, and in particular a Baptist pastor named Claude Leavitt, who had established himself and his family among the recently contacted Trio a decade earlier (Conley 2000), organized a series of contact expeditions to the remote area around the headwaters of the Oeremari River near the border with Brazil in search of an elusive group of Akuriyo hunter-gatherers then known as *wajiarikure*, a Trio ethnonym used to refer to wild, semihuman beings living in the forest (Forth 2008).

Trio people generally consider forest dwellers to be barbaric in everyday practices such as cooking and the treatment of their bodies, but they also fear them for their fierceness and predatory capacities (these capacities are known as *ëire* in Trio, a word also used to describe the aggressive, magically strengthened bodily state of a warrior). The Trio feel ambivalent towards wild people, considering them individuals of reduced capacity for socialization who nonetheless enjoy superhuman predatory and transformational aptitudes. This helps to explain the way Trio-Akuriyo relations unfolded after contact, and particularly how this relationship came to be considered mutually beneficial and construed in terms of ownership and tutelage. As we shall describe, the Akuriyo became the Trio's property through capture and then became the creatures of the Trio, in the sense that the latter endeavoured to make them into 'real people'.

In 1968, the first of a series of Trio and Wayana expeditions led by North American missionaries located a group of Akuriyo. On subsequent expeditions, some Trio remained with the Akuriyo to gain their confidence and learn their language. After various sedentarization schemes (including planting fruit trees and manioc, and starting a Maroon-run manioc 'farm' to encourage trade) had failed and progressive contact had led to major health problems among the Akuriyo, the missionaries decided to cut their losses and make the Akuriyo settle in Tëpu with the Trio (Crocker n.d.; Yohner 1970; Schoen 1969, 1971; Conley 2000: 393).

This was not the first time Leavitt had embarked upon a contact expedition; as a member of the Unevangelized Fields Mission, he had gained some experience in southern Guyana with the three Hawkins brothers, who had founded the mission of Kanashen among the Waiwai in the early 1950s. It was in southern Guyana that the technique of 'cumulative evangelism' (Grotti 2009) was developed, whereby resident missionaries accompanied by converted Amerindians organized expeditions to contact other groups and encourage them to sedentarize alongside the indigenous expedition members. This procedure worked well among the populations of the central Guiana region, which at the time were typically constituted by relatively mobile extended cognatic groups. The process of cumulative evangelism involving the Waiwai was well documented by Catherine Howard (2001). Howard describes the Waiwai perspective on these expeditions to contact those whom they referred to as the 'unseen tribes'. She stresses in particular that the Waiwai's willingness to take part in these expeditions reflected an enthusiasm for the capture and assimilation of other people, and that both capture and assimilation were expressed through the missionary idiom of evangelization.

The men who embarked on these first contacts were all in the prime of life. Without exception they were young heads of households, most of whom had developed a special relationship with the missionaries, making them their *jipawana*, their friends or trading partners. All later rose to become prominent elders as plant and chant healers, village leaders or pastors. In the Trio case in particular, the initial search for trails or camps in the forest and the establishment of first contacts were solely a male enterprise.

During the initial interactions between the Trio and Akuriyo, the hunter-gatherers expressed restraint and a desire to cut bonds by moving on and trekking back into the forest. The Trio expedition members nevertheless immediately took the initiative to develop a form of ongoing interaction, and some stayed for months with the Akuriyo, following them on their treks between camps and communicating with the use of a portable radio.² Almost immediately after the first contacts, the missionaries stood back and let the Trio engage in most transactions with the Akuriyo. From catalysing and organizing the first expeditions, they went on to provide logistical support. As three main groups of about thirty people each were contacted between 1968 and 1971 (Jara 1990: 17), Trio men also tracked down the entirety of the remaining scattered nuclear families.

When diseases started to spread, the Akuriyo were eventually flown in a light aircraft to Tëpu, where they were settled, each family unit closely supervised by a Trio expedition member. The Akuriyo families were to provide services such as hunting and wood fetching for the families of their 'captors', and in return they would be taught how to live as the Trio do. As captive wild people, the *wajiarikure* became Akuriyo, after the name for one of the Akuriyo groups, Akuriekare (or agouti people). In this new, domesticated guise they were incorporated into village life as children: they were given the front benches in Church and were encouraged to go to school, were taught how to make gardens and prepare manioc bread and manioc beer, and were shown how to cook (and eat) 'real food' – thoroughly cooked meat stew eaten with manioc bread. The Trio held that all of these activities wrought bodily change upon the Akuriyo, but they most obviously and visibly changed their bodies by cutting their hair and plucking their eyebrows the way the Trio do.³

Partial Familiarization

The Akuriyo were domesticated by the Trio but have never been fully assimilated by them, in contrast to comparable cases in the region.⁴ The reasons for this seem to lie in Trio narratives of Akuriyo identity, which emphasize their barbarity. Primarily because they were nomadic hunter-gatherers, the Akuriyo were considered particularly wild and inhuman by their captors – indeed, were it not for the influence of the missionaries, the Trio and Wayana would not have contacted them at all for the purposes of trade or alliance. Although the Akuriyo had deliberately and completely isolated themselves, hoping to exclude themselves from the Janus logic of war and trade (the one giving way to the other),⁵ the result was a prolonged Hobbesian war – effectively a 'cold' war with a constant (though rarely realized) threat of violence.

This account of the capture of some Akuriyo, told to us by one of the Trio expedition members in Tëpu, shows how this threat of violence crystallized into fear:

Then we searched for them, they ran and hid, they went this way and that way, they went running off again. We looked for them on the path, they ran. Sïlawo and his mother were frightened of us, and they ran on the path. Muloto ran alone, she got lost in the forest. During the night she ran and also stayed there in the forest because she was frightened of us. Epoti waited for her, with the others in the little house: 'She is coming', said Epoti. Polowpa waited for her too; Muloto was still frightened of us. Then Polowpa and Epoti hid to catch her. She came back to look for fire, it was almost evening, she was all alone, that's why Polowpa ran towards her to catch her, but Muloto ran to the river. Then, Polowpa caught her. 'No, no, let me go', said Muloto. 'No, we won't do anything, we won't hurt you', I said. But we didn't know how to speak their language. Their language is different from ours. … We brought them all back; we had already caught the other two … Sïlawo was really scared of us; he defecated because he was so afraid of us.

The sudden transformation of the relations between Trio and Wayana on the one hand and Akuriyo on the other from those of enemy-strangers to those of coresidents has had far-reaching consequences. The Akuriyo in Tëpu today are effectively servants of the Trio. Akuriyo nuclear families live away from each other in different parts of the village, each attached to the household of a Trio family. Although they are spoken of as children, Akuriyo men are also often treated in some respects as though they were sons-in-law, implying as subservient a relationship as is possible between adults in traditional kinship terms, but also implying indebtedness.[6] Despite this, it is rare to find an Akuriyo man actually married to a Trio woman.[7]

This situation of partial familiarization, or domestication without assimilation, is extraordinary in a region where coresidence usually leads to social absorption. Domestication of the Other in Amazonia is of vital importance for the constitution and reproduction of the group, its identity and its vital energy (Fausto 1999a; Santos-Granero 2009; Vilaça 2002). Such a state of affairs therefore cannot simply be attributed to missionary activities. It can instead be partially understood through narratives of identity that have defined certain 'peoples' as fierce and cannibalistic. Since sedentarization, these narratives have come to differentiate 'superior', riverine, sedentary, horticulturalist, trading people from 'inferior', forest-dwelling, foraging people. But the narratives also mean that the domestication of such peoples differs in character from the domestication of other horticulturalist peoples (Howard 2001).

Akuriyo are in a constant state of becoming, but partly as a result of this they are also reduced socially. The special advantage of the relationship with the Akuriyo, from the Trio's point of view, is that the Akuriyo can still be rendered their agency when they go into the forest, where they can become powerful hunters who can 'see' as no Trio can. With Akuriyo to hunt for them, the Trio are therefore able to concentrate on cultivating their familiarity with the more powerful knowledge held by white people.

The Trio's aversion to marriage with Akuriyo may be due to the contrived nature of their coresidence, which resulted from outside influence – as we have mentioned, the Trio would never have shared the same villages with the Akuriyo had it not been for the intervention of missionaries.[8] An ordinary alliance would not have occurred between Trio and Akuriyo because the Akuriyo lacked the quintessentially humanizing food, bitter manioc. The Akuriyo may have had gardens and bitter manioc in the past, and they were, long ago, allies of other *jana* or historic subgroups who cannot have considered them fierce, but these facts appear irrelevant to their current unequal alliance with the Trio. Even though they are now learning to grow and process manioc, the Trio still portray them as hunter-gatherers whose ignorance of this vital cultivated food is the ultimate evidence of barbarity, compared to which the inferior knowledge of Christianity is a mild stigma.

The Trio see the Akuriyo as fitting into categories that imply transformation and domestication. Carlos Fausto (1999b) has argued that a mode of social interaction and transformation central to native Amazonia is 'familiarizing predation', whereby 'other' people are ritually transformed into kin through a process of domestication following capture in warfare in the case of humans, or capture during forest expeditions in the case of pets. Put another way, the dialectic of predation and familiarization allows the production of persons and the reproduction of society. It provides the mechanism and the reason for domesticating the Other through nurture. The object of familiarizing predation is treated as a consanguine and referred to like an adoptive child (rather than a son-in-law, a distinction we will discuss shortly). Fausto (2008, 2012) has shown that the relationship also constitutes a form of ownership or 'mastery'. Today, the Trio refer to the Akuriyo attached to their households in terms of ownership, or *entume*: they say that they 'own' (*entume wae*) an Akuriyo. Ownership and mastery are in fact synonymous: *entu* signifies 'leader/owner/master' as well as 'source' or 'base of mountain', and *entume wae* means 'I own/control'. Akuriyo call their Trio masters *Tamu* – a word with a set of meanings that overlaps with those of *entu*, for it corresponds closely to the category of 'master/owner' that Fausto has identified across Amazonia. It signifies consanguineous asymmetry and is most commonly used to address both paternal and maternal grandfathers. It is also used to address a village leader or any senior man familiar to the speaker. In the possessive form, *itamu*, it is also the term used to refer to the spirit masters of animals. The significant point here is that the Akuriyo use a term of consanguinity to address their Trio masters. The latter treat their Akuriyo as servants and do not address them using kinship terms; instead, they address them by name (which they never do to each other) or as *jahko*, a neutral term meaning something like 'comrade' whose use appears to be an outcome of the Trio's sedentarization in large villages where they frequently come into contact with affines. They also refer to their Akuriyo servants with an affinal term, *pëito*, which we shall now discuss.

Familiarization, Subjugation and Affinity

The Trio appear to see the domestication of the Akuriyo as a form of familiarizing predation and to treat them as a form of 'pet', following a pattern found elsewhere in Amazonia, according to Fausto (2008). The Akuriyo themselves say that they regard themselves as children in relation to the Trio, and that the Trio teach them about living in a civilized way, much as fathers teach sons. Yet the Trio also refer to the Akuriyo as their *pëito*, a word associated with affinity. In Wayana (many Wayana living in Tëpu have intermarried with the Trio), it means 'son-in-law'. It is also the equivalent of the Carib *poito*, which was commonly used by both Caribs and Europeans in the colonial period to refer to 'red' or Amerindian slaves, for which European demand peaked in the eighteenth century (Whitehead 1988: 181). Neil Whitehead (1988: 181) explains the relationship between slavery and affinity in terms of warfare and trade:

> Amerindian slaving can be understood as an extension of Carib trading activities, for only by trade and intermarriage would those populations from which the captives were taken be defined as poitos. Thus the Caribs would have stood in an affinal relation to the people they raided in virtue of the fact that they married the women and sold their 'brothers-in-law'.

The Trio's use of *pëito* seems to be a recent adoption from the Wayana. The corresponding Trio term *pito*, which has less asymmetrical connotations, is also still used today. Commenting on these words and their cognates among different Carib groups, Peter Rivière (1977: 40) notes that they '[have] variously been translated as slave, servant, client, brother-in-law, son-in-law, and sister's son', adding that 'this range of meanings covers a continuum from the potentially equal (brother-in-law) to the totally inferior (slave) ... however, slave and servant are concepts that are out of keeping with the nature of Carib societies as we know them today'. Whitehead also emphasizes the historical variation in the intensity of the asymmetry of the relationship with *poito*, underlining that 'the "slave" status of the *poito* became more pronounced under European influence, both on account of the enhanced exchange value of such captives and because of the political advantages that accrued to the Caribs through their European alliances' (1988: 181) Whitehead further argues that this effect was especially strong in the Dutch colonies because the Dutch relied more heavily on trade to maintain 'access to, and control of, the Amerindian population', lacking the 'manpower and religious infrastructure of the Spanish' (184).

The case of the Trio's subjugation of the Akuriyo shows that since Rivière's own fieldwork, things have changed in ways he did not anticipate. More recent scholars of the Trio have struggled to understand the relationship between the terms *pito* and *pëito* as used by the Trio in the wake of these changes. The linguist Sergio Meira (1999: 590) disagrees with Rivière's suggestion that *pito* is a cognate of the widespread Carib term denoting 'slave' or 'servant', on the grounds that there is a more convincing case for arguing that *pëito* is the Trio equivalent, and thus *pëito,* not *pito,* would derive from the ancient Carib word *poito*. Meira does not seem to have been aware that *pëito* was a recent introduction in Trio. However, even without this knowledge, he might not have doubted that the two terms had a common origin had he been aware of the relationship between social subordination and affinity in Guiana Carib societies. *Pëito* means 'son-in-law' as well as 'follower/servant' in Wayana, and the Trio seem to have adopted the term from them in recent decades (indeed, after Rivière's fieldwork) during which the two groups have had sustained close contact including coresidence, mixed villages and intermarriage. Among the Trio, *pito* can refer to brothers-in-law as well as sons-in-law, and even to fathers-in-law. This is related to the traditional ideal of marriage with one's sister's daughter (Rivière 1969), which blurs the distinction between symmetrical (brother-in-law) and asymmetrical (son-in-law) relations. In other words, the differences between traditional Wayana and Trio marriage practices and political relations correspond to the differences between *pëito* and *pito*. The two terms in Trio and Wayana play equivalent roles, taking into account the greater emphasis on endogamy and individual autonomy among the Trio.[9]

Pëito was thus adopted from the Wayana to enable Trio people to express – and reproduce – new, more asymmetrical kinds of relationships. It is interesting that Rivière believed that the more extremely asymmetric forms of meaning for *pito/pëito* cognates on the continuum he described were more likely to be 'postcontact adaptations of indigenous ideas modified by European influence' than reflections of 'an earlier, more complex, and more hierarchical form of society that has now disappeared', although he recognized that these two explanations were not necessarily mutually exclusive (Rivière 1977: 40). This belief may seem to be supported by the fact that the capture and subordination of the Akuriyo (which resulted in the clearest example of asymmetrical relationships in Trio society today) would almost certainly not have happened without the missionaries' intervention. On the other hand, Santos-Granero's recent study of indigenous Amazonian forms of slavery (2009 and this volume) shows that the pre-contact thesis should not be dismissed too lightly.

One might expect that carrying out fieldwork among the Trio would make Rivière more alert to the more 'equal' end of the continuum of meanings of *pito/pëito*. Yet he recognized that 'in all Carib societies the relationship between affines – and specifically between parents-in-law and their children-in-law – is always asymmetrical in nature, and this being the case, affinal relationships offer the best idiom for expression of political relationships that involve domination and subordination' (1977: 41). Here, then, we have the social category which allows the domestication of the *wajiarikure*, the wild people, and in the Trio's case *pëito* seems to have been adopted to refer to the new and exceptionally asymmetrical relationship with the Akuriyo.

It is worth noting that this shows that familiarizing predation among the Trio seems to be constituted affinally as well as consanguineally, rather than in unequivocally consanguineal terms. This difference may be partially explicable in light of the symbolic importance of the father-in-law among the Trio. In many myths a Trio man meets a jaguar or another forest person who entices him to marry his daughter, and only by avoiding eating the food of his host does he escape turning into a jaguar himself. Of course such myths express affinity, but they also express the dangers of marrying distant Others – one risks losing one's human perspective and in some cases may even have to attack and kill one's own former kin. They also express the ideal of marrying close, in which consanguinity and affinity shade into each other. And the risk of losing one's own perspective, as attested in numerous cases from all over Amazonia, derives from the fact that commensality and conviviality can lead to becoming kin: as Fausto (2007) has pointed out, by eating *with* each other (rather than eating each other), we come to share the same perspective. Indeed, as Lévi-Strauss argued in his article on the Nambiquara brother-in-law relationship (1943), the term (equivalent to *pito*) for the brother of a potential wife serves to create kinship relations between previously unrelated groups.

What is occurring in the case of the Akuriyo is precisely the opposite: they have been domesticated and made into servants, but neither marriage nor kinship relations have been created. That they are referred to as *pëito*, but never as *pito*, seems significant for understanding this. Santos-Granero (2009: 174) notes that slaves eventually tend to intermarry with their masters: 'captive slaves, servant groups and tributary populations were integrated, and eventually assimilated, into their masters' societies', yet '[e]nemies are equated to affines and game meat, whereas captive children are associated with consanguines and pets'. On one hand, the Akuriyo engage in a constant attempt to assert themselves as consanguines, describing themselves as being like the children of the Trio and thus implicitly bidding for their eventual integration into Trio society. On the other hand, the Trio maintain them as affines, placing them in a category, *pëito*, which demands service, and meanwhile withholding the only means by which Akuriyo may be familiarized as kin: intermarriage. They never call Akuriyo *pito* because this term would imply the potential, if not the realization, of marriage. In the Akuriyo case, intermarriage has not occurred in the forty years since their capture, except in certain rare cases. When such marriages have occurred, the relationship has always favoured the Trio. Trio 'ownership' of Akuriyo always trumps the usual behaviour expected of wife-givers and wife-takers, and if an Akuriyo should become a father-in-law to a Trio then it is the Akuriyo who performs services for his son-in-law, in a reversal of the traditional practice of bride service. Even when intermarriage occurs and affinity in this sense is thus realized, the relationship of mastery persists.

Fausto (1999a: 949) writes that 'to be powerful, shamans and warriors must ensure that the subjectivity of their wild pets is preserved, which means that they can never become entirely tamed'. This ambivalence is at the heart of mastery. But it seems that a similar ambivalence lies at the heart of asymmetric relations of control – an ambivalence that can itself take the form of chronic slippage between the two forms of asymmetry, consanguineal and affinal, in native Amazonian social relations.

Nurture

The Trio mastery over the Akuriyo can also be read in terms of feeding and nurture. The image of the prestation of manioc – the quintessential humanizing food, associated with maternal nurture – constantly recurs in the contact narratives of missionaries and Amerindians alike, and is the key image in the idiom of 'care for the Other' as constituting the driving force behind contact (Crocker n.d.; Schoen 1969, 1971). Certainly Amerindian and non-Amerindian views on this idea of 'care', the word used by missionaries in their accounts, differ in a way that reflects diverging views about the nature of these other people and the underlying reason for their need for care. The missionary notion of care found resonance in a set of Trio processual kinship practices that we can understand in terms of nurture. Nurture in this sense implies a relation that engenders regressive control because it places contacted peoples in the social position of children who need to be fed and educated.

The 'domestication' or 'taming' of other groups occurs throughout the Guianas. The Waiwai, following their contact expeditions to sedentarize and 'domesticate' neighbouring groups (Howard 2001), maintain their relationship with these groups through various prestations clearly expressed in the institution of the alliance feast, at which the exchange of manioc beer or bread plays a key role. These alliance feasts today differ significantly from those recalled in oral narratives of the more distant past. For example, when the Apalai, having had enough of war, decided to accept the equivalence of the Wayana's culture, they exchanged both beer and women with them (Barbosa 2002: 180–82).[10] In contrast, the Waiwai and the Surinamese Trio and Wayana, as Christian converts, were convinced of the superiority of their newly modified way of life; therefore their prestation of manioc was not to be reciprocated. Their expeditions to contact other groups were not for the purpose of alliance in the conventional sense. Their purpose was evangelical, and as such it was to give culture, not to receive it; correspondingly, they were to give manioc,[11] not receive it. The result was integration, or in the case of the Akuriyo, incorporation and subjection: an unequal alliance. This should be seen in conjunction with the fact that in such cases knowledge, in the form of evangelization, is also primarily passed from manioc-giving hosts to manioc-receiving guests, reversing the usual direction.[12]

Although they were not 'tamed' by the Trio or Wayana in the same sense in which other Amerindian groups were, it is useful to compare the case of the Maroons – the descendants of slaves who escaped Dutch plantations in the eighteenth and nineteenth centuries and were, for over a hundred years, the Trio's privileged trading partners. The Trio say that Maroons, like the Akuriyo, do not 'know about' manioc (although in fact they do grow it); also like the Akuriyo, Maroons are not considered suitable marriage partners. The modalities of the relationship between categories of people are thus expressed in the reciprocal or nonreciprocal prestation of beer and women: 'real' people gave manioc to Akuriyo and Maroons, who are classified as 'lacking' manioc; this marks them out as unsuitable wife-takers.

During our field research Trio people often contrasted their past life in the forest, characterized by warfare and spirit attacks, with their present living conditions in large, sedentary villages near rivers, where former enemies intermarry and live in peace with one another. In this new way of life they attach great importance to a capacity for extended socialization, the quintessential symbol of which is manioc production and processing. But additionally, in the eyes of our Trio interlocutors, wildness implied greater exposure to the spirit world and to body-strengthening techniques that the Trio gradually gave up as a compromise to live in larger sedentary settlements. So the Akuriyo did not represent an Amerindian version of the intellectually inferior Aristotelian natural slave who could be captured with ease, but rather an ambivalent, highly transformative Other whose wildness had to be carefully controlled. In accounts of first encounters, whereas the missionaries emphasize the Trios' willingness to tell the recently contacted hunter-gatherers about the Bible and God, the Trio remember the importance of handing over manioc bread and teaching the rudiments of garden clearing and manioc planting – manioc being the substance from which the bodies of 'real people' are made. In short, whereas the missionaries wanted to humanize the Akuriyo by inculcating Christian knowledge, the Trio wanted to socialize the Akuriyo by inculcating moral convention through action on their bodies rather than on their minds. Both cases, however, entailed an insistence on caring for these wild people as a motivating force.

Securing the Akuriyo well-being implied both healing and educating them. Upon being sedentarized, the Akuriyo were exposed to many infectious diseases for the first time. Adding to the trauma of their radical change of lifestyle, health problems had a major impact: about a quarter of those contacted died within the first year of their sedentarization (Kloos 1977a, 1977b). The wives of Trio expedition members got involved in caring for the Akuriyo, especially by treating them for their illnesses. This was very much encouraged by the missionaries, who considered this form of dedication a true demonstration of the altruistic potential of the Trio, revealed by their conversion to Christianity (Schoen 1969; Yohner 1970).

Educating was as important as healing. When we asked our host why he went to the Akuriyo, he answered that it was because they did not know how to live properly and needed to be taught. When telling us this, he used the words *enpa*, which the Trio use to describe the kind of education that a father gives to his son (see also Kloos 1977a), and *arimika*, which describes the nurture of children by mothers. While the notion that the Akuriyo needed to be taught how to live might well owe something to missionary influence, its expression in the idiom of consanguinity is at least consistent with the principle of familiarizing predation. Bringing up a child among the Trio is associated less with doing than with undoing: *arimika*, the word for a mother's upbringing of her child, means 'to undo the spider monkey', as at birth the ontological status of an infant is still indeterminate; consequently, any traces of wildness have to be gradually undone to secure it as a human and a relative.

After their incorporation into Trio social networks, the surviving Akuriyo appeared more than ever to have this need to be cared for. In both Amerindian and non-Amerindian discourse, the predator gradually becomes a carer who secures the well-being of his prey. This change evokes the relationship between control and protection underlined by Fausto, who observes that 'the owners control and protect their creatures, being responsible for their well-being, reproduction and mobility. This asymmetry implies not only control but care'. He goes on to comment that 'from the perspective of whoever is adopted-captured, being or placing oneself in the position of an orphan or a wild pet is more than just a negative injunction: it may also be a positive way of eliciting attention and generosity' (2012: 32). As if to confirm this view, an Akuriyo hunter described to us that he considered himself to be like a child, and that when he and his kin lived in the forest they were ignorant of the things they were now being taught in Tëpu. However, this version of Trio-Akuriyo relations exemplifies only one dimension of a complex web of relations; one may see it as the 'official line' given in discourses in which Trio or missionaries are present. When alone, our host's Akuriyo helper abandoned the discourse of the child benefiting from education to complain bitterly about the rough treatment inflicted upon him daily and tell about intimidation, beating and theft.

From the missionaries' point of view, the mere fact that these discourses of nurture were still repeated to non-Amerindians like ourselves thirty years after the Akuriyo were brought to Tëpu shows that something has gone amiss and the process of assimilation has in effect stalled into mere incorporation. These peculiar 'children' never became civilized but remained servants undergoing a perpetual nurturing and humanizing process, neither processual kin nor attractive marriageable partners. Trio themselves consider the Akuriyo effort to adopt Trio social conventions as a failure in many regards. Today they still see Akuriyo gardens as primitive and unproductive, their cooking and manioc processing as dangerously incompetent, and their treatment of their bodies as far from sufficient to make them 'proper'. But whereas their socialization has failed, their wildness has allowed them to maintain a certain supremacy in the world of the forest. Hunting and gathering remain their domains of excellence, something the Trio candidly admit they cannot be as good at simply because their bodies are not as strong and fierce anymore. They associate this 'softening' with their sedentarization and their conversion to Christianity.

Predators of unerring strength and skill, the Akuriyo are a unique source of services and goods for their Trio guardians, who enjoy increased influence and status through them by enlisting their services. At times of large-scale celebrations in particular, they rely on Akuriyo hunting skills to provide game for the participants. Trio men with trading partners in the city enlist Akuriyo hunters to obtain game, which the former can send to the market by air for a considerable profit. Yet the Akuriyo remain marginal and subject to the Trio's surveillance and control, although their mistreatment at the hands of the Trio is somewhat restrained by fears that they may put powerful curses on their tormentors. In short, from this perspective the Akuriyo typify a form of servitude that presents aspects of a situationally reversable asymmetry – a form of reciprocal hierarchy that depends upon the social surroundings, with the village at one end of the spectrum and the forest at the other.

Conclusion

The modes and effects of the nurturing relationships that were sealed at the time of contact and have evolved up to the present day between expedition members and contacted 'wild people' – that is, the relations between captors and captives, between carers and cared for – can shed light on the expression of a peculiar form of Amerindian ownership that may have resonance elsewhere in native lowland South America. This is especially clear from Santos-Granero's work on captive slavery, which is based on a study of multiple early sources that was undertaken in such a way as to exclude the possibility of European influence on the practices described (2009; also see Santos-Granero this volume). In his analysis of the 'process in which slaves shifted from a marginal condition as recent war prisoners to their integration as subordinates and, eventually, to their (or their descendants') assimilation into their masters' kinship networks', Santos-Granero (2009: 200) equates wildness with lack of humanity, arguing that wild or enslavable Others are treated like game that can be preyed upon – they are 'total strangers uncontaminated by links of consanguinity, with whom ... one does not marry but rather makes war'. Captives were treated much like pets, except that they were to be turned into people and ultimately into kin. Their role was not merely material but more importantly allowed the reproduction of society. It was ultimately more concerned with the creation of sameness rather than the maintenance of otherness – slavery was about the conquest and acquisition of symbolic vitality (207).

Santos-Granero understands the capture and appropriation of persons in native Amazonian societies in terms of the renewal and reproduction of society, accomplished by making enemies into real people. It involves the creation of relations of ownership through the capture of wild Others. These relations of ownership are an effect of social reproduction, which is a process of transformation from Other into kin. But the case presented here suggests something more complicated. Before contact was established between Trio and Akuriyo, the Trio did indeed regard the *wajarikure,* as they called them, as wild enemies rather than potential affines. After contact was established, Trio and Akuriyo each sought to fit the other into relationship categories that best suited their interests. The Trio adopted a Wayana term to affirm the Akuriyo as affines, placing them in a role that would require the Akuriyo to serve them. The Akuriyo, meanwhile, responded to the Trio's nurturing actions by reaffirming the consanguineous relationship they implied, calling the Trio *tamu*. These distinct Trio and the Akuriyo points of view can explain why the relationship terms each uses for the other are not terms that one would ordinarily expect to be mutually reciprocated. Here, words are not exchanged for words, but for actions. The Trio address their Akuriyo captives as *pëito,* and the Akuriyo respond with work. The Akuriyo call their Trio captors *tamu*, and are rewarded with care.

This divergence between the Trio and Akuriyo understandings of the relationship between them is precisely what allows the relationship to be perpetuated. But it also illustrates something more general about native Amazonian societies. Historical accounts of Guiana Carib slavery have emphasized the affinal relationship expressed in the term *poito*. Meanwhile, accounts of war captives from elsewhere – such as, most famously, those of the Tupinambá – have emphasized the 'familiarizing predation' that functions in the idiom of consanguinity. Both cases involve an openness towards alterity, which Viveiros de Castro contends does not concern 'the creation of sameness rather than the maintenance of otherness'. He argues instead that the Tupinambá and other Amerindian societies are founded on 'the relationship to others, and not self-identity'. He then goes on to quote James Clifford:

> Stories of cultural contact and change have been structured by a pervasive dichotomy: absorption by the other *or* resistance to the other.... Yet what if identity is conceived not as a boundary to be maintained but as a nexus of relations and transactions actively engaging a subject? The story or stories of interaction must then be more complex, less linear and theological. What changes when the subject of 'history' is no longer Western? How do stories of contact, resistance, and assimilation appear from the standpoint of groups in which exchange rather than identity is the fundamental value to be sustained? (Clifford 1988: 344, cited in Viveiros de Castro 2011: 17–18)

In the 1970s, the missionaries – and the anthropologist Peter Kloos – predicted that the Akuriyo would quickly become Trio, that the Trio would impose their identity upon them. This did not happen, and we might hope to find that acts of resistance performed by Akuriyo people are the reason. It is indeed gratifying to watch Akuriyo hunters as they enter the forest: they stand taller, their eyes brightening as they begin to enjoy some short-lived autonomy. Similarly, when an Akuriyo complains to an anthropologist about being mistreated by his Trio owner, we may or may not interpret this as some sort of act of resistance. However, we suspect that such resistance plays little or no role in the actual relationship between Trio and Akuriyo. When Akuriyo complain to an outsider of petty acts of violence that Trio perpetrate on them, they call for pity, appealing to the anthropologist, in this case, to engage or continue to engage in another paternalistic and nurturing relationship. Meanwhile the violence itself no doubt reiterates and helps maintain the Akuriyo's lowly status.

The relationship between the Trio and Akuriyo is fundamentally ambivalent. From the Trio point of view, the Akuriyo are servants and bride servants without brides. They are objects of property that are to be nurtured but never allowed to become full and proper Trio persons. The

Akuriyo meanwhile cling to the potential of the Trio's nurturing role to transform them into Trio and dissolve the affinal difference between the two groups. They address their Trio masters as *tamu* and emphasize that they are to become civilized. The emphasis is on *becoming*: the Akuriyo are continually becoming kin. Trio and Akuriyo have found a way of maintaining a relationship of exchange and continual transformation that is premised upon, and perpetuates, their divergent points of view.

Coda

During field research in 2011 we discovered that a group of Trio men from Suriname had visited a remote group of Zo'é, a Tupi-speaking group living in isolation in a remote part of the Brazilian state of Pará, under the protection of FUNAI, the Brazilian Indian agency. The Trio delegation took trade objects – fishhooks, metal tools, clothes. They brought a young Zo'é boy to visit their home villages in Suriname and took video footage of his adventure with their mobile phones. Stories circulate about other isolated groups and further plans for contact expeditions. According to the missionaries still active in Suriname, the Trio, of their own initiative, are carrying out their own evangelical missions to reach uncontacted peoples with the goal of converting them to Christianity. While this may be true, we hope that we have shown that this missionary zeal is founded upon a more ingrained desire to embrace alterity – that is, to help Others to become Trio and thus to become white themselves – for the Trio relationship with the Akuriyo, and perhaps in turn the Zo'é, reproduces that of the missionaries with the Trio themselves, in which nurture and alterity are perpetuated together.

Vanessa Grotti is Part-Time-Professor at the European University Institute in Florence. She is the co-editor, with Marc Brightman and Olga Ulturgasheva, of *Shamanism in Rainforest and Tundra: Personhood in the Shamanic Ecologies of Contemporary Amazonia and Siberia* (2012) and *Rethinking the "Frontier" in Amazonia and Siberia: Extractive Economies, Indigenous Politics and Social Transformations* (2007). Her monograph *Living with the Enemy: First Contacts and the Making of Christian Bodies in Amazonia* is due to be published by Berghahn Books.

Marc Brightman is Lecturer at the Department of Anthropology, University College London, and author of *The Imbalance of Power: Leadership, Masculinity and Wealth in Amazonia* (in press). He co-edited (with V. Grotti and O. Ulturgasheva) *Shamanism in Rainforest and Tundra: Per-*

sonhood in the Shamanic Ecologies of Contemporary Amazonia and Siberia (2012) and *Rethinking the "Frontier" in Amazonia and Siberia: Extractive Economies, Indigenous Politics and Social Transformations* (2007).

Notes

This chapter is a synthesis of the authors' separate contributions to the workshop, 'Relações (Im)próprias', which we co-organized with Carlos Fausto at the Museu Nacional in Rio de Janeiro, Brazil in 2010. An early version was presented at the Research Seminar on Anthropological Theory at the London School of Economics in March 2013, convened by Matthew Engelke. We are grateful for the comments and suggestions of participants on both occasions. We are immensely indebted to our Trio, Akuriyo and Wayana friends and hosts. We also wish to express our gratitude towards Peter Rivière for sharing with us unpublished documents from his personal collection.

1. There are just over 2,000 Trio and just under 2,000 Wayana. The Akuriyo number less than 40.
2. Radios were clearly an important tool for the contact expedition. Unfortunately the missionary accounts offer no indication of how the Akuriyo thought of these objects, although one may easily imagine that they perceived them as powerful and mysterious. What we can say is that today, Akuriyo people, in contrast to their Trio neighbours, do not use the radio, for two reasons. First, there are few Akuriyo in other villages, and Akuriyo travel little except in the forest – they therefore have virtually no kin, trading partners or friends to speak to on the radio. Secondly, speaking on the radio requires adoption of a 'strong talking' idiom and confident deployment of protocol such as the English term 'over', or the Trio *'meta'* ('you hear' [i.e. 'do you copy?' in radio protocol]). The Akuriyo are extremely reserved and timid; to adopt this mode of speech would be almost unthinkable for them.
3. At the time, the characteristic Trio hairstyle was long at the back and sides with a short, straight fringe. Today this remains the hairstyle of choice for older Trio men who wish to affect a traditional appearance. Then as now, the most respected Trio men pluck all of their body hair, including not only eyebrows but also eyelashes.
4. Particularly the Waiwai, see Howard (2001).
5. Prior to missionization, the Trio were by their own account engaged in more or less constant war with their neighbours in cycles of vengeance alternating between shamanic spirit attacks and warrior raids. They thus maintained a form of negative reciprocity with their enemies. The *wajarikure*, in contrast, isolated themselves, remaining mysterious and frightening to the Trio, who in turn avoided making contact with them.
6. A key institution in Trio kinship (though ideally cancelled out by marrying ego's sister's daughter) is the practice of bride service: marriage tends to be uxorilocal, at least for an initial period during which the new husband carries out services such as building canoes and houses, clearing gardens, hunting and fishing for his parents-in-law (see Brightman 2007 and Rivière 1969 for further discussion).
7. In one or two instances Akuriyo men have married old Trio women, and Trio men have married Akuriyo women, but otherwise no intermarriage has occurred. In practical terms, it is favourable for a Trio man to be married to an Akuriyo

woman because he can hardly be obliged to carry out bride service for an Akuriyo father-in-law. In exactly the same way, the Makú, whom the Tukanoans treat as servants, only intermarry with Tukanoan men: 'Whilst Tukanoans sometimes take Makú wives, Makú men do not marry Tukanoan women' (Silverwood-Cope 1972: 200).
8. See Keifenheim (1997) on 'wild' Mashiku Indians 'pacified' by the Kashinawa: their status is ambiguously poised between 'brother-in-law' and 'slave'.
9. We are grateful to Luiz Costa (pers. comm. 14 July 2010) for his detailed comments and notes on this point. For further discussion see Brightman (forthcoming).
10. The exchange of women and food to end conflict is a recurrent theme in Wayana mytho-historical narratives (Chapuis and Rivière 2003: passim).
11. Protestant missionaries, unlike the Catholics in Missão, have attempted to eliminate the production of beer wherever they have had influence (among the Wayana, Trio, Waiwai and Wapishana). They have completely succeeded only in the case of the Waiwai, who replaced it with a non-alcoholic alternative also made from manioc that is called *pënkuhpë* by the Trio, who therefore also call the Waiwai *pënkuhpësawa*, 'drinkers of *pënkuhpë*' (C. Koelewijn, pers. comm. 2004).
12. Knowledge of the forest, hunting skills and shamanic knowledge are passed from guest to host under such circumstances. We observed this in the case of the Trio-Akuriyo relationship, as did Howard (2001) in the case of the Waiwai and the 'unseen tribes'.

References

Barbosa, G. 2002. 'Formas de Intercâmbio, Circulação de Bens e a (Re)Produção das Redes de Relações Aparai e Wayana', Masters dissertation. São Paulo: Universidade de São Paulo.
Brightman, M. 2007. 'Amerindian Leadership in Guianese Amazonia', Ph.D. dissertation. Cambridge: Cambridge University.
———. forthcoming. *The Imbalance of Power: Leadership, Masculinity and Wealth in Amazonia*. Oxford: Berghahn Books.
Chapuis, J. and H. Rivière (eds). 2003. *Wayana Eitoponpë: (Une) Histoire (Orale) des Indiens Wayana*. Paris: Ibis Rouge.
Clifford, J. 1988. *The Predicament of Culture: Twentieth-Century Ethnography, Literature, and Art*. Cambridge, MA: Harvard University Press.
Conley, J. 2000. *Drumbeats that Changed the World: A History of the Regions beyond Missionary Union and the West Indies Mission*. Pasadena, CA: William Cavey Library.
Crocker, W. n.d. 'Notes from Two Telephone Calls between Ivan E. Schoen and William H. Crocker'. Tapescript.
Fausto, C. 1999a. *Inimigos Fiéis: História, Guerra e Xamanismo na Amazônia*. São Paulo: Editora da Universidade de São Paolo.
———. 1999b. 'Of Enemies and Pets: Warfare and Shamanism in Amazonia', *American Ethnologist* 26(4): 933–56.
———. 2007. 'Feasting on People: Eating Animals and Humans in Amazonia', *Current Anthropology* 48(4): 497–530.
———. 2008. 'Donos Demais. Maestria e Domínio na Amazônia', *Mana: Estudos de Antropologia Social* 14(2): 329–66.

———. 2012. 'Too Many Owners: Mastery and Ownership in Amazonia', in M. Brightman, V. Grotti and O. Ulturgasheva (eds), *Animism in Rainforest and Tundra: Personhood, Animals and Non-Humans in Contemporary Amazonia and Siberia*. Oxford and New York: Berghahn Books, pp. 29–47.

Forth, G. 2008. *Images of the Wildman in Southeast Asia: An Anthropological Perspective*. London: Routledge.

Grotti, V. 2009. 'Protestant Evangelism and the Transformability of Amerindian Bodies in Northeastern Amazonia', in A. Vilaça and R. Wright (eds), *Native Christians: Modes and Effects of Christianity among Native Peoples of the Americas*. London: Ashgate, pp. 109–26.

Howard, C. 2001. 'Wrought Identities: The Waiwai Expeditions in Search of the "Unseen Tribes" of Northern Amazonia', Ph.D. dissertation. Chicago: University of Chicago.

Jara, F. 1990. *El Camino del Kumu: Ecología y Ritual entre los Akuriyó de Surinam*. Utrecht: ISOR.

Keifenheim, B. 1997. 'Futurs Beaux-Frères ou Esclaves? Les Kashinawa Découvrent des Indiens Non-Contactés', *Journal de la Société des Américanistes* 83: 141–58.

Kloos, P. 1977a. *The Akuriyo of Surinam: A Case of Emergence from Isolation*. Copenhagen: IWGIA.

———. 1977b. 'The Akuriyo Way of Death', in E. Basso (ed.), *Carib-Speaking Indians: Culture, Society and Language*. Tucsan: University of Arizona Press, pp. 114–22.

Lévi-Strauss, C. 1943. 'The Social Use of Kinship Terms Among Brazilian Indians', *American Anthropologist* 45(3): 398–409.

Meira, S. 1999. 'A Grammar of Tiriyó', Ph.D. dissertation. Houston, TX: Rice University.

Rivière, P. 1969. *Marriage among the Trio: A Principle of Social Organisation*. Oxford: Clarendon Press.

———. 1977. 'Some Problems in the Comparative Study of Carib Societies', in E. Basso (ed.), *Carib-Speaking Indians: Culture, Society and Language*. Tucson: University of Arizona Press, pp. 39–41.

Santos-Granero, F. 2009. *Vital Enemies: Slavery, Predation and the Amerindian Political Economy of Life*. Austin: University of Texas Press.

Schoen, I. 1969. 'Report on the Second Contact with the Akuriyo (Wama) Stone Axe Tribe, Surinam, September 1968'. Washington, DC: Center for Short-Lived Phenomena, Smithsonian Institution.

———. 1971. 'Report on the Emergency Trip made by the West Indies Mission to the Akoerio Indians, June 1971'. Washington, DC: Center for Short-Lived Phenomena, Smithsonian Institution.

Silverwood-Cope, P. 1972. 'A Contribution to the Ethnography of the Colombian Maku', Ph.D. dissertation. Cambridge: Cambridge University.

Vilaça, A. 2002. 'Making Kin out of Others in Amazonia'. *Journal of the Royal Anthropological Institute* 8(2): 347–65.

Viveiros de Castro, E. 2011. *The Inconstancy of the Indian Soul: The Encounter of Catholics and Cannibals in 16th Century Brazil*. Chicago: Prickly Paradigm Press.

Whitehead, N. 1988. *Lords of the Tiger Spirit*. Dortrecht: Foris.

Yohner, A. 1970. 'Contact with a New Group of Akurijo Indians of Suriname'. Washington, DC: Center for Short-Lived Phenomena, Smithsonian Institution.

CHAPTER 3

Fabricating Necessity

Feeding and Commensality in Western Amazonia

Luiz Costa

> If someone were to come here and they had no place to stay and I took them in and fed them, they would be relatives to me; if you feed someone, if they depend on you, they are related to you.
> —Yanktonai Sioux woman to Raymond DeMallie, 'Procrustes and the Sioux'

This chapter investigates how relations of 'ownership' or 'mastery' affect the creation and perpetuation of kinship through human action and intention. 'Ownership' and 'mastery' are here used interchangeably to designate an asymmetrical bond involving control, protection, dependency and care, which is lexically and/or conceptually present among a wide range of native Amazonian peoples. Ethnographers have long drawn attention to the importance of this bond, but only recently has it been the object of general or comparative studies (Fausto 2008; Sztutman 2012). The bond is often expressed in terms of the parent-child relation, an idiom of filiation, though it articulates with kinship in complex and ethnographically variable ways.

My aim in this chapter is to show how ownership articulates with kinship among the Kanamari, a Katukina-speaking people of western Amazonia for whom the 'social fabrication of kinship' (Viveiros 2002: 354) depends on a bond of ownership that is both elementary and indispensable. If, as Sahlins (2013) has proposed, kinship is everywhere 'the mutuality of being', then for the Kanamari, mutuality is preceded by dependency and kinship amity is preceded by ownership asymmetry. By 'precedence' I refer to two related facts: that in terms of the life cycle, people are first embedded in relations of ownership before being distributed in other relationships; and that in terms of Kanamari conceptions of kinship, ownership is a precondition of and for mutuality. Ownership generates the space where the intersubjective qualities of kinship are lived, and there are no kinship relations that are not derived from ties of ownership.

Since I cannot discuss all aspects of how ownership determines kinship, I limit myself to how kinship is articulated with the distinction between two ways of distributing and consuming food: 'feeding', defining or expressing an ownership relation; and 'commensality', characterizing communal meals that propagate kinship relations and are only possible as a consequence of previous acts of feeding. This distinction is explicitly and lexically recognized by the Kanamari, and it implies two different but interdependent orientations towards others.

For present purposes, 'kinship' defines two overlapping qualities that the Kanamari consider integral to the relations between those who are 'kinspeople' (*-wihnin*) to each other. The first is 'coresidence', *-wihnin-to* ('to live together/with kin'). Coresidence may, but need not, refer to joint residence in a single village. It must, however, minimally delineate joint residence within a cluster of villages linked to a longhouse, a unit I term a 'subgroup' (Costa 2010: 173–75). Coresidence defines a range of people with whom nonritual interactions are ongoing. The second quality of kinship I will emphasize is encapsulated in the Kanamari expression *ityonin-tikok*, 'to know the land'. *Ityonin-tikok* is the Kanamari variant of a commonly reported native Amazonian concept that is often rendered as a 'state of communal well-being', translations of analogous terms sometimes being 'living well', 'good life', 'tranquillity' or 'conviviality' (e.g. Belaunde 2001; Overing and Passes 2000). People who 'know the land' are those who live together harmoniously through 'love' (*wu*), 'beauty' (*bak*) and 'happiness' (*nobak*). *Ityonin-tikok* is a complex concept immersed in a complex ethics of social life, elucidation of which would require a different study. In this chapter I will therefore take *ityonin-tikok* to be synonymous with one of its facets, 'love' (see Lepri 2005: 714).[1]

I will first show that relationships that are based on commensality and love spring from feeding and ownership. I will then demonstrate that a relationship's cycle of development from feeding and ownership to commensality and love unfolds within a structure that is itself determined by the priority of the feeding bond. The conclusion will analyse the origin of feeding in myth, showing that whereas feeding is phylogenetically and ontogenetically precedent over commensal ties, it is itself derived from a prior relation of predation that constitutes the primordial ownership bonds from which the present is derived.

My fieldwork was carried out between 2002 and 2006 among the roughly 430 Kanamari who inhabited the banks of the Itaquaí River in the Vale do Javari Indigenous Reservation. The Itaquaí is a tributary of the Javari River, but its upper course is accessible, via the watershed, from the Juruá River basin, where the majority of the more than 3,100 Kanamari still live. There are important ethnographic differences between the Kanamari of different regions (see Reesink 1993; Carvalho 2002), so I must stress that my analysis refers primarily to the Kanamari of the Itaquaí. Its eventual pertinence for the remaining Kanamari would need to be demonstrated through further fieldwork.

Feeding

The Kanamari word for 'to feed [someone]', *ayuh-man*, contains the root *ayuh*, which refers to a need for something or someone. In verbal phrases it often acts as a modal verb, such as in *ayuh-dok*, 'to need to defecate', and *ayuh-pok*, 'to need to have sex'. In these examples, *ayuh* indicates a mechanical necessity over which people have little control. Portuguese-speaking Kanamari always translate *ayuh* in these phrases as *precisar*, 'to need'.

Like its Portuguese and English translations, *ayuh* can also be used as a nonmodal verb. This is the case of *ayuh-man*, in which *ayuh* is bound to *–man*, a polysemic verb that means 'to make/to do/to fabricate/to get', but also 'to say'. In *ayuh-man*, *–man* functions as a causative.[2] In contrast to other verbal phrases incorporating *ayuh*, the Portuguese word *precisar* does not figure in translations of *ayuh-man*. Instead, the Kanamari always translated it to me as *dar comida* ('to give food [to someone]'), though it literally means 'to cause need' or 'to fabricate need'.

As with any causative event, *ayuh-man* expresses a 'macro-situation' that encodes two 'micro-situations': the causer feeds, the causee is fed (see Comrie 1981: 165–66). *Ayuh-man* generally results in the fed participant 'eating' (*pu*) food offered by another, or made possible by that other, but, as the analysis of the verb implies, *ayuh-man* does not stress the causation of 'eating' as the primary goal of feeding. If *ayuh-man* is a causative that does not (only) cause another to eat, then what does *ayuh-man* cause in another?

To cause another to eat is a method for causing a need in the fed person in relation to the person doing the feeding. The Kanamari call this need *–naki-ayuh*, *–naki* being the postposition 'in'. *–Naki-ayuh* is literally an 'internal need' or 'urge' of the subject of the verbal phrase; we may call it a 'dependency'. *Kamanyo na-naki-ayuh awa niama*, for instance, means 'Kamanyo needs [depends on] his mother'. What is conveyed is a constitutive and at times vital need that follows from feeding. Thus the act of feeding does not cancel a previously existing need (i.e. hunger), but rather creates or perpetuates a need. In other words, while both the English verb 'to feed' and the Kanamari verb *ayuh-man* are causatives, the first causes eating and the second causes a need or a dependency.

'Feeding' connotes a rather heterogeneous assemblage of acts and events, including breastfeeding, giving food to pets, transforming raw food into cooked meals for collective feasts, providing the physical setting (e.g. house or longhouse) in which raw food is distributed to others, supplying others with the physical means to obtain food for themselves (e.g. rifles, fish hooks, machetes) and knowing and singing the chants that make possible the reproduction of forest flora and fauna. Acts and events spoken of in terms of feeding are characteristic of certain relations, but it should not be assumed that feeding defines a set of relations to the exclusion of others. On the contrary, feeding can potentially be instated between people who stand in the most varied relations, though its instatement alters the nature of any prior relationship. Some of the relations most often associated with feeding include those between women and their pets, parents and children, shamans and their familiar spirits, chiefs and followers, and the Brazilian National Indian Foundation (FUNAI) and the Kanamari; however, it can also characterize elements of the relationship between husband and wife,[3] as well as that between teacher and pupil (e.g. an experienced hunter and his companion; a shaman and his apprentice). In all of these cases the former term in the relation is said to feed the latter, but again, feeding is a necessary, though not always sufficient, aspect of these relations.

A glance at this list – itself composed of shorthand labels for complex phenomena – is evidence enough that a substantive or exhaustive definition of feeding is unproductive. Instead, feeding is more readily defined in opposition to acts of 'exchanging food' (*tyawaihmini hom*) between non-kin, or 'commensality' (*da-wihnin-pu*) in daily meals among kin. In contrast to these interactional contexts, feeding is not sharing or exchanging food between adults who have the capacity to make or obtain food for themselves or others, nor is it a subsistence practice that is common in regular, quotidian interactions. Rather, what the Kanamari call 'feeding' creates or conveys an asymmetric relation between the participant who feeds and the one who accepts being fed. This does not mean that feeding cannot characterize bonds between fully productive adults in certain contexts. What it means is that prescinding such a bond from other relations brings into relief the supplementary productive capacity of the feeder over the fed. A focus on this bond to the detriment of others renders an otherwise fully productive adult into a dependent, construing that adult as someone who is not fully productive, at least in the context of the feeding event.

Although the Kanamari translate *ayuh-man* as 'to feed', many of the actions I have listed here do not look very much like what we think of as feeding, even if they all have some link, however slight, to at least providing the physical means or the raw materials for others to produce food for themselves. At its limit, however, *ayuh-man* need not be related to eating or subsistence activities at all. Causing another to eat by giving them food or the means to produce food is only a privileged instance of a much more general asymmetry that involves one participant making available for another what was previously unavailable, thereby creating or furthering the latter's dependence on the former.

Pets

Like many Amazonians, the Kanamari often tame and raise the captive offspring of animals that they kill. Raising pets is an example of what Fausto has termed 'familiarizing predation', which he defines as 'the process through which alien subjects are consumed and controlled in order to produce new subjects on the inside of the group' (Fausto 1999: 949). For the Kanamari, feeding is both the means by which this control is established and an important moment in the production of persons (or, moving ahead a bit, the production of persons who produce and/or consume). A study of how pets are raised is a suitable place to start an ethnographic discussion of feeding because the relationship between master and pet is primarily, and at times only, defined through feeding. As a paradigmatic instance of feeding, pet-keeping allows us to clearly identify its effects and isolate them in contexts in which feeding may be intertwined with, or replaced by, other relations.

I have said that the Kanamari who speak Portuguese translate *ayuh-man* as 'to give food [to someone]', but when directly asked 'what is *ayuh-man*?' many respond with an example: it is when a woman chews food, takes it from her mouth and places it in the mouth of a pet that she is raising. The Kanamari word for 'pet', *bara o'pu*, literally means 'small game' and is used to refer either to the young of wild animals or to pets (i.e. formerly wild animals), regardless of their age. Although Kanamari pets rarely live for very long, even fully grown pet animals are called 'small game', which here denotes their condition as animals being raised by humans.

The root *bara*, 'game/animal', may be substituted for the name of the species in concrete cases.[4] Although men hunt, it is mostly women and sometimes children who feed and raise pets, a division of labour that is common in Amazonia (see Erikson 1987; Taylor 2001; Cormier 2003: 114–15). The role of women in taming is encoded in the Kanamari term for pets: *o'pu*, 'small', when preceded by a possessive prefix, is the kinship term for 'son' in female kinship terminology (see also Vander Velden 2012: 165). *Bara o'pu* can be translated as either 'small game' or 'game son (w.s.)', highlighting an association between parent-child (in this case, mother-son) and owner-pet relations that is widespread in Amazonia (see Fausto 1999).[5]

Another common name for 'pet' is *ityowa tyuru-tiki-yan*, 'that which we cause to grow/thrive', which stresses the vital bond between the animal and its human owner that is established by feeding.[6] By 'vital bond' I mean that the pet would not survive without being fed by its caretaker. Feeding is the central technique in taming: when the infant animal accepts being fed, it is deemed to have lost the potential to feed itself and therefore to no longer be able to exist outside of the emerging bond. Feeding is furthermore not simply the provisioning of food, but a process that forces a change in diet upon the pet, which must learn to accept food that humans eat, prepared by human culinary techniques – including, occasionally, meat from the very same species being reared (Erikson 2011: 22). The pet's newly acquired palate further identifies it with its new owner, supplying an additional deterrent to escape (see also Déléage 2009: 191; Goulard 2009: 215–16).

Although it is the central technique in taming, feeding occurs alongside a series of other operations. When a hunter brings a young animal to a village, it has its teeth removed, and, if necessary, its claws; birds immediately have their wings clipped. The pet is then tied to a house post if it is a mammal or a reptile, or stored in a loosely woven basket that is kept warm if it is a young bird. Periodically, the pet is freed in order to be passed over the smoke of the hearth so that it grows accustomed to the smell of the house and will lose the will to run away. All pets are initially fed banana porridge, sweet manioc drink or *Bactris* palm fruit drink. These meals often include pieces of banana, manioc dregs or the flesh of *Bactris* fruits, all of which are chewed by women before being placed directly into their pet's mouth or beak. Progressively, birds learn to eat food placed in the palm of their owner's hands, and toothless mammals to eat food intentionally thrown on the floor near the house post to which they are tied. Later, when they no longer need to be kept tied up, they receive their share from their owner's plate. During the first days in which the pet is fed, the woman responsible for its well-being (or, according to some, everyone in the household) must refrain from eating game, particularly meat from the same species being reared (when it is an edible species).

Submitted to this process, the animal gradually shifts from being 'from the forest' (*ityonin-warah*) to being 'from the house' (*hak-warah*) and it is untied from the house post and allowed to move freely within the village. The pet is tamed as it comes to need its new owner and its ability to survive outside of the household is extinguished. As the relationship develops, feeding can become laced with sentiments that seem at first to eclipse the originary dependency, or at least to add other possible orientations to it. One of these sentiments is 'love' (*wu*). The Kanamari verb *wu* implies a mutual and reciprocal orientation between those who love each other. It thus denotes a symmetry that is apparently contrary to the asymmetry of the feeding bond, and an elective and performative dimension which is apparently contrary to the mechanical and ineluctable character of dependency. In relation to pet-keeping, what concerns me in the remainder of this section is how, in the development of the master-pet relation, feeding is a precondition for pet and master to love each other, though it need not result in love.

When a woman begins feeding a pet she may state that she will 'produce its old age' (*kidak-bu*), meaning that she intends to care for the pet as she and it age together. After some months of taming, some women begin to sleep with their pets in their hammocks, and they are fond of pets that follow them around the village in their daily chores. People, in turn, pointed out to me that a pet follows its owner because it loves her. At this stage in their relationship, most women will refer to their pets with an established pet vocative term.[7] Pets called by these vocatives are rarely fed directly. Instead, they simply 'eat' (*pu*) food that people prepare for themselves, sometimes receiving or taking food directly from peoples' plates or the pans where food was prepared. At the death of a beloved pet, women sometimes enter periods of 'mourning' (*mahwanin*, literally 'longing'), which involves suspending work, eating less and periodically bursting into laments in which the appropriate pet vocative is repeated. On one occasion, when I showed a man a picture of his wife and her late pet woolly monkey, I was told that under no circumstances should I show it to her lest she resume mourning, even though it had been more than a year since the pet died.

While all pets are created through acts of feeding, not all receive the love of their owner in this way. Many pets die young, sometimes a few weeks or months after being brought to the village, and are unceremoniously tossed into the river or the forest. Others that are fed sporadically and heedlessly eventually die or run away without causing any commotion or sadness. At other times, pets remain unloved. Their owner continues to feed them to some extent but no further care is given, nor is any intimacy shared. These pets may be exchanged with other Kanamari or with the neighbouring whites, who may kill and eat them.[8] Some pets are ignored by those who originally fed them and become virtually ownerless. These pets, the Kanamari say in Portuguese, are *da comunidade*, 'the community's'. Rather than meaning that they are 'everyone's' pet, being 'the community's' means that they are in fact the responsibility of no one. These strays wander from house to house eating leftover scraps, begging for food or stealing it.[9]

Where love between master and pet exists, it can be traced back to an originary feeding bond, but not every act of feeding results in love. What every act of feeding does result in is dependency (*–naki-ayuh*). The relation between a woman and the pet she feeds is one in which she establishes control over its fate, where she is the source of its life. As long as feeding is prolonged, the pet's dependency on its owner is sustained and the development of other relations remains a possibility.

Ownership

Shifting our discussion from the causative acts that establish asymmetry to the categories generated through them, we encounter the Kanamari variant of the widely attested Amazonian category of the 'owner-master' (Fausto 2008). For the Kanamari, anyone who feeds another is an 'owner' of whomever or whatever he or she feeds. The Kanamari word that I gloss as 'owner' is *-warah*, but its semantic range is wider than this English translation allows. If it were translated into standard English, it would have at least two meanings: the 'living body' of people and animals; and the 'owner' of something or someone.[10] In the Kanamari language, these meanings are not alternatives but always occur simultaneously. I will render *-warah* as 'body-owner', a composite of the two Portuguese words, *corpo* and *dono*, that the Kanamari most often propose as translations of *-warah*. To be more precise, then, anyone who feeds another is a body-owner of that other (see Costa 2010).

A woman, for example, is the body-owner of her pet. Anyone who wishes to refer to this woman in relation to her pet will call her *a-warah*, 'its body-owner'. The pet, in turn, is not the body-owner of anyone or anything. There is no way of referring to the pet through the concept of the body-owner without subsuming it to the woman who feeds it, although it can simply be called 'pet' (*bara o'pu*, a condition that implies an ownership relation) or, in the case of pets who have lived in the village for some time, by its vocative term. This means that the body-owner of the pet is the woman who feeds it, and it lacks a body-owner outside of this relation.

-Warah is the only Kanamari word that can possibly refer to the whole, living body of humans or animals. It may thus seem odd to claim that a pet lacks a 'body' outside of a relation. The *-warah*, however, signifies the objectification of an asymmetrical relation, and not a substantive entity defined through its physicality.[11] The asymmetry that the *-warah* objectifies is not just a feature of structural positions in a relational scheme; rather, it has real effects on how the terms put into relation are constituted. *-Warah* is the term (in a given relation and context) whose referent has the capacity to act with and for those that he or she subsumes by aligning their activities to his or her own (see also Strathern 1988: 274–88). The body-owner is hence a figure of what late twentieth-century anthropology calls 'agency' (see Ortner 2006: 134–37). 'Agency', in this anthropolog-

ical sense, is a variable concept, 'a culturally prescribed framework for thinking about causation' (Gell 1998: 17). For the Kanamari, referring to a person as 'X-*warah*' indicates that the person thus referred to has greater power over social processes than those who are implicated or included in his or her acts. Such power does not, therefore, inhere in individuals but is always a matter of objectifying – channelling and coordinating – the activities of others towards some collective end. The *–warah* emerges from a bond, and within that bond it dictates the nature of activities.

In his recent discussion of kinship as 'the mutuality of being', Sahlins stresses that just as kinship makes experience 'transpersonal' by diffusing it among those who are kinspeople to each other, so is agency 'a function of the conjunction, located in and as the relationship it also realizes in action. Agency is in the unity of the duality' (Sahlins 2013: 52–53). For Sahlins, agency has a quality of 'we-ness', being distributed across those who are conjoined in action. In contrast to the diffuse agency posited by Sahlins, Kanamari render the capacity to act as a function of one term of the relation, the body-owner, whose position is constructed through a vested asymmetry. For any action performed in the context of this bond, one of the terms of the duality, namely, the one who feeds the other(s), will display greater initiative and power, or be attributed these qualities by others. Thus, agency is not equally distributed in each of the terms that constitute the *–warah,* since the person who occupies the encompassing limit of the duality will ultimately (be held to) determine the direction of future actions.

Sahlins (2013: 53) proposes his definition of agency as 'shared intentionality', distributed along relations rather than objectified in the actor, as an alternative to Strathern's emphasis on agency as a quality of the singular person who 'acts with another in mind' (Strathern 1988: 272). Regardless of the relative scope of each approach as social theory, for the Kanamari agency lies in the 'singular person' as constituted in an asymmetric relation of feeding another or others, thereby subsuming their will into his or her own.[12] 'Bodies' are hence referred to only when they are the *loci* of activity, i.e. when a subject acts in specific asymmetrical relations to others. This means that for the Kanamari, an individual, solitary body never actually materializes, for any activity in which the body-owner is manifest requires at least two participants, one of whom will be the body-owner of the other.[13]

I have already shown how the ensuing dependency upon the superordinate term operates in the pet-keeping relation, but it applies to all body-owner bonds established through feeding, although certain variations must be taken into account. To speak, for instance, of the relationship between a mother and her child, and to emphasize the body-owner bond over other relations that may be maintained by mother and child, one will refer to the superordinate term, in this case the mother, as *a-warah* (his/her/its body-owner), *awa opatyn-na-warah* (her child's body-owner) or X-*warah*, where X is the name of the child. There is no way to refer exclusively to the 'body' of a newborn (just as there is no way to refer exclusively to the 'body' of a pet) since it is not yet involved in relations in which it can be a body-owner to others. The mother is the body-owner of the child because she feeds it, at first with breast milk and later with food she has cooked. The child contributes very little to the subsistence economy or to the daily upkeep of the household. Even when children are old enough to contribute food on certain occasions, 'the labour of these children does not circulate in their names for they are treated as extensions of their parents in terms of production', as Gow (1989: 578) has observed for the Piro. In this sense, whatever tasks a child may perform are 'simply an adjunct to adult activity' (ibid.).[14]

To grow and thrive the child must be fed by its mother – or more accurately, any woman who so feeds it becomes its mother (*niama*) by enabling it to grow and thrive.[15] In the first years of its life, the child's mother is its most proximate body-owner, although the father and other close kin may also be referred to as its body-owner on some occasions. In the process of growth, however, the child progressively develops body-owner bonds of his or her own by learning to provide some food (i.e. fish or forest fruits) for his or her younger siblings or becoming responsible for the care of one or more pets. The development of body-owner bonds is a feature of maturation, part of the life cycle of all persons. To be an adult human being is to enter into and maintain body-owner bonds with others.

As one becomes a body-owner in relation to others and hence progressively becomes a productive person, many of the body-owner bonds that previously constituted the person in question meanwhile slacken or drift towards more symmetrical and mutualistic relations, including love, which elide the earlier asymmetrical bond of dependency. An adult man may love his mother, but he does not need her in the same way that a child needs its mother: she no longer feeds him because he can produce his own food and is able to feed others, thereby becoming a body-owner to them. This does not mean he will not find himself in a subordinate position to others acting as his body-owner in certain contexts, but that these situations lessen as opportunities to assume a superordinate position as a body-owner increase.

Lest there be any confusion about the language I am using to describe the bond between a Kanamari mother and her child, I take the opportunity to reiterate that 'love', 'dependency', '(body-)ownership', 'feeding' and so forth stand in for the Kanamari concepts described above. My use of English language glosses is inevitably imperfect, whether they be my own translations from the Kanamari language or my translation of glosses provided by Kanamari who speak Portuguese. The reader should hence always defer to the analysis of the Kanamari words involved.

Likewise, it would be presumptuous of me to make any claim about what a mother actually feels for her child and vice versa. My concern is not, at any rate, with the affectionate way Kanamari mothers tend their newborns, nor with those basic aspects of the mother-child bond that develop through the attachment generated by nurture. My concern relates to a discursive and pragmatic fact of Kanamari social theory, one that conveys (my understanding of) Kanamari understandings of the life cycle. In light of this, I can state that the use of *wu*, 'love', to characterize the relation between a mother and her newborn is unusual. Indeed, this is a truism, because although I follow the Kanamari in translating *wu* as 'love' (Portuguese *amor*), it designates a reciprocal relation in which both parties contribute to their mutual wellbeing. Since in the mother-child bond, particularly during the first years, it is exclusively the mother and her kinspeople who produce for the child, and since nurturing flows unidirectionally from mother to child, the Kanamari frame the mother-child bond by the 'feeding/dependency' pair and downplay references to 'love' (and other orientations) from their theories of this relation. The word *wu* comes to be used frequently once the child is able to contribute, however little, to productive activities, or at the very least displays its intention to do so (i.e. plays with a toy bow, follows its mother when she fetches water, etc.). Concomitantly, interpretations of the mother-child through the 'feeding/dependency' pair become less salient as they are replaced by the idiom of love.

I also note that, once the particular slant of Kanamari theories of ontogeny are taken into account, the facts I describe are fairly current in the literature on Amazonian child rearing practices. It is widely reported in Amazonian anthropology that being born to human parents is no guarantee of the child's humanity, a condition echoed in the ambivalent attitudes that adults display towards young children. These ambivalent attitudes tend to be mitigated as the child reveals its capacity for learning and interacting (see Vilaça 2002 and Santos-Granero 2011 for reviews of indigenous Amazonian attitudes to children). Humanity is thus constructed and positional, in that it is dependent on how one acts in relation to others (Gow 1997). The Kanamari achieve this construction of the child's humanity gradually, the first act being to fabricate the child's necessity through maternal feeding, which is a humanizing procedure. At the same time, it should come as no surprise that in some cases, certain affectionate bonds established between adults, such as those that an anthropologist might render as 'love', will be absent from the relation between parents and newborn children. Indeed, the ambivalent nature of children and the corresponding reticence of adults is hardly restricted to Amazonia. Among the Korowai of West Papua, for instance, where newborns are categorized as inhuman and their attachment to adults needs to be created, women are often heard to say that "on the birth scene, there is no love" (Stasch 2009: 152; see also Course 2011: 27–28).

Similarly, the fact that having children is an integral component of the development of the person is widely attested in Amazonian anthropology. Children often establish the couple as a stable, productive unit and ensure the success of matrimonial unions, which are sometimes considered fickle prior to the birth of children (e.g. Da Matta 1982: 123–24). A first child may mark the end (or a relaxing) of the husband's period of bride service in uxorilocal regimes (Kensinger 1995: 106; Rival 1998; Santos-Granero 1991: 173), and having children enables the passage between age grades, where these exist (Seeger 1981: 112–15). But although hunting, pet-keeping and marriage have been analysed as partaking of shared symbolic premises (Taylor 2000, 2001; Walker 2013), the wider implications of the fact that raising pets can likewise be an integral part of maturation have generally been excluded from comparative considerations.[16] Although Fausto's model of familiarizing predation, for example, draws on the language of pet-keeping, actual pet-keeping practices remain a somewhat silent element in his scheme, which veers towards less prosaic relations between the killer and his victim or the shaman and his familiar spirits, all of which clearly accrue capacities to those who display mastery over others (Fausto 1999). Yet, as Taylor (2001) reminds us, human relations with their pets may be antithetical to animal procreativity, insofar as pets do not reproduce in captivity, but they are an integral part of the development of human creativity through the appropriation of foreign vitalities. In the case of the Kanamari, raising pets, like providing food for younger siblings, is likely to spark the first moment in which a child who so far has been fed by others develops his or her own ability to feed.

But there is evidently an important difference between raising pets and raising children. The altricial nature of children and pets obliges both to exist through their body-owners, but the ability to create body-owner bonds through feeding (and hence to mitigate former bonds of dependency) is a feature of the maturation of the former that is absent for the latter. Although both children and pets are new individuals that enter the space of everyday relations, kinship with pets can only go so far because they never feed others and never produce food. Owner-pet relations that develop into love and commensality are, in this sense, a public fiction because there is no way to fully extricate the bond from its underpinnings in the way that a child disengages itself from its mother's ownership as it instates body-owner bonds with others through feeding.[17]

Before discussing how commensality differs from, and is articulated to, feeding, I would like to reiterate four aspects of the Kanamari idiom of the master-owner. First, a single word applies to both the owner and to the body. Second, mastery relations are clearly articulated with feeding. Third, mastery relations are conveyed through an imagery of containment: to feed is to contain that which is fed; to be fed is to be inserted in a relation with a body-owner (see Sztutman 2009 and Cesarino in this volume for similar cases). Finally, being owned by someone, as a child or a pet is owned by its *niama*, is the ineluctable start of a life cycle that allows other relations to develop as these bonds weaken or follow their trajectory towards different dispositions. The weakening of the body-owner bonds that constitute the child is coterminous with the child's instatement of body-owner bonds through feeding as he or she matures. As the child ceases to be fed, he or she feeds others; and as the former bond gives way to other sentiments and social orientations, the latter creates new relations of dependency that constitute the feeder as an adult person.

Commensality

The problem with ontogenetic arguments like the one I have just advanced is that it is ultimately impossible to establish the primacy of one relation over others without falling into the difficulties of infinite regress. While the love one has for pets, for instance, emerges from a bond of dependency (and before that an act of cynegetic predation), a woman will raise pets only after she is herself involved in relations of mutual love and care with her kinspeople. Kanamari social theory solves this problem by positing less immediate feeding bonds that are articulated with more encompassing body-owners. These are structural preconditions for the relations that occur within the province of kinship (see Gordon in this volume). In other words, both the feeding bonds that tie *niama* to children and pets and the love that can emerge from the development of their relations are dependent on the existence of a further feeding bond at the origin of social life. This is the bond between chiefs and followers.[18]

The most salient feature of the people who follow a given chief is precisely that they all are, to different degrees, 'kinspeople' (*-wihnin*) to each other. In order to understand the Kanamari concept of 'kinspeople' and its relation to chiefs, it is necessary to discuss 'commensality', a modality of consumption that can only occur among kinspeople. I have already mentioned commensality when considering some of the possible developments of the master-pet or mother-child bond as it drifts from more direct feeding into less determined instances of sharing meals. But since I am claiming that the course of these developments is determined by a structural relation between chiefs and followers, I must now specify what exactly commensality entails.

The Kanamari word for 'commensality' is *da-wihnin-pu*, which can be decomposed into the verb *pu*, 'to eat', proceeded by *da-wihnin-*, which the Kanamari gloss as 'together' (Portuguese *juntos*). *Da-wihnin-* can be further decomposed into the root *wih*, 'bunch', inflected by the suffix *-nin*, which here subordinates the root to *da-*, a perfective prefix. *Da-* marks for durative aspect (Comrie 1976: 41–44), indicating that an action occupies a set segment of time, having the general meaning of 'for a while', 'for some time', in contrast to an unspecified duration designated by unmarked verbs. When *da-* inflects the verb *pu* directly (*da-pu*), it has the meaning of 'to snack' rather than 'to eat'. *Da-* has a similar effect on other verbs: 'to sleep' is *kitan* but 'to take a nap' is *da-kitan*; 'to give' is *nuhuk* but 'to lend' is *da-nuhuk*. When *da-wihnin-* precedes a verb, it signifies that two or more participants carry out the action of the verb in unison within the duration specified by the aspectual marker. *Da-wihnin-pu* can thus be literally translated as 'to eat together (for the duration of a meal)'.

Commensality occurs between fully productive adults. In other words, it characterizes the productive and consumptive activities of people who produce all the food required of them by the Kanamari sexual division of labour: adult men hunt, fish and clear gardens; women gather forest fruits and garden crops, butcher game meat and cook. People who produce food and share meals should live together harmoniously through an ethic of 'knowing the land' (*ityonin-tikok*) that has love as one of its central features. The word *-wihnin*, which composes the word for commensality, is the same word that the Kanamari use to refer to 'kinspeople'. *Da-wihnin-pu* can thus equally be translated as 'to eat as kin (for the duration of a meal)'. Commensality is a correlative of love and kinship.

I have shown that the development cycle of Kanamari relations includes a transitory period in which dependency and love overlap. Thus love is not an orientation occurring exclusively between productive adults but is also a feature of adult relations with unproductive children and pets. Both children and pets may be loved, and they may love their *niama* in turn, but neither is able to contribute food towards daily meals. They may partake of these meals, but young children and pets are not given plates of food; instead they are allowed to take their share from anyone's plate, particularly their *niama*'s. In this way 'a gloss of mutuality is put upon the unequal, asymmetrical relationship' (Strathern 1988: 90), and through this gradual widening of mutuality, the asymmetrical relationship will ultimately shift towards other relations – even if these other relations always remain partial and ambivalent, as in the case of pets. It is not required that children and pets 'eat together' with adults because they are directly fed. The commensality that they thus share with adults is tempered, if not determined, by feeding relations that are more basic and immediate.

This ambiguity in the overlap of feeding and commensality is expressed in jokes. Pets (particularly monkeys) that take their food from their *niama*'s plates or from pans in which food has been prepared and join people for meals in households are a farce. 'Is it human (*tukuna*)?' the Kanamari will ask, and add, bursting into laughter, 'Is this pet our kin?' Seeing the pet next to its *niama* eating from her plate, others may get up and, taking food from their own mouths, place it in the mouth of the pet, saying, 'Here, take your food', as if to remind it (or others) that it is not a commensal.[19] Children are subject to similar jokes. When boys start to bring home fish that they have caught in the nearby stream, or when girls help their mother with cooking, adult Kanamari will jokingly refer to them as 'grandfather' (*paiko*) or 'grandmother' (*hwa*). Here the emphasis is not on what the child may think he or she is, but rather on what he or she will one day become. The point of the joke is to ironically situate children at the opposite end of the life cycle, shifting them from nascent commensals to (soon to be) ex-commensals, thereby stressing their incipient and negligible participation in communal meals by equating it with the reduced contributions of elderly kin.[20]

In contrast, coresident adults who contribute towards daily meals 'eat together' on a regular basis. But adults are not thereby exempt from being the subordinate parties to ownership bonds. If commensality is isolated from other relations, it will appear to differ from feeding in that feeding establishes the body-owner as a figure of agency, whereas commensality diffuses agency through the many acts of those who participate in communal meals. Because it is both temporally and spatially enacted away from the immediate and unmediated feeding bond, commensality creates the illusion of being independent from it. Among the Kanamari, however, commensality never occurs in isolation and is never a voluntary manifestation of a simple desire to share meals. Instead, it must occur within a space created by prior acts of feeding. What distinguishes adults from pets and children, then, is not that the latter are fed while the former are not. It is that adults exist at a remove from feeding that is greater than the dependency that ties children and pets to their mothers (see Bonilla in this volume).

Chiefs

The Kanamari recognize two chiefs.[21] One is a village chief, linked to a nucleated settlement (a village); the other is a subgroup chief, linked to a longhouse and associated with a number of nucleated settlements. Both chiefs are called –*warah*, 'body-owner', by those to whom they are chief, although each defines a different scale of collective life. These two chiefs and the settlement patterns associated with them make up the subgroup.

Most commensal events occur in villages, spaces that are inseparable from their chiefs. A Kanamari village is composed of a variable number of thatched houses arranged near a stream and a garden. It is the identification of a suitable garden plot and the first efforts at clearing it that mark the site of the future village. The village chief is invariably the man who identifies a plot and who organizes the work of clearing. People who work towards clearing a garden and building the houses of a village do so *da-wihnin*, 'together', but also, literally, 'as kin' for the duration of the activity. The aspectual *da-* stresses the contingency of the 'togetherness' of making a village, but people do not necessarily disperse when work is concluded. Postmarital uxorilocality ensures that a village chief's unmarried sons and sons-in-law have little choice but to remain in the new village. Meanwhile, others who worked towards building it may choose to live in the village if they consider the village chief to 'know the land' (i.e. behave ethically), and if his 'beautiful speech' (*koni baknin*) is capable of dissipating the 'angry speech' (*koni noknin*) that sometimes emerges among people who work together. Because of their close genealogical or marital ties, common labour and the ethically correct relations they establish through their chief's example, the residents of a village are 'true kin' (*–wihnin tam*).

A 'true kin' aggregate is maintained by the chief's ongoing generosity. Although the garden plot is cleared collectively and divided into subplots associated with each household in the village, the Kanamari say that the garden is the chief's, because it was his initiative that mobilized people to clear it and hence to coreside (*–wihnin-to*, literally 'to live together/as kin'). The term *baohnin-warah*, 'garden body-owner', is perhaps the only expression in the Kanamari language that exclusively designates what I have called 'the village chief' (in contradistinction to other body-owners). For the residents of the village, he is simply *tyo-warah*, 'our body-owner'. His name, followed by *–warah*, is how non-residents of the village refer to the chief and to his followers, as well as to the village, its gardens and everything that is associated with it.

The village chief also plays a pivotal role in processing game. All the game animals brought to the village are laid on the floor of the chief's house, where they are skinned, butchered and redistributed (Costa 2012). The chief's house is furthermore a place where there is always some cooked meat available for consumption. Before setting out on hunting trips, hunters gather there at dawn to eat and to make themselves 'strong' (*waman*) enough to 'withstand' (*kima*) the hardships of the hunt.

The commensality that characterizes day-to-day meals is therefore made possible by the village chief: it is his garden that draws a village together, his garden that is divided into household plots that feed the village, his house where game carcasses are transformed into pieces of meat that can be cooked, his house's abundance of food that supplies hunters with the strength to procure game. Any commensality between the coresidents of the village is the outcome of the consumption of food that the chief's activities make possible. Indeed, the contingency of 'commensality', indicated by the perfective *da–*, can only be converted into regular acts of sharing meals through the chief's continuing ability to feed those who live in his village, that is, to ensure that food will be available for collective meals.

The bond between chiefs and followers is hence a condition for establishing kinship between coresidents through, among other mechanisms, commensality. There are no settlements without chiefs, and there is no kinship without settlements. This is the inescapable conclusion of the conjunction of two widely attested facts of Amazonian societies that are closely associated among the Kanamari: that kinship is generated or maintained through coresidence (Gow 1991: 165–67; Overing 1993: 55; McCallum 2001: 32), and that a settlement is indissoluble from its chief (Rivière 1984: 72–73; Heckenberger 2005: 255–90; Brightman 2010: 145–47). If kinship emerges from proximal living, then the absence of the conditions for proximal living must result in the impossibility of making kinship relations (Guerreiro Júnior 2011: 119–20). For the Kanamari, two people can make themselves kin only if both are, on some level, subsumed under (i.e. fed by) the same chief.

Kanamari villages are articulated into subgroups. These are named, endogamous units localized to the basins of the tributaries of both banks of the Jurua River. Subgroups are physically composed of two different settlement types, organized along the hydrology of these basins. Villages are always built on the streams and headwaters that flow into the main channel of a river basin, but never on the main channel, which is the site of the longhouse. Only one man and his family build a thatched house in the vicinity of the longhouse. This man is the subgroup chief, and he is called *tyo-warah*, 'our body-owner', by all residents of the different villages that compose the subgroup.

The subgroup is the sociocentric horizon of Kanamari kinship. Coresidents in a village, who recognize the same village chief as their body-owner, are 'true kin', but they are 'distant kin' (*–wihnin parara*) to the residents of other villages of their subgroup, who reside with other village chiefs. The distinction between true and distant kin is effaced in reference to the subgroup chief, in relation to whom everyone in the river basin, regardless of his or her village, is simply 'kin' (*–wihnin*) to one another. There are no kinspeople outside of the area synthetically expressed in a river basin, its longhouse and the subgroup chief.

The subgroup chief is sometimes also called *hak nyanin-warah*, 'the longhouse body-owner'. The longhouse is associated with both a 'large garden' (*baohnin nyanin*), cleared and used by everyone in the river basin, and extensive fallows containing palm trees that are essential for Kanamari livelihood (Costa 2009: 160–62). The large garden plays a crucial role in Kanamari subsistence: when a village is terminated, the large garden will sustain those who previously coresided there while they decide their future course of action; and it is from among the cultigens planted in the large garden that the residents of a future village will choose the varieties they will plant in their new gardens (Costa 2010: 180–81). The large garden of the subgroup chief is hence the condition for the smaller village gardens.

The defining trait of the subgroup chief, however, is his knowledge of the 'Jaguar songs' (*Pidah owaik*), which are integral to the 'Jaguar-becoming' (*Pidah-pa*) ritual, performed in periods when all the villages of the river basin coalesce in the longhouse. The Jaguar-becoming ritual guarantees the regeneration of the forest flora and fauna. At the same time, the ritual marks a period in which large communal meals involving everyone in the subgroup are possible thanks to abundant crops from the large garden and fallows, and meat obtained from collective hunting and fishing expeditions. These communal meals, like all meals, are made possible by the existence of feeding bonds. While the village chief feeds those of his village, the subgroup chief feeds everyone in the subgroup by ensuring, through his ritual knowledge – or, in the words of Santos-Granero (1986), his control over 'the mystical means of reproduction' – that the basis of Kanamari livelihood and the raw material out of which kinship is made is available to all those who, through commensal acts, continue to be kinspeople to each other. If the subgroup defines the domain in which kinship operates, then the subgroup chief, a hyper-feeder, is at the same time the source and extent of kinship.

The Origin of Feeding

Although anthropologists have drawn attention to the articulation of asymmetrical and symmetrical orientations in Amazonian politics and social ethics (e.g. Gow 1989, 1991: 161; Santos-Granero 1991), few have focused on the distinction between feeding and commensality. The exceptions I am aware of concern differences between food distribution and consumption in ritual and nonritual events. Vanessa Grotti, for example, stresses the difference, for the Trio of Suriname, between quotidian commensality, 'cloistered within cognatic units' (Grotti 2009: 80), and ritual nurture, where commensality is enlarged to enable a temporary fusion of unrelated peoples who participate in ritual beer drinking ceremonies (Grotti 2009, 2012). 'Nurture' functions as a form of control exercised over a given group of people and is held to be distinct from the practices of nonritual commensality, which have a much more limited scope with regard to the sorts of relationships they can generate.[22]

The majority of studies of Amerindian alimentary practices, however, have concentrated on the difference between commensality and cannibalism, the latter understood as 'any devouring (literal or symbolic) of the other in its (raw) condition as a person' (Fausto 2007: 504). Whereas commensality is a 'primary vector of identity' (502), cannibalism is a vector of transformation that must be kept distinct from commensality if kinship is to be produced. In Amazonia, cannibalism is a manifestation of what Viveiros de Castro has called 'generalized predation', which far exceeds cannibalism in that it is 'the prototypical modality of Relationship in Amerindian cosmologies' (1993: 184). If, among the Kanamari, feeding is the condition for commensality, what is the relation of feeding to predation and cannibalism?

Despite its axiomatic nature, feeding is absent from the world delineated in the set of ancient myths that the Kanamari call 'stories of the Jaguar' (*Pidah nawa ankira*). In one of these myths we learn that the Jaguar is a 'fish-body-owner' (*dom-warah*) that used to live in the headwaters of the Jurua River with all of the fish, which it ate and never released. Ancestor Heron was reluctantly allowed to fish, but his brothers-in-law were told by the Jaguar that they would be killed were they to try and do so. Hungry, since there were no fish anywhere else, they decided to go to the Jaguar anyway, and he mercilessly killed all of them. Ancestor Heron killed the Jaguar in revenge, whereupon it became many groves of rubber trees (*Hevea brasiliensis*), its falling leaves transforming into *piau* fish and its seeds into *pacu* fish that proceeded to swim downriver. Fish now travel through different parts of rivers, but they still gather in areas close to concentrations of rubber trees, where they feed on the compost that gathers in the riverbed.

The first lesson of this and related myths is that whereas feeding is a feature of the present world that is extracted from myth, ownership existed before it. The Jaguar is explicitly said to be a *-warah*, embodying a hierarchically ordered predatory scheme that constrains the movement of the fish it eats. This means that ownership is inseparable from feeding only when the creation of necessity and kinship are isolated from a wider cosmological backdrop. Once this backdrop is taken into account – as it must be, if we are to investigate the passage from 'the absolute discourse' of myth (Viveiros de Castro 1998: 483) to the 'world of multiple domains' of the present (Fausto 2008: 339) – it is evident that feeding, from whence kinship is derived, is itself derived from predation within a structure in which ownership remains constant.

But whereas the architecture of ownership remains constant in both the mythical and postmythical worlds, in the former it does not rest on the

Jaguar 'making the necessity' (*ayuh-man*) of the fish, which are likewise not 'dependent' (*–naki-ayuh*) on the Jaguar in any way. Instead the Jaguar 'kills' (*–ti*) the fish, who 'die' (*tyuku*) in order to satisfy their master. The Jaguar does not imbue in the fish any disposition towards it, but simply situates them through a sort of predatory terror, directed both at the fish that compose their body-owner and the characters who crave these fish. There is no kinship in the world of the Jaguar because there is no relationship of feeding, only generalized predation that is both internal and external to the characters of myth.

The emergence of feeding in the phenomenal world is precisely the transformation that the myth sets out to narrate. After its demise, the predatory Jaguar body-owner is transformed into a multiplicity of biomes that are the body-owners of the fish they feed. Fish are drawn to the *Hevea* groves just as pets and children are drawn to their mother, or adults to their chiefs. Furthermore, *Hevea* groves actually generate, through falling leaves and seeds, the fish that they then feed, generative capacity being one of the hallmarks of ownership in lowland South America (Déléage 2009: 117–21; Santos-Granero 2009: 168–70).

For kinship to exist, body-owners must feed others and thus emerge as agents in relation to the passivity or defencelessness of those who are fed. Love, knowing the land, and commensality are possible only within a restricted space whose parameters are delimited by an owner and the dependency the owner generates in others. Commensality and love are not *sui generis* relations and dispositions, for symmetrical orientations always reveal their asymmetrical origins in feeding.

But feeding is itself possible only in a world that is extracted from violence, where the global parameter of a singular unit is predation. This is clear in the ritual activities of the subgroup chief. The Jaguar songs known to the subgroup chief are precipitates of the world of the Jaguar. The Jaguar-becoming ritual that the subgroup chief sponsors in order to guarantee the kinship of his 'children' is a dangerous undertaking that reveals some of the precariousness of the feeding bond, poised as it is between a primordial world of universal predation and a phenomenal world of localized commensality. Commensality and kinship ultimately depend on the subgroup chief's ability to replicate, in ritual, the same transformation of predation into feeding that was effected in myth.[23]

Having started with a description of pet-keeping – a paradigmatic, inexorable feeding bond – it is appropriate to conclude with the subgroup chief's feeding of his children through ritual, which is the less vertical or imminent extreme of the same bond. Whereas it is virtually impossible to transform feeding into commensality in pet-keeping, the Jaguar-becoming rituals enmesh feeding with commensality: one blurs into the other. Gathered before the people of his subgroup, the chief must impel others to accompany him in singing the songs that regenerate the forest's abundance, thereby ensuring that commensality and kinship will not lag behind. After the ritual, people return to their villages and continue to hunt the animals that ritual made available, share meat and, supplementing it with manioc from the village chief's garden, eat together as kin.

Lacking the obvious violence that characterizes the taming of pets, Jaguar-becoming rituals nonetheless point to the violence that characterizes the primordial world from which the present is extracted. Irrespective of its immediacy, feeding is always both the hinge between predation and commensality and the means through which generalized predation is processed as kinship. Its derivation from predation marks its ambivalence, while its orientation towards kinship confirms its necessity.

Luiz Costa is Associate Professor of Anthropology at the Institute of Philosophy and Social Sciences, Federal University of Rio de Janeiro. Among other articles and chapters, he has recently published 'The Kanamari Body-Owner: Predation and Feeding in Western Amazonia' (2010), 'Making Animals into Food among the Kanamari of Western Amazonia' (2012) and 'Alimentação e Comensalidade entre os Kanamari da Amazônia Ocidental' (2013).

Notes

This chapter has benefited from the comments of Luisa Elvira Belaunde, Marc Brightman, Carlos Fausto, Marco Antônio Gonçalves, Cesar Gordon, Vanessa Grotti, Paul Kockelman, Els Lagrou and Joana Miller. It is based on twenty months of fieldwork with the Kanamari of the Itaquaí River (Vale do Javari, Brazil), most of which was carried out between 2002 and 2007. My deepest gratitude lies with the Kanamari, and particularly with Poroya, Tiowi, Dyumi and Dyan, all of whom taught me much about dependency and care. Fieldwork was made possible by the Wenner-Gren Foundation for Anthropological Research, the Conselho Nacional de Pesquisa e Desenvolvimento (CNPq), the Coordenação de Aperfeiçoamento de Pessoal de Nível Superior (Capes), the Programa de Pós-Graduação em Antropologia Social (PPGAS-MN), the Núcleo de Transformações Indígenas (Nuti-Pronex) and the Centro de Trabalho Indigenista (CTI).

1. *Wu*, which I translate as 'love' but which could also be translated as 'affection', designates a reciprocal orientation between people who participate in the domestic or subsistence economy. In the words of Peter Gow (1989: 580), it is a relation of 'mutual demand' or 'mutual desire' that is central to productive relations in the Amazonian regime of the sexual division of labour. *Wu* always includes traces of mutuality, reciprocity and symmetry. When a relationship with predominantly asymmetrical traits is expressed in the idiom of 'love', this implies that: (1) the

asymmetrical relation is in the process of being transformed into a symmetrical relation; (2) the asymmetrical traits are obviated in favour of a symmetrical language within a specific discursive context in which this gloss is desirable.
2. Causatives in the Kanamari language can be formed by *–man* or *–bu,* factitive stems that indicate 'to make' or 'to produce', or else by the causative suffix *–tiki*. While *–tiki* is strictly limited to causative constructions, *–man* and *–bu* have wider semantic scopes (on *–bu* see Costa 2012: 104). The two sets of causative constructions do not appear to be grammatically interchangeable. Although I am unable to affirm with any certainty why one form is chosen over another, the difference appears to me to be related to the distinction between direct (*-man* or *–bu*) and indirect (*-tiki*) causation (Comrie 1981: 171–74).
3. Although the relation between husband and wife tends to be more symmetrical and egalitarian than the other relations listed, the Kanamari say that husbands feed their wives and never vice versa. An understanding of the marital tie, and gender relations more generally, through an asymmetry seems to be a recurring feature of southwestern Amazonian societies. E.g. Kensinger (1995: 51–52) states that among the Kaxinawá women may refer to their husbands as *xaneibu,* a term otherwise used for headmen, and Lorrain (2000: 303) writes that among the Kulina, neighbours of the Kanamari, men are the primary givers and women the primary receivers in the most diverse spheres of activity, referring to the 'encompassing character of male agency in production [which] is correlated with a primary access of men to all products, whether male or female'.
4. The Kanamari raise a wide range of animals as pets, including tapirs, peccaries, otters, boa constrictors and all varieties of birds and monkeys. The only animals that they explicitly told me were not suitable as pets were felines, poisonous snakes, anacondas or caimans.
5. Although the Kanamari show little interest in the sex of their pets (in contrast to the great interest shown in the sex of the game animals they hunt), the term *bara o'pu* seems to imply that 'pets' are associated with sons rather than daughters. In fact, however, in the Kanamari language 'sons' is the unmarked form for 'sons and daughters', a feature it shares with Romance languages. When a woman speaks of *i-o'pu hinuk,* 'my sons', she may thus mean her sons and daughters.
6. Throughout Amazonia, native terms for pets often register their passive status in relation to acts of feeding. For example, the Huaroani of Amazonian Ecuador call their pets *queninga,* which means 'that who is fed' or 'that who has received food from humans' (Rival 1999: 79); the Tukanoan Barasana call their pets *ekariera* which means 'those whom we feed' (Stephen Hugh-Jones in Fausto 2007: 502).
7. Like many western Amazonian societies, the Kanamari have an established set of vocative terms for pets that distinguish them from wild individuals of the same species (see Erikson 1988: 28). All pets of the same species are called by the same term. The nature of pet vocatives varies across species, but they can be abbreviations of the Kanamari word for the animal in the wild, the names of mythical characters, the names of parts of the animal (like 'beak'), or the words that neighbouring Pano- or Arawá-speaking people use for the wild species in question. Regardless of the nature of the pet vocative, the Kanamari say that they are always the name of the wild species in the language of the *adyaba* spirits, which in myth raise captive Kanamari as their children. See Dienst and Fleck's (2009) excellent survey of western Amazonian (including Kanamari) 'pet vocatives', an expression coined by them.

8. One neither kills nor eats pets that one feeds, although pets can be given to or exchanged with others in the knowledge that they will be killed and eaten. In some cases an exchanged or given pet is raised by the recipient, who feeds it and thereby reorients the pet's dependency towards a new owner.
9. Many ethnographers of native Amazonia have noted the ambivalence owners display towards their pets, which they treat with a 'rather brusque affection' (Descola 2013: 253), both caring for and ignoring, loving and disdaining them (see also Erikson 1987). At the start of the taming process among the Kanamari, it is impossible to predict whether a pet will be actively raised or passively ignored, but the ambivalence other authors have noted is, in this ethnographic case, inseparable from a consideration of whether the pet is fed regularly by its owner or sporadically by a number of people.
10. *-Warah* has at least one further meaning: it refers to the largest part of any entity constituted of multiple parts, such as the trunk of a tree in relation to its roots, leaves, seeds and branches, or the main channel of a river system in relation to its tributaries and headwaters. The *-warah* thus conjoins disparate elements into a singular entity, as will become evident shortly.
11. *-Warah* is a bound morpheme that must always be preceded by a noun or pronoun that specifies what is owned through the relation, as indicated by the hyphen. Its relational quality is therefore given in its linguistic usage as well as in practice. Many *-warah* relations are vocatively nonreciprocal because they involve relations between adults, on the one hand, and entities lacking speech capacity, such as pets and newborns, on the other. However, it also encodes the relation between chiefs and followers, where followers call a chief 'my body-owner' (*i-warah*) and are called 'my children' (*atya opatyn hinuk*) or 'my people' (*atya tukuna hinuk*) in return (see Fausto 2008: 332–33 on reciprocals for ownership relations). In these cases, the name of a chief (or a personal pronoun) followed by *-warah* designates not only the chief, but everyone that lives with the chief and the place where they reside (see below).
12. For some examples of how the agency of the body-owner is construed, see Costa (2009: 162–65, 2010: 181–85). I would need more space to reflect on the applicability of Strathern's (1988: 273) distinction between the 'agent' (the one who acts) and the 'person' (the one who causes others to act). Nonetheless, the body-owner has both greater leeway and flexibility in acting and is more capable of influencing how those who depend on him or her come to act (see also Agha 2007: 230–31; Kockelman 2007: 379–82). Even in contexts where agency appears more diffuse, seemingly closer to Sahlin's preferred mutual "we-ness", mutuality is still, ultimately, derived from a feeding bond, as we will see shortly.
13. The Kanamari word that translates as 'alone', *padya,* literally means 'empty'. People who are 'empty' lack relations in which they feed others or are fed by them. Therefore they are not the body-owner of others and do not themselves have a body-owner. Such a state is dangerous, befalling people who, for example, become lost in the forest. Lacking asymmetrical relations, they run the risk of becoming a 'spirit-soul', *ikonanin,* errantly wandering from place to place. The same applies to wild animals, the prototypical example being the peccary who gets lost from a herd and finds itself 'empty' (see also Fausto and Costa 2013; Lagrou 2000; Rodgers 2013: 93–94; Sterpin 1993: 59–60).
14. The overlap between relations of kinship and ownership is a classic theme in anthropology (see Strathern 2006) that has undergone certain interesting develop-

ments in Amazonia. Among the Kaxinawá, for example, McCallum (2001: 33) reports that the word *ibu*, 'owner', also means 'parents' and 'encompasses both possession and legitimate authority'. Oddly, McCallum then goes to some lengths to dissociate the idiom of ownership from relations between persons (2001: 92). See Brightman (2010: 152) on some of the contradictions she thereby incurs.

15. One child, for example, was being raised by his grandmother (MM) even though both his parents lived in the same village, an arrangement that is not uncommon among the Kanamari (see Bonilla 2007: 338–44 for the importance of this practice among the Paumari). Although he sometimes called his grandmother by the genealogically correct term *hwa*, he sometimes also called her 'mother', *niama*, all the while continuing to call his birth mother *niama*. A formal analysis of Kanamari kinship terminology shows that it is theoretically impossible to simultaneously call two women *niama*. Although their terminology is of the 'Dravidian' type, it establishes certain noncanonical terminological distinctions in G1 between M and MZ (and F and FB) – a distinction that may be related to the focal and exclusive nature of the body-owner bond. By using a denotative term in a classificatory manner and using *niama* for both his M and MM (the latter alternatively called *hwa* in certain contexts), the child was expressing the conflicting ownership bonds established through feeding that his predicament created.

16. See Cormier (2003: 116–17) and Howard (2001) for ethnographic descriptions of pet keeping as a component of the life cycle among the Tupi-Guarani-speaking Guajá and the Carib-speaking Waiwai, respectively. See Vander Velden (2012) for an innovative description of the life cycle of pets as they age alongside adults among the Arikem-speaking Karitiana. The role of domestic or familiar animals in socializing children has been described for other regions. See e.g. Ulturgasheva's (2012) discussion of how, among the Siberian Eveny, children's 'personhood' is developed in their relation to one reindeer that they nurture from an early age.

17. Coelho de Souza (2002: 381) draws attention to the limits imposed on Amerindian kinship processes by different regimes of alterity and corporality (see also Santos-Granero, this volume). The difference between children who are rendered productive through the consumption of food made possible by others and pets that always remain consumers is the Kanamari manifestation of this wider problematic. The difference between the effectiveness of the kinship processes to which children and pets are submitted is explicit among many Amazonian peoples, such as the Trio, who (like the Kanamari) can exchange or sell their pets, but not their children (Grotti 2007: 169–70).

18. I realize that this robust claim may seem like a case of the gullible anthropologist falling victim to chiefly mystification of productive processes. However, I never actually heard any chief boast of chiefly prominence in Kanamari society in this manner. What I did hear from every Kanamari with whom I discussed the matter (chiefs or nonchiefs, men or women) was that without the Jaguar-becoming fertility ritual (discussed below), there would be no game in the forest or fruits to be gathered, and crops would not grow. Although all adults should participate in (and contribute to) this ritual, they do so at the chief's instigation (*a-nobu-nin*, 'he orders it', i.e. he bids people to participate) by collectively singing Jaguar songs that only he can conduct. As the sponsor of the ritual, the chief is referred to as *Pidah-Nohman*, 'the Jaguar Chanter', or as *Pidah-Warah*, the 'Jaguar Body-Owner'. It is thus accurate to claim that chiefs are the condition of the possibility for Kanamari social life because, as the Kanamari acknowledge, without chiefs

they would lack the material and economic basis of their livelihood (see Santos-Granero 1986) and hence all other feeding bonds would be impossible.
19. The Huaulu of Seram studied by Valerio Valeri have a similar attitude to dogs that cease to be effective hunters. These dogs continue to live alongside humans and have to be fed, even though they no longer keep their end of the mutual obligations established between dogs and humans. Here, however, the register in which their pitiful position is made explicit is not that of the joke, but the insult (Valeri 1992: 158).
20. The joke is also at the expense of the elderly, who, like children, have to be at least partly fed by adults. I am unable here to describe the global symmetry of the life cycle, which makes ageing adults cease to be productive as they gradually come to be fed once again. See Costa (2007: 319–23) on the associations between children and the elderly among the Kanamari.
21. My discussion concerns Kanamari descriptions of precontact social organization. For the changes this organization has undergone, see Costa (2007; forthcoming).
22. Grotti has recently turned to an analysis of how 'nurture' operates in situations of interethnic contact (Grotti 2012; Brightman and Grotti this volume). In a series of ethnographic studies that resemble my description of feeding among the Kanamari, Guerreiro Júnior (2011, 2012) has also shown how among the Kalapalo of the Upper Xingu, asymmetrical relations of feeding are characteristic of chiefs who are 'trunks' or 'mainstays' of social aggregates, enabling kinship to exist among those who rely on their activities. Santos-Granero's (1986) discussion of the economic basis of Amerindian leadership and Lorrain's (2000) arguments concerning gender hierarchy in the productive sphere among the Kulina also resonante with Kanamari ethnography.
23. On the Jaguar-becoming ritual, see Costa (2007: 386–92).

References

Agha, A. 2007. *Language and Social Relations*. Cambridge: Cambridge University Press.
Belaunde, L.E. 2001. *Viviendo Bien: Género y Fertilidad Entre los Airo-Pai de la Amazonía Peruana*. Lima: CAAP.
Bonilla, O. 2007. 'Des Proies si Désirables: Soumission et Prédation pour les Paumari d'Amazonie Brésilienne', Ph.D. thesis. Paris: École des Hautes Études en Sciences Sociales.
Brightman, M. 2010. 'Creativity and Control: Property in Guianese Amazonia', *Journal de la Société des Américanistes* 96(1): 135–67.
Carvalho, M. do Rosário. 2002. *Os Kanamari da Amazônia Ocidental. História, Mitologia, Ritual e Xamanismo*. Salvador: Fundação Casa de Jorge Amado.
Coelho de Souza, M. 2002. 'O Traço e o Círculo: O Conceito de Parentesco entre os Jê e os Seus Antropólogos', Ph.D. thesis. Rio de Janeiro: Museu Nacional, Universidade Federal do Rio de Janeiro.
Comrie, B. 1976. *Aspect*. Cambridge: Cambridge University Press.
———. 1981. *Language Universals and Linguistic Typology*. Chicago: The University of Chicago Press.
Cormier, L. 2003. *Kinship With Monkeys: The Guajá Foragers of Eastern Amazonia*. New York: Columbia University Press.

Costa, L. 2007. 'As Faces do Jaguar: Parentesco, História e Mitologia entre os Kanamari da Amazônia Ocidental', PhD thesis. Rio de Janeiro: Museu Nacional, Universidade Federal do Rio de Janeiro.
———. 2009. 'Worthless Movement: Agricultural Regression and Mobility', *Tipiti: The Journal of the Society for the Anthropology of Lowland South America* 7(2): 151–80.
———. 2010. 'The Kanamari Body-Owner: Predation and Feeding in Western Amazonia', *Journal de la Société des Américanistes* 96(1): 169–92.
———. 2012. 'Making Animals into Food among the Kanamari of Western Amazonia', in M. Brightman, V. Grotti and O. Ulturgasheva (eds), *Animism in Rainforest and Tundra: Personhood, Animals, Plants and Things in Contemporary Amazonia and Siberia*. Oxford: Berghahn Books, pp. 96–112.
———. forthcoming. 'Becoming FUNAI: a Kanamari Transformation', in P. Virtanen and H. Veber (eds), *Creating Dialogues: Indigenous Perceptions and Forms of Leadership in Amazonia*. Boulder: University Press of Colorado.
Course, M. 2011. *Becoming Mapuche: Person and Ritual in Indigenous Chile*. Urbana: University of Illinois Press.
Da Matta, R. 1982. *A Divided World: Apinayé Social Structure*. Cambridge, MA: Harvard University Press.
Déléage, P. 2009. *Le Chant da l'Anaconda: L'Apprentissage du chamanisme chez les Sharanahua (Amazonie Occidentale)*. Nanterre: Sociétéd'Ethnologie.
DeMallie, R. 2011. 'Procrustes and the Sioux: David M. Schneider and the Study of Sioux Kinship', in Richard Feinberg and Martin Ottenheimer (eds), *The Cultural Analysis of Kinship: The Legacy of David M. Schneider*. Urbana and Chicago: University of Illinois Press, pp. 46–59.
Dienst, S. and D. Fleck. 2009. 'Pet Vocatives in Southwestern Amazonia', *Anthropological Linguistics* 51: 209–43.
Erikson, P. 1987. 'De l'apprivoisement à l'approvisionnement: chasse, alliance et familiarisation en Amazonie amérindienne', *Techniques et Culture* 9: 105–40.
———. 1988. 'Apprivoisement et habitat chez les amérindiens Matis (langue Pano, Amazonas, Brésil)', *Anthropozoologica* 9: 25–35.
———. 2011. 'Animais demais ... Os xerimbabos no espaço doméstico matis (Amazonas)', *Anuário Antropológico* 5(2): 15–32.
Fausto, C. 1999. 'Of Enemies and Pets: Warfare and Shamanism in Amazonia', *American Ethnologist* 26: 933–56.
———. 2007. 'Feasting on People: Eating Animals and Humans in Amazonia', *Current Anthropology* 48: 497–530.
———. 2008. 'Donos demais: maestria e domínio na Amazônia', *Mana. Estudos de Antropologia Social* 14(2): 329–66.
Fausto, C. and L. Costa. 2013. 'Feeding (and Eating): Remarks on Strathern's Eating (and Feeding)', *Cambridge Anthropology* 31(1): 156–62.
Gell, A. 1998. *Art and Agency: An Anthropological Theory*. Oxford: Clarendon Press.
Goulard, J.-P. 2009. *Entre Mortales e Inmortales: El Ser Según los Ticuna da la Amazonía*. Lima: CAAP/IFEA.
Gow, P. 1989. 'The Perverse Child: Desire in a Native Amazonian Subsistence Economy', *Man* (N.S.) 24: 567–82.
———. 1991. *Of Mixed Blood: Kinship and History in Peruvian Amazonia*. Oxford: Clarendon Press.

———. 1997. 'O parentesco como consciência humana: o caso dos Piro', *Mana. Estudos de Antropologia Social* 3(2): 39–65.
Grotti, V. 2007. 'Nurturing the Other: Wellbeing, Social Body and Transformability in Northeastern Amazonia', PhD thesis. Cambridge: Cambridge University, Department of Social Anthropology.
———. 2009. 'Un corps en movement: Parenté, "diffusion de l'influence" et transformations corporellesdans les fêtes de bierre Trio, Amazonie do nord-est', *Journal de la Société des Américanistes* 95(1): 73–96.
———. 2012. 'Happy with the Enemy: Kinship, Pacification and Corporeal Transformation in Trio Beer Feasts, Northeastern Amazonia', *Anthropology and Humanism* 37(2): 191–200.
Guerreiro Júnior, A. 2011. 'Esteio de gente: reflexões sobre assimetria e parentesco a partir de depoimentos de chefes kalapalo', *Revista de Antropologia Social dos Alunos do PPGAS-UFSCAR* 3(1): 95–126.
———. 2012. 'Ancestrais e suas sombras: uma etnografia da chefia kalapalo e seu ritual mortuário', PhD thesis. Brasília: University of Brasília.
Heckenberger, M. 2005. *The Ecology of Power: Culture, Place and Personhood in the Southern Amazon, AD 1000–2000*. New York: Routledge.
Howard, C. 2001. 'Wrought Identities: The Waiwai Expeditions in Search of the "Unseen Tribes" of Northern Amazonia', PhD thesis. Chicago: University of Chicago Press.
Kensinger, K. 1995. *How Real People Ought to Live: The Cashinahua of Eastern Peru*. Prospect Heights, IL: Waveland Press.
Kockelman, P. 2007. 'Agency: The Relation between Meaning, Power and Knowledge', *Current Anthropology* 48: 375–401.
Lagrou, E. 2000. 'Homesickness and the Cashinahua Self: A Reflection on the Embodied Condition of Relatedness', in J. Overing and A. Passes (eds), *The Anthropology of Love and Anger: The Aesthetics of Conviviality in Native Amazonia*. London and New York: Routledge.
Lepri, I. 2005. 'The Meanings of Kinship among the Ese Ejja of Northern Bolivia', *Journal of the Royal Anthropological Institute* (N.S.) 11: 703–24.
Lorrain, C. 2000. 'Cosmic Reproduction, Economics and Politics among the Kulina of Southwest Amazonia', *Journal of the Royal Anthropological Institute* 6: 293–310.
McCallum, C. 2001. *Gender and Sociality in Amazonia: How Real People Are Made*. Oxford: Berg.
Ortner, S. 2006. *Anthropology and Social Theory: Culture, Power and the Acting Subject*. Durham, NC, and London: Duke University Press.
Overing, J. 1993. 'The Anarchy and Collectivism of the "Primitive Other": Marx and Sahlins in the Amazon', in Cris Hann (ed.), *Socialism: Ideals, Ideologies and Local Practice*. London and New York: Routledge, pp. 43–58.
Overing, J. and A. Passes. 2000. 'Introduction: Conviviality and the Opening Up of Amazonian Anthropology', in J. Overing and A. Passes (eds), *The Anthropology of Love and Anger: The Aesthetics of Conviviality in Native Amazonia*. London: Routledge, pp. 1–30.
Reesink, E. 1993. 'Imago Mundi Kanamari', PhD thesis. Rio de Janeiro: Museu Nacional, Universidade Federal do Rio de Janeiro.
Rival, L. 1998. 'Androgynous Parents and Guest Children: The Huaroani Couvade', *Journal of the Royal Anthropological Institute* (N.S.) 4: 619–42.

———. 1999. 'Prey at the Centre: Resistance and Marginality in Amazonia', in S. Day, E. Papataxiarchies and M. Stewart (eds), *Lilies of the Field: Marginal People Who Live for the Moment*. Boulder: Westview Press, pp. 61–79.

Rivière, P. 1984. *Individual and Society in Guiana*. Cambridge: Cambridge University Press.

Rodgers, D. 2013. 'The Filter Trap: Swarms, Anomalies, and the Quasi-topology of Ikpeng Shamanism', *Hau: Journal of Ethnographic Theory* 3(3): 77–105.

Sahlins, M. 2013. *What Kinship Is – and Is Not*. Chicago: University of Chicago Press.

Santos-Granero, F. 1986. 'Power, Ideology and the Ritual of Production in Lowland South America', *Man* (N.S.) 21: 657–79.

———. 1991. *The Power of Love: The Moral Use of Knowledge Amongst the Amuesha of Central Peru*. London: Athlone Press.

———. 2009. *Vital Enemies: Slavery, Predation and the Amerindian Political Economy of Life*. Austin: University of Texas Press.

———. 2011. 'Hakani e a campanha contra o infanticídio indígena: percepções contrastantes de humanidade e pessoa na Amazônia brasileira', *Mana. Estudos de Antropologia Social*. 17(1): 131–59.

Seeger, A. 1981. *Nature and Society in Central Brazil: The Suya Indians of Mato Grosso*. Cambridge: Harvard University Press.

Stasch, R. 2009. *Society of Others: Kinship and Mourning in a West Papuan Place*. Berkeley: University of California Press.

Sterpin, A. 1993. 'La chasse aux scalps chez les Nivacle du Gran Chaco', *Journal de la Sociétédes Américanistes* 79: 33–66.

Strathern, M. 1988. *The Gender of the Gift: Problems with Women and Problems with Society in Melanesia*. Berkley: University of California Press.

———. 2006. *Kinship, Law and the Unexpected: Relatives Are Always a Surprise*. Cambridge: Cambridge University Press.

Sztutman, R. 2009. 'De nomes e marcas – ensaio sobre a grandeza do guerreiro selvagem', *Revista de Antropologia* 52(1): 47–96.

———. 2012. *O profeta e o principal: A ação política ameríndia e seus personagens*. São Paulo: EDUSP.

Taylor, A.-C. 2000. 'Le sexe de la proie: Représentations jivaro du lien de parenté', *L'Homme* 154–55: 309–34.

———. 2001. 'Wives, Pets and Affines: Marriage among the Jivaro', in L. Rival and N. Whitehead (eds), *Beyond the Visible and the Material: The Amerindianization of Society in the Work of Peter Rivière*. Oxford: University Press, pp. 45–56.

Ulturgasheva, O. 2012. *Narrating the Future in Siberia: Childhood, Adolescence and Autobiography among the Eveny*. Oxford: Berghahn Books.

Valeri, V. 1992. 'If We Feed Them, We Do Not Feed on Them: A Principle of Huaulu Taboo and Its Application', *Ethnos* 57(3–4): 149–67.

Vander Velden, F. 2012. *Inquietas Companhias: Sobre os Animais de Estimação entre os Karitiana*. São Paulo: Alameda.

Vilaça, A. 2002. 'Making Kin out of Others in Amazonia', *Journal of the Royal Anthropological Institute* 8: 346–65.

Viveiros de Castro, E. 1993. 'Alguns aspectos da afinidade no dravidianato amazônico', in E. Viveiros de Castro and M. Carneiro da Cunha (eds), *Amazônia: Etnologia e História Indígena*. São Paulo: FAPESP, pp. 150–210.

———. 1998. 'Cosmological Deixis and Amerindian Perspectivism', *Journal of the Royal Anthropological Institute* 4: 469–88.

Walker, H. 2013. 'Wild Things: Manufacturing Desire in the Urarina Moral Economy', *Journal of Latin American and Caribbean Anthropology* 18(1): 51–66.

CHAPTER 4

Parasitism and Subjection
Modes of Paumari Predation

Oiara Bonilla

> All lines go in one direction, none in the other.
> They literally go to one opening:
> the gaping maw of the universal parasite.
> Or to a common misery:
> the broken back of the universal victim.
> —Michel Serres, *The Parasite*

This chapter is inspired by two field observations that form the basis for an exploration here of Paumari relational sociology. The first observation is that Paumari insist on defining their relations with others in 'commercial' terms. Thus the term by which they refer to themselves, *pamoari*, is also the term used to designate the client position vis-à-vis a *patrão* or boss (*kariva*) in a commercial context. In other relations, the Paumari also systematically position themselves as clients (*pamoari*), sometimes shifting to adopt the position of employees (*honai abono*) of a boss. The second observation is that Paumari describe themselves as prey (*igitha*) in their relations with others, whether wild Indians (*Joima*) coming from afar to devour them, or white people (*Jara*) coming to kill, enslave or convert them.

Given the history of the region and the Paumari involvement in the debt peonage economy of *aviamento* introduced along the Purus River during the late nineteenth-century rubber boom, neither of these two observations is surprising.[1] Aside from the fact that absolutely everything is and must be negotiated (in exchange for either money or commodities), what is noteworthy is the indifference the Paumari typically show for the goods obtained in exchange for a favour, information, a fish or the like. It is as though asking for something were much more interesting than actually obtaining it. Besides bargaining for everything, the Paumari insist on placing themselves systematically in the service of their interlocutors, very often transforming simple questions from the latter into orders or requests that must be duly remunerated or compensated.

On the other hand, they complain about their health and current life almost constantly, contrasting the present with the 'boss era' and the 'mission era' with an air of nostalgia.[2] Both this description of themselves as victims and the apparent definition of all relations in commercial terms are recurring themes in everyday life, observed in a variety of forms throughout my research. While still in the field, I tended to relate these two themes to the history of the Paumari involvement in the region's violent social and economic history (Bonilla 2005, 2007, 2009). As I have shown in my subsequent work, however, what appears to be a form of subjection can in fact be conceived of as a particular variant of ontological predation, one of its potential actualizations being precisely the shift the Paumari make from the position of prey (*igitha*) to that of pet (*igitha*)[3] and the position of client (*pamoari*) to that of employee (*honai abono*).

My objective here is not in any sense to deny or minimize the effects of colonization and the violent impact of the rubber economy on the peoples inhabiting the region. On the contrary, I wish to add to the discussion of these events by exploring the issues raised by the apparent 'subjection' of the Paumari. The ethnographic data allows us to move beyond our own understandings of the terms 'submission' or 'subjection' so that Paumari meanings can surface. What subjects are these, who define themselves as pacific prey and place themselves systematically in the service of another? What types of relations are actualized in this movement?

Since the publication of my earlier article (Bonilla 2005), a number of other ethnographic cases have been described and analysed, each suggesting that indigenous peoples' definition of themselves as prey or pets can afford insights into various aspects of Amazonian ontologies, especially their ongoing historical transformations (see Costa 2009, 2010 and this volume; Deturche 2009: 118, as well as Fausto's (2008) comparative study of notions of mastery and ownership in Amazonia).[4] At the same time, although this apparent victimization is related in the Paumari case to a certain market-based 'consumerism' (Hugh-Jones 1992: 43), it is not the commodities themselves that appear to be the focus of desire, but the relations that exchange and indebtedness allow to be actualized continuously (Bonilla 2005: 42).[5] My aim here is to show that subjection, and its extreme limit as expressed in the ideal of parasitism, are also forms of predation and full-blown actualizations of the Paumari dynamic of relationality and sociality.

Clienthood

The Paumari today number around 1,500 people living along the lakes and shores of the middle Purus River in the south of Amazonas state. They speak variants of the same language, which belongs to the Arawá family (Dixon and Aikhenvald 1999: 294). In day-to-day life they frequently use Portuguese to communicate among themselves and with white people (*Jara*), generally merging the grammatical and lexical structures of the two languages. The Paumari live primarily from fishing and cultivating small swiddens where they grow various plant crops, particularly manioc, yams and bananas. They also plant crops on the river beaches during the Amazonian summer and trade most of this harvest with river traders journeying up and down the Purus, or with the bosses and traders in Lábrea and Tapauá.

The Paumari interest in commerce was attested by the first white travellers to explore the Purus during the second half of the nineteenth century. Their 'facility for trading' also tended to coincide with a description of the people as 'peaceful' or 'fearful', and as 'great lovers of song'. At that time the Paumari, or Pammarys, like the Juberi, were still known as the Puru-Puru, the 'blemished' or 'blotchy-skinned Indians', since they suffered from the endemic skin disease *pinta,* a nonvenereal form of syphilis (*Treponema carateum*) that causes skin-colour alterations and seems to have played the role of an identity marker for the group (Bonilla 2007: 65–70, 2009: 130). They lived in floating houses on the shores and lakes of the Lower and Middle Purus and were described early on as skilled traders who were peaceful and inoffensive, and disposed to singing:

> They are peaceful. ... They are happy, fun-loving and adore singing, ... Some traders who employed an entire village of them managed to obtain 200 to 300 turtles in one day's work. (Chandless 1949: 26)

Labre (1872: 27) describes them as '"true canoeists" who work on extracting natural products, which they exchange for commodities and drink', while Silva Coutinho (1863: 71) emphasizes their disinterest in war and describes their relations with the river traders:

> Some river traders exploit the fears of the Pammarys to obtain better deals. They would say that the Muras were coming to strike them, which was enough for the entire maloca to accompany the traders in trepidation of their enemies ...
>
> ...
>
> Naturally fearful, they flee at the slightest sign of aggression, not only from the Muras but also from any other tribe, and will find resources through the means they have at their disposal for navigation.

The Paumari recall that before the arrival of white people (*Jara*) and more specifically the bosses (*kariva*), they lived like the gulls (*tihi*) that come to roost on the beaches of the Purus at the start of the Amazonian summer.[6] Hence they were much more numerous than today, occupying beaches from the Tapauá downriver to the Sepatini upriver, but were also consequently exposed to attacks from other Indians, the *Joima*, as we shall see later. After the appearance of the figures of the *kariva* and *Jara*, the Paumari abandoned the beaches, considered too exposed, and entered the forest in search of *terra firme*, though still choosing sites close to lakes and streams.

In the 'rubber era' and until the arrival of the mission in 1964, the Paumari were able to work seasonally for one or other boss (mainly rubber estate owners, but also loggers or fishermen) as either employees (*honai abono*) or clients (*pamoari*). Depending on context, the auto-denomination *pamoari* is used to refer to someone occupying the client position, that is, a client linked to a boss by debt. Employees are a somewhat different kind of client, able to repay their debts through work and services provided directly to the boss. As clients, the Paumari typically became indebted to various bosses (whether rubber estate owners, merchants or river traders) in order to obtain a single commodity from each one, which led to their insertion in a dense and complex network of relations of indebtedness with no guarantee of continuity (Kroemer 1985: 136).

For example, a family head would work for some months for a boss (as an employee), but still owe others (as a client), whom he would pay with his *produção*, a term used in Portuguese to designate any product extracted from the forest environment. In this way the Paumari obtained clothing, work tools and food, mostly in exchange for salted fish (pirarucú and other scaleless fish), turtles or timber, and more sporadically extractivist products like Brazil nuts, andiroba, copaíba or small quantities of latex. As a result the Paumari were primarily recognized as suppliers of fish and turtles to the regional market.

Before marrying, young men would frequently leave the village to work as employees extracting rubber or timber at a *colocação* (forest settlement), or sometimes to join the crew of a river trader or a fishing boat, usually for several years at a time. This still happens today and, Paumari men say, allows the young man to learn the '*Jara* ways' (*Jara kahojai*) by 'being raised by him' and to obtain regular access to white people's goods (*inisika*). The '*Jara* ways' include the ways white people work, tap rubber, extract timber, plant and hunt, and above all speak Portuguese, barter, eat, drink and dance. The relationship established between the youth and his employer is long-lasting and in many cases amounts to a form of adoption. Hence many men today say that 'I was raised by *Jara*', meaning they grew up and lived with the whites.

Generally the young man returns to the village to marry without clearing his debt but having obtained privileged access to the commodities his boss supplies by living with him and becoming his adoptive son or godson, thereby obliging the boss to become his provider and protector. Today men of all ages tell of how they grew accustomed to the food and habits of the *Jara*, learned to pilot a boat and travelled along the length of the Purus and beyond, visiting other Amazonian towns, learning about other peoples and so on. They also explain how they gained their *Jara* surnames and were raised by a particular boss who today resides in the town.[7] This practice is still common among the Paumari of the region of the Tapauá and Cuniuá rivers. By mobilizing these fictitious kin relations with the Paumari, the fishermen and traders themselves also guarantee their access to the region's lakes and streams for exploration (Bonilla 2010: 221–23).

Until the end of the 1960s, the bosses prevented the Paumari from planting, acquiring goods from the river traders, or fishing in waters that the bosses claimed as their own, except when the Indians were working to pay back their debts. With the decline of the rubber market, the arrival of the first mission (in the 1960s) and FUNAI (in the 1970s), and the gradual legalization of indigenous lands in the region (at the end of the 1990s), the debt peonage system gradually vanished and the power of the bosses waned. Even today, though, the Paumari run up debts with the 'little bosses' (*patrõezinhos*) along the river shore to obtain basic goods or sometimes flour and manufactured foods. They repay these debts with their own produce or provide some kind of service: the men clean the traders' yards or repair the roofs of their houses, while the women wash clothes and so on.

It is important to note that the Paumari do not evoke the era of submission to the rubber bosses with any particular expression of displeasure or revolt. On the contrary, they usually manifest a strong nostalgia for this period, recalling the time of the bosses as an era of plenty and relative peace.[8] In terms of abundance of merchandise, that time cannot be compared to the 'mission era', that is, the period after the arrival of the Evangelical mission, which to a large extent took over the function of supplying the kinds of goods previously distributed by the bosses (Bonilla 2009: 137–39). This nostalgia is relative, of course. Although they have not forgotten the violence suffered during the era of the bosses, what older people like to recall is how good the bosses were when they provided an endless supply of goods and looked after the Paumari 'like their own children', sharing food with them and giving them clothes and sometimes medicines. Above all, the bosses gave them Christian names and surnames ('people's names'). Hence, besides receiving commodities, protection and symbolic goods, the Paumari extended their relations beyond the limits of the village, establishing fictitious kinship ties through both Catholic baptisms – which were organized by the priests who visited the region – and fire baptisms in the Festivals of São João held by the bosses and *ribeirinhos*.[9] Nowadays, they say, everything is much more difficult to obtain: you need money, and you have to travel to town to indebt yourself to supermarket and trade store owners who offer only manufactured goods and provide no guarantee of continuing the relation (Bonilla 2013).

–*Kapamoarihi*: The Human Form

The regional population consider the Paumari to be 'tame' Indians *par excellence*, a people who were 'pacified' and quickly learned 'civilized' ways (a quality invariably associated with the possibility of trading, at least in this part of the Purus region). According to the *ribeirinhos*, the two biggest dangers the Paumari pose to white people are their capacity to provoke skin diseases – their shamans may attack Others by sending spells in the form of a contaminating powder – and the possibility that the Paumari will become permanently indebted without ever repaying what they owe.

For the Paumari themselves, the term *pamoari* can be used to formulate an expression indicating the potential human quality – the 'pamoari-ness' – of any being or object. The expression is composed of a noun followed by a construction involving the self-denomination *pamoari*, which is preceded by the possessive prefix *ka–* and followed by the suffix *–hi*, indicating the human form or quality of the preceding substantive. All animals, plants and inanimate objects can be perceived in human form and as a collective. The river dolphin, for example, is potentially human and social: it can appear in a human form that lives in the rivers and lakes of the Purus, dwelling in its own village with its own people, performing festivals, speaking its own language, marrying and having children.

When someone refers to the river dolphin, they use the term '*basori*. However, when talking about the dolphin's own kind, its social life and habits – its '*pamoari*-ness', as it were – people use the expression '*basori kapamoarihi*, referring to dolphin social life and dolphins as a collective (Bonilla 2005: 50, 2007: 301–5). In this context the Paumari translate the expression as 'dolphin people' or 'dolphin nation'. Here we can identify the typical expansion of Amerindian perspectivism, through kinship and alliance, to the cosmos as a whole – everything in the world is potentially human in the sense that any entity can be manifested in a collective, humanized, anthropomorphized form, and above all can express a world in which each species is a point of view (Viveiros de Castro 2002: 351, 384–85).

The idea of *pamoarihi* – the human form of animals, plants and objects – has sometimes been translated by myself as, and associated by other authors with, the idea of owner. In my doctoral thesis I translated the concept at various points using the term 'master', noting that this was one of its potential applications (Bonilla 2007: 53). This semantic approximation attempted to explain and translate the concept of 'human form'. When the Paumari refer to the human form of a being or thing, they do not evoke or refer to the figure of an 'owner' in the sense, for example, of the Yudjá *iwa* described by Lima (2005: 94–96), let alone the idea of the owner-controller appearing in other ethnographic contexts (Fausto 2008: 329–31). Nor do they conceive of this human form as a type of magnified person (ibid.; Cesarino this volume) or suggest that the human form possesses or controls the species in question, or that the borders of each species delimit some form of domain. Instead, when people use the term *pamoarihi*, they are referring primarily to an exemplar of that species, a generic example of its human form, and to the expression of its point of view, its subject position (Viveiros de Castro 2002: 353). As well as comprising its human form – meaning its people form, its collectivity – the *pamoarihi* of the prey animal is also and above all the locus of its point of view. It amounts to its human subjectivity, actualized through the gaze of shamans – who in turn pass this viewpoint on to their audience. The human form of the manatee is the subject position of the manatee's human perspective of the world; what the *pamoarihi* expresses is the human point of view of the manatee species. Hence Fausto's (2008: 339) affirmation that the postmythic world is a 'world of multiple domains' where 'everything has or can have an owner' can be redefined in Paumari terms: 'everything is potentially *pamoari*' and therefore everything in the postmythic world has or can have a point of view.

It should be noted that while the term *pamoari* designates a being's humanity, it is also the term used to designate the client in a relation of subjection or commercial exchange with a *kariva* (boss). So would the human form (*pamoarihi*) of a being also be its client form? Could we say that people are clients of a boss? I think so, and would add that the way this relation can be actualized varies. How should we conceive of a perspectivist world in which the point of view is expressed by the weaker pole of the relation, by the world of the prey and the client?

Bosses and Employees

Let us explore more closely the different terms at play in Paumari commercial relations. As we have seen, the term *pamoari* assumes, on the one hand, the general meaning of the Paumari collective and, on the Other, the positional meaning of client in the context of commercial relations between bosses and clients. But there is another term that plays a constitutive role in commercial relations: the position of employee (*honai abono*). Although *pamoari*, signifying client, also designates Paumari as a whole, the Paumari seem to emphasize the position of employee much more, both in everyday life and in rituals.

The term *honai abono* designates a boss's employee, someone in the service of someone else, under orders (where *honai* designates a command or order, and *abonoi*, the person's soul-body[10]). The same expression is used to designate various professions of white people – a teacher is *ojomo'ihi abono* (*ojomo'ihi*: lesson, teaching), cleaner is *jahahi abono* (*jahahi*: cleaning) – as well as physical activities: planter is *rakhajahi abono*, fisherman is *araba abono* and so on.

The client (*pamoari*) is someone who, indebted to a boss, has to produce or extract something to pay back the debt. What links the client to the boss is debt and debt alone. For the Paumari, this seems to be humanity's generic position. But the employee (*honai abono*) is in a sense located one step ahead in terms of commitment to the boss, and vice versa. An employee is also linked by debt, but debt that will be repaid by services provided to the boss (which may eventually develop into a more long-term relationship). Employees place themselves at the boss's disposition in order to repay their debts, usually living with or near him, which in return obliges the boss to provide certain forms of care and support.

It should be stressed that the difference between the positions of client and employee is not always evident or marked. White people, for example, do not seem to distinguish the two terms, using them as synonyms. Among the Paumari, I also observed this oscillation between synonymy and the distinct use of the two terms. But when the terms are used in Paumari, the ambiguity evaporates and what is emphasized is precisely the difference between the two positions. Hence what differentiates *pamoari* from *honai abono* is the degree of mutual implication that each position enables with the bosses. While the term *pamoari* refers to any client, whether or not Paumari, in commercial relations it designates the position of the client as a debtor. This is the default by definition: in the face of a boss, the generic position is that of client. It therefore makes sense to say that *pamoari* (Paumari/client) is the generic position and *honai abono* (employee), as a transformation or a potential shift from the former to a new position, is more interesting relationally speaking. Indeed, the relation between the boss (*kariva*) and the employee (*honai abono*) seems more interesting to the Paumari, since it is described and emphasized both in interethnic contexts and in their cosmology, rites and mythic narratives.

For example, bosses and employees appear in the *ihinika* rituals, which primarily involve the shaman's introduction of the *abonoi* (soul-body) of all foods (plant, animal or manufactured) into the soul-bodies of newborns, children and their mothers (Bonilla 2007: 169–217). Along with these *ihinika*, which take place almost daily, the soul-bodies of the foods invited to the festival arrive in their human form (*kapamoarihi*) and are preceded by the soul-bodies of other species described as their employees (*honai abono*).

The employees of the soul-bodies of the foods announce their arrival by addressing them directly as *bi'i*, father, or indirectly as their *kariva*, boss. In the eyes of the shamans, all these beings are people, who arrive in their human form. Some are employees, others clients and others bosses. Thus the manatee appearing in the ritual in human form (*boma kapamoarihi*) is a boss who plies the bottom of the river in his boat with all his employees on board: the human form of the *'daki'daki* bird (wattled jacana, *Jacana jacana*) is the manatee's employee who plants his swidden, the human form of the *kamokia* bird (horned screamer, *Anhima cornuta*) makes his flour, the human form of the *vaikajaro* (tucuxi dolphin, *Sotalia spp.*) works as his rower, the human form of the *viraka'da* frog (unidentified) as his cook and the *id'oki* bird (great kiskadee, *Pitangus sulphuratus*) as pilot of his boat. The human forms that present themselves as bosses (being preceded by employees) are generally large animals or occupy a prominent place in the Paumari diet. The species described as employees, meanwhile, are generally associated with species considered to be bosses because of their specific habitat and/or dietary habits. Hence the horned screamer bird (whose human form is the employee of the manatee human form) lives in the marches and lakeshores and feeds on floating plants that are described precisely as the 'manatee's swidden'.

In the manatee *ihinika*, for example, the great kiskadee, its employee, appears first, announcing the manatee's arrival:

> Let's go to this festival,
> Before the boss arrives,
> Let's go first[11]

The manatee soon arrives saying (singing):

> Let's go to this festival
> To which we were invited
> Let's go to watch

To see if they arrive
Where they told us to go

The *viraka'da* bird, which the manatee sees as his cook, then announces:

Let's go first to the festival
Because after
I have to make coffee for the boss

And the *kamokia* bird, who tends the manatee's swidden and makes its flour, chants:

Cousin, let's go to the festival
Because the boss is already there
Commemorating with our people.

Its cousin (another cook) replies:

Cousin, let's go,
Because now we have to plant
The swidden of the boss (*kariva*).

During the *ihinika* ritual of the tapir ('*daama*), a similar cortege announces the arrival of the tapir's human form, another boss. This time the cortege is formed by the *fifi* bird (striped cuckoo, *Tapera naevia*), the tick (*kajapa*) and the *matiroro* bird (red pileated finch, *Coryphospingus cucullatus*).[12]

The Paumari describe the tick as a human form – an employee of the tapir-boss human form. The striped cuckoo – also a kind of parasite, since it uses other birds' nests – is the employee announcing the boss's arrival (Bonilla 2007: 200–201). In everyday life parasites are generally described as the *honai abono* of their hosts. This ethnographic detail strikes me as important since it expresses a subtle idea, frequently expressed in ambiguous form by the Paumari themselves, partly due to the oscillation in the use of the terms client or employee to describe it. The interest resides, I think, precisely in this alternation. Indeed, the difficulty I encountered in defining and translating the position of the tick highlights precisely the interesting ambiguity of its position. Is the tick a client who lives on/inside the boss, or an employee who only receives and never has to provide a service in exchange? According to the Paumari logic, it is evidently both and neither at the same time. Or better, the relation can be actualized as one or the other.

To return to our earlier question, how do we understand a world from the viewpoint of prey, victims or employees, that is, a world expressed by the viewpoint of the prey-client or the pet-employee? The position of the parasite and parasitism as a relation appears to provide an interesting line of analysis (Bonilla 2007: 216–17). As we have seen, subjection, as conceived here, amounts to the shift from the more generic position of client (*pamoari*) to that of employee (*honai abono*) – the person under orders, the subject of a boss – in order to obtain goods and forms of care and to establish relations. In parasitism, though, as conceived through the ritual figure of the tick, subjection becomes a specific ideal mode of predation exercised by a client-employee who only obtains and never pays or works, but 'lives with', annulling the temporality and distance presumed by the debt and therefore neutralizing his or her own subjection. In other words it involves the predation and capture of a boss who becomes colonized by the client-employee. Unlike the employment relation between the cook and the manatee, which involves an exchange or circulation of goods and care, the parasitic relation (conceived here as the ideal, intensive background of a world of clients-employees) is unidirectional. The parasite feeds on, sucks from and may even eliminate the boss host, definitively annulling the relation and thus its own condition of existence.[13]

Captures, Adoptions and Employment

In Paumari cosmography the relations between bosses and employees also determine the relations between soul-bodies (*abonoi*). Hence shamans leave in search of the soul-body of a child who has been captured by a food-spirit.[14] This capture of the child's soul-body by the soul-body of a food-spirit causes the child to sicken immediately. The shaman must then ingest or inhale snuff and hallucinogens and then (with the help of auxiliary spirits and female singers) leave in search of the soul-body to negotiate its return. While this is happening, though, the child's soul-body is being adopted and consequently transformed into an employee of the soul-body of the food-spirit that captured it. If the negotiation attempted by the shaman and his assistants fails, the capture may become definitive and the child remain forever with his or her new boss, the food soul-body (an eventuality that translates as the child's death). This employment-subjection of the child is also translated into the language of kinship and more specifically that of adoption: the child becomes an adopted pet son or daughter (*najivava,* or 'adoptive child') of the soul-body of the food-spirit and its *honai abono,* employee. Consequently the child starts to address its captor as father, becoming accustomed to the 'ways' (*hojai*) of its new kin, learning their language and adopting their food habits, but also providing them with services. The more the soul-body becomes accustomed to its new kin, the more difficulties the shaman will encounter in retrieving it (Bonilla 2007: 191, 216, 358).

It is crucial to emphasize that the relational equivalence between adoption and employment is a key aspect of Paumari kinship relations (Bonilla 2007: 339–56). In fact, internal adoption (of Paumari children by their real grandparents or by classificatory parents) is common, and a form of fostering, or temporary adoption, also exists. This temporary adoption can equally be compared to the familiarization of animal young, a process that, as we shall see below, is understood as temporary by definition. The fact that adoption is conceived as a form of employment can also be linked to the question of affinity, that is, of affinal adoption, and the position of the father-boss as a potential affine-father (Bonilla 2007: 367–70).

After death, the person's *abonoi* detaches from its bodily envelope (*toba bo'da*) and follows the path to the Lake of Renovation[15] (*Aja'di ka'dako*). This is where the unevangelized Paumari dead live, resuscitated after a magical bath and the removal of the food residues accumulated in their soul-bodies over the course of life. After receiving a new envelope (*toba ja'dini*), the dead are asked to choose between two types of seat: the mat (*jorai*) or the rocking chair.

The deceased who choose the mat remain in the lake, where they will live for the rest of eternity, able to eat and dance tirelessly. But those who choose the rocking chair (a regional symbol of the Amazonian boss) are immediately employed by the human form of the rainstorm (*Bahi kapamoarihi*), a meteorological spirit that, like the sun, is described as a very powerful, rich and generous boss. This power is translated in the spirit's strong, corpulent appearance and irascible temperament, but also in the quantity of boats it possesses, all piloted by Paumari soul-body employees who fetch water in the reservoirs of Manaus to pour onto the land.[16] These same soul-bodies – employees of the human-rain form – also enable communication between Paumari shamans and the dead via thunder. Asked about their interest in working for yet another boss after death, the Paumari reply unanimously that the human-rain form, besides being powerful, is also kind and generous, possessing and providing endless quantities of diverse commodities.

Here, then, something is offered that the generic position of client does not guarantee: regular access to goods, their continuous flow, the boss's commitment to employees, and their relative geographic and corporal proximity to the boss. 'To be serving someone' is to be under their protection, living with them (or nearby) and being directly or indirectly fed by them. This immediately raises the questions of commensality in Amazonia, the process of kinship and the familiarization of animals and people, and the centrality of eating/not-eating (what and with whom) as a relational mode in the region (see among others Costa 2010 and this volume; Fausto 2002, 2007; Gow 1989, 1991, 1997; McCallum 2001;

Vilaça 1992, 2002; Viveiros de Castro 2012). To explore this idea in more depth, though, we need to analyse both the terms in which the Paumari conceive the prey position and the contexts in which this positioning most clearly appears.

The Prey Condition

Here it should be recalled that the Paumari describe themselves in many contexts as victims and prey, and often say that in the past they were like *igitha* – the prey of wild Indians (*Joima*) – or the pet animals of particular bosses (Bonilla 2005, 2007: 142–43). When telling of attacks by voracious Indians coming from afar to 'enjoy their flesh', the Paumari describe their reactions using details that evoke prey fleeing from predators (e.g. hiding in a hollow log, the canopy of a tree or an armadillo hole, or fleeing into the forest). Only their shamans (*arabani*) and the ancient *Jobiri* managed to escape the voracity of these Others.[17] The shamans were saved by their songs and transformational powers, whereas the *Jobiri* survived thanks to their physical training, agility, skill and capacity to camouflage themselves: they would dodge the arrows of the *Joima*, recover them and then shoot them back at their enemies (Bonilla 2007: 57–65).

In these accounts, the Paumari always appear as targets of attacks who are unable to retaliate directly. They are always defended or avenged by Others – distant similars with transformational powers, particularly *Jobiri* or captive children (whether Paumari adopted by enemies or enemy children who have been Paumarized). Here adoptive children serve as intermediaries between the Paumari and their aggressors or defenders. This amounts, therefore, to a pacifism mediated by third parties[18] rather than a categorical rejection of aggression and revenge. Getting to know one's enemies and have some chance of transforming or dislocating their predatory perspective involves seducing them and allowing oneself to be (partially) captured. Given that it is usually the young of animal prey who are familiarized, it makes sense that the ideal subject to be captured is the child.

Shamans are also great defenders of the Paumari. But they are not described as soldiers like the *Jobiri*; instead, their transformational power is emphasized. More specifically, they protect the Paumari from external attacks by tricking aggressors or turning them into prey (*igitha*) (Bonilla 2007: 86–87). People say that the Paumari shamans freed a village from a siege by *Joima* who had surrounded one of their upriver encampments during a puberty ritual. To trick the enemies, the shamans imitated the cries of children, making it seem as though they were coming from one side of the village; meanwhile everyone escaped from the other side.

When white people came from Manaus to capture the Paumari and force them to do construction work in the city, a shaman called *Badori Titxatxa* (Grandfather Titxatxa) transformed them into otters as soon as their boats entered the lakes, or sent hordes of ants to invade the holds of their ships and devour all the stored food.[19] In this case the Paumari weapon against voracious enemies is the transformational power of shamans, and above all their trickery and cunning.

Direct violence and revenge are replaced, at least in the Paumari accounts, by agility, cunning and their capacity, as prey, to seduce predators through the mastery of bodily techniques (e.g. the agility of the *Jobiri* and their capacity to transform into children) and verbal techniques (e.g. shamanic songs or imitation of children's crying and foreign languages). Attracting an *igitha* means observing it, knowing how to imitate its song (the Paumari consider all animals to have their own song and therefore to possess the capacity to communicate) and recognizing its habits, such as by knowing where it drinks water or where it roams, what type of fruits it eats and how to recognize its tracks (Gow 1989: 570). This also recalls the various techniques for attracting prey and familiarizing animals, and their relation to amorous seduction and kinship (Taylor 2000: 314–16).

There is not enough space here to list or detail the techniques the Paumari use to seduce, attract and adopt prey.[20] However we can note that the inversion of roles that they actualize by positioning themselves as prey with the aim of being partially familiarized by Others, establishes ties of commensality that force the Other to approach and assume the position of boss-father, 'affinizing' this figure and transforming it into a potential affine (Bonilla 2007: 367; on the ambiguity between affinity and consanguinity, see Brightman and Grotti this volume). The position of boss-father, seen from the viewpoint of predation, is a transformation of the enemy into a potential father-in-law, reflecting the 'function of dynamic mediation exerted by potential affines' (Viveiros de Castro 2002: 162). Forcing the boss-predator to become an adoptive father/potential father-in-law also involves forcing this Other to recognize the possibility of the viewpoint, unstable by definition, of a shared world. Hence the ambiguity and instability Fausto evokes over the course of his text – regarding both the definition of the of 'master' or 'owner' position, and adoption and ownership relations (Fausto 2008: 335, 341, 352) – seems to me to express precisely the background of enmity and affinity intrinsic to the perspectivist dynamic, a background that conditions and actualizes the relations (Viveiros de Castro 2002: 157, 166).

Finally, returning to the Paumari, this apparent inversion also has to be considered in relation to their descriptions of their supposed pacifism. In these accounts, the Paumari compare themselves to birds (or prey) that prefer singing and coexisting peacefully to making war. This comparison of themselves to prey (*igitha*) is especially frequent in historical contexts. When describing the eventual departure of the first Summer Institute of Linguistics (SIL) missionary to work in the area, for example, the Paumari recall their despair, comparing themselves to orphans who had been left 'like motherless ducklings'. At one level these comparisons are clearly metaphoric images that serve to emphasize the Paumari's present-day concern with establishing and maintaining peaceful relations with white people and other ethnic groups. At another level, though, they are absolutely literal affirmations that describe not only the relations of proximity and dependency that unite them with Others (the ideal of endogamy and commensality), but also their dispersed occupation of the region's beaches (they compare themselves to gulls who flock to the beaches in summer).

The analogies drawn between Paumari and *igitha* (prey, birds, pets) are also observed in several accounts I collected of the arrival of the first SIL missionary at Marahã Lake. Like the *Joima,* who had come from afar to 'relish the flesh of the Paumari', the *americanos* – foreigners coming from far away – were feared, as they were notorious for capturing Paumari children to make corned beef, which is still sold in the region today.[21] The accounts evoke the first contact with the foreign woman, followed by the flight of the Paumari and then their gradual familiarization with the missionary (notably through gift giving; the exchange of goods for Paumari produce, especially craftwork; and the treatment of their skin diseases), until her eventual final departure and the consequent feeling of abandonment it provoked in the Paumari.[22]

From this we can ascertain that when the danger is one of being devoured, the favoured viewpoint is that of the *igitha*-pet, but when the danger stems from exploitation and economic domination, the favoured perspective is that of the employee. It is this voluntary subjection on the part of the Paumari that enables the countercapture of foreigners seen as potentially dangerous and voracious. In other words, by placing themselves in the position of prey-client, the Paumari force the interlocutor to adopt the corresponding position of familiarizer, thus diffusing the imminent threat of being preyed on and devoured, at least temporarily, while also creating the possibility of subjection and ideally parasitism as forms of unlimited and univocal access to desired goods.

Hence, bosses who did not provide goods generously or refused to supply anything before being paid were killed by shamans through sorcery attacks (Bonilla 2007: 101–2).[23] Taking this idea to its ultimate consequences, the predatory weapon of the Paumari is undoubtedly their capacity to be subjected, forcing the interlocutor placed in the position of domination to take pity on them and adopt them as though they were indeed 'motherless ducklings'. Potential predators are dislocated from a position of exclusive domination to a more paternalist position, more dependent on their subjects and committed to caring for them. This capacity to subvert predatory danger contains exceptional potency and force, not only to neutralize danger but also to obtain what one desires and define the relation in one's own terms, diverting the authority and power exerted by predatory bosses in one's own favour and preventing hierarchy from becoming consolidated by continually multiplying the relations of subjection and debts with diverse bosses (Bonilla 2013). Here pacifism, self-victimization and subjection appear to echo what Serres describes in his essay on parasitic practices (1980: 109–12, 390–91).

Living Well and Parasitism

One of the characteristics of the dynamic animating the Amazonian perspectivist world is precisely the ability to change the Other's viewpoint – that is, to dislocate oneself in order to provoke the dislocation of the Other, changing the latter's view by moving to affect the Other's perspective and thereby transform the relation, ideally to one's own benefit (Taylor and Viveiros de Castro 2006: 169). Thus the idea of subjection and parasitism as forms of micropredation and subversion of domination and hierarchy seems crucial to conceptualizing those collectives that, rather than present themselves as predators, warriors or the only truly human and brave peoples, tend to position themselves as victims or to submit voluntarily to the Other. Hence, the Paumari might say: 'to warriors, predation; to clients, parasitism'.

I wish to make clear that the concept of parasitism as a form of predation, constructed through the ritual figure of the parasite (the tick, the tapir's employee), is my own abstraction and remains to be explored and defined more carefully and in more depth. As I have shown elsewhere, certain aspects of the potency that the Paumari exert through their own subjection recall Deleuze's analysis of sadism and masochism in terms of humour.[24] Indeed, Deleuze shows how the masochist's use of humour to subvert and deny any submission to the law and punishment enables the attainment of his or her objective: pleasure (Deleuze 1991: 77–79, 105–15). As I suggested above, subjection-parasitism can be conceived of as a form of ontological predation that has the Paumari relational figures of prey-client and pet-employee as its potential forms of actualization. The subjection to the Other as a mode of existence, or an actualization of a lived world – far from reflecting a de facto submission to an Other or the actualization of a hierarchy established by fixed and given positions (bosses and clients, owners and domains, masters and slaves), transcendental values and positions – is a subversion of the very possibility of domination. Hence, following Deleuze, the subject's literal submission to the law 'nevertheless conceals elements of irony and humor which made political philosophy possible, for it allows the free play of thought at the upper and lower limits of the scale of law' (Deleuze 1991: 81). Thus humour 'is the attempt to sanction the law by recourse to an infinitely more righteous Best' (82). Systematically revealing oneself to be the victim of atrocities perpetrated by others and presenting oneself as the most defenceless being possible allows authority to be underlined in a more ferocious humoristic form (Bonilla 2007: 391–99). Talking specifically about the position of the parasite, Serres (1982: 26) also identifies its political potential: 'One day we will have to understand why the strongest is the parasite – that is to say, the weakest – why the one whose only function is to eat is the one who commands. And speaks. We have just found the place of politics'.

Pursuing the same logic, if being human means being a prey-client and living means being captured, this is because being subjected and familiarized-employed enables the ideal of micropredation and parasitism. As Serres (1982: 79) also emphasizes: 'The parasite is the essence of relation. It is necessary for the relation and ineluctable by the overturning of the force that tries to exclude it. But this relation is nonrelation. The parasite is being and nonbeing at the same time'. To be or not to be, in Serres' sense, is to be or not to be in a relation – or, in Paumari terms, 'to be captured' or 'not to be captured' (equivalent to not existing: Bonilla 2007: 215–17, 259–60). Hence, in Taylor's (1996: 210) words, '[b]eing a live human person is not a state defined as such ... yet it is nonetheless precisely circumscribed by the articulation of a set of non-explicit premises. Being a person is thus an array or cline of relational configurations, a set of links in a chain of metamorphoses simultaneously open and bounded'.

What the Paumari aim for, more than the control of Others and predation itself – as I initially suggested (2005) – is the parasitic ideal, the desire for a world where bosses become continually captured and apprehended captors, making them eternal providers not only of manufactured goods but of everything deemed indispensable to living in the world: kin, names, food, exchanges and enemies. In a world of prey, the ideal form of predation is parasitism. However, it is essential to remain aware of the instability of what defines these positions, so as not to lose track of the dynamism of transformations that never close in on themselves or fix positions, but rather 'multiply the mediations' (Serres 1982: 220). For the Paumari, then, living well is different from what has so often been understood or described as living in peaceful coexistence among kin, following ideals of 'tranquillity', 'conviviality' and 'emotional comfort' that exclude predation and alterity, and banishing difference and expelling it beyond the boundaries of the group (Belaunde 2000: 209; Overing and Passes 2000: 1, 7–19).

In sum, this ideal limit of parasitism is where the Paumari person lives well, but there is a price to pay: it involves living well among Others and thus an exposure to risk and danger, 'living dangerously as the existential condition of the social form' (Viveiros de Castro 2012: 29, 32). Submitting oneself – being captured – forces the predator to become a host and thus constitutes oneself too as a discrete, invisible, relentless predator.

Oiara Bonilla is Associate Professor of Anthropology at the Universidade Federal Fluminense. Her publications include 'O Bom Patrão e o Inimigo Voraz: Predação e Comércio na Cosmologia Paumari' (2005), 'Topographies cosmiques et démarcations de terres indiennes au Brésil: le cas des Paumari' (2006) and 'The Skin of History: Paumari Perspectives on Conversion and Transformation' (2009).

Notes

Translated by David Rodgers.
1. On the debt peonage system in Amazonia, see Geffray (1995, 1997), Léna, Geffray and Araújo (1996) and Rezende Figueira (2004), as well as the collection edited by Carneiro da Cunha and Almeida (2002).
2. As is common in this region, the native conception of time and history refers to a past divided into 'times' or 'eras': see Costa (2007: 48), Gow (1991: 59–90), Grotti (2013: 17–19), Santos-Granero (2007: 48), Taylor (2007: 155).
3. The Paumari use the same word, *igitha*, to denote both pet and prey, and the distinction is usually clear from context, though speakers frequently play upon the ambiguity that the single term affords.
4. Rival (1999) describes the Huaorani identification of themselves as prey in a pioneering article that I found extremely valuable when thinking through the Paumari data.
5. For a similar situation among the Urarina, see the recent analysis by Walker (2012).
6. The term *–Jara* is probably taken from Língua Geral, though it should be emphasized that it does not have the same acceptation as the Tupi-Guarani term *–jara*, meaning 'owner' or 'master' (Fausto 2008: 331). *Jara*, in Paumari, designates the category 'white people' and more specifically *ribeirinho*, 'river dweller', contrasting with the categories *americano* (foreigner) or *Joima* (wild Indian). It is also important to stress the difference between *Jara* and *kariva*, the former designating the *ribeirinhos* and the second the *patrões* (bosses). They are not synonymous. In no context in Paumari is *Jara* used to designate the category 'owner' or even '*patrão*.'
7. The main bosses for whom the Paumari worked later settled in Lábrea, where they became store owners. Many of the former white clients of these bosses remained on the river shore, becoming the so-called little bosses, *patrõezinhos*, while others became river traders.
8. This nostalgia or positive recollection of the period of subjection to the bosses is also found in other ethnographic contexts. e.g. the Piro say that subjection to the

bosses allowed them access to the 'civilized world', i.e. to knowledge, history and kinship (Gow 1991, 1993: 332–34).

9. See Santos-Granero (2007: 60) for a description of the ritual appropriation of San Juan fireworks by the Yanesha. In the Paumari case, the São João event is and continues to be a *Jara* (white people's) festival during which people obtain godparents (*compadres* and *comadres*), though it is sometimes held conjointly with certain *ihinika* rituals.

10. Here I use the term soul-body to translate *abonoi*, a term that contextually designates both the trunk (of the tree and the body) and the body's parts as a whole, as well as the soul, and which could be taken to designate something like an animated body or a personified soul (Bonilla 2007: 145–49). See Lima (2002) for a discussion of the perspectival and relational complexity of Amerindian terms for soul and body.

11. See Bonilla (2007: 200–205) for a gloss of the songs.

12. Another food spirit that comes to its *ihinika* in human-boss form is the pirarucu fish (*babadi*), one of whose employees is the bird *bikiakia* (unidentified). Meanwhile the tambaqui fish (*i'oa*) in its human form is a river dweller (*Jara*) who likes sugar cane, rum and forró music. The human forms of the fish live in villages and towns located at the bottom of the Purus River and the region's lakes.

13. The theme of parasitism and the figure of the parasite have been discussed in other Amazonian contexts, including rituals, as in the case of the Miraña described and analysed by Karadimas (2003). Adopting a different but no less thought-provoking approach, works on Chinese Mongolia and Tibet have also explored the theme of parasitism (see Da Col 2012).

14. This usually (though not only) occurs when the parents fail to respect the prescriptions (*kaaji*) that apply after the *ihinika* has been held (e.g. parents should not hit their child, allow her to be hurt or scared, or let him fall, and generally are to take exceptional care of the child).

15. For the Evangelicals, the dead follow an entirely different path before finally arriving at the House of God (*Deus gorana*) (Bonilla 2009).

16. This description of the human form – the rain boss, the meteorological spirit of the rainstorm – is a transformation of the mythological figure of *Bahi*, father of *Jakoniro*, father-in-law of *Jamapitoari* and insatiable eater of manatee flesh (see Bonilla 2007: 34–35 and Menendez 2011). Here the mythic position of the boss/father-in-law clearly expresses the language of potential affinity.

17. The *Jobiri* are probably the Jubery or Juberis, described by travellers as a Puru-Puru subgroup. The *Jobiri* are described as warriors, and belonging to this category was hereditary (transmitted both patrilineally and matrilineally). I discuss this topic in another work.

18. This position recalls that of the included third (or "thirdness") as a position of 'complex effectuation of potential affinity', described by Viveiros de Castro (2002: 153–154).

19. The Paumari always categorize insects that bite or sting as predators and sometimes call them *feras* (wild beasts) in Portuguese. This reinforces the idea of micropredation as a potentially full predatory act.

20. The difference between definitive capture and temporary or partial capture should be established here. The Paumari model of adoption of children (i.e. internal adoption, generally of grandchildren by G+2) is that of fostering, in which the child spends a long time living with and helping his or her adoptive parents.

However, such children may go back to living with their real parents and never cease to recognize them (and often refer to them) as such. Likewise, I observed the Paumari treating their pets as adoptive children, raising them to adulthood before releasing them, explaining that they had to return to their original kin but (at least in the case of birds) would come back to visit them. This once again evokes the idea of the instability of the position of familiarizable prey and the person in general (Taylor 1993, 2000; Vilaça 2005). In my view, capture and predation in this context are not dynamics that can be subsumed by the concept of 'property', even if it is defined as temporary or 'relational' (Santos-Granero this volume).

21. The theme of the cannibal stranger (*pelacara, sacacara, pishtaco*) recurs throughout the region and the entire Andean foothills (see Gow 2001: 41, 256–60).
22. The conception of the self as 'orphaned' or 'abandoned' is not exclusive to the Paumari, just as it is not necessarily related to their ontological particularity: it may also be read through the themes of capture and sickening (Taylor 1997: 151; Viveiros de Castro 1986: 184–96).
23. There is yet another twist here with regard to shamanism and the relation between shamans and auxiliary spirits, since it is precisely in this relation that predation is expressed and realized in affirmative form (Bonilla 2007: 351–56).
24. For an analysis of subversive humour and laughter in Paumari rituals, see Bonilla (2007).

References

Belaunde, L. 2000. 'The Convivial Self and the Fear of Anger Amongst the Airo-Pai of Amazonian Peru', in J. Overing and A. Passes (eds), *The Anthropology of Love and Anger: The Aesthetics of Conviviality in Native Amazonia*. London: Routledge, pp. 209–20.

Bonilla, O. 2005. 'O Bom Patrão e o Inimigo Voraz: Predação e Comércio na Cosmologia Paumari'. *Mana: Estudos de Antropologia Social* 11(1): 41–66.

———. 2007. 'Des Proies Si Désirables: Soumission et Prédation pour les Paumari d'Amazonie Brésilienne', Ph.D. dissertation. Paris: École des Hautes Études en Sciences Sociales.

———. 2009. 'The Skin of History: Paumari Perspectives on Conversion and Transformation', in A. Vilaça and R. Wright (eds), *Native Christians: Modes and Effects of Christianity among Indigenous Peoples of the Americas*. London: Ashgate, pp. 127–45.

———. 2010. 'Os Paumari do Rio Tapauá e Cuniuá', in G. Mendes (ed.), *Album Purus*. Manaus: EDUA, pp. 206–27.

———. 2013. 'Be My Boss! Comments on South African and Amerindian Forms of Subjection', *Journal of the Royal Anthropological Institute* 19(2): 246–47.

Carneiro da Cunha, M. and M. Almeida (eds). 2002. *Enciclopédia da Floresta: O Alto Juruá: Práticas e Conhecimentos das Populações*. São Paulo: Companhia das Letras.

Chandless, W. 1949 [1869]. 'Notas Sobre o Rio Purus'. *Arquivos da Associação Comercial do Amazonas* 9(3): 21–29; 10(3): 29–40.

Costa, L. 2007. 'As Faces do Jaguar: Parentesco, História e Mitologia entre os Kanamari da Amazônia Ocidental', Ph.D. dissertation. Rio de Janeiro: PPGAS-Museu Nacional, Universidade Federal do Rio de Janeiro.

———. 2009. 'Worthless Movement: Agricultural Regression and Mobility', *Tipití: Journal of the Society for the Anthropology of Lowland South America* 7(2): 151–80.

———. 2010. 'The Kanamari Body-Owner: Predation and Feeding in Western Amazonia', *Journal de la Société des Américanistes de Paris* 96(1). Retrieved 27 October 2012 from http://jsa.revues.org/index11332.html.

Da Col, G. 2012. 'The Poisoner and the Parasite: Cosmoeconomics, Fear, and Hospitality among Dechen Tibetans', *Journal of the Royal Anthropological Institute* 18(S1): 175–95.

Deleuze, G. 1991 [1967]. 'Coldness and Cruelty', in G. Deleuze, *Masochism*. New York: Zone Books, pp. 9–142.

Deturche, J. 2009. Les Katukina do Rio Biá (AM). Histoire, organisation sociale et cosmologie. Ph. D. dissertation. Paris: Université Paris X-Nanterre.

Dixon, R. and A. Aikhenvald (eds). 1999. *The Amazonian Languages*. Cambridge: Cambridge University Press.

Fausto, C. 2002. 'Banquete de Gente: Comensalidade e Canibalismo na Amazônia', *Mana: Estudos de Antropologia Social* 8(2): 7–44.

———. 2007. 'Feasting on People: Eating Animals and Humans in Amazonia', *Current Anthropology* 48(4): 497–530.

———. 2008. 'Donos Demais: Maestria e Domínio na Amazônia', *Mana: Estudos de Antropologia Social* 14(2): 329–65.

Geffray, C. 1995. *Chroniques de la Servitude en Amazonie Brésilienne: Essai sur l'Exploitation Paternaliste*. Paris: Editions Karthala.

———. 1997. *Le Nom du Maître: Contribution à l'Anthropologie Analytique*. Paris: Hypothèses, Ed. Arcanes.

Gow, P. 1989. 'The Perverse Child: Desire in a Native Amazonian Subsistence Economy', *Man* 24(4): 567–82.

———. 1991. *Of Mixed Blood: Kinship and History in Western Amazonia*. Oxford: Clarendon Press.

———. 1993. 'Gringos and Wild Indians: Images of History in Western Amazonian Cultures', *L'Homme* 33(126–28): 327–47.

———. 1997. 'O Parentesco como Consciência Humana', *Mana: Estudos de Antropologia Social* 3(2): 39–65.

———. 2001. *An Amazonian Myth and Its History*. Oxford: Oxford University Press.

Grotti, V.E. 2013. 'The Wealth of the Body: Trade Relations, Objects, and Personhood in Northeastern Amazonia', *Journal of Latin American and Caribbean Anthropology* 18(1): 14–30.

Hugh-Jones, S. 1992. 'Yesterday's Luxuries, Tomorrow's Necessities: Business and Barter in Northwest Amazonia', in C. Humphrey and S. Hugh-Jones (eds), *Barter, Exchange and Value: An Anthropological Approach*. Cambridge: Cambridge University Press, pp. 42–74.

Karadimas, D. 2003. 'Dans le Corps de Mon Ennemi: L'Hôte Parasité chez les Insectes Comme un Modèle de Reproduction chez les Miraña d'Amazonie Colombienne', in E. Motte-Florac and J.M.C. Thomas (eds), *Les Insectes dans la Tradition Orale*. Paris: Peeters, pp. 287–506.

Kroemer, G. 1985. *Cuxiuara: O Purus dos Indígenas, Ensaio Etno-Histórico e Etnográfico sobre os Indios do Médio Purus*. São Paulo: Loyola.

Labre, A.R.P. 1872. *Rio Purús. Noticia*. Maranhão: Typ. do Paiz.

Léna, P., C. Geffray and R. Araújo (eds). 1996. 'L'Oppression Paternaliste au Brésil', *Lusotopie* 1996. Retrieved 16 June 2013 from http://www.lusotopie.sciencespo bordeaux.fr/edito.html

Lima, T.S. 2002. 'O Que é Um Corpo?' *Religião and Sociedade* 2(1): 9–19.

———. 2005. *Um Peixe Olhou para Mim: O Povo Yudjá e a Perspectiva*. São Paulo: Editora UNESP, ISA; Rio de Janeiro: NuTi.

McCallum, C. 2001. *Gender and Sociality in Amazonia: How Real People are Made*. Oxford: Berg.

Menendes, L. 2011. 'A Alma Vestida: Estudo sobre a Cestaria Paumari', Ph.D. dissertation. São Paulo: Pontifícia Universidade Católica de São Paulo.

Overing, J. and A. Passes. 2000. 'Introduction: Conviviality and the Opening up of Amazonian Anthropology', in J. Overing and A. Passes (eds), *The Anthropology of Love and Anger: The Aesthetics of Conviviality in Native Amazónia*. London: Routledge, pp. 1–30.

Rezende Figueira, R. 2004. *Pisando Fora da Própria Sombra: A Escravidão por Dívida no Brasil Contemporâneo*. Rio de Janeiro: Civilização Brasileira.

Rival, L. 1999. 'Prey at the Center', in S. Day, E. Papataxiarchis and M. Stewart (eds), *Lilies of the Field: Marginal People Who Live for the Moment*. Bolder, CO; Westview Press, pp. 61–79.

Santos-Granero, F. 2007. 'Time is Disease, Suffering, and Oblivion: Yanesha Historicity and the Struggle against Temporality', in C. Fausto and M. Heckenberger (eds), *Time and Memory in Indigenous Amazonia: Anthropological Perspectives*. Gainesville: University Press of Florida, pp. 47–73.

Serres, M. 1982 [1980]. *The Parasite*. Baltimore/London: The John Hopkins University Press.

Silva Coutinho, J.M. da. 1863. 'Relatório da Exploração do Rio Purus', in *Relatório Apresentado na Abertura da 2ª Sessão da Assembléia Legislativa da Província do Amazonas*. Manaus, pp. 40–85.

Taylor, A.-C. 1996. 'The Soul's Body and Its States: An Amazonian Perspective on the Nature of Being Human', *Journal of the Royal Anthropological Institute* 2(2): 201–15.

———. 2000. 'Le Sexe de la Proie: Représentation Jivaro du Lien de Parenté', *L'Homme* 154–55: 309–34.

———. 2007. 'Sick of History: Contrasting Regimes of Historicity in the Upper Amazon', in C. Fausto and M. Heckenberger (eds), *Time and Memory in Indigenous Amazonia: Anthropological Perspectives*. Gainesville: University Press of Florida: 133–68.

Taylor, A.-C. and E. Viveiros de Castro. 2006. 'Un Corps Fait de Regards (Amazonie)', in S. Breton (ed.), *Qu'Est-ce Qu'un Corps?* Paris: Musée du Quai Branly/Flammarion, pp. 148–99.

Vilaça, A. 1992. *Comendo Como Gente: Formas do Canibalismo Wari'*. Rio de Janeiro, Editora da UFRJ.

———. 2002. 'Making Kin Out of Others in Amazonia', *Journal of the Royal Anthropological Institute* 8(2): 347–65.

———. 2005. 'Chronically Unstable Bodies: Reflections on Amazonian Corporalities', *Journal of the Royal Anthropological Institute* 11(3): 445–64.

Viveiros de Castro, E. 1986. *Araweté: Os Deuses Canibais*. Rio de Janeiro: Jorge Zahar Editora.

———. 2002. *A Inconstância da Alma Selvagem e Outros Ensaios de Antropologia*. São Paulo: Cosac and Naify.
———. 2012. 'Immanence and Fear: Stranger-Events and Subjects in Amazonia', *HAU: Journal of Ethnographic Theory* 2(1): 27–43.
Walker, H. 2012. 'Demonic Trade: Debt, Materiality, and Agency in Amazonia', *Journal of the Royal Anthropological Institute* 18(1): 140–59.

CHAPTER 5

How Much for a Song?
The Culture of Calculation and the Calculation of Culture

Carlos Fausto

> When I argued that having given the fish away meant that he would have less fish than before, Robtokti replied: 'When the Suya give something to somebody, it doesn't mean we are going to have less of it. When I give my brother fish, he always pays me back. So if I have 10 and give him 3, he will give me more fish when he goes fishing. So that is 10 + 3, and not 10 – 3'.
> —Kawall Ferreira, 'When 1+1 ≠ 2'

The first missionary to visit New Zealand, Samuel Marsden, suggested that the Maori had originated from wandering Jews, providing as evidence the fact that they possessed 'a great natural turn for traffic; they will buy and sell anything they have got' (Hanson 1989: 892). Had Marsden disembarked in the Upper Xingu, in the same year of the Lord 1819, he probably would have suggested that the Xinguanos too were descendants of one of the lost tribes of Israel, due to to their equal propensity 'for traffic'. Gertrude Dole (1956–58: 125), the first researcher to work with the Kuikuro, one of the peoples forming the multiethnic Upper Xingu system, wrote in the 1950s that they 'are constantly preoccupied with the exchange of goods and services and with equalizing accounts'. Further on she added: 'Virtually every gift or service requires a return. Sharing and pure gift-giving are almost non-existent among the Kuikuro' (126).

The image of an indigenous Amazonian society obsessed with the exchange of goods and services, and with balancing accounts is fairly uncommon. At the start of my research among the Kuikuro, I suffered a culture shock, writing on 23 July 2000 that 'paying' is always necessary – in general immediately, since whenever this doesn't occur, they observe something like 'you can think of the payment'. Today, for example, when Bruna [Franchetto] took a present to grandpa [Agatsipá], he apologized straight away for the lack of payment; Bruna insisted that the present was a free gift and that this was the way of the *kagaiha* [whites]. (2000, field notes)

The notion of the free gift as a tradition of white people is not without its irony.

I had previously worked among the Tupi-speaking Parakanã, who had very few objects, none of them with transcontextual value. The numeric system was limited to four quantities: single, even, uneven and many. There were no standards of value, nor any ritualized forms for distributing goods. There was a verb designating the exchange of identical things (*–ponekwan*), as well as a term meaning 'to compensate' or 'to pay back' (*–wepy*), but the actions described by these verbs did not define a code of conduct enacted in everyday relations. Even I, a researcher-stranger, had no need to constantly calculate the payment for the questions and requests I directed at my 'informants'.

When starting my research among the Kuikuro, I felt plunged into another world, incapable of dealing with a logic in which everything had a retribution. Some of these demands pertain to spheres or relations in which there is a fixed standard of value; others, though, have to be calculated on the spot, always with the risk of giving too much or too little.[1] Almost all services and objects can be inserted into this system of 'payment', the term by which the Kuikuro usually translate the word *ihipügü*. Services provided by shamans, singers, messengers, as well as body painting, ritual wailing, the end of the mourning period, sexual favours – each of these has its 'price.' The only item that almost always remains excluded from this system is fresh or cooked food.[2] And here lies another irony: although in my experience the village was the place where 'everything had a price', the Kuikuro, on the contrary, had this same feeling about the city, where they have to pay to eat and sleep.[3]

A clearer understanding of this world where 'everything has its price' and nothing is 'free' requires a description of the various spheres and subsystems of the value regime. In this chapter I provide a very general account of this system, beginning with ritual activities that involve a standardization of value. Subsequently I turn to a ritualized 'commercial' activity in which equivalences are negotiated on the spot, and then focus on the payment for shamanic services, marriage compensation and knowledge transmission. Finally I conclude with a description of contemporary situations in which standards of value are renegotiated according to a new logic and by new actors (including myself).

The Time Between Giving and Receiving

The Upper Xingu system comprises a set of autonomous political units congregated in one or more villages. What defines their political autonomy is the presence of a head chief and the capacity to sponsor an intertribal ritual or be invited to take part in one held by another political unit. These units tend to be marked by linguistic differences, whether in language or dialect, although these do not necessarily coincide with the political units.[4] Language distinguishes but also identifies. Macroblocks formed by speakers of the same language partially coincide with the monopoly on certain craftwork specialities: hence the Carib peoples are producers of snail-shell necklaces and belts, the Arawak are potters and the Tupian Kamayurá and Aweti are, respectively, specialists in the manufacture of blackwood bows and vegetal salt.[5]

An equivalence exists between the more refined and prestigious products of each of these industries. For example, a large Wauja pot for cooking manioc porridge is equivalent to three Carib snail-shell necklaces (*inhu aketühügü*); a black bow is equal to one large shell belt (*uguka*); a small basket of salt is exchanged for one or two shell belts while a large basket can be exchanged for a necklace. Prestigious items also include the full headdress (*kahokohugu*) with its diadem of toucan and oropendola feathers topped by red macaw and eagle tail feathers, as well as necklaces made from jaguar claws. In the past granite axe blades were also part of this system of luxury goods, but these were rapidly substituted by the metal tools that arrived with the German expeditions of the late nineteenth century. Vegetal salt lost some of its importance upon the introduction of industrial salt, yet it did not vanish completely. Meanwhile the shell necklaces and belts found a complement, rather than a replacement, in glass beads from Czechoslovakia. In fact the snail-shell industry flourished with the arrival of new tools – knives, needles, stones for polishing – that lead to technical enhancement and probably a certain devaluation in relation to the manufacture of pottery. The latter, in turn, was only partially substituted by another luxury good: 100-litre aluminium pans (Figure 5.1).[6]

What determines the value of these objects – whether or not they are 'expensive' (*tihipükoinhü*) – is not their utility or their rarity. Nor is it an abstract labour time needed to produce them. At least, these are not the terms used by the Kuikuro. They usually refer to the fatigue, the suffering and the difficulty involved in their manufacture, a concern that is closer to the juridical notion of *pretium doloris*, 'the price of pain', than to the labour theory of value. So, for instance, they say that the necklaces are expensive because the material is very hard to perforate and very difficult to cut,

Figure 5.1 *Aluminium pans received by the owners of the Takwaga festival. Kuikuro village of Ipatse, Xingu Indigenous Park, Brazil, 1998. Photo: Carlos Fausto*

hurting the artisan's hands a lot. Meanwhile, the Aweti charge a lot for salt because its production involves tiredness and danger: not only does it require lengthy exposure in the sun, but there is also the risk of being bitten by a snake, stung by an electric eel or finding oneself covered in leeches.[7] The expensiveness of these objects is explained in the same terms even today, even though metal tools, guns and clothing have facilitated their manufacture enormously.[8]

Snails shells and clay continue to be the main raw materials for the confection of artefacts serving as intertribal ritual payments. Every festival involving more than one political unit requires an invitation made by three messengers, which, if accepted, will prompt the invited village to choose three chiefs to head the designated group's journey to the host village. At the closure of the festival, soon after the end of the wrestling, each of the chiefs places 'things' (*engiko*) on the ground for the messengers who invited them, respecting each other's hierarchical order (the first chief offers items to the first messenger, and so on).[9] This cannot appear as a simple exchange of goods: each messenger must first take what he has received to his house and then return to the plaza to ask the invited chief: 'You came in search of what?' (*tü kaema egei enhügü?*).

Typically a Kuikuro visitor will bring belts made from disks of snail shell and, if participating in a festival in a Wauja village, ask for pottery in return. This exchange does not involve any evaluation of quality. Well or poorly made, small or large, the exchange is compulsory and without haggling. This is why people say that the messenger from the host village, in the obligatory time-span between receiving and reciprocating, walks back to his house anxiously trying to guess what the chief of the guests will solicit from him.

Industrial goods are beginning to enter this system. Some years ago a Matipu woman, after offering snail-shell belts, asked a Kuikuro messenger to give her an old bicycle, which in the language of ritual requests means a bicycle in good condition. In 2010, a young Kuikuro woman who headed the guests to a Yawalapiti village – known for its mixture of different Xinguano peoples and for possessing many industrial items – asked the messenger for 150 litres of petrol in exchange for the two belts she had given him.

Intrahouse Markets

At the top of the ritual exchange system, there exists a certain standard of value that regulates the relation between political units. In the case of the Kuikuro, this value system is expressed primarily in terms of snail-shell belts or necklaces. Of all their objects, the snail-shell adornments, owing to their durability, transportability and divisibility (counted in the number of bands), are the best equivalent to the idea of currency, as a Kuikuro man explained when I asked him if I could use money to take part in the formalized exchanges known as *luki*: '[O]f course, money is the shell belts of the whites' (*tamatehe, kagaiha ugukasü hegei tinhegui*).

Luki is a ritualized intravillage trade practice that can also be performed as an intertribal public ritual. *Luki* means 'swallow', a name that conveys the image of a flock of people moving from house to house like a flight of swallows. It occurs more frequently in the rainy season but can be held at any time of year, especially when a group of people return from the city laden with new industrial goods. As a public ritual, it happens when the inhabitants of one village go to another one to trade: the mechanics of exchange are basically the same, but the market moves from within the house to the central plaza.[10]

As ritualized domestic practice, *luki* is a form of immediately balancing accounts, thereby reducing expectations and limiting the claims that one person can make on another. The practice begins as a casual chat between people expressing their collective desire to trade. If the idea takes hold, they seek out someone who has already 'been on the stool' (*tahaguho tütegatinhüpe*) – that is, someone who has already acted as chief of the guests at an intertribal festival – in order to lead the group. They then head to the house of one of the village chiefs, who fetches a stool for the leader to sit on. One by one, the members of the household place objects on the ground in front of him (Figure 5.2). The act of placing the object on the ground is called 'to make sit' (*–akanenügü*), an expression also used to designate sales of craftwork in the city. The leader then asks, 'What do you want for this?' (*tü kaema?*) and the 'seller' sets a price, normally expressed using a first-person possessive form: 'my belt', 'my football boots' and so on.[11] At this point the people gathered around have to decide whether to pick up the object. If nobody does so, the 'seller' immediately fetches another object and expresses a new desire. There is pressure for this to unfold quickly and without pause, forcing the residents to expose their most desired goods, invariably hidden away in bags and suitcases in the darkest recesses of the house. When the pace of the traded objects starts to drop, the cycle has been exhausted. Trading stops. The group moves to the next house, travelling in an counterclockwise direction around the central plaza, repeating the same actions until they reach the final dwelling.[12] The 'swallows' forming an itinerant market inside each house finally disperse.

Almost any kind of object can be traded in *luki*: shell necklaces and mobile phones, fishing lines and pequi oil, money or even food. But no haggling is allowed: the one who is 'price labelling' is the person depos-

Figure 5.2 *A young woman with chiefly status leading an internal* luki. *Kuikuro village of Ipatse, Xingu Indigenous Park, Brazil, 2013. Photo: Carlos Fausto*

iting the object on the ground. The only form of calibration is to place something and ask for the desired return object; if nobody accepts, the first object is removed and replaced by another of higher value, asking for the same object.[13] There also exists a certain standardization of value expressed in bands of Czech beads. At the start of the 2000s, for example, one bar of soap was equivalent to four necklace bands, while one length of fabric was traded for eight bands.

Although almost everything circulates in the *luki* marketplace, a few exceptions do exist. Excluded items include shamanic artefacts, ceremonial objects and tape recordings of ritual songs. If you paid to record a set of songs, you cannot sell this knowledge materialized in a cassette tape. You can only transmit it to a third party (and receive a payment for it) through your own voice. The knowledge needs to have become part of your own memory, or as the Kuikuro say, incorporated in your belly.

Shamanic Services

The standardized system of value in ritual exchange is replicated at lower levels of inclusion and in other contexts, ritual and otherwise.[14] So, for example, in the shamanic therapy to recover the sick person's soul, normally undertaken by three to five shamans, there is a well-established expectation for payment: the main shaman will normally receive a high-quality shell necklace or belt, while the shaman who holds the doll used to recover the sick person's soul will receive a bead necklace with various bands (Figure 5.3). The remaining assistants receive a few bands of beads or a belt made from cotton.[15] If no necklace is available, people can improvise: I once saw a man pay the main shaman with a used bicycle (when they were still a rarity in the village). Unlike most payments for goods or services, these payments cannot be called *ihipügü*. Instead they are called *ihatoho*, which could be translated as 'made to (re)count'.[16] If the payment is not made immediately at the end of the shamanic session, the shaman's auxiliary spirit may turn against his master (the shaman).[17]

The payments made to shamans maintain a fairly stable value, and every adult is careful to maintain at least a small stock of shell or bead adornments to cover the costs of treatment. Even the most trivial therapies, in which just one shaman is summoned to extract 'spirit arrows' from the patient, may involve a substantial payment of a shell necklace or belt.[18] In the case of newborns, action is taken before a crisis point is reached. When the baby becomes sick for the first time, the parents choose a shaman-paediatrician (*ipagisü*), making a standard payment of a shell necklace or belt. This payment is valid until the child begins to run. During this period the shaman can be asked to perform cures without any new payment.

Figure 5.3 *Matü confects the* akunga, *the shamanic doll. Kuikuro village of Ipatse, Xingu Indigenous Park, Brazil, 2002. Photo: Carlos Fausto*

If they wish, parents can offer a new payment to extend the covered period to around the age of five. Like other payments to shamans, these goods are denominated *ihatoho,* but they have a peculiarity: the shaman must keep them until the end of the covered period – if the child dies, he must return the very same item, not one of equivalent value.[19]

All these *ihatoho* are seen as payments to the shamans and to their 'children', meaning the spirits who confer on them the power to cure and who are consubstantial with them.[20] The payments made to these dual people follow a regular pattern well known to everyone, including the spirits. Over recent years, though, outbreaks of prophetism in the region have, among other things, thrown this scale of values into question. The most significant of these took place about five years ago when a former wrestling champion suddenly began to cure in the name of God, creatively combining traditional elements of shamanism with innovations inspired by either Christianity or free interpretations of elements from the Xinguano world. Prices paid for his services underwent an inflationary burst: a Kuikuro man who was ill for more than a year after a failed shamanic initiation ended up paying him thirteen shell necklaces. At the peak of his pan-village success, he started to claim that his spirit – God – would only accept *ihatoho* in paper money. Thus, for example, he apparently charged 2,000 reais to treat the Kĩsêdjê (Suyá) chief, an amount that would have been supplied by the local council in Querência, a small town at the edge of Xingu Park where Indians comprise a large section of the electorate.

There is no space here to describe the process by which traditional shamanism responded to the innovations of this prophet or self-styled 'Master'.[21] Suffice it to say that one factor in his fall from grace was precisely the deregulation of the payments system and the introduction of money into its circuits. God's demand to be paid *only* in money vexed a lot of people who found themselves excluded from therapy due to the difficulty of obtaining the 'leaves' (*tagü*) of the whites, as the Kuikuro originally called paper money.[22] Though the Xinguanos have bank accounts, people do not accumulate money as they do shell necklaces and belts. They prefer to spend everything they earn, converting the money into industrial goods that enter the system of circulation, linking them to their kin. They are not concerned with the moral significance of money but with how to gain access to it. Money is just the whites' shell belts, and though I was refractory about paying for services with money (for moral reasons), this was exactly what they expected from me.

Compensations: The Cost of a Wife

Besides serving as counterprestation in intertribal ritual relations and for shamanic therapy, luxury goods are used in marriage compensations. In an abstract way, the Kuikuro affirm that the son-in-law must pay all his parents-in-law, including classificatory ones, with snail-shell necklaces to compensate them for the fact that he will have sons with the wife.[23] The payment must be made by the bridegroom's mother and applies to a girl's first marriage, especially when she leaves post-menarche seclusion and has her fringe cut. When a girl marries after having had various sexual relations already, her husband is expected to pay only her real parents. As a man once explained to me, 'it's like among the whites: used is cheaper'.

The paradigmatic situation occurs in marriages between 'chiefs' (*anetü*), which involve a matrimonial arrangement prior to the girl's seclusion. At the end of a major intertribal ritual, an uncle (MB) or a wrestler takes the girl to the groom's house, where the young man's hammock is taken down; then it is carried to her parents' house, where he will live from then on. On the same day the boy's mother presents the payment to the girl's family.[24] The payment is sometimes called the 'price of the vagina' (*igügü ihipügü*) (Franchetto 1996: 41), at other times, the 'price of raising' (*inkgukipügü ihipügü*) – referring to the fact that what is being repaid is the joint effort of the parents-in-law in raising the girl. As in the case of the shaman-paediatricians, the goods paid on this occasion – normally shell belts – must be kept by the parents-in-law until the birth of the first grandchild, for if the marriage is dissolved, they must be returned to the former son-in-law. After the birth of a child the paid goods do not need to be given back because, as people say, the girl has already been 'spoilt' (*ihetsüpügü*) by her husband.[25]

From the viewpoint of the girl's family, the payment is for the 'care' spent in raising her: the worries, the sleepless nights, the affection, the food – in sum, everything contained in the Kuikuru notion of 'care' (*ig-ikasi–*). The compensation is made with objects whose value expresses the suffering and difficulty involved in their fabrication. The equivalence between people and things does not imply an abstract calculation, an 'exchange rate' in which a certain quantity of a product has a value numerically expressed in 'shell necklaces' qua currency. What is placed in relation is a human quality inscribed in the object: the payment is a recognition of the ties uniting a girl with her parents as a result of their long-term 'care', rather than the simple annulment of these ties and their transference to the groom. Hence bride service and uxorilocal residence are combined with the bride wealth rather than being cancelled by it.

From the viewpoint of the boy's family, the transfer of luxury goods is a prolongation of the care involved in his upbringing, since the payment to the parents-in-law reduces the 'shame' (*ihüisu*) felt by the son-in-law in the house of his affines.[26] He acquires greater freedom, including being able to remove his wife temporarily from living with her parents. In the eyes of the boy's parents, the payment is above all meant to mitigate the years of bride service and reduce the time of uxorilocality, though this always depends on the families' relative hierarchical position and the contingencies that every interpersonal relation imposes. The payment does not imply an immediate transference of 'rights' over a woman (from the parents to the husband), cancelling a standing debt. Rather, it opens up the possibility of creating a new relational field in which the ties between spouses (who will themselves become parents) progressively overlap the ties of debt between affines.

There are other forms of compensation that aim at cancelling debt incurred by accident. A few years ago, for instance, when a boy playing with fire set off a blaze that razed five houses to the ground, his father compensated each of the house owners with shell belts and necklaces.[27] Here there is no attempt to draw an equivalence between what was burnt and what was paid: the belts do not compensate for the goods lost in the fire. Like the 'bride price', no calculation of value or account balancing is possible. Instead the aim is to re-establish equilibrium in relations distorted by an excessive debt that generates a profound sense of 'shame' – this time not in a young son-in-law, but in the person carrying the burden of the debt. Compensations for accidental injuries or deaths follow the same pattern, serving to soften the excessive and unbalanced connection suddenly created between the parties.[28]

Deceiving: Knowledge Transmission

Like most services, formal transmission of knowledge must also be repaid. This applies especially to the specialized knowledge of shamans and singers, but is likewise true for more diffuse sets of knowledge such as that involving spells and medicines, which are not exclusive to shamans. In the polished language of formalized relations, these payments to acquire knowledge are never called *ihipügü*, except outside the context of the relation. For example, the correct way to request instruction from a singer is to say 'deceive me with that thing you didn't hear well' (*uinkguhike hõhõ ahangahesügüki*). The singer will agree in a self-derogatory manner to indeed deceive the pupil with 'the little that I have learnt' and asks for nothing in return, expecting precisely that the apprentice will not behave deceptively in the future when the first suite of songs has been learned and the first payment should be made. The interval between the request and this payment can vary considerably in length depending on the intensity of the apprenticeship. During this period the singer, in theory, should not trick the pupil, or at least should only partially trick him or her, in the expectation of receiving a repayment matching the efforts and knowledge expended on the instruction. When offering it, the pupil will repeat the formula, saying that this time she or he is the one who is deceiving the master.

The 'deception' (*augene*) is more than inverted speech whose actual meaning is its symmetrical opposite. It is a virtuality of the relation, made explicit in a formulaic mode. The agents' expectations are calibrated by the virtual existence of deception: on one hand, it is possible that the knowledge will not be transmitted correctly; on the other, the payment might not correspond to the value of what was transmitted. One factor lessening the uncertainty of this relation of double deception is the existence of a certain standard of measure shared by everyone and expressed, once again, in terms of snail-shell necklaces and belts (or goods equivalent to them). However, people are diverse, some being more inclined to 'deceive' than others; moreover, not all transmitted knowledge has the same value – some songs are worth more than others.

The Kuikuro have fifteen ritual song sets internally divided into named suites, each composed of between ten and a hundred different songs (Fausto, Franchetto and Montagnani 2011). The value of a suite does not depend on how many songs it contains, but on a particular quality: that of being more than simply music. All ritual songs are, by definition, a manifestation of the 'spirits' (*itseke*), but some of them are themselves said to be 'spirits' and/or are associated with crucial moments of ritual action, indexing certain acts that invoke risks in relations with the 'spirits'.[29] These songs are said to be *tainpane*, a term the Kuikuro usually translate as 'sacred', though actually it is closer to the anthropological notion of taboo. In most cases only some of the songs in a suite are *tainpane*; some suites, though, are entirely 'sacred'. Thus, for example, out of the nineteen suites for *kagutu* flutes – which women are prohibited from seeing – one, with just ten songs, is considered the most valuable. This suite is performed at special moments and elicits considerable tension, since any error by the performer may lead to his own death or that of a relative.

In sum, the standardization of value does not guarantee that, as Gertrude Dole would say, accounts are equalized. The main constraint to ensure that expectations converge is kinship ties, which are responsible for the continuity in relations between master and apprentice. Consequently families of singers tend to form, with musical knowledge being transmitted between kin, especially from parents to children. Even in these cases, though, the teaching must be repaid – although in a less strict manner – otherwise, people say, the student will be unable to properly hear the songs or correctly memorize them. Whoever pays, pays attention.

The advent of tape recorders some decades ago enabled a new mode of transmission: recording an unrelated singer resident in another village, who is paid immediately with goods promised beforehand. Thus any long-term involvement or risk of being 'deceived' is avoided. Singers are often heard saying that they do not teach young people today because the latter do not ask them; the youth in turn say that they feel ashamed and are afraid to commit themselves to a master and become entangled in a cycle of learning and debt payments they might be unable to meet. The tape recorder allows them to 'equalize the account' immediately, transferring to tape the lengthy relation with a master and his or her expectations.

Pricing Songs

Becoming a great singer is a source of prestige in the Upper Xingu. Singers play a central role in all rituals. When they start to be called upon to perform 'sacred' songs in the host village, during intertribal rituals, their name becomes well-known. Renown is a fundamental concern for Xinguano people, and is conceived of, as Munn has argued for Gawa, as a 'spatiotemporal expansion of self' (1986: 117). As a name circulates among different villages, its bearer becomes *tikagi*, 'much talked about'. A famous person exerts influence over other minds, as his or her name extends in time and space. Names are transmitted between alternating generations, and a chiefly name – one that was bore by an eminent chief who left good memories imprinted in peoples' minds – is a living chief's most important asset.

In Kuikuro a singer is designated *eginhoto,* a conjunction of *egi* ('song') and *oto,* which can be translated as 'owner' or 'master'. Like the Trio *entume* (Brightman and Grotti this volume) or the Kĩsêdjê *kandê* (Coelho de Souza this volume), this is a very productive category that applies to a number of contexts ranging from a people's relation to its territory, to a person's connexion to his or her material or immaterial possessions (one can be the owner of a tape recorder or a specific ritual).[30] Most specialists are named by a noun followed by *oto,* except for the shaman, who is called *hüati.*[31] Thus, the herbalist is *embuta oto* ('master of medicine'), the wrestling champion is a *kindoto* ('master of wrestling'), the storyteller is an *akinha oto* ('master of story'), as the singer is an *eginhoto* ('master of song'). In all these cases, the translation 'master' is more adequate than 'owner', since it implies possession of a certain knowledge rather than ownership of an object. Both knowledge and ownership are transferred by means of payment.

As I argued in the last section, musical knowledge is almost always transferred against payment in luxury items like shell ornaments or highly valued industrial goods. The great female singer Kanu, for instance, who learned most *Jamugikumalu* songs from her mother, paid a 100-litre aluminium pot to the male singer Agaku in order to also 'have' (*ngipi*) a very valued suite known as *Auga imitoho* that her mother did not know (Figure 5.4). When you obtain an item of musical knowledge – when you have it 'in your belly' and become capable of performing it publicly in a ritual, you acquire the right to transmit it to someone else. You become an *eginhoto,* independent from the original source of your knowledge. When you are paid by a new apprentice, you owe nothing to the master who first taught you.[32]

In the last few decades, the ways of becoming renowned have multiplied and shifted away from the more traditional area of ritual. Becoming a teacher, a healthcare assistant, a filmmaker, a university student, learning Portuguese, handling money – all of these have begun to eclipse the traditional pathways to fame. Names circulate now through the Internet; young people have profiles on Facebook, and they also travel around a lot. When I began my research more than a decade ago, the chief Afukaká feared the end of Kuikuro musical knowledge since, according to him, young people no longer wanted to learn the songs. In another text (Fausto 2011) I have described how this feeling of 'culture loss' led us to elaborate a documentation project focused especially on the universe of songs, whose dimension and specificities comprise a huge challenge to individual and collective memory. I shall skip over this particular point, for what matters

Figure 5.4 *Kanu sings during a Jamugikumalu festival. Kuikuro village of Ipatse, Xingu Indigenous Park, Brazil, 2010. Photo: Carlos Fausto*

here are the dilemmas that surfaced once we decided that we should pay the singers to record their knowledge. This payment would be made by the Indigenous Association itself, created in 2002 to manage the project, while the recordings would be made by indigenous filmmakers trained in our video production courses.

Four years passed from the project's conception and creation of the association to making the first recordings, whereupon two questions needed answering. First, how much does a song cost? And second, to whom do the songs belong once recorded – that is, who can learn them and retransmit them? Had I proposed that the songs would belong to me, the second problem would have been solved, but the first would have triggered an inflationary spiral capable of rendering the execution of the project unviable.

Chief Afukaká understood the recordings as belonging 'to everyone', 'as our things' (*kukengüko*). From most people's standpoint, though, there is nothing that clearly belongs to the 'community' (*comunidade*) in opposition to the 'private person' (*particular*) – two concepts that, in Portuguese, now blend into Kuikuro discourse. Everything the chief sees as everyone's stuff (*tatutolo engü*) tends to be seen as the chief's by everyone else. This has both positive and negative aspects. The chief is in fact the singular form through which the collective appears, and his absence is experienced as a lack. Hence the chief is said to be *tühüninhü*, 'something one doesn't abandon'. But at the same time, every chief has two bodies, so a common accusation against him is that he is acting as a 'private person', or more precisely, thinking only of his family. Consequently, as years went by and the problem remained unresolved, Chief Afukaká confided to me that his people were distrustful of him.[33]

I once naively asked a great singer how much he would charge to record everything he knew. He told me he had no idea but would ask his son. Some time later, with pen and paper in hand, the son handed his father a quote of R$ 40,000. Having little or no idea of the structure and scale of this knowledge, I was startled and quickly changed the subject. Today I regret not having tried to understand how he arrived at this figure, which in fact no longer seems absurd, given the extent of his father's knowledge. After this misunderstanding, I decided to research the topic better in order to reach a standard of value. I began studying the internal structure of the set of songs, their division into suites and their rigorous organization, as well as the ritual practices and narratives co-indexed to them. I imagined that it would be possible to create a hierarchy of ritual sets and convert the traditional payments into monetary values. Yet in meeting after meeting, talk after talk, we continued to go round in circles. The question remained: how much should songs be worth?

Eventually I hit upon two proposals. First, each recorded hour of 'simple' songs would be worth 100 reais and each hour of 'sacred' songs, 200 reais. Second, we would record everything but would not let anyone listen to the recordings. We would deposit one copy in the archives of the Indian Museum in Rio de Janeiro, and another in a Documentation Centre to be built in the village.[34] At last, under these terms, the deal was done. The project finally took off, along with a new standard of value that, once up and running, began to constitute its own reality to the point that it become part of the taken-for-granted environment in which these relations were negotiated. In 2010 we were still following the same payment system and singers were coming to us of their own accord, sometimes from other villages or even from other peoples living in the region.[35] Then the chief could say: 'they believe me'.

The story does not end here, though, since we had swept the second obstacle under the carpet: to whom do the recorded songs belong? Subjecting them to a regime of museological mutism would betray the project's very goal of reinvigorating the process of song transmission. Following the inauguration of the Documentation Centre in 2007, young people started exerting pressure to make the recordings available, but the singers refused to simply release them to all and sundry. Did the fact that the Indigenous Association paid for the songs mean it had them in its belly? Had it also acquired the right to transmit them to third parties? To put it in more contemporary language: who owns their copyright? And how much is it worth?[36]

Conclusion

This chapter has offered an ethnographic description of a place in Amazonia where a logic of 'payment' pervades numerous social fields. This description contrasts with the standard anti-market image of Amazonian societies as a universe of sharing and gift-giving. But I do not take it as just another example of the conflation of gifts and commodities. Instead I prefer to think of this example as an Amerindian way of expanding the social field through the circulation of objects (material and immaterial) rather than the circulation of parts of persons. In previous work, I have tried to theorize the latter case through the notion of 'familiarizing predation', the process through which alien subjectivities (in the form of trophies, songs and souls) are violently captured outside to be transformed into wild pets inside, thus engendering an ownership relation, in the Amazonian sense of the word. Now, I strive to theorize an object-oriented regime as a transformation of the predatory one.

The constitution of the Xinguano constellation required putting predation in the background and promoting a sort of 'relational interweaving;' that is, the production of ever more cordial relations through visits, gifts and marriages that gradually build up a network of identity denser than the array of differences without, however, effacing all meaningful differences, which are preserved in language and in certain craft specialties (Fausto, Franchetto and Heckenberger 2008). Objects thus came to play a key role in the mediation between peoples of different ethnic and linguistic origin. This example is not unique in Amazonia. The Upper Rio Negro system, composed of Arawak-, Tukano- and Hupdá-speaking peoples, is also an ethnographic case in point (Hugh-Jones 2013). In terms of standardization of value, the best historical example comes from the Arawak and River Pano system on the Andean piedmont, where in colonial times, rock salt in bars of fixed size served as a sort of general 'currency' throughout a vast region of the forest (Renard-Casevitz 1993).

The conversion of relations into things that are evaluated according to certain standards is quite a different process from the conversion of objects into subjects – a more commonly discussed topic in the Amazonian literature. Obviously, the latter conversion also applies to a great number of objects in the Upper Xingu, where we find two different anthropomorphic effigies in addition to a number of masks, musical instruments and other ritual paraphernalia (see Barcelos Neto 2008; Fausto and Penoni 2014). In this chapter, however, I have focused on objects because they connect people through their transference and not because they contain, to use Santos-Granero's (2009) expression, any 'soul-stuff'. These transferences imply forms of calculation and establishment of equivalences, which may be interpreted as a rudimentary currency-based system, as Gertrude Dole hypothesized.

Here though I have tried to show that these equivalences do not result from the computation of an abstract quantity but from the type of relations involved. At this point, it is pertinent to mention that the Kuikuro's numerical system (as well as spatial and geometrical thinking) is fairly sophisticated and would permit them to calculate abstract quantities. That is why I thought my arithmetics would serve to calculate the value of a suite of songs. But it would not, for the relation I was proposing was new – not by virtue of the recording technology (which they already used), but because no one was learning on the other side: the owner of songs was simply relinquishing knowledge to no one or to every one. It thus fell to me to decide the value of this relation. Once decided, this value became part of its own context of enactment, and nobody asked me for more. It became the standard of *our* relationship, or as they say, 'The Project' relationship. This standardization did not result from a computation of labour time or rarity, but from an equivalence between one tape and a quantity of money. Tapes, of course, have a built-in time dimension, but this was not important to the computation. We just counted tapes, no matter what.

Such operation disassembled the recording and the learning of songs into two different relationships. There is now an owner of the tapes (The Project, represented by myself, the Association or the chief), but no new song owners. This is why singers now demand to be paid once more whenever people are allowed to learn from the tapes. This is not a ruse, but the computation of a new relation in the age of digital reproduction. What they are counting is not a right to copy, but their capacity to make someone else embody a knowledge, 'to have the songs in his/her belly', which can only result from a relationship between people.

Carlos Fausto is Associate Professor of Anthropology at the Museu Nacional, Federal University of Rio de Janeiro, and Senior Fellow of the National Council for the Development of Science and Technology (CNPq). He is the author of *Os Índios antes do Brasil* (2000), *Inimigos Fiéis: História, Guerra e Xamanismo* (2001), and *Warfare and Shamanism in Amazonia* (2012). He co-edited (with M. Heckenberger) *Time and Memory in Indigenous Amazonia* (2007) and (with C. Severi) *L'Image Rituelle* (2014).

Notes

An initial version of this chapter was written for the colloquium 'New Perspectives in Economic Ethnography: Modalities of Exchange and Economic Calculation', held at the Museu Nacional, Rio de Janeiro, in 2011. I thank Federico Neiburg and Fernando Rabossi for their kind invitation. A later version was presented at the London School of Economics in 2012 at the invitation of Hans Steinmuller, whom I also thank. David Rodgers translated it into English. This final text, based on twenty months of discontinuous fieldwork in Ipatse village in the Xingu Indigenous Park, could not have been written without continuous dialogue with Takumã Kuikuro and Mutuá Mehinaku in Rio de Janeiro and via the Internet. I thank FAPERJ and CNPq for financing most of the research. I also thank Petrobrás Cultural, PDPI-Ministry of the Environment and IPHAN-Ministry of Culture for their additional support. Finally I thank Bruna Franchetto for first taking me to the Kuikuro (and continuing to help me with the language) and the Kuikuro for maintaining me there for so many years.

1. At the start of my fieldwork, I observed the following scene: the house owner's son-in-law, who had recently arrived from the FUNAI post where he was responsible for operating the communications radio, had brought with him a large assortment of technological paraphernalia, including a stereo, a television and a satellite dish. Without any brothers to help him fix the antenna, he asked a young lad for assistance. After the latter had completed the work, I saw the son-in-law enter the house quickly and start to rummage through his things somewhat anxiously. I asked him what was happening and, pulling out a new pair of bermuda shorts from his bag, he told me that he had to provide payment (*ihipügü*) for the boy's work. Having moved to the village recently as a junior affine, he was trying to impose himself through his control over the world of manufactured goods and ended up overpaying for a task that would normally cost a couple of bars of soap or a few batteries.
2. Food is fundamental as a return for collective work. This counterprestation, known as *endugu*, is not considered a payment. The food and drink is offered by the owner of the swidden or house where the work is executed.
3. The spectre of the monetization of village life only casts its shadow over the alimentary sphere. The problem is not the insertion of money in the 'traditional' circuits of exchange, but its interference in food sharing. A Kuikuro friend once told me the story of a Xinguano man who went to visit a Bakairi village and went hungry because the food there, rather than being shared, was sold at a small market located in the indigenous territory. In a Kuikuro village, the everyday sharing of food among close kin and affines is also supplemented by ritualized forms of asking for food, or for the loan of a swidden or an area of river with a fish trap from more distant kin. These formulas are called *inko ihatoho* ('for recounting things').
4. E.g., there are two autonomous Kalapalo political units corresponding to the villages of Aiha and Tanguru.
5. The Mehinaku also produce vegetal salt. I presume that they relinquished their monopoly over its production during the process of including the Aweti within the Xinguano system. In regards to the snail shell adornments, it seems there was once a distinction between the Kalapalo necklace and the Kuikuro belts.
6. The 70- and 100-litre aluminium pans became objects of payment, but not utensils to cook manioc porridge. On receiving a pan as payment for the festival, the owner of the ritual must offer food to the community one more time before using this object as s/he wishes.
7. The Kuikuro's perception coincides with Aweti's views on the value of their salt. According to Figueiredo (2010: 99), the Aweti always explain its high 'price' in

intercommunal exchange in reference to 'the dangers and the physical hardships that women face in its production process'.

8. E.g. in the past the stone used to pierce the snail shell had to be acquired from the Kalapalo, who embarked on long journeys up the Culuene River to a site named *kugugi*, which I estimate to be 60 to 70 km south of the present-day border of the Xingu Indigenous Park.
9. These 'things' are not described as 'payment' (*ihipügü*). The chiefs of the visitors refer to them as *uakandokongo* ('the companion of my stool'), since the stool is their status symbol: the chief of the guests (*hagito anetügü*) is the one who goes 'on the stool' (*tahaguhongo*). The messenger-hosts, on the other hand, may refer to this payment as *uetidzingagü* (which can be glossed as 'my having been a messenger'). The necklaces and belts must be placed vertically on the ground, forming a line between the chief of the guests and the messengers.
10. In intertribal *luki*, men dominate the scene. On arrival, the chiefs of the guests place their items on the ground without stating what they want in return. The chiefs of the hosts are thus obliged to take them. They agree on a 'price' only afterwards, in private. The next day another *luki*, this time held by the women, takes place inside the houses (see Basso 1973: 135–38).
11. The person may also simply say 'think about it' (*eingunkgike*), letting whoever takes the object decide what to give in return.
12. The circuit may also be completed in another way: by starting between two houses, if someone enters the circle, the participants go to the house of this new person, tracing out diagonal lines that cut across the village circle.
13. Some people, feeling compelled to display their goods but wishing to keep them, ask for a high-value item in return. This practice, though, implies that the person is overly attached (*tüitunginhü*) to his or her own things – evidently not a compliment per se.
14. During the finale of a ritual, it is customary to pay the festival owner for having fed the community of people and spirits over so many years. Among the Kuikuro, each of the people called 'bodies' (*ihü*) – that is, those who asked the owner to assume responsibility for the festival – must give him a large pan, today made from aluminium, in which other people may deposit their own presents.
15. The system allows for variations: ideally, the main shaman makes a soul-doll, another shaman casts a spell (*kehege*) for the doll to come alive, while a third places the doll on his chest in order to fetch the soul from wherever the 'spirits' (*itseke*) have taken it. The fourth and fifth shamans are assistants who carry the things offered to the spirits. It is more common, though, for the shaman who makes the doll to cast the spell too. Whatever the case, the payment also depends on the length of time spent reciting the spell. Consequently, the sick person's kin must pay close attention when the spell is cast to know how much they have to pay. In any case, all the shamans must receive a payment lest their spirit harm them (i.e., the shamans).
16. The root *–iha* means 'to tell (a story)' and 'to show'. When used in a phrase with the quantifier *hisundu*, it also means 'to count'. The word *ihatoho* designates the index finger, and could be glossed as 'made to show or point'. In this text, I provisionally translate it as 'made to recount'.
17. The spirits who took the soul of the sick person also receive objects. During the cure, various prestigious items, including the ritual feather headdress, are hung in the centre of the house and taken by the assistant shamans to the location that

provides access to the abode of the spirits. These take the 'double' (*akunga*) of these objects.

18. When the shaman is summoned to the sick person's house, the payment is made and he must then return two or three times every day until the patient has completely recovered. No further payment is necessary. A patient who goes to the shaman's house for a single consultation pays with more prosaic items.

19. According to Mutuá Mehinaku, who is a Kuikuro person and holds a master degree in Anthropology, this necklace *is* the child and hence cannot be given to anyone else. However, the equation between the necklace and the child evaporates when the latter begins to run (toddling is not enough).

20. One of the crucial stages of a shaman's initiation is the transmission of a substance called *nguto* from initiator to initiate. This viscous substance pertains to (and also is) the spirit. The initiator removes *nguto* from his hands, mouth, chest and knees and applies it to the same parts of the initiate. It is this substance that will allow the new shaman to remove 'spirit arrows' (*itseke hügi*) from a sick person's body. A direct form of transmission also exists: when a person becomes very ill, the *itseke* places *nguto* in the patient, who thereby acquires a special relation with the spirit concerned. To become a practising shaman, though, that person still must go through the entire training and initiation process with an established shaman. In addition to this form of consubstantialization, shamans, like some chronically sick people, possess another family in the world of the spirits, including a spouse and children.

21. On this prophetic movement see Cardoso, Guerreiro and Pereira Novo (2014), Fausto and Vienne (2014).

22. In 2012, a pan-Xinguano meeting was held in the town of Canarana to discuss paying shamans through the state health service. Some people argued that they, like indigenous health agents, should receive a salary and not demand any payment from patients. According to the account related to me by Takumã Kuikuro, himself the son of a shaman, there was no consensus. He argued that money should not be used to pay a shaman, since the money, as he put it in Portuguese, 'does not appear, does not come into sight'.

23. Ideally a man should pay his parents-in-law when a male child is born, because this son will be his 'substitute' (*itakongo*), the one who will replace him. This replacement occurs at any time, but it is especially visible in regards to ritual roles.

24. The payment can be made to various 'parents-in-law', including all those who the bride's mother and father consider close 'siblings' (including parallel and cross-cousins). The parent-in-law/child-in-law relation implies strict avoidance and, in cases where the distance allows some degree of choice, the parent-in-law may prefer not to be 'respected' (*itsankgijü*) by his/her junior affine. Upon a marriage, the parents of the bride and groom go to the houses of their kin with firewood, asking them whether they wish to be respected by the child-in-law. During the first months of marriage, the young couple must learn all the names of their respective in-laws, which they cannot pronounce anymore.

25. The verb applies to material contexts, as when someone damages (*ihetselü*) a particular object. In the intransitive form (*epetselü*), the term is employed to say, e.g., 'the photographic camera broke'. Should the wife die in labour, the goods are not returned either.

26. Shame is a central category in the Upper Xingu. It is the core notion/emotion defining moral behavior. For the Kalapalo, see Basso (1973) and Guerreiro

(2012); for the Mehinaku, see Gregor (1977: 219–23); for the Wauja, see Ball (2007).
27. The child's grandfather is a shaman, so the father was able to turn to him to make the payments quickly and then, little by little, make new necklaces to repay the loan.
28. Many years ago, the harpy eagle of a Kuikuro chief killed a child when the latter got too close to its cage. The chief 'paid' the family as a form of compensation for their suffering. This is a form of resolving a situation in which feelings of shame (*ihüsu*) and suffering (*egitamine*) are produced. The compensation is a way of recognizing this pain, not an objective responsibility. Some years ago, a woman who had gone to take part in a show in a leisure centre in São Paulo was run over by a car and left paralysed. The parents demanded a 'payment' from the owners of the leisure centre, who argued that they had no responsibility for the accident: she had come to São Paulo of her own will and gone out to look around the city equally of her own will. To compound matters, the driver was apparently blameless in the accident. Hence, according to the centre, it would not be fair to pay anything to her parents. The problem for the latter, though, was very different and had nothing to do with objective responsibility. Rather, the question was one of shame and the recognition of the family's suffering.
29. Most of the time these are songs obliging the 'owner' of the ritual to bring special food that is then shared by elders and spirits only.
30. The term Kuikuro comes from the name of the lake they inhabited in the nineteenth century. Then they were said to be *Kuhi ikugu otomo*, 'the owners of the fish *kuhi* lake'.
31. The term does not apply to a shaman's relation with his auxiliary spirits, although the genitive form is commonly used to refer to them: 'my spirit is the *boa*' (*konto uitsekegüi*), a shaman might say.
32. There is no issue here concerning authorship, as in the case described by Cesarino (this volume). Although there exist rituals that involve the composition of joking songs, these are not considered part of traditional knowledge and are not transmitted via payment.
33. The transitive verb *ikeni–* means 'to believe', but in this context also 'to trust'. One can say, for instance, *tikenitümbüngü ekisei anetü, inhalü anetü ikeninümi ihekeni*, 'that chief is not someone who can be trusted; they do not trust the chief'.
34. We also paid daily fees for all the services associated with the project: cinematographer, transcriber, translator, drivers – in sum, any job required by the project.
35. A fundamental moment in establishing this standard of value came in 2006, when the brother-in-law of Chief Afukaká, an important village leader, decided to record his entire repertoire of *kagutu* flute music. Thereafter everyone began to trust the project.
36. From my perspective, there was an additional question: the recordings elided the pragmatics of transmission, causing a loss of the content essential to the actualization of the songs in ritual situations. The recordings the Kuikuro had made spontaneously on old cassette tapes did not suffer from quite the same problem because the owners of the recordings were adults with good knowledge of ceremonial life. The new generations, however, run the risk of gaining extensive knowledge of a musical universe without the skill base to transform this knowledge into concrete ritual actions. The working solution we envisaged was to make each of the musical sets available to specific people, associating their apprentice-

ship with the singer responsible for the recording. The apprentice would have to consult the singer during the learning process, and upon the memorization of a complete suite of songs, the Indigenous Association would make a new payment to the singer. Hence, once again, the circuit of deceptions would be activated: we would ask the singers to trick us, accepting the risk of ourselves being tricked too, but certain that we too could in the end trick them, given that we again would not know how much a song would cost.

References

Ball, C. G. 2007. 'Out of the Park: Trajectories of Wauja (Xingu Arawak) Language and Culture', Ph.D. dissertation. Chicago: University of Chicago.
Barcelos Neto, A. 2008. *Apapaatai: Rituais de Máscaras no Alto Xingu*. São Paulo: EDUSP-FAPESP.
Basso, E. 1973. *The Kalapalo Indians of Central Brazil*. New York: Holt, Rinehart & Winston.
Cardoso, M., A. Guerreiro Jr. and M. Pereira Novo. 2012. 'As Flechas de Maria: Xamanismo, Poder Político e Feitiçaria no Alto Xingu', *Tellus* 23: 11–33.
Dole, G. 1956–58. 'Ownership and Exchange among the Kuikuru Indians of Mato Grosso'. *Revista do Museu Paulista* N.S. 10: 125–33.
Fausto, C. 2011. 'Mil Años de Transformación: La Cultura de la Tradición entre los Kuikuro del Alto Xingú', in J.-P. Chaumeil, O. Espinosa and M. Cornejo (eds), *Por Donde Hay Soplo: Estudios Amazónicos en los Países Andinos*. Lima: IFEA-CAAP-PUCP, pp. 185–216.
Fausto, C., B. Franchetto and M. Heckenberger. 2008. 'Ritual, Language and Historical Reconstruction: Towards a Linguistic, Ethnographical and Archaeological account of Upper Xingu Society', in A. Dwyer, D. Harrison and D. Rood (eds), *Lessons from Documented Endangered Languages*. Amsterdam: John Benjamins, pp. 129–58.
Fausto, C., B. Franchetto and T. Montagnani. 2011. 'Les formes de la mémoire: Art verbal et musique chez les Kuikuro du Haut Xingu (Brésil)', *L'Homme* 197: 41–69.
Fausto, C. and Penoni, I. 2014. 'L'Effigie, le Cousin et le Mort : Un Essai sur le Rituel du Javari (Haut Xingu, Brésil)'. *Cahiers d'Anthropologie Sociale* 10: 14–37.
Fausto, C. and E. de Vienne. 2014. 'Acting Translation: Ritual and Prophetism in 21st Century Indigenous Amazonia'. *Hau: Journal of Ethnographic Theory* 4(2): 161–91.
Ferreira, M.K.L. 1997. 'When 1+1 ≠ 2: Making Mathematics in Central Brazil'. *American Ethnologist* 24(1): 132–47.
Figueiredo, M.V. 2010. 'A Flecha do Ciúme: O Parentesco e seu Avesso Segundo os Aweti do Alto Xingu', Ph.D. dissertation, Museu Nacional, Universidade Federal do Rio de Janeiro.
Franchetto, Bruna. 1996. 'Mulheres Entre Os Kuikúro'. *Revista de Estudos Feministas* 1(1): 35–54.
Gregor, T. 1977. *Mehinaku: The Drama of Daily Life in a Brazilian Indian Village*. Chicago: University of Chicago Press.
Guerreiro, A.R., Jr. 2012. 'Ancestrais e suas Sombras: Uma Etnografia da Chefia Kalapalo e seu Ritual Mortuário', Ph.D. dissertation. São Paulo: Universidade de São Paulo.

Hanson, A. 1989. 'The Making of the Maori: Culture Invention and Its Logic', *American Anthropologist* 91(4): 890–902.
Hugh-Jones, S. 2013. 'Bride-Service and the Absent Gift', *Journal of the Royal Anthropological Institute* 19(2): 356–77.
Munn, N. 1986. *The Fame of Gawa: A Symbolic Study of Value Transformation in a Massim (Papua New Guinea) Society*. Cambridge: Cambridge University Press.
Renard-Casevitz, F.-M. 1993. 'Guerriers du Sel, Sauniers de la Paix'. *L'Homme* 33(2–4): 25–44.
Santos-Granero, F. 2009. *The Occult Life of Things: Native Amazonian Theories of Materiality and Personhood*. Tucson: University of Arizona Press.

CHAPTER 6

The Forgotten Pattern and the Stolen Design
Contract, Exchange and Creativity among the Kĩsêdjê

Marcela Stockler Coelho de Souza

In April 2006, news came to the Kĩsêdjê that the top model Giselle Bündchen was thinking of using indigenous designs in the next collection of her footwear brand Ipanema, produced by the shoe manufacturer Grendene. She was interested in supporting an environmental cause, and the Xingu River, with its exuberant sceneries and the colourful cultures of the Xingu Indigenous Park under threat from an infrastructure project, was an obvious candidate. She had contacted the Instituto Socioambiental (ISA), an NGO involved in many projects in the Xingu area, including the Y' Ikatu Xingu ('Good Water of the Xingu', in the language of the Kamayurá, one of the native peoples of the region) campaign to protect and restore the headwaters of the river. ISA, a long-standing partner of the Kĩsêdjê, mediated negotiations, and an agreement was reached. The contract included authorizing the use of indigenous graphic patterns on the sandals and a TV ad to be filmed in the village, featuring Giselle, decorated by the Kĩsêdjê, as its star.[1] I will focus on two moments of this experience. The first was the solution the Kĩsêdjê found for a problem they faced from the start: how to paint Giselle, if the female body painting designs they ordinarily use are all part of the graphic repertoire of the Xinguanos, belonging thus not them, but to their neighbours? The second involved the negotiations that followed what the Kĩsêdjê interpreted as a breach of contract when, a year later, designs they recognized as theirs were reused in a different line of sandals by the same company.

The first moment – the re-creation of an old pattern never seen before by any living member of their communities – will serve as starting point for a tentative outline of the mode of creativity characteristic of Kĩsêdjê knowledge practices. Subsequently, focusing on the episode of the non-authorized reuse of the designs, I will discuss different understandings regarding the nature of the products of such creativity and the form of the transaction sustained by the Indians and the company, contrasting what I will call the *contract model* and the *exchange model*. In conclusion I propose these be seen as corresponding to two different creativity modes, which, following James Leach (2004), I call 'appropriative' and 'distributed' creativity. These imply, as we shall see, different concepts of ownership.

The Kĩsêdjê

The Kĩsêdjê (a Northern Gê-speaking group formerly known as Suyá) comprise today a population of around 450 people living in four communities in the Terra Indígena Wawi, next to the Xingu (Indigenous) Park (Mato Grosso state, Brazil). This is a small piece, reclaimed in the 1990s, of the vast territory they used to occupy before their transferral to the park at the moment of contact, in 1959. Their main village, Ngôjhwêrê, stands at the exact site of one of the two contact villages, on the Pacas River to the west of their traditional territory but on the eastern limits of their presently recognized lands.

The Kĩsêdjê probably entered the Xingu basin at the beginning of the nineteenth century. There are today two groups, speaking very close, mutually intelligible languages: the Kĩsêdjê (Eastern Suyá) and those that became known as Tapayuna (Western Suyá, self-denomination Kajkwakratxijê). They maintain the memory of a single past. Coming west from the centre of dispersion of the Northern Gê (somewhere in the north of the state of Goiás and in Maranhão), they divided after crossing the Xingu River (perhaps two hundred years ago). Turning east again, the Suyá arrived at the Xingu via the Arraias or the Ronuro River, and were partially integrated into the Xinguano regional system. The Tapayuna settled by the Arinos River, where they tried, after decades of conflict, to establish peaceful relations with Brazilians, with disastrous results. Reduced to forty-one persons, they were flown to the Xingu Park to be reunited with the Kĩsêdjê (Seeger 1980: 160, 1981: 49–55). Some are still living in Kĩsêdjê villages; most live with the Kayapó Metyktire in the Terra Indígena Capoto/Jarina.[2]

Throughout this period, relationships between the Kĩsêdjê and the Xinguanos (the Kamayurá and Trumai, notably) as well as other peoples later brought together in the park, were intense and unstable. The Kĩsêdjê incorporated captives and survivors from groups now extinct (Manitsawa,

Yaruma). Conflicts with the Yudjá (Juruna) and Kayapó seem to have motivated their movement west along the Suiá-Miçu River at the start of the twentieth century. Later, coresidence in the park resulted in important relations with the Panara and Kayabi. All this history appears in the mixed ascendancy of many individuals and in the presence of Indians from these ethnic groups who married into Kĩsêdjê communities.

In anthropological literature the Kĩsêdjê are known mainly from the writings of Anthony Seeger, who has worked among them since the 1970s. They are the only Gê-speaking group that participates (in an unstable, peripheral and complex manner) in the multiethnic and plurilingual system of the Upper Xingu area, the so-called 'Upper Xinguano society'. The most important effect of this was their 'xinguanization', a process visible in a variety of domains: technology and material culture, body decoration, musical and ceremonial repertoire. One of the most interesting aspects of this 'acculturation' is perhaps its differential influence upon the sexes (derived, at least in part, from the capture of women from Xinguano villages). Xinguano influences are concentrated in the feminine sphere, for instance in the technology of manioc processing and its related cuisine, and especially in body decoration (Figure 6.1) of women, who have also adopted Xinguano practices and ceremonies (the long seclusion period for young women and the Jamurikumã ceremony). As the xinguanization process proceeded, more visible transformations occurred also in the masculine sphere (haircut, the abandonment of auricular and labial disks). Even so, the Kĩsêdjê retained a significant part of their ceremonial and musical repertoire, as well as the associated onomastic groups, on which they confer a value and sense clearly differentiated from what they assign to Upper Xinguano songs and ceremonies (on all this, see Seeger 1980, 2004).

The adoption of elements from Upper Xinguano culture depended on appreciation of their beauty or utility. Thus the Kĩsêdjê, in a diffusionist spirit of sorts, conceived this cultural equipment as a set of features to be separately embraced or refused. This indigenous perception of culture as acculturation is modelled by mythology itself – an account of the way in which, through the adoption of resources and techniques from other peoples and beings, 'the Suyá became true human beings. Nothing was pre-established by a cultural hero; everything was adopted because it was "good" or "beautiful"' (Seeger 1980: 169). From the Kĩsêdjê point of view, this acculturation process is not only open-ended but also reversible. One such reversion occurred when they were reunited with the forty-one Tapayuna survivors brought to the Xingu Park, an event that seems to have caused a revival of pre-Xinguano Kĩsêdjê culture. It is only natural that this culture would flourish, even strongly, upon the reconquest of '

The Forgotten Pattern and the Stolen Design   159

Figure 6.1 *A Kĩsêdjê couple in full regalia.* Kĩsêdjê Kapẽrẽ: alfabetização na língua suyá. *São Paulo: ISA/Fafo, 1999*

Kĩsêdjê traditional territory, as an officially recognized Terra Indígena separated from the park, now equipped with a FUNAI post,[3] a health centre and a public school.

This cultural renaissance continues to unfold, apparently propelled by another acculturative pressure (besides the good old 'intertribal acculturation' [Schaden 1965]) that is felt more strongly every day by the Kĩsêdjê: the vertiginous intensification of their relationship to nonindigenous society, its objects and its knowledge. The moment is of intense, if ambivalent, experimentation. On one hand, an emerging series of purgative actions aims to preserve the Gê (as opposed to Xinguano) and indigenous (as opposed to white) character of local culture – a kind of cultural fundamentalism, we might say, if it were less dependent on context and more attached to 'fundamentals', as we will see. On the other hand, a passionate effort to acquire these alien goods and resources seems to pervade a great part of their everyday life. This crossroads is the site of the experience that is the object of this story.

The Forgotten Pattern: Creativity

In March 2006, when I was living in a house in Canarana[4] that was also the office of the Kĩsêdjê Indigenous Association (AIK), the association received a proposal from the footwear company Grendene regarding the use of indigenous designs on a collection of sandals for Giselle Bündchen's line Ipanema. The proposal included a TV commercial to be produced by Conspiração Films and directed by the award-winning movie and video clip director Andrucha Waddington. The commercial would be filmed in the village, with Giselle as the star and the Indians, or perhaps whites representing Indians, as figurants. Indigenous ornaments, body painting, artefacts and music would of course appear in the commercial and advertising campaign, and the promotional material would include the name of the Kĩsêdjê and a little information on their 'culture'.

I was able to follow the negotiations from the beginning. One question worried me from the start: Which designs could be suggested to the company? Compared with their Xinguano neighbours, the Kĩsêdjê have a rather limited repertoire. A few months earlier, trying to obtain a comprehensive sample of designs, I had collected three named patterns for the body (see Figures 6.2, 6.3 and 6.4) and two for the face, all of them exclusively male. Women invariably used Upper-Xinguano patterns (for reasons already mentioned). Grendene had proposed a workshop to produce a sample of designs, from which the company would select a limited number. So, a month after we heard of the proposal all of us (the people from the ISA, myself – a little anxious – and the Kĩsêdjê with their unshakeable self-confidence), ready to face the challenge, were at Ngôjhwêrê to meet representatives of Grendene, staff from the advertising agency and the Conspiração Films team.

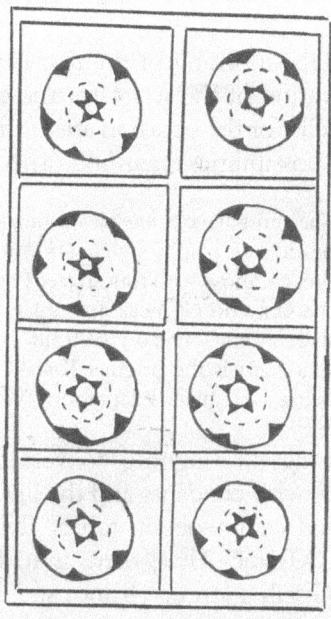

Figure 6.2 Anhi ro kũtêmtêm, *'a spiral on me'*. Drawing: Wetanti Suyá, 2006

Figure 6.3 Tepsôk nhõ sôkô, *'wooden lip plug design'*. Drawing: Wetamtxi Suyá, 2006

Figure 6.4 Anhi ro roptxi, *'a jaguar on me'*. Drawing: Wetantxi Suyá, 2006

Recreating the Pyj Design

On the morning of the first day, following the advertising agency's presentation of the script for the commercial, a debate on how to decorate Giselle for the occasion arises among the Kĩsêdjê. The chief, Kuiussi,[5] lists the possibilities regarding ornaments:

> She must have a *mbrata* (a pendant for the back). Women do not wear feather headdresses; only the *khrãkit hrõ* [a feminine ritual position] may put on headdresses, those with toucan [red] down. On the wrists, strings of tucum palm beads; the same on her neck and ankles. She may wear cotton strings on her knees, or make a *kasin* – tied on the front, with loose ends [another man interrupts to explain that *kasin* is the original Kĩsêdjê style, the hidden knot, now more fashionable, being a Xinguano adaptation]. Women do not wear armbands.

During the ongoing conversation, necklaces of many types, bracelets, belts with pendants and the like are brought to the Men's House and disposed over wooden tables. Two things seem to be non-negotiable for the Kĩsêdjê. First, there is to be no inclusion of masculine ornaments in Giselle's attire: '[S]ince she is a woman, she must wear only feminine ornaments; if the commercial were with a man, we would use masculine decoration', said Kuiussi. Second, items adopted from their Upper Xinguano neighbours and thus not considered to belong to the 'old Kĩsêdjê' will not be included either. We shall see that both restrictions, albeit very simple, had to be slightly relaxed in the end.

The relative poverty of Kĩsêdjê female decoration, compared to the exuberant male ornaments – an aspect of the lesser ceremonial involvement of women as well as of the 'xinguanization' process already mentioned – posed a problem. There are no collective women's ceremonies that the Kĩsêdjê recognize as their own. Women often, and enthusiastically, perform the Xinguano Jamurikumã (exclusively female) and Djuntxi (in which both sexes participate) ceremonies, which are among the favourite dances at Ngôjhwêrê. On such occasions they are painted and dressed as perfect Xinguano women. They may also join in singing Kĩsêdjê music, like the Khahran Ngere songs that were part of the male initiation cycle, which has not been held for more than sixty years. Some songs of this cycle are now performed on occasions such as New Year commemorations, Dia do Indio (national Indian Day), birthdays, political meetings and so on (a practice that has both defenders and opponents). At such events the women form a line in front of the singing men and strive to stress the 'Gê' (as opposed to Xinguano) quality of their appearance: tucum necklaces are preferred (instead of beads) and tend to be crossed over the chest instead of worn around the neck. Nevertheless, the body designs are still Xinguano, for there is not – or there was not, up to the events I am discussing – any alternative.

The problem with the body paint design emerges almost immediately. As Kuiussi expresses it,

> The thing is that there are no [Kĩsêdjê] women designs; we only have patterns for important rituals for men, like *tutwakandêjê wisôkô, kupēkandêjê wisôkô, tepkradjê wisôkô* ... There was a design, which was called *pyjkango*, but it is lost, we have no way to recover it. Last night, *tuwáj* ['grandmother'] Mbeni was telling us about this design, the same way our father used to describe it. But they only described it to us, never painted anybody for us to see. They trace the *si* first and then fill with the *kango*; this is what my father told me, what I heard.

The Kĩsêdjê then start to evaluate their options, talking in their language (as this is not a subject non-Indians are supposed to have a say in): should they 'draw it on paper to *find out* [what it looked like]', or try to paint it directly a woman's body? Agreeing that solving this problem will take more time than the decision regarding ornaments, they decide to focus on the latter so the production team can test the alternatives on their model. The pattern to be painted on Giselle will remain undisclosed until the day of the shooting, for they have to wait for the old people to 'find out [the design] in their heads'[6] so they can paint a girl and then present it. The company and the advertising agency are spared; nothing is said to them about the dilemma. If they later ask, Kuiussi reflects, 'we can explain that this is the only female design there is for ceremonies'. During the lunch break, Kuiussi calls Mbeni (a lady about ninety-five years old who is an accomplished, respected storyteller) to his house to describe the Pyj ceremony and the associated design. The ornaments are tested on one of Kuiussi's daughters, Ngajsôjgrântxi, this same afternoon. The following day, again by late afternoon, Mbeni, Kuiussi and his family, the board of the indigenous association and myself meet again at the back of the chief's house to test the design on the body of the same girl. While Mbeni and Kuiussi rememorate descriptions of the ceremony and designs they had heard from their parents, the chief's wife, based on these narratives, guides one of her daughters-in-law, to execute the painting (Figures 6.5 and 6.6).[7]

The orienting axes are the shape of the *si*, traced like a framework to be filled; and the form of the filling, called *kango*. As Kuiussi explains, you start 'making the *si*, tracing it uniformly; the *kango* comes to the same point, and meets it without error [*ajmen kãm kango ro tê*]. This is the women's design, the design of the Pyj'. When drawing or painting, the Kĩsêdjê usually start with this framework or *si* – 'bone'. The meaning of *kango* is more elusive. They first tell me that *kango* refers to striped or scratched objects when the lines are thin and proximate. Later, confronted with two sets of stripes, one horizontal and the other vertical, roughly traced on paper, a research assistant explains to me that surfaces or ob-

Figure 6.5 *Recreating the Pyj design: the* si *pattern. Ngójhwéré village, Xingu Indigenous Park, Brazil, 2006. Photo: M.S. Coelho de Souza*

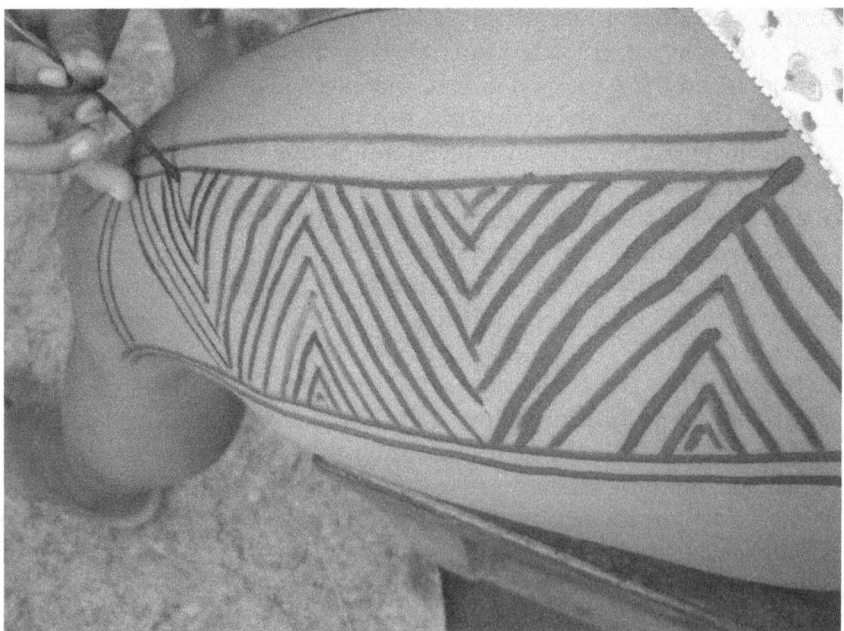

Figure 6.6 *Re-creating the Pyj design: filling in the* si *with the* kango *pattern. Ngójhwéré village, Xingu Indigenous Park, Brazil, 2006. Photo: M.S. Coelho de Souza*

jects with vertical stripes are referred as *sĩpê* (or *sĩpê kryre*, if the stripes are thin); those covered with horizontal stripes are *kajngoro* (or *kajngoro kryre*).[8] What is *kango*, then? This assistant tells me that 'when you are making a club for someone, he may ask you: "make it *kango*". This means with scratches like that [along the length of the club, vertical], made not with paint, but by scraping it. If you use paint, it is *sĩpê*' (Figure 6.7).

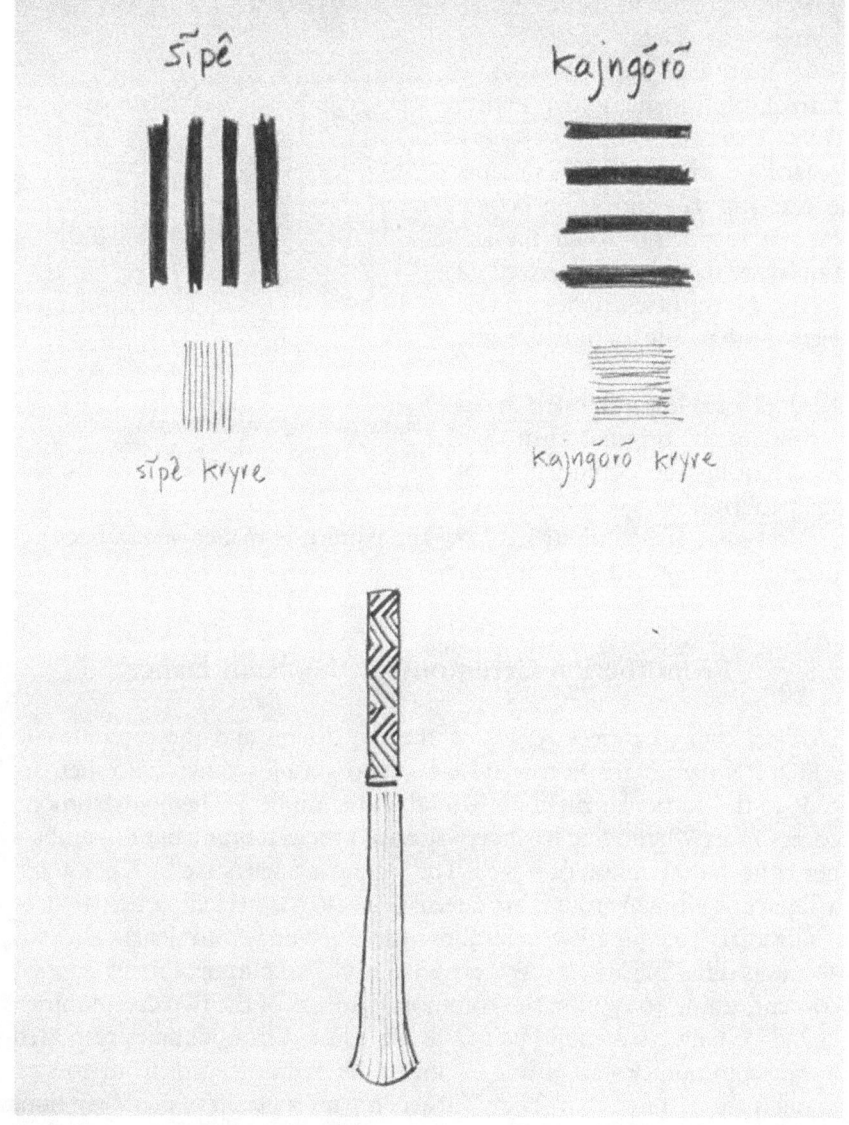

Figure 6.7 *The* sĩpê *and* kajngörö *design patterns. Ngôjhwêrê village, Xingu Indigenous Park, Brazil, 2006. Photo: M.S. Coelho de Souza*

I am not sure what this says about the Pyj design – can it be linked to scarification practices, for instance (my assistant was not impressed by the suggestion)? Be that as it may, the ambiguity may help explain the recent fate of the pattern, which, in being transferred to artefacts (stools, bracelets, etc.), has undergone some formal transformations (Figure 6.8). There is some uncertainty regarding which of the variants is the original, and some people express scepticism about the antiquity of the pattern as executed today. Nevertheless, the general view is that any of the variants would be a fair candidate, and the Kĩsêdjê seem less interested in determining the original form than in exploring the potentialities of the pattern.

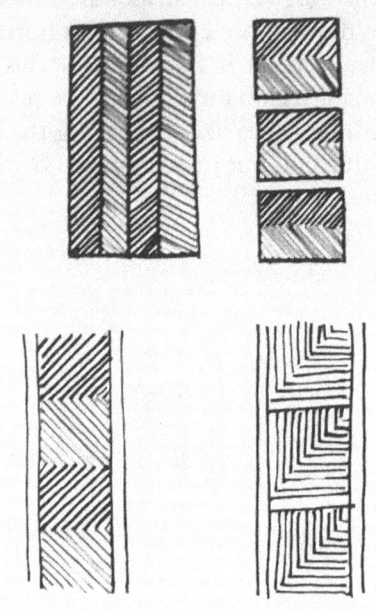

Figure 6.8 *Formal transformations of the Pyj pattern. Drawing: M.S. Coelho de Souza, 2009*

Now that I have discussed how the pattern is made, or has been remade, I will now ask what it *makes*.

From the Pyj Ceremony to the 'Rain Dance'

I collect two narratives regarding the Pyj design and the ceremony in which Pyj names are bestowed on the two young women who then accede to the particular ritual position the title implies.[9] The first testimony comes from Mbeni. She has never attended the ceremony but remembers her father's description of it well. The second is a narrative by Khôkhôtxi, a Tapayuna woman around her late sixties who has herself participated, in a subsidiary role, in a Wyj ceremony (the Tapayuna equivalent). The two accounts differ in various respects: detail, style, amplitude. I focus on their content, trying to capture the common elements of the two ceremonies.

Pyj/Wyj always come in pairs and are selected from families respected by the community – according to one of the narrators, girls from gossipy families are never chosen. They will accompany a group of men on a hunt or a fishing expedition (a pattern that applies to many female ritual positions). Mbeni's story focuses on the events that precede the expedition;

Khôkhôtxi's, on those that follow. In both cases, the installation of the Pyj/Wyj girls involves the application of a specific body painting pattern and the donning of a set of ornaments. These operations are executed in the Men's House (*ngá*), by the men. One expression used to refer to this is equivalent to 'stay in their [the men's] midst' (*to ajmen nhi hôk to pa*). The girls' return to their houses is prepared: radial paths are excavated between the *ngá* and the houses and covered with mats, so the girls' feet will not touch the earth. Another crucial element is the chants. I transcribe one (the Tapayuna version). Like the one featured in the commercial (and almost any other Kĩsêdjê song [Seeger 2004]), it has two parts:

Krari (Beginning)
inty ra kuwe ne he wõ õ
I painted my rattle and we went
kuwẽ nhõ wẽj nty
little Indian honeybee
nhõ wári kawe wã
before my tree
inty ra kuwe
I painted my rattle
inky ra kuwe ne ne wõ ne he ha
I painted my rattle and we went
djyyy dja

Sindo (Closing)
inty ro atite ne he wõ
dancing with my rattle, we went
ké weni re nty
jataí bee
nhõ wári kawe wõ
before my tree
djyyy dja

The girls sing the song as they dance in front of each house in the village circle – like the mentioned bees in front of their trees. Khôkhôtxi's narrative (from which the song has been extracted) emphasizes the importance of 'good memory': to correctly execute the designs or the songs, you have to be one of the 'people with good memory' (*me tumbaj mbet ta – mbaj* being a root that refers to thinking, understanding, listening, remembering and imagining).

The girls who pass through this accede to a special position that affects their everyday life. The transition is marked by the imposition of a new name starting with the prefix Pyj (Wyj). In the two ceremonies described by the older women – both referring to specific historical instances – the girls received the names Pyj-kango-txi and Pyj-kango in one case, and Wyj-nty-txi [*nty*, 'rattle'] and Wyj-nhĩtep-txi [*nhĩtep*, 'point'] in the other.

From this moment on, they will be called 'wives' of the set of men who chose them, took them to the forest and above all gave them their names and ornaments. The mothers of those men, with specific functions in the ritual, all become 'mothers-in-law' to the girls. The men, in turn, will respect (through name avoidance, among other obligations) the mother and father of the Pyj as if they were their parents-in-law. This is a very peculiar kind of marriage, though, and not only because it is 'collective': unlike real wives, Pyj/Wyj women do not work. As Khôkhôtxi tells us:

> The girl who is a Wyj does not touch fire, does not clean game animals, does not eat their entrails, this is our custom …
> … The woman who is a Wyj-kuwêrê [real Wyj] does nothing but take care of her hands, comb her hair, paint herself with urucum, her hair is shining … Only later, after she marries and have children, will she become ugly.

This exemption from everyday female work in kitchens and gardens, and the focus on body care and decoration, is reaffirmed by Mbeni's narrative; both narrators also mention the custom of criticizing and teasing lazy girls by means of these figures. As Mbeni says:

> [a Pyj girl] does not work, stays there without working, with her ornaments, with 'necklaces' on their arms and ankles; when the mother goes to the gardens, 'let's get some manioc', she goes, but she sits on the fallen trunks and stays there, she cannot carry anything, the mothers carry manioc on their head but she doesn't. This is why when girls get lazy, mothers say: 'have you ever been amidst the people [men], is this why you do not work'?

The Pyj status can be revoked, and when a girl gets older and her career comes to an end, it may happen that one of their lovers decides to take her as his wife. Until this moment, however, all her efforts must be to remain beautiful.

In a certain sense, the shooting of the commercial corresponded to the installation of Giselle Bündchen as Pyj: Pyjmberi – 'Pyj-beautiful' – is the name by which she is now known among the Kĩsêdjê. (The name is also used to baptize the truck bought with the payment received from Grendene). It is hard to ignore the parallel between the Pyj category and that of our top models. Many times the Kĩsêdjê pointed it out to me, and although the parallel was not explored in the advertising material, it was not lost on the whites in, for example, the commentary in the entertainment and gossip magazine *Caras*: 'For the most majestic top model of the planet, they [the Indians] suggested traditional designs destined to women noted in the community for their beauty'.[10] Nevertheless, this was an ad hoc correspondence: the choice of the design was not conditioned by the analogy between those two 'roles', but was entirely due to the unavailability of any other female Kĩsêdjê pattern. Was this mere coincidence?

Here I will introduce a parallel with the music chosen by the Kĩsêdjê for the ad. The screenplay is clear: there has to be a 'rain dance'. The Kĩsêdjê choose the following song:

Krari
uu kukryrytxi na wa mõ ne pâj ne amã kê ingere roj iwi kameni ro mõ ne
we, king vultures, came, arrived, and danced to and fro for you
kukryrytxi na wa mõ ne pâj ne amã kê ingere roj iwi kameni ro mõ ka amã kini ro nhy na
we, king vultures, came, arrived, and danced to and fro for you, sitting there and watching

Sindo
ntonirytxi na wa mõ ne pâj ne khôkhô mã ká ra jatá ne
We, king vultures, came, arrived, and dressed the *khôkhô* [feminine ceremonial position] with clothes/skin
ntonirytxi na wa mõ ne pâj ne kôkô mã ká ra jatá kê kãmã anhi mbari kêt anhi jarêni ro ta na
We, king vultures, came, arrived, and the *khôkhô* said she was lost with the clothes/skin we dressed her with ['she said she didn't know how to wear it', the translator explains]

The choice of the song was, according to various reports, motivated by practical reasons: it was a well-known song that all men could easily sing, and it was not too long. A few incongruities were ignored: its belonging to the repertoire of 'bad water-turtle songs' (*khahrân kasáká*) traditionally performed during the dry season and the apparent contradiction in its performance as a 'rain song' were explained away by one Kĩsêdjê man who remarked that it was in fact a very appropriate choice, for these songs were performed in the dry season so that the rains may come again.[11] In any case, the important point is that a posteriori explanations of this sort – that is, to justify apparently or initially arbitrary choices of cultural elements (songs, designs, ornaments) to be transacted with non-Indians – are in fact recurrent. As a research assistant working on the transcription and translation of the song above observed: '[S]ee, that song tells of a woman that, putting on the clothes of the vulture, did not know how to wear it correctly. The same as Giselle with our body paint and ornaments'.

Two years after these events in 2008, in a completely different context, one of the indigenous teachers spontaneously offered to other, non-Indian interlocutors (Rafael Nonato, pers. comm. 25 May 2008) the following commentary on the choice of this song for the commercial:

> The song tells of a person who was ill. The birds took the soul to the sky. The person is sick, knows nothing of the soul. The birds dance with the soul. The person did not know, he was just sick. It was only after that he, feeling ill, slept and saw the soul up there, with the birds. He woke up and told the people: 'look, I think I will

live no more, I will die. Because my soul is up there with the birds.' Then he told of this dance to the people. 'Look, my soul dances like this with the people there [birds]. I will show you the dance, you must perform it.' Then his soul came back, and he survived again. This person almost died.

This is why we chose this dance for the ad. Because we thought: let's do this dance, since Giselle will in the future leave us and we will feel sad. Because she is the one who is famous, and we will be left with nothing. She will continue to receive more [money?] with her ad, we will receive nothing. She will pay only once, we will be left with nothing. Let's show this dance. So it was, this is the story.

I believe such remarks represent more than mere artificial or 'secondary' rationalizations of choices that, though arbitrary from a 'cultural' point of view, would follow from a purely instrumental logic commanded by the need to satisfy white partners with minimum effort and damage. Although factors of this sort were hardly absent, the interesting thing is that the symbolic meanings associated with the transacted cultural elements conditioned the interpretation the Kĩsêdjê came to make of the transaction itself. In this way, specific relations established by means of these transactions take form through those elements, and the objects transacted acquire new meanings. They now evoke, for instance, the new relations they worked to establish.

Coming back to Giselle's installation as Pyj, I believe that, as in the case of the song, they are not mere coincidence, nor mere manipulation, nor a deliberate intention to 'represent' one thing with the other (Giselle standing for the Pyj category or vice versa). What is at stake here is a certain form of creativity by which the rearrangement of certain cultural elements in the context of new social relations make those relations possible and give them an intelligible, meaningful form for the subjects. Giselle, the top model, in being painted as Pyj, is redefined as a kind of Pyj; but the Pyj design, once painted on Giselle, is itself redefined, for now it means also the relationships between the Kĩsêdjê and Giselle, Grendene and other non-Indians (since it will circulate among them as the signifier of a Kĩsêdjê 'identity'). This 're-signifying' process does not constitute an 'appropriation' in the proprietary sense of the term. Changing hands, in the transaction process, the cultural objects in question are themselves transformed, since they are constituted – reinvented – in terms of the new relations they now signify. In this sense, the Kĩsêdjê's careful choice and the control they tried to maintain over the 'appropriation' of their designs, ornaments, music and image by Grendene and the film producers were not aimed primarily at 'preserving the authenticity', the original form, of these elements taken as fixed, immutable, 'traditional' objects. More, they were meant to identify which aspects of their creations could be re-created in ways that would make the transaction meaningful – and make the objects thereby generated capable of signifying the same transaction for both the Kĩsêdjê and their partners. This same transaction would, of course, be signified *differently*: the Kĩsêdjê do not require (knowing it to be impossible) that the whites attribute to those objects the same meanings they do. A Pyj is not a top model. But if the Kĩsêdjê may treat Giselle as a Pyj and in this way have her stand 'amidst the people' while the whites continue to see her as a top model, then the transaction will have been successful. What is important is that the objects remain significant for both sides – not that their significance be the same. As in marriage exchanges: what is a wife to for me, is a sister for you, and it is this difference of perspectives that connects us (Viveiros de Castro 2004: 18–19).

The point of this creativity mode is to make this connection, which is essentially an exchange (of perspectives). This does not always work. Connection by means of separation supposes on the other hand that the alternate meaning attributed by the other be recognized and maintained as such: as an *other* meaning.[12] To suppose that it must be the *same* meaning is to make the exchange (which depends precisely on difference) impossible. Instead of giving rise to potentially productive equivocations (Viveiros de Castro 2004), it may cause very disabling disagreements. Let us look at one.

The Stolen Design: Contract and Exchange

The mode of creativity implied in this sort of *exchange* 'produces' objects with a social form that differs greatly from the commodity form apprehended in terms of property relations. Whereas 'property' refers to 'relationships between people with respect to things' (a traditional legal definition of some importance in anthropology), what distinguishes it from the social form of objects discussed here is precisely the strict distinction between people and things it supposes – a point to which I shall return below. Nevertheless, the objects in question here – 'intangible cultural assets' such as graphic designs and songs – have their owners, and just like the property rights we are familiar with, the 'rights' of those owners may be acknowledged, violated and transacted. Before discussing the episode the Kĩsêdjê interpreted as a breach of their rights, I will describe some events that may further the understanding of what kind of 'property' might be at stake for them.

Headdresses, Songs and Beads: Other People's Creations

As noted above, the Kĩsêdjê negotiating with Grendene over Giselle's decoration saw two things as non-negotiable: decorating a woman with male ornaments, and employing items not considered 'of the old Kĩsêdjê'. In the process, both constraints proved more flexible than they appeared.

The Kĩsêdjê know that the element of indigenous attire that most impresses whites is feathers, especially on headdresses. However, headdresses and feathers do not ordinarily form part of a woman's ensemble. Exceptions include one type of headdress for some female ritual positions (normally held by two women in each ceremony, accompanying the men in the performance of specific songs), and myth. But the Kĩsêdjê understand that, for whites, an Indian *must* wear feathers. Therefore they put a male headdress on Ngajsôjgrãtxi's head to assist in the composition of Giselle's decoration. But this flexibility has its own limits. The contract with Grendene provided that all materials, including indigenous designs, objects or images, should be previously approved by the Kĩsêdjê. So, a few days after the workshop, the advertising agency sent for their consideration a series of photographs featuring a 'clone' of Giselle dressed in different compositions of the various ornaments obtained in the village and elsewhere (from other indigenous groups).

The need to respond within two days made things difficult for the Kĩsêdjê – for practical reasons to start with, since it can take a full day to get from Canarana to the village, where the elders could see the pictures. More importantly, the period of time that is required for maturing positions and achieving consensus is often ignored by outsiders who expect that decisions can be taken through predefined hierarchical structures and representative positions. In any case, the Kĩsêdjê mobilized, took the photographs to the village, discussed the matter and communicated their impressions to me so that I could transmit them to Grendene on time. With one important exception, their objections were respected. Their message went like this:

> We think the photographs are in general beautiful and we liked the result. Our single reservation concerns the picture with the red/yellow [glass] beads necklace, that we think should not be used since beads are not an originally indigenous item – as we had already said to you in the village, during the workshop. About the black beads under the tucum necklaces, we think they are ok, since they don't show much and are there just to create volume. The headdress in that same picture does not seem to be worn properly. We would prefer headdresses to be worn as they are in the other pictures.

The objection to glass beads was bound to cause some surprise, given their wide diffusion among indigenous peoples. Their foreign origin should not be a problem in itself, since almost everything the Kĩsêdjê (like many other Gê peoples) consider part of their 'culture' (artefacts, ornaments, songs, ceremonies, names) has, ostensibly, in their own view, a 'foreign origin' (in encounters with other peoples or beings). The very designs that are the object of the transaction discussed here were, as we will see, acquired from fish and other peoples. So why did they object to beads?

Because, well, 'they are not an originally indigenous material', Winti Suyá, the then president of AIK, told me as he dictated the email to Grendene. This indicated we were dealing with a question of indigeneity, that is, identity. Indeed, the objection to beads echoed other reservations expressed during the shooting of the commercial (recommendations to avoid filming water tanks, electric wires, goal posts, etc.). But beyond this, beads were excluded for the same reason as were those cultural elements considered to belong to other indigenous groups. These exclusions express what I have called above the 'cultural fundamentalism' now prevalent among the Kĩsêdjê: the effort to extirpate, *in certain contexts,* 'foreign' elements (be they indigenous or nonindigenous). These contexts arise when such foreigners are themselves partners, actual or potential, in the transactions at stake. The problem with the headdresses – as with the body paint pattern – was precisely this. The objection to the picture of the Indian girl with the yellow headdress is its emblematic Xinguano character – 'everybody' has seen pictures of Xinguano Indians wearing those. The Kĩsêdjê make and wear such headdresses often, when they perform Xinguano ceremonies among themselves or with Xinguano guests. But they do not present themselves wearing them before white people – this is a Xinguano prerogative, since the presence of whites implies, as it were, the presence of the Xinguanos.[13]

This, by the way, was the motive for the first dissatisfaction the Kĩsêdjê expressed regarding the transactions with Grendene. In August, the advertising material – now the actual images of Giselle, instead of test photographs of her 'clone' – were sent to the Kĩsêdjê for their final approval. At first the chief denied the authorization because the model exhibited an impressive Xinguano headdress, against the recommendation expressed in the email. It is impossible to know whether Grendene did not understand the recommendation, or ignored it because of the aesthetic effect of the piece. The Kĩsêdjê ended up overlooking the problem, accepting the excuse that the advertising agency had included the headdress without Grendene's knowledge, and that those photographs would only appear in the packages – not on the TV commercial. A Kĩsêdjê friend commented: 'It didn't go wrong because in the small towns [around the Park] the sandals were not sold in their boxes with the photographs, they just hung them in the supermarkets, and the pictures with the headdress appeared only in magazines, not on TV. The people of the Upper Xingu did not see it, or else ...'

Interesting here is the specific way 'identity' is constructed by means of cultural objects and elements that are barely 'diacritical' and even less 'arbitrary'. Their selection may be contextual and relational, but is no less motivated because of that. A parallel may be traced with the negotiations for the publication of the Portuguese translation of Anthony Seeger's book, *Why Suyá Sing*. The second U.S. edition (2004) included a CD (the first, 1987 edition came with an audiocassette). The Brazilian edition will be accompanied by a DVD, a first version of which was presented to the community so they could authorize the images. I participated in the process, and noted in my journal:

> This morning we wrote the authorization for Tony's DVD. They asked him: a) to cut the voice and image of Ng. [a woman who had passed away in February 2005]; b) to suppress a Juruna song performed by Kĩsêdjê women. Kuiussi explained to me that this song was learned very recently, it is new, it belongs to the Juruna. It is different from the Upper Xingu songs, such as Tawarawanã or Djuntxi, and also from their designs, learned by the [Kĩsêdjê] people a long time ago: 'those are already ours'. He goes on: 'Aritana [an important Yawalapiti chief, sometimes presented as paramount chief of the Upper Xingu] has authorized us, he said "it is yours too."' This applies, he says, to graphic patterns used in body painting, but not the same designs when applied to objects (stools, paddles etc.). He comments that even the whites who come to buy these artefacts recognize the patterns as Upper Xinguano. This is why people here are using only Kĩsêdjê designs: *anhiro kutemtem, anhiro roptxi,* and the Pyj pattern.

Graphic patterns and ornaments such as headdresses, of Xinguano origin, learned more than a hundred years ago through dense, if ambivalent, social relationships, 'are already yours too', as Aritana said – but only in specific contexts and transactions. Objects made for sale, or images that will be transacted between the Kĩsêdjê and outsiders, are another matter. This was made clear to me when the president of AIK reported on the debate that the Grendene commercial had sparked at the meeting of the Indigenous Associations of the Upper and Middle Xingu in November 2007 at Diauarum. As I recorded in my journal:

> Winti tells me that they discussed ('seriously argued') about 'image rights': graphic patterns, ornaments.... The Wauja complained about the Xinguano armbands and body painting designs [used by the Kĩsêdjê extras in the movie]; the Kayabi complained about the necklaces.... They decided to debate the matter further at the next meeting / someone mentioned they should call an anthropologist for the discussion. [Another leader told me later that Winti said to the people there they could, on a future occasion, pay other people with similar claims (like the Wauja)].

No doubt the language of 'rights' must be refined to contemplate such distinctions. The objects and patterns in question 'belong' to the Upper Xinguanos as they belong to the Kĩsêdjê – and in this they differ from the Yudjá songs, which the Kĩsêdjê perform 'privately', but never 'in public'. In Seeger's DVD, they will appear singing Xinguano songs (Jamurikumã), but regarding transactions like those with Grendene more severe restrictions seem to apply. If the vocabulary of 'rights' must be improved, it is because there are many ways of 'owning' an object, and the differences among them go well beyond the right to alienate it or not. To whom it should be alienated, with what purpose, for how long and in what circumstances are primordial, not secondary, considerations. The form and nature of the transaction defines the relationships between transactors and objects transacted. The property model is obviously too poor to deal with such a logic.

The Cost of Nonpayment

The contract between the Kĩsêdjê and Grendene represents, perhaps, a model case of contractual transfer of 'cultural rights'. From the outset, all parties insisted on the need to ensure the community's broad control over all aspects of the process and project. This included not only control of the images to be publicized (which images, for how long, in which media, etc.) but control over the image of the Kĩsêdjê as a people – how they would be portrayed or represented. The contract, elaborated with the assistance of ISA lawyers, contemplated all those aspects.[14]

Before going into the episode of the 'theft' of the designs, I will briefly describe the latter. Of the drawings produced during the workshop, representatives of Grendene's product development department selected three patterns (all part of the five-pattern repertoire I had previously collected):[15]

1. *Anhi ro kũntêmtêm* ('[I made] a spiral on myself'): an element of male body painting used exclusively by initiated men that have already been through the ceremony of the *tutwa kandêjê* ('owners of the scarifier'), and so are allowed to use this title. They are painted this way every time they go *me sáktxêrê* (literally, 'call people'), that is, sing individually, walking the village circle for a whole day. It was learned from fish (Figure 6.9).

2. *Ndo sôkô* ('face design'): a facial pattern used by initiated men when performing individual songs (*me sáktxêrê*). It accompanies the body pattern described above (Figure 6.10).

3. *Tepsôk nhõ sôkô* ('lip plug design'): pattern applied to the lower face of the lip disk, which is made of a light wood (*tepsôkô*) that grows on the shores of the river. The Tapayuna acquired their design from the fish, through a shaman; the Kĩsêdjê acquired theirs from the Tapayuna (long ago, before they separated for the first time). It is

Figure 6.9 *The chief Kuiussi painted with the* anhi ro kũntêmtêm *and the* ndo sòkò *patterns. Ngójhwêrê village, Xingu Indigenous Park, Brazil, 2007. Photo: M.S. Coelho de Souza*

Figure 6.10 *The facial pattern* ndo sòkò. *Drawing produced during the Grendene workshop, Ngójhwêrê village, Xingu Indigenous Park, Brazil, 2006. Photo: M.S. Coelho de Souza*

worn only by initiated men. Today, with lip disks falling into disuse, it is being applied to the body and objects (Figure 6.11).

Of these three patterns chosen by Grendene and licenced for use under the terms of the contract, only the first was effectively applied to the sandals – the others appeared only in the packaging (boxes, labels) and

Figure 6.11 *The lip plug design painted on the Wadubati's back. Ngôjhwẽrẽ village, Xingu Indigenous Park, Brazil, 2007. Photo: M.S. Coelho de Souza*

advertising materials. Two other designs were presented but not chosen (they were left out of the contract). The first, *anhi ro roptxi* ('[I] made a jaguar in/of myself'), a prerogative of warriors (that is, men who have killed an enemy), has fallen into disuse, and there is some uncertainty about the correct manner of its execution. It is applied on the chest, stomach and back for log races and other ceremonies. It was learned from the Mesândjê, a people of similar language and culture with whom the Kĩsêdjê maintained close, sometimes matrimonial relationships, and from whom they also learned the practices of killers' ritual seclusion. The second corresponds to a basket weaving pattern (generally called *to syry,* 'woven') that the Kĩsêdjê themselves discarded, considering it to be pan-indigenous and thus unsuitable to figure in a transaction exclusively between themselves and Grendene.

Besides control over the 'images', the other critical question for the Kĩsêdjê was the payment for the graphic patterns applied to the sandals and for the use of their images to market the product. According to the company's proposal, the Indians would receive around a third of the total payment and the Y' Ikatu Xingu campaign would keep the rest. The ISA's counterproposal, which had Kĩsêdjê support, provided for an equal division of the total amount. There was also some discussion among the Kĩsêdjê over the absolute value of the payment, which they perceived as insufficient as it was understood that it would be made only once, whereas the designs would be available to the company for a lengthy period. However, the proposed amount would allow them to make reasonable investments on a then unprecedented scale, so they decided to accept the offer and leave the question of the time span of the permission open for later negotiations. As we will see, their apprehension was not unfounded: although a temporal limit was fixed by the contract, it was not respected.

Other ticklish details besides the amount complicated the payment. The contract included the following clause:

> The amount specified in the previous clause will be employed in community development projects executed by the Kĩsêdjê Indigenous Association, and may not be directed to the individual patrimony of any one of its members ('Instrumento particular de avença sobre direito autoral e de imagem' – preliminary version, clause 6.2).

This clause had already been relaxed. The company's initial proposal was to condition payment on the development of *specified* community projects with certified environmental sustainability and other such features, but it had been met with a counterproposal to apply similar requirements to the company's profits. Still, even the relaxed provision posed some difficulties for the Kĩsêdjê. This became clear soon after the shooting of the commercial, when the indigenous association realized it would need to pay the 'actors' – men and women who had participated in the shoot and whose images appeared in the ad – individually. The producers refused to pay them, arguing that despite their original proposal to contract with extras (who, being non-Indians, would of course have to be paid), the decision to participate had been taken by the Indians themselves. The total amount of the payment was therefore divided: half went to the purchase of a F4000 truck – baptized Giselle or Pyjmberi – and the other half to a fund to be distributed among participants according to their age and family status (unmarried youths received less than married adults).

The visit of the international top model boosted Kĩsêdjê prestige in the region. On the day she arrived, the mayor of the municipality rushed to the village to 'welcome' the celebrity, trying to take advantage of his diplomatic relationships with the real hosts (photos of him with Giselle in the village decorate his office in Querência and were published in the local newspaper). Besides the TV film, the advertising campaign, launched in September 2006, featured ads in magazines and outdoors. In the following months, Grendene sandals with Kĩsêdjê designs could be found in every supermarket in Brazil, including those in Canarana and Querência, and were soon on the feet of many Indian and non-Indian girls in both towns. The Kĩsêdjê received their share of the sandals and used the payment as they saw fit. The transaction seemed to have been a total success.

A year later in 2007, however, the Kĩsêdjê identified transformed renditions of their designs among Grendene's new collection. They called ISA, and a meeting with Grendene was arranged in Brasília. The company alleged that lack of communication between their creative department and the people that had arranged the contract with the Kĩsêdjê had resulted in an unfortunate 'error', given that the contract provided that any reuse of the designs would require a new contract, with new payments, approval of the product and accompanying material and so forth. It also argued that since one of the designs in question – a weaving pattern of embedded squares that had not been included in the original contract but now appeared on sandal straps – was pan-indigenous, it owed the Kĩsêdjê nothing on this account.

All parties agreed that a new contract, with a new payment, should be made, but the Kĩsêdjê also called for separate compensation for the breach of the first contract, as they had been unpleasantly surprised to find their designs stamped on the new sandals without their knowledge and with no acknowledgement of their origin. The company, however, considered payment of 'compensation' tantamount to an admission that the commercial relationship had been a failure. The transfer of money as reparation, they said, would be 'to sever' the relationship between the parties. So although agreement was reached on a total amount that was close enough to what the Kĩsêdjê intended, their effort to obtain some sort of recognition of the damages suffered was in vain. Nothing was paid in compensation. Even the letter of apology to the community that the company had promised to send – a document that would not be published – proved too much of an embarrassment for Grendene and never came. The Kĩsêdjê, as many people told me during the following months, did not find the agreement satisfactory. They had acquiesced in part because the association needed the money, and in part because other relationships were in question, notably Grendene's participation in the Y' Ikatu Xingu campaign and its partnership with the ISA. They did not say the experience was entirely negative, but they did say that if they repeated it, they would be more careful and assertive in their claims. I doubt that they would work with Grendene again. But things would be different if the company had materially demonstrated its good intentions and feelings, and its regret for the 'error', through compensation that, for the Kĩsêdjê, would precisely *not* sever the relationship, but facilitate its continuity instead.

From the indigenous point of view, subjective dispositions have to materialize in objective and visible correlates so that intentions, as well as knowledge, are clearly demonstrated. The intention is what counts, but payments are needed to 'count' it, that is, to objectify it. Therefore the name of the payment – compensation, not remuneration – more than its pecuniary value, became the focal point of disagreement. It was necessary to concretely distinguish the different dispositions activated in and through the transaction, that is, the past and the future of that transaction. A payment indicating the expectation of future increment (the renewal of the contract) was not the same thing, and could not mean the same thing, as a compensation signalling acknowledgement that damage had been inflicted and deserved reparation. What Grendene regarded as a contractual transfer of property-like rights to objects was seen by the Kĩsêdjê as an exchange in which those objects were indexes of intentions, subjective dispositions and the relational status of the partners and their mutual entanglement. These were what needed to be demonstrated.

Distributed Creativity

The 'protection' and 'preservation' of culture and knowledge (particularly knowledge associated with biodiversity or genetic resources) have became a prominent concern both for indigenous peoples and organizations, and for those who, inside or outside the state apparatus, are involved in the development and implementation of policies regarding those peoples. Public debate, largely organized in terms of notions such as heritage, tradition and property rights, often tends to ignore or minimize the specificity of indigenous regimes of knowledge production and circulation, reducing it to two aspects: the presumed 'collective' character of the subjects (the creators or holders of knowledge), and the supposedly 'traditional' nature of the objects involved (the cultural productions and the content of knowledge). Nevertheless, neither subject nor object, neither creator nor creature, normally behaves according to the expectations embedded in those assumptions.

The instability of the subjects that are being created as holders of rights through contracts and legislation concerning access to traditional knowledge – the proverbial difficulty of deciding who, that is, what persons or groups (peoples, communities etc.) are ultimately 'the owners' of the cultural knowledge or asset in question – corresponds, evidently, to the nature of Amerindian political constitutions, which know not, or better (according to Clastres' famous hypothesis), refuse the centralizing and unifying impulse that constitutes the principle of what we know as the State. So when rights are at stake – cultural or knowledge rights, for instance – they never arise as collective rights that can be unequivocally ascribed to peoples or groups, but rather as a vast network of heterogeneous prerogatives, entitlements and obligations that does not fit easily in the moulds of legal representation required by the contract form (Carneiro da Cunha 2009: 335–39). The way the Kĩsêdjê conceive of their 'rights' over songs, performances and ornaments, in relation to the 'rights' of Upper Xinguanos, Kayabi or Yudjá, reveals such a heterogeneity. The transaction, realized via the form imposed by the commercial contract, forcibly reduces and fixes this heterogeneity in ways that inevitably give rise to contestation. The Upper Xinguanos, Kayabi and Yudjá, for instance, have contested it. The debate between the Kĩsêdjê and Grendene concerning the weaving motif is symptomatic: not included in the contract because the Kĩsêdjê themselves considered it pan-indigenous and therefore not theirs to transact, it acquired a new meaning a year later, when the company used it with other, contracted designs now being reused without authorization. Along with the stolen designs, the motif – now called pan-indigenous *by the company* – seems to the Kĩsêdjê to be something they can claim as theirs because they showed it to Grendene – its ultimate origin is irrelevant. As the AIK president told me (in August 2007):

> Before our designs appeared to the world, they [Grendene] did not have all this variety; now, they modified our design and they do have it. The motif on the straps is everybody's [all Indians']; but before they [Grendene] didn't use it, after [they got] our designs they are using it.

It is not easy to harmonize this logic with a concept of 'collective rights' of a preconstituted subject over the object of its creation. First of all, as Amazonian ethnology has shown in recent decades, here, for the Kĩsêdjê as for other Amerindian peoples, almost everything that defines human culture came from the outside, or was obtained from exterior forces, in a movement that is essential to the mode of constitution and differentiation of entities and identities in Amazonia. This prevalence refers us back to a wide set of ethnographic topics (war, shamanism, death and the afterlife, etc.) and, in general, to the mythic theme of the acquisition of 'culture' itself, the obtaining of the apparatuses and practices that define a properly human life. In the Kĩsêdjê case, maize came from the mouse; fire from the jaguar; names, moieties and ornaments from a race of cannibal dwarves; lip plugs from the Tapayuna; songs from bees, vultures, trees and water turtles; manioc processing techniques and implements from the Upper Xinguanos, along with ceremonies like the Tawarawanã and Jamurikumã, and the practice of seclusion for adolescents. If Kĩsêdjê culture belongs to the Kĩsêdjê, it is surely *not* because they are its creators. Maybe creation and creativity need to be understood differently here.

The rooting of Euro-American notions of property in a certain conception of creativity, according to which created objects attest to the activity of the intellect and the labour of the human subject, appearing as extensions of that subject's own identity, is well known (and generally credited to John Locke). This 'appropriative creativity' (Leach 2004) depends on the abstraction of agency, will or purpose (human or, originally, divine) in relation to matter – matter that, recombined by this transcendent force containing in itself all and any innovative principle, must remain inert. Realized in the object, creativity cannot inhabit (and emanate from) it, because it is a prerogative of the subject, remaining thus contingent in relation to a world previously structured (Leach 2004: 162). In this difference between creative subjects and created objects, property is anchored as a relation among people with respect to (mediated by) things.

We are talking, then, about 'appropriation' in a 'proprietary' mode. This is very different from Amerindian appropriations, in which objects are less passive registers of a subject's capacities than personified objectifications[16] of their relationships, appearing not as simple *things* but as *persons,* for it is the mutual constitution of persons, their relational constitution, that is objectified in the objects they transact in their interactions. It is the relations that are creative, and this creativity is distributed in and by the objects. We can see this in the case of the shells, pigs and yams Melanesians famously exchange so passionately, but also of the rituals, cults, songs or myths that they keep, exchange, steal and licence among themselves with equal obstinacy, as they do people, like women given to other clans. If Melanesian practices are a 'gift' anthropologists have for some time now been circulating as a concept with very important *returns,* it is apposite, then, that I finish with a *return* to a Melanesianist, invoking the mode of 'distributed creativity' that Leach contrasts with the 'appropriative' one. In this distributed mode, recombinations are not the work of an intellect separated from matter; here, subjectivity exists distributed in objects, forming 'an animated landscape composed of different kinds of bodies in which change and effect are events with meaning on the same level as human actions' (Leach 2004: 169) – an 'intersubjectively constituted landscape [in which] all effects are caused by the actions of other subjects' (170). 'People' and 'things' appear then as indexes of capacities and powers the apprehension of which becomes the focus of the explicit practice of subjects.

Such a landscape is not unfamiliar to Amerindians, to whom every object is potentially a subject, or to whom, as has been suggested, an object is nothing but an incompletely interpreted subject, and '[t]o know is to personify, to take on the point of view of that which must be known' (Viveiros de Castro 2004: 468–69). Because of this, science here is shamanic – the aim of shamanistic interpretation being to access the 'covert agency' (Sztutman 2005: 158) behind phenomena. '[A] good interpretation, then, would be one able to understand every event as in truth an action, an expression of intentional states or predicates of some subject' (Viveiros de Castro 2004: 470).[17] And what such interpretations afford is a new relationship (with the subject or agent in question). The same is true of any creation: what the Kĩsêdjê 'discovered in their heads' by recreating the Pyj design – the knowledge they actualized – was not a pre-existing graphic pattern: it was a specific transformation of a pre-existent repertoire of forms and meanings in order to produce an object capable of signifying, to themselves and to their partners in that transaction, the intentions and dispositions capable of sustaining their new relationships. This was an operation that Grendene executives, unsurprisingly, did not know how to imitate.

Exchange against contract: Mauss saw the gift as the key to a theory of the origins of contract, whereas I am using the concept here in opposition to it, observing the contrast forced by Strathern between those two economies of the gift and of the commodity – one in which 'people and things assume the social form of things', and another in which they 'assume the social form of persons' (1988: 134) – in order to measure the impropriety of certain concepts, such as our concept of property, to appropriately determine and activate certain relations.

Marcela S. Coelho de Souza is Associate Professor of the Department of Anthropology at the University of Brasília. Her published works include 'The Future of the Structural Theory of Kinship' (2009), 'A Cultura Invisível: Conhecimento Indígena e Patrimônio Imaterial' (2009), 'A Vida Material das Coisas Intangíveis' (2012), and 'The Making and Unmaking of Crow-Omaha Kinship in Central Brazil(ian Ethnology)' (2012).

Notes

1. The commercial 'Rain Dance' is a Conspiração Filmes production, directed by Andrucha Waddington. It may be watched on YouTube. <http://www.youtube.com/watch?v=Jx9qVK0xLpA>.
2. In 2009 the Tapayuna resident among the Metyktxire built a separate village, Kawêrêtxikô, inside the Terra Indígena Capoto/Jarina ('Relações com outros povos' n.d.).
3. With the restructuring of FUNAI (Fundação Nacional do Índio, National Indian Foundation) in 2010, Indian posts were converted into Coordenações Técnicas Locais subordinated to a Coordenação Regional that manages the whole Xingu Indigenous Park. The Kīsêdjê have now an exclusive Coordenação Local, corresponding to the Wawi Indian post created in 2007.
4. A town of twenty thousand inhabitants at the border of the Xingu Park that flourished during the 1990s due to the expansion of soybean production in Mato Grosso. It is the main entrance to the park, and FUNAI, NGOs and most indigenous associations have offices there. I was based in Canarana throughout 2006.
5. Kuiussi Suyá is a man in his late sixties who, when still a teenager, became cacique, chief, of the Kīsêdjê following the death of his father (an important chief) and other older leaders in the first years of contact.
6. This is the translation provided by a research assistant for the expression *ataj karai kwã atumbaj kôt*, which refers, literally, to 'discover with/by means of thought'.
7. Ngajsôjgrātxi had left seclusion – a practice adapted from the Upper Xinguanos that aims at fabricating a beautiful and capable body endowed with the knowledge and moral dispositions that define a 'good girl' – less than a year before. She represented an ideal of beauty and exemplary behavior, and was in a category similar to that of the girls traditionally selected to receive Pyj names and designs, as we shall see.
8. Seeger (pers. comm.) also heard *kajngoro* as a term for striped objects – e.g. a species of fish with stripes that are, however, vertical (*tep kajngoro*). One of the chief's dogs is called Kaingoro; his stripes are also vertical, at least to my eyes.
9. The term is a cognate of the *wyty* [*wītī*, *vu'té*] timbira, which also indexes an important female ceremonial role (and secondarily a male one), associated with age moieties (see Crocker 1990: 278ff.; Melatti 1978: 302ff.; Nimuendajú 1946: 92).
10. Giselle Bündchen, A Top Dos Kīsêdjê, *Caras OnLine*, 17 October 2006. Retrieved from http://caras.uol.com.br/noticia/gisele-bundchen-a-top-dos-kisedje#image0.
11. Seeger specifies (pers. comm.) that those songs were performed at the end of the dry season, in September and October before the heavy rains – corroborating the explanation given to me. But the events described happened in May.
12. '[T]he aim is to avoid losing sight of the difference concealed within equivocal "homonyms"' (Viveiros de Castro 2004: 7).
13. That is, given the context of the Xingu Indigenous Park, it is impossible for the Kīsêdjê to relate to whites, or vice versa, without taking into account the existence of Upper Xinguanos (see Coelho de Souza 2010).
14. After the shoot, a supplementary clause was added to the contract, regarding the rights to (and payment for) the song performed in the commercial.
15. The names of the designs and their stories were narrated by the elders during the

workshop; from the recordings, indigenous teachers prepared texts that were later used in the advertising materials.
16. 'By objectification, I understand the manner in which persons and things are construed as having value, that is, are objects of people's subjective regard or of their creation. Reification and personification are the symbolic mechanisms or techniques by which this is done.' (Strathern 1988: 176).
17. Thus here, as in Melanesia, '[w]hat one encounters in making interpretations are always counter-interpretations' (Strathern 1999: 239).

References

Carneiro da Cunha, M. 2009. '"Cultura" e Cultura: Conhecimentos Tradicionais e Direitos Intelectuais', in M. Carneiro da Cunha, *Cultura com Aspas e Outros Ensaios*. São Paulo: Cosac and Naify, pp. 311–73.
Coelho de Souza, M. 2010. 'A Vida Material das Coisas Intangíveis', in E. Lima and M. Coelho de Souza (eds), *Conhecimento e Cultura: Práticas de Transformação no Mundo Indígena*. Brasília: Athalaia Editora, pp. 97–118.
Crocker, W.H. 1990. *The Canela (Eastern Timbira): I. An Ethnographic Introduction*. Washington, DC: Smithsonian Institution.
Leach, J. 2004. 'Modes of Creativity', in E. Hirsch and M. Strathern (eds), *Transactions and Creations: Property Debates and the Stimulus of Melanesia*. New York: Berghahn Books, pp. 151–76.
Melatti, J. 1978. *Ritos de Uma Tribo Timbira*. São Paulo: Atica.
Nimuendajú, C. 1946. *The Eastern Timbira*, trans. R. Lowie. Berkeley: University of California Press.
'Relações com outros povos'. n.d. *Povos Indígenas no Brasil*, Verbete Tapayuna, Instituto Socioambiental. Retrieved 18 November 2015 from http://pib.socioambiental.org/pt/povo/tapayuna/2259.
Schaden, E. 1965. 'Aspectos e problemas etnológicos de uma área de aculturação intertribal: o Alto Xingu', *Aculturação Indígena*. *Revista de Antropologia* 13: 65–102.
Seeger, A. 1980. 'A Identidade Etnica Como Processo: Os Indios Suyá e as Sociedades do Alto Xingu', *Anuário Antropológico* 78: 156–75.
———. 1981. *Nature and Society in Central Brazil: The Suyá Indians of Mato Grosso*. Cambridge, MA: Harvard University Press.
———. 2004 [1987]. *Why Suyá Sing: A Musical Anthropology of an Amazonian People*. Urbana and Chicago: University of Illinois Press.
Strathern, M. 1988. *The Gender of the Gift: Problems with Women and Problems with Society in Melanesia*. Berkeley: University of California Press.
———. 1999. *Property, Substance and Effect: Anthropological Essays on Persons and Things*. London and New Brunswick, NJ: The Athlone Press.
Sztutman, R. 2005. 'Sobre a Ação Xamânica', in D. Gallois (ed.), *Redes de Relações nas Guianas*. São Paulo: Associação Editorial Humanitas / NHII, pp. 151–226.
Viveiros de Castro, E. 2004. 'Perspectival Anthropology and the Method of Controlled Equivocation', *Tipití: Journal of the Society for the Anthropology of Lowland South America* 2(2): 3–23.

CHAPTER 7

Doubles and Owners
Relations of Knowledge, Property and Authorship among the Marubo

Pedro de Niemeyer Cesarino

> "Everything ought to have an owner"
> (Henry Maine, *Ancient law*)[1]

On the coast of Papua New Guinea, an anthropologist observed something familiar to visitors to Amazonian villages. A fruit tree that seemed to her to have 'grown there of its own accord', notes Demian (2004: 60–61), was revealed during her interactions with the local population to be 'an index not only to a land boundary but the history of one or more lineages who have resided upon that land'. Something similar occurs with the Marubo, a Panoan-speaking people of the Vale do Javari Indigenous Reservation (Brazil).[2] At most, everything for the Marubo has a master or owner: trees, whether they be the wild kapok or the cultivated mango, but also peccaries, tapirs or oropendolas, are indexes of social relations. The relationship involved in the notion of ownership implies, of course, presuppositions that differ as much from those held by Maine (see epigraph) as from those of the peoples of Papua New Guinea on whom Demian reflects. Under what regime of relations can an element of the landscape be an index here? What set of concepts is expressed in the notion of master/owner?[3] 'Owner' is a translation of the Marubo term *ivo*, cognate of *igbo* (Shipibo-Conibo), *ibo* (Kaxinawá), *ifo* (Sharanawa), among others found in the Pano family of languages.[4] A married man is said to be master of his longhouse, *shovõ ivo*), or of a section of the house in which he lives. Although there is no fixed rule, Marubo houses are usually composed of a shaman-chief (*kakaya* and *kēchītxo* respectively), his sons and daughters, and sons- and daughters-in-law.[5] Each of the nuclear family units has its own swidden (garden) and its own responsibility to obtain game meat. Food is shared in collective household meals on the central patio (*kaya naki*): men eat sitting on parallel benches, *kenã*; women, on the floor. At mealtimes, the owners of the family sections carry their plates of food out to the collective space. The plates are put at the feet of the other relatives and, little by little, are refilled up by the children and women, who move from behind the backs of the men. At the end of the meal, the cups, cutlery, plates, baskets and bags of salt must be quickly removed and put away. Each person is responsible for taking her or his things – each spoon or cup must go back to its original section of the house. There is nothing that belongs to a supposed 'collectivity' (except, and according to a particular position, the space itself in which the commensals sit).

It is unacceptable to take the fruit of any tree without first asking permission from its owner, that is, the inhabitant of the nearest house who planted it. One does not randomly enter the swidden of another. Creeks, river beaches, hunting trails: everything is subject to the sphere of influence of a particular house. Hunting in the territory of a neighbouring chief can lead to political complications, which feed into old disputes between the segments of Marubo social morphology, the *–nawavo*. There is no no-man's-land, and the territorial delineations brought about by the dynamic of ownership extend beyond the reach of the visible *socius*. The link that is established there certainly cannot be described in terms of either the modern notion of private property or its opposite, the myth of primitive collectivism. When investigating other possible formulations of possession or property as they are elaborated by the Marubo, one must keep sight of their specific relationship with the problem of authorship in shamanic knowledge.[6]

A forest tree whose wood can be used to construct a canoe can only be cut down by a particular house owner's relatives or allies, at the risk of invading other people's area of influence. While doing so, they must also be careful of possible retaliations (*kopía*) caused by the doubles (*vaká*) – the masters of what, to the living, appears as a tree. I never witnessed blessings or prayers before the cutting of a tree, but there is always a risk that its double may avenge itself on the person who cuts it down and in future manifest itself as an acute pain in the wrists or arms of the worker. Something similar might be observed with the treatment of game. Peccaries are killed in droves and brought to villages without further care over the possible suffering of the animals – they are merely 'his animal' (*awẽ yoĩni*) or 'his carcass' (*awẽ shaká*), meaning the animal or carcass of his humanoid master. It is this animal extension of the humanoid doubles that provides meat (*nami*) for meals.

The expression I have just used to describe the relationship between 'animals' and 'doubles' is less simple than it appears. An 'animal' will always be the animal *of* and *for* somebody, that is *of the double* who, together with the carcass, composes what I have elsewhere called 'singularity' (see

Cesarino 2011a). A singularity is something made up of the carcass/animal and the double, whether this be personified in a human-like aspect (*kayakavi keská,* 'like a human') or not (*kayakavima,* 'different from a human'). When a singularity has a human-like aspect, the double may well repay any aggression against its animal, which usually is the meat consumed by humans. The relationship between the two terms is one of *possession* and *reflexivity*: the Marubo language uses possessive pronouns and reflexive suffixes to express this type of relationship. In Marubo, one does not say anything along the lines of 'every animal is a person', a universal proposition. One says that 'for themselves [e.g. tapirs] understand themselves as people': *ari ã tanáro yorarvi.* To understand oneself as person immediately implies *having* a double, that is, a human-like subjectivity. Having a double implies in turn establishing a possessive link with a particular body. 'This is its carcass, its double is really a person' (*aro awẽ shaká, awẽ vakáro yorarvi*). A double is conceived of as a person, but the same term that refers to 'people', *yora,* is also used to say 'body'. The 'doubles' are not ethereal or fleeting entities, evanescent and immaterial souls, but rather (and reflexively, that is 'for themselves') bodies.

Some animals do not possess a defined 'human' image. There is not exactly a village of peccary-people or of tapir-people. Tapirs, in any case, are under the influence of a spirit-person, *Mīshō,* the 'master of animals' (*yoĩni ivo*) (Viveiros de Castro 2002: 354). *Mīshō* keeps them enclosed in a kind of corral (*kene*) and frees them from time to time – or else withholds them (*wachia*) from an incautious hunter who may have wasted its meat or thrown away its entrails. Peccaries and tapirs are *involved* by their masters in the corrals that enclose them, in a way that is homologous, as will be seen, to the way in which humans shelter themselves in their houses. Birds, meanwhile, have a defined 'human' image and a prototypical sociality. Several narratives of a markedly perspectivist stamp develop the relations established between their doubles and humans.[7] To shoot an oropendola (*isko*) in flight can be extremely risky: from far off, in its house, its double watches over its carcass through a snuff inhaler (*rewe,* a tubular instrument of mediation). It then sends a *rome* projectile to the person, who falls ill. The doubles of birds (*chaĩ vaká*) are their masters and their 'carers' or 'protectors' (*awẽ vesoyavo*). They are also shamans and house masters, frequently visited by the *romeya* shamans, whom I shall discuss shortly. The myriad bird-peoples are in turn under the influence of *Chai Roka,* Roka-Bird, the master of them all. His human correspondent is *Shokô Roka* (Roka-Shed, who receives the doubles of the dead in the Home of the Sky-Shed, *Shokô Naí Shavaya*).[8] Here too he lives in the celestial plane as a house master, together with his wife and his brood of peccaries.[9]

Note that this personifying cosmology does not presuppose a hierarchization of entities (as a counterexample, Leibniz's *Monadology* postulates

God as the omniscient point of convergence of the hierarchized infinity of monads), but rather a replication of the intensive field of 'human' and its generic form, that is, 'master'.[10] 'Masters' agglomerate social spaces and dynamics of kinship. Masters involve or encompass potentially dispersive multiplicities, but they do not unite or totalize parts and fragments, confer vitality to inanimate matter, represent individuals, exercise authority by the transfer of right, or impose property relations upon 'things' (though they might upon 'relations', if this provisional approximation to a certain anthropological definition applies [Hann 1998: 4ff.]). 'Master' refers to the prototypical form of personified doubles, that is, of that species of entity 'equipped with an intentionality analogous to the human' (Viveiros de Castro 2002: 354) that, together with the body-carcass, completes a singularity.

The break between the two aspects of any particular singularity implies distance in time and in space. Very often, the doubles/masters are distant from their corresponding corporeal bodily supports. Kanãpa, a prayer shaman, told me once that the masters of gasoline (*gasorĩ ivo*), for example, are its makers (*a shovimaivo*), who live far off in the cities of the white people while the liquid is stored in jerry cans in the village. The internal doubles of a person also have a different time of growth from the bodily support that envelops them. Very often – as in the case of gasoline, or of a house, whose owner is the person who inhabits it – the master/double is described as *its maker*, that is, that subjectivity that originates or forms the corporeal support or the visible carcass for the human position or the relational field.

It is from this point that Marubo cosmology presents a self-similar pattern, once the unlimited *socius* replicates itself through the division between doubles and bodies. The multiplicity that constitutes the Marubo cosmos is a multiplicity of owner-masters, whether they be those of the collectivities referring to the bodies of anacondas, peccaries, the ultramarine grosbeak birds, the kapok tree, houses, or those of other elements that we habitually call 'materials'. Doubles can also at this point be translated as 'spirits', if by this we refer, as Viveiros de Castro (2006: 321) suggests, to a notion of 'intensive virtual multiplicities'– of the 'infinitesimal citizens of the virtual arqui-*polis*' (323), in an expression used to describe certain homologous entities, the *xapiripë* of the Yanomami. This is not merely a matter of ethnographic rhetoric. It reflects how one Marubo decided to visualize the body of a *romeya* shaman in a drawing, in response to questions from anthropologist Delvair Montagner, who pioneered fieldwork at the Upper Ituí villages. (Firmínio Marubo, apud Montagner 1996, republished in Cesarino 2011).[11] The drawing was, at once, a cosmogram and a diagram of the shaman-person. The form 'house master' is replicated throughout the infinite multiplicity of 'spirits', animal doubles and other entities. A man outfitted with two *paka* lances, bandoliers crossed on his chest, feather headdress and various ornaments: this is the image of the owner/chief of the house, consistently represented in designs by the shamans I worked with almost three decades after Montagner. 'In this sense', writes Fausto (2012: 32), 'rather than being a representative – that is, someone occupying the place of another – the master-chief is the form through which a collectivity is constituted as an image: it comprises the form in which a singularity is presented to others' (also see Viveiros de Castro 2006: 325). Indeed, although consistently described in the singular in designs and *iniki* shamanic songs, a master/chief carries with him or embeds within himself all of his collectivity, that is, his relatives, those with whom he resides in a house. There are no solitary individuals, only members standing out from a collectivity. This is evident in various drawings produced by the Marubo at my request,[12] including the following:

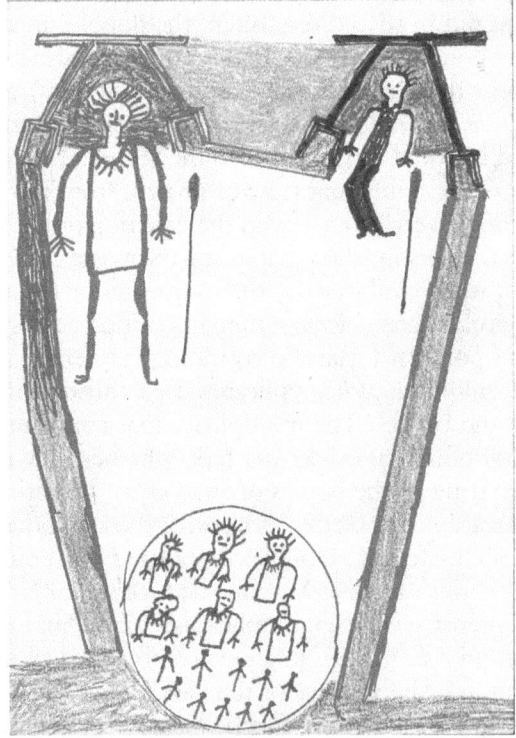

Figure 7.1 *Paulino Joaquim Memãpa, 'Earth Planting Spirits' (coloured pencil, graphite and watercolour on paper, 210 x 297 mm, 2005), collection of Pedro Cesarino*

The *yovevo* spirits keep the prototypical image of the ancestors (*shenirasĩ*). Despite unlimited variations, they maintain all of their bodily adornments, facial tattoos and paraphernalia: this is how their chief (*awẽ kakaya*) comes to present himself to his relatives in the shamanic sessions that occur in the houses. Not all of the spirits/doubles/masters possess this ancestral image: the sun's double (*varĩ vaká*), for instance, is also a house owner, but his house is of stone; he is bearded, hunts with dogs and guns, wears clothes and a straw hat, and indeed is a stranger, *nawa*. The same applies to the doubles of gasoline (*gasorĩ yochĩ*), who, as we have seen, are its makers and live in white people's cities. Whether they have an image of ancestors or of strangers, what matters above all is that the owners maintain a sociopolitical configuration: they are maloca owners, 'magnified singularities' (Fausto 2012: 32) who envelop or enclose their relatives.

It has been thus since the times of the emergence. In Marubo mythology a series of episodes describe the deeds of owner/masters. Kana Voã, the demiurge, was already a house owner before these 'humans' (the Marubo) came into existence. The way the shaman Paulino Memãpa chose to represent him is significant: he appears as a male owner and chief holding spears in front of his house. To his right is his nephew, Roe Iso. Both spirits emerge from the circle that is at the bottom of the image and then go on their way until they establish themselves in their villages, represented in the upper section of the drawing:

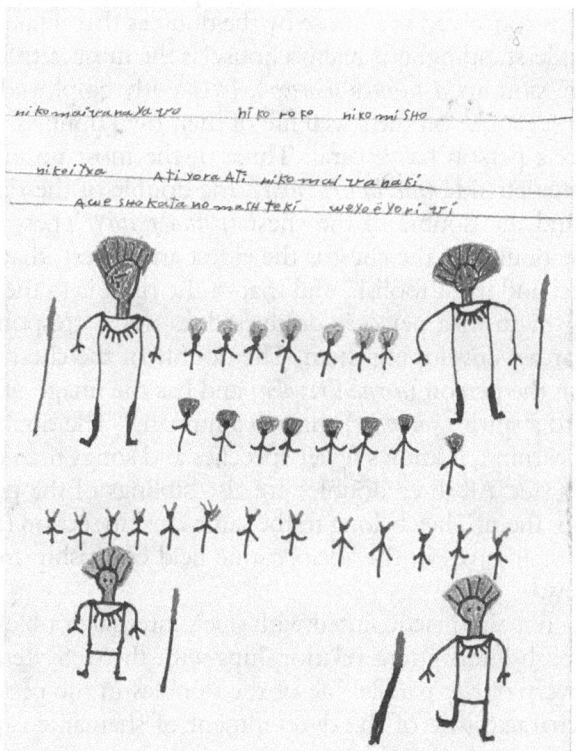

Figure 7.2 Paulino Memãpa, 'The Emergence of Kana Voã' (*coloured pencil, graphite and felt tip pen on paper, 210 x 297 mm, 2005), collection of Pedro Cesarino*

This is why Kana Voã, Roka and other important demiurge spirits in this cosmology resist the translation as 'god', to which the Marubo nevertheless sometimes resort – always, however, making use of similes (*matõ deos keská,* 'it is like your god', meaning they are already *something else*) (Cesarino 2011a). The owners and positions that constitute the pre- and post-emergence cosmos configure an ontology of multiplicity that is radically distinct from Western conceptions of private property and metaphysical monisms.[13]

Internal Multiplicities

The replication unleashed by the split between doubles and bodies does not extend only to animals, distant spatial dimensions or the dominions of the *yovevo* spirits, who live, from their own point of view, as chiefs of their houses in the celestial, terrestrial planes and many other locations. The Marubo person itself ('living' or 'human') is also a configuration marked by the break between doubles and bodily support. Our body (*yora*) or carcass (*shaká*) is conceived as a house by the doubles that inhabit it. 'According to its understanding, it is really a house' is the most faithful translation of the expression *ari ã tanáro shovorvi,* frequently employed by Marubo shamans to speculate on the social life of their own doubles.

Of these, a person has several. Three of the most important are the double of the left side (*mechmiri vaká*), the double of the right side (*mekiri vaká*) and the double of the chest (*chinã nató*). These are a trio of siblings: the double of the chest is the eldest and wisest, that of the left is the youngest and most foolish, and that of the right is in the middle. The period of growth of a person's doubles does not correspond to that of the body/carcass enveloping them. The double of the chest for example, is older than the person (*a vaká vevoke*) and has the image of an ancestor; it is closer to a spirit (*yovepase*) than to a human.[14] The double of the left side is still learning, it knows fewer speeches and songs than does its elder brother or sister. All three doubles are also siblings of the person-carcass that envelops them. They belong to the same kinship section (the *–nawavo*) and orient themselves in the sociocosmic field of kinship from a similar point of view.[15]

One may remain unacquainted with one's internal doubles throughout life or establish intermittent relationships with them. Systematic contact – the discovery of the parallel life of the doubles in the person's internal *house* – is characteristic of the development of shamanic capacities. The doubles live in this body, which they regard as a *house.* There they develop the same social relationships we do: they live with their children and relatives; they are 'owner/chiefs' of their (internal) collectivities; they leave the house, visit other people and call them to into their homes. Hence the problem of shamanism: how to mediate the 'excess of owners' and collectivities that populate the multiplicities?

When it comes out of the house, the 'chest double' of the person establishes relationships with the other *yovevo*[16] spirits that live in their houses. There they acquire songs and rituals, choreographies and graphic patterns, names, narratives, and many other forms of knowledge, which they transmit to the people upon returning to their domains. The shamanic sessions are moments in which a *romeya*, lying in his hammock, allows his double to come out of his internal *house* so that other spirits go in there to sing. The doubles come out of their internal house to live elsewhere and learn. The person-carcass is thus favoured: he/she becomes more intelligent, better able to memorize the long and complex curing songs.

'Every theory of property', writes Simon Harrison (1992: 238), 'is necessarily a theory of the person'. The possible reinventions of the notion of property for the present case depend on contemplation of the composition of the multiple person, which illuminates the status of creation and authorship in a shamanistic regime of knowledge. But the particular notion of the person that is being outlined here is different from the presupposition of 'identity' that, even in Harrison (1992: 238, 239), seems to dominate. The person is above all a point of confluence for the alterities suspended in the virtual.[17] The circulations of knowledge realized through a gift regime refer here not to identitary reifications but to recursive dynamics and to processes of transformation.[18]

Authors and Changers

Marubo epistemology is associated with an ontology of multiplicity and its intrinsic connection to the process of personifying replication. Knowledge does not come from an individual creative subject, but from the displacements that doubles establish in an undefined field of positions. The replication of the *socius* in the internal dimension does not lead to idioms of interiority that refer to modern metaphysics, in which the figure of the author tends to gravitate around individuals and regimes of appropriation. Moreover, songs, graphic patterns and rituals originating in various positions in the cosmos penetrate Marubo 'culture' or 'people' in a complex way. On different levels, Marubo shamanistic thought seems as much opposed to processes of appropriation of discourses as it is to identitary reifications and the problems of solipsism. Then again, an additional complexity emerges when shamanism finds itself confronted with the Western lexicon and starts to formulate its own translations of dilemmas, concepts and impasses brought into relationship with the nonindigenous world (Carneiro da Cunha 2009; also see Coelho de Souza this volume).

The examination of this (imminent) meeting of conceptual regimes must be accompanied by an investigation of the possible meanings of 'authorship' before Marubo shamanism arrives at a more radical confrontation with the institutions of copyright and intellectual property. The elements coming from the outside are responsible for the formation of the meaning of what tends to be called (often by Marubo themselves) Marubo 'culture': kept or transmitted by their shamans, these elements suggest a possible idea of authorship that has nothing to do with the generic image of primitive collectivism still present in Brazilian and Western common sense.

We are, after all, quite far, in the words of Antonio Risério (1993: 29), 'from the belief that these "pre-logical" poets had not dislocated themselves sufficiently from their social milieux to raise themselves to the level of creative individuality ... as though they were nothing more than mere ventriloquists of culture'. Risério is correct to underline this still-common presupposition. He refers to Anthony Seeger and his well-known ethnography of the *akia* songs of the Suyá to list some manifestations of 'authorship' in the 'creative texts' (this is his expression) of others: the existence of a 'repertoire in progress, not stationary' (argument of creativity and innovation); the correct execution that is not later forgotten; the 'individual intention' discernible in the musical structure and style of a song, not to mention signatures (repetitions of names) that appear in certain non-Western creative texts (Risério 1993: 30). Risério rightly points out the existence of authorship in such domains, but I think that the reflection needs to be taken further. It is not enough to describe immediate expressions like style, novelty, intention or signature. Its meanings and effects must also be investigated, starting with the presuppositions that underlie Amazonian creative regimes.

Let us deepen this reflection through an examination of structures and strategies of enunciation mobilized in the verbal arts pertaining to Marubo shamanism (Cesarino 2011a). For now I will limit it to a few dilemmas, such as those related to the inadequacy of the notion of the individual for the comprehension of the multipositionality and multiplicity constituting the Marubo person and its reflections in the enunciative structure of shamanic songs. It is significant that a possible 'novelty' does not originate in the creations related to any individual author, let alone in a reified 'culture', but comes from other sources – the Inca, from Kapok Spirit-People, from anaconda-shamans, from school, from Brazilians – before they are familiarized in the field of kinship. The 'signatures' that a possible author inscribes on his or her aesthetic expressions certainly serve to augment the image of their magnified person (generally a shaman and chief) and that person's performative efficacy and locquaciousness. Even thus, they do not make reference to the random and contingent traces of the creative capacity of the person or his or her[19] internal intellectual abilities, but instead to the capacities of connection with the virtual field of knowledge, based on the tasks of quotation, mediation and transmission, which roughly characterize the epistemological constraints involved in the verbal arts and their respective ritual dynamics. The person must make or construct him or herself in a determined way, through specific rituals involving the consumption of psychoactive agents, in order to become capable of carrying out these tasks of translation (Carneiro da Cunha 1998).

At different points in its development, the idea of authorship in the West itself has offered relevant contrasts with this case. Of course, one cannot posit Western thought as a monolithic counterpoint to Marubo shamanism. Foucault (2009: 47), for instance, says that even in the West, discourse was first conceived as an act and only thereafter as a thing of commodity. In the *Vocabulaire des institutions indo-européennes,* Émile Benveniste (1974) observed that the semantic field of 'author' is related to an action, movement or promotion, as in the power of words performed by a position of authority. A formulation of the problem of authorship in a different context from that of Benveniste's work serves here as another counterpoint to the present case. In one of the founding texts of modern political thought, Hobbes (1996: 112) formulates the problem in the following terms:

> Of Persons Artificiall, some have their words and actions *Owned* by those whom they represent. And then the Person is the *Actor*; and he that owneth his words and actions, is the AUTHOR: In which case the Actor acteth by Authority. For that which in speaking of goods and possessions, is called an *Owner*, and in latine *Dominus,* and Greeke χύριος; speaking of Actions, is called an Author. And as the Right of possession, is called Dominion; so the Right of doing any Action, is called AUTHORITY and sometimes *warrant*. So that by Authority, is always understood a Right of doing any act: and *done by Authority,* done by Commission, or Licence from him whose right it is.

Thus, in a reflection on the social contract, the figure of the author is equated with that of the owner. In the case at hand, it seems coherent to say that shamans effect a movement: they 'promote' certain events in which songs, choreographies or teachings come to the surface. They constitute a certain regime of authorship that differs radically from the institutions projected by the Hobbesian regime of property, for example. The meeting or the occurrence of the personified myriad in the figure of the shaman does not transform him into a political figure marked by unity, that is, by the transferral of multiple authorities into a determined representative. The shaman does not speak for others, does not represent the original authority of another as an agent, but rather replicates the words of others, transporting or mediating like a radio.[20] Hence the special discursive strategies of shamanistic poetics. The use of the reportative *–ki*, in Marubo and other Pano languages, indeed serves to circumscribe or maintain the authority of the words of others in their own registers, even when they are integrated into complex polyphonic enunciations (Cesarino 2011a; Viveiros de Castro 1986).

Once, however, the shaman Armando Cherōpapa, from whom I was recording *iniki* spirit songs, suddenly made a request: 'I want to hear *my* songs'. The same figure who had several times told me that songs were from others, that they were the words *of the spirits* (*yovevo vanarivi, atō narvi*),[21] seemed at that moment not to regard himself as a holder of the enunciations of others. More than the property of particular intangible goods, though, what Cherōpapa seemed to want to indicate was a movement capable of circumscribing a certain dominion of authority in his mediations of the words of others – a 'bringing-into-play', so it seemed, to use the terms of Agamben's (2007: 61ff.) consideration of the reflections of Foucault referred to above. The categories relating to literature and to the work of art may not translate so easily into the dilemmas of shamanic thought, but the *position* granted there to a certain figure of authorship is nonetheless interesting. The movement in question, however, is precisely contrary to the immediate image of anonymity and absence of authorship transmitted by shamanistic regimes of attribution: this is indeed why the shaman (or his body/carcass) remains *apart*, allowing other voices to come onto the scene (not as literary characters, but as actual persons) and recognizes himself (and must be recognized) as the author of his songs. Such a position, in fact, is what guarantees the functioning of the complex polyphonic configurations and their enunciative amalgamations characteristic of shamanic songs such as the Marubo *iniki*, the Kuna *ikar* and the Kayabi and Araweté *maraká*, among others.

Not coincidentally, the *romeya* are named *yove vana ikiya*, 'those who cite the speech of spirits' Their imprinting of memory and experience with knowledge that is transmitted is another element associated with the regime of authorship involved there. With their inaugural gesture, they promote and make possible a particular ritual event and thus differ from the solipsistic modern (but not necessarily contemporary) creation.

Modes of Creativity

This brief overview of some aspects of the problem of authorship only aims to map some dilemmas concerning the decentralization of the 'author function' related to Marubo shamanism. Directly associated with such dilemmas are the specific types of creation that are linked to Marubo mythopoesis. Every owner is also a *shovimaivo,* something like 'maker' or 'creator': the maker of a canoe, a house, a necklace. But there is not exactly one *shovimaivo* of *iniki, shoki* or *saiti* songs or *kene* graphic patterns, which are reproduced or imitated (*tekia, naroa*) through a network of knowledge.[22] The *saiti* myth-songs refer, however, to deeds of the *shovimaivo,* which are spirits who once 'made' or 'assembled' the land and might return to sing in shamanic sessions. The mythical process by which the world was assembled does not resemble creation *ex nihilo* or the monological imperatives of Genesis.[23] Moreover, the 'makers' of the time of emergence used existing elements to mount/compose the first landscapes. This was not exactly done through a 'mysterious quality or power' like that which substantiates Indo-European conceptions of creation and authorship, as Benveniste showed. Or was it? The Marubo themselves translate *chinã* as 'life'; it is an attribute of animals and of the house (*shovo chinã aya*), but not of a canoe (*noti chinã yama*; see Cesarino 2011a). It comprises, as we have seen, the name of the person's eldest double, the *chinã nató*. Although it assumes the features of a *mana*-term, its role in the creative configurations in question is rather peculiar: those who use it in a competent way (shamans) do not project themselves over other people as 'teachers of truth' or keepers of dynastic and courtly knowledge (see Detienne 1967). On the contrary, they justify their competence by their ability to articulate in a horizontal and intensive field where 'owners/masters' proliferate to infinity. *Chinãivo yora,* 'thinking people,' is a fairly rough translation for the designation of shamans (real and virtual) who, with their 'thought-words' (*chinã vana*), constantly change the processes, agencies and configurations of the world.

The owners/chiefs, as we said, have been present in their sociological form since mythical times. The protagonists of the *Koĩ Mai Vana saiti* narrative, the 'Foreign Earth-Mist' song-myth, correspond to those of a drawing (see Figure 7.2) highlighted above: chiefs equipped with spears and body adornments standing in front of their *houses*; visual extensions of their collectivities. The *saiti* song, which deals with the formation of the world (see Cesarino 2013a for full translation), is composed of scenes of dialogues between spirits of ancient times who then decide to 'make' (*shovima*) or 'cause the emergence' (*wenima*) of the world, first through the use of certain psychoactive substances (ayahuasca (*Banisteriopsis caapi*), the angel's trumpet flower (*Brugmansia sp.*) and tobacco).[24] But such psychoactive agents or elements precede the emergence of the spirit demiurges themselves from their 'winds'. With regard to contemporary shamanism, the connection between 'plants', or psychotropics, and forms of knowledge and emergence also comes to the foreground. The 'owner of ayahuasca' (*oni ivo*), called Ayahuasca Bud (*Oni Shãko*), is one who thinks (*chinã*) through the shaman by blowing into his ear (*Oni Shãko mĩ peshotka*, 'Ayahuasca Bud comes up behind him') the complex chain of poetic formulas that compose a healing song. The person who is not familiar with Ayahuasca Bud – which is possible only through the progressive intake of tea made from *his* plant – cannot learn to speak and does not understand the songs and words codified in ritual speech. Here, once again, the image of the master is mobilized in central dynamics of the shamanic 'creative' process. This image, by the way, is not restricted to the Marubo, as we can see in Déléage's (2006: 270–71) account of Sharanawa shamanic songs. Although the recursive model that applies to the Marubo case is less explicit in Sharanawa ethnography, the complex status of spatiality, interiority and exteriority that also characterizes this shamanism remains notable.[25] There is here a pervasiveness that is of great importance: the same entity can be located in two places (the masters are in their homes but are also in the belly of the singer). It is as if the two references coincided at one and the same point of actualization (the shaman's body) – in other words, as if the visionary experience were an ability to change or perceive that the kernel of knowledge is elsewhere, though nevertheless potentially within the person. The privileged image for this external source of knowledge is, again, that of the owners/masters, yet they are moved or displaced from their centres, susceptible to extending or replicating their positions for those of the singing shamans.

Marubo shamanism and mythopoesis are thus based on processes of transformation (in relation to complex *shōki* song-thoughts as much as to the *saiti* song-myths and the *iniki* spirit-songs). In *shōki*, the singers make use of an 'agentive thought' accomplished through poetic formulas belonging to a virtual inventory (Cesarino 2011a, 2011b). Although I cannot enter into the details of this scheme and its processes of transformation, it is worth noting that the stock of formulas (visible in the song fragments quoted above) are not exactly found at the boundaries of Marubo 'culture' or 'tradition', or of the individual creativity of a shaman (unless one reinvents the notions of culture, tradition and creativity). The poetic formulas were conceived in mythical times by the spirits. They constitute an open structure of combinations, substitutions, concatenations and recompositions updated at any time by shamanism. They come from a wide variety of speakers, some identifiable to the visible *socius* (the Marubo) and some belonging to the multiplicity of entities and spirits that often come to sing on earth. Mythopoesis configures a two-way process of descent and ascent between virtual and actual, in which information and schemes of combination are at all times retrieved from the background of the sociocosmos and simultaneously sent back to the virtual in the form of innovations.

The source of such knowledge will always be attributed to another: the shaman's own brother/double who, living in far-off places, has become a powerful entity and teaches him to sing from a distance or within his body/longhouse; the double/owner of ayahuasca, snuff or angel's trumpet flower; an undefined person (*yora wetsa*) who, in dreams, brings certain implements (radios, macaw and parrot chicks, *paka* spears) that transmit *chinã* to a singer; his dead relatives, who in other contexts continue to teach songs to the living. All, it is worth stressing, possess the image of house owners – shaman/chiefs of distinguished speech, knowledge of which the aspiring shaman has access to only if, as already mentioned, he changes (*wetsakea*, 'becomes other'; *yovea*, 'becomes spirit') his 'body-person' (*yora*) so that his double becomes pleasing to the convivium of the various entities of the cosmos. But in the process of sedimenting or familiarizing virtual knowledge through kinship as well as through its coincidence with a given 'Marubo' collective, some obstacles begin to appear.

Cosmopolitics and Authority

Before the name Marubo and the current distribution of longhouses, kin and social segments became consolidated, a set of remnants of Pano-speaking peoples lived in the region located between the headwaters of the rivers Ituí and Curuçá called *Kapi Vana Wai*, Mata-Pasto Plantation.[26] Under pressure from the economic exploitation of the Vale do Juruá (Acre State and internal disputes, the fragments of Panoan peoples, who spoke different languages, gathered gradually under the influence of great leaders and shamans. Prominent among them is João Tuxáua Itsãpapa, who in the early twentieth century began to develop the society now called Marubo. João Tuxáua, with his shaman brothers, persuaded the warlike subjects gathered there to adopt a kinship perspective and abandon war.[27] He taught everyone songs and rituals that he had learned from other beings, as he was an anaconda shaman: his *chinã natõ* was the son of the doubles of the anacondas and thus had the ability to circulate through the various positions of the cosmos.

In the first half of the twentieth century, disagreements and mutual witchcraft attacks deriving from disputes over women caused the Marubo to divide between the channels of the two rivers and thus abandon the old 'Mata-Pasto Plantation' and the leadership of João Tuxáua. However, he remained the de jure authority for the inhabitants of the upper Ituí: even though the old chief died and his kin now do not have effective authority over the longhouses of a given river, they are always reported as the main source of specialist knowledge even today. Meanwhile, the presence of

João Tuxáua and of the former village remains only in memory. After his death, the double of the respected head migrated to the 'infinite background of social virtuality', in the words of Viveiros de Castro (2002). The village itself continues to exist in its parallel reference; it became a possible posthumous destination for those who manage to avoid the dangerous Death-Path (*Vei Vai*) that connects this earth to the House of Sky-Death (*Vei Naí Shavaya*).

It is no coincidence that Tekãpapa, a respected praying shaman of the upper Ituí, attributes the source of his knowledge to those relatives of Curuçá River metaphorically called 'our government', an explicit translation of the Brazilian authorities that so captivate the Marubo (Cesarino 2011a: 287ff.). In other discursive contexts, the translation is made to contrast with 'your' government, that is, that of white people or *nawa*, in a way analogous to the comparisons that reappear in his discourses: 'he is like God' (*yos keská*), 'he is like the father of us all' (*noke ashkãsh papa keská*). The fact that the comparison is based precisely on prototypical figures of authority in Western culture – and consequently of authorship and of creation – should not obscure the webs of reverse anthropology that are woven here. Tekãpapa speaks about the 'double of the government': the doubles of João Tuxáua and his brothers, who continue to live 'for themselves' in the Mata-Pasto Plantation (note once again the use of reflexive suffixes). In former times, such a house owner involved or spanned the collection of people who lived there, thus preventing their possible dispersion – a risk analogous to that of the body/chiefs (*warah*) of the Kanamari, neighbours of the Marubo, as Luiz Costa shows (2007).

The strategic use of 'father' (*papa*) for Tekãpapa should not, of course, be confused with the lexicon of paternity and procreation related to the constitution of copyright (Strathern 1998: 214–45). The usage is for my benefit, as the anthropologist who recorded and transcribed the testimonies in question – someone who should understand the terms 'god' and 'government' well.[28] We must therefore ask why, among the Marubo and other lowland South American societies, the nature of the bond between owners and things or persons (e.g. children) that derive from their efforts (*meiki* 'work', *shovima* 'making/building' and *wenima* 'to emerge/appear') leads not to private property and copyright, but on the contrary to an instability that may conflict with Brazilian institutions and forms of contract.

Owners and chiefs confirm their authority exactly when they project themselves towards others, that is, in the virtual plane. Hence the infinite regressions characteristic of this and other Amazonian regimes of knowledge and authorship, averse to the distinction between mind and world upon which modern metaphysics is founded and its 'appropriative mode of creativity', as James Leach writes (2004: 162). Consequently, these regimes have no way to imagine any kind of intellectual property attributed to the mind and individual creativity of an author. The regime of authorship and the criteria referring to relationships between people and knowledge are related to the ritual technologies of access to the virtual, that is, the ways of constituting a 'body-people', the peculiar transformation of the *romeya* into a kind of recursive space or multipositional event in which the multiple voices of others are brought into play. The field of authorship outlined there demands specific strategies of shielding or protection, independent of criteria based on identity (and their resulting politics of segregation) or on individuality (and its regime of appropriation).[29] Ritual technologies are responsible for putting the person in contact with the sociocosmic relational field ruled by the gift, whose connective capacities are by definition undefined, unlimited and averse to separation into dominions. Marubo shamanism aims mainly to make the person capable of establishing relationships with the virtual through which new knowledge enters into 'culture'. How, though, should we think about their interfaces with the reifications of the increasingly present commodity regime?[30]

To say that the Marubo mode of creativity rests on the virtual replication of subjectivities does not, once again, bring us to some kind of primitive collectivism (Brightman 2010; Kirsch 2004) or signify that there is no claim of ownership over knowledge such as songs and graphic patterns. Nor does the mode of creativity investigated here share the romantico-nationalist ideology that Brazilian culture attributes to indigenous peoples.[31] Marubo shamanic knowledge does not equate to the criteria underpinning the cybernetic politics of Creative Commons, which indeed is based on a common domain supported by the idea of freedom (as opposed to the restrictions of private property). Shamanistic virtuality is a replication of owners/masters and not exactly a free zone of circulation of knowledge.

The idiom produced by the infinite replication of gifts, that is, of networks of alliance and of influence, is not one of ownership over things or ideas, but of the apprehension of things and ideas of others, potential candidates for the dynamics of familiarization. Even so, the apprehensive movement is not a mere theft of the things of others, but the establishment of a relational field that potentially extends to infinity. This alliance demands a whole series of constraints on the part of anyone who takes the knowledge of others (such a person is a relative of the spirits that are visited and will be charged by them upon, for example, disappearing for a long time), in contrast to the unimpeded circulation of collective information. But who says, anyway, that cybernetic virtuality is something merely free? Every participant in a virtual network who is not just selfishly motivated knows that reciprocity is the rule of the game. Strathern (2004) showed something similar occurring in the circulation of knowledge in academic life. This is what drives the peer-to-peer dynamic, among other contemporary experiences that also fall within the regime of the gift.[32] At this point, Strathern's analysis of Papua New Guinea proves revealing: 'if anything needs protection it is the perpetual reminder of sources in others' (2004: 102). To borrow Strathern's words, also among the Marubo (and many other lowland peoples, such as the Kĩsêdjê; see Coelho de Souza this volume), the weight appears to lie less in things (songs, designs etc.) and more on the conditions of relationship by which knowledge becomes possible – less, therefore, on property, but more on the technologies or modes of transformation that allow access to the field of relationships (Leach and Aragon 2008: 621).

The Problem of Circulation

It is against this background that dilemmas related to the circulation of knowledge (and their respective creative reinventions) have emerged in recent times. Praying shamans have always been jealous of their *shōki* songs and worry that they may circulate among their affines, who could render the songs powerless or else steal (*keroma*) some 'shamanic technology' owned by a specific social category. Today, some also fear that the knowledge of their ancestors (*nokẽ shenirasĩ tanáti*) may fall into the hands of Panoan peoples such as the Katukina or the Yawanawa. This reflects a fear shared by some Marubo who, when establishing more systematic contact with the idiom of 'culture' and 'identity' present in the nearby cities (Atalaia do Norte in Amazonas, and Cruzeiro do Sul in Acre), must navigate relationships with certain nonindigenous agents and with other peoples more implicated in the 'commerce of cultures' (Harrison 1993). In meetings held in Upper Ituí villages to reflect upon the increasingly constant processes of circulation of knowledge (through the visits of filmmakers and documentarists, exchanges between Marubo teachers and other indigenous peoples, the activity of researchers and the progressive articulation of a regional shamanistic network), there is slowly emerging an idiom of protection of knowledge that approaches the logic of goods, and of closure in the discourse of protection of identity and 'culture'.

In other instances, such as the case of the micropolitics of the city of Atalaia do Norte and its 'projects market', this discourse indeed seems to be dominant. However, in the *houses* of the Ituí it is still something new, subject to polemics, misunderstandings, dissent and processes of translation. Who should regulate the circulation of knowledge, where there is no central point of representation (a paramount chief, or even an NGO) and where owners/masters proliferate in their *houses* and their respective networks of kinship? Where should the split occur between the inside and outside of what is less a closed 'people' or a self-sufficient monad than a conglomerate of relationships? From arguments for protection and closure (ranging from discussions of the presence of outsiders in the villages to the journeys of young people to visit neighbouring peoples), there follow long discussions of the processes by which, for example, the knowledge related to the architecture of the Underwater-People's *houses* was acquired (*viá*) in distant times. It was feared, in certain circumstances, that the Katukina and the Yawanawa might 'steal' this knowledge (perhaps useful for their processes of reinventing tradition or, as they say, of 'cultural rescue'): a knowledge that the Marubo's ancestors had taken from others in turn.

Although the influence of the metropolitan lexicon of ownership and culture (Carneiro da Cunha 2009) has in recent years become more apparent on the Upper Ituí, the Marubo system carries a *savoir faire* when it comes to processes of transaction and circulation: the challenge is to understand the intersection of the two registers. The ancestors had already established relationships with outsiders who often seemed to escape a gift logic, for instance in the acquisition of axes from the Inca, as told in the *saiti* 'Asking the Inca for Axes' (*Inka Roẽ Yõká*) (Cesarino 2013a). However much they resemble commodity exchanges (Harrison 1993), these transactions form the fabric of mythic narratives: they show that Marubo culture was always 'acculturated' (Carneiro da Cunha 2009; Coelho de Souza this volume; Viveiros de Castro 2002), composed of acquisitions familiarized through process of kinship. The system in question establishes a complex interplay between 'exo-orientation' and the configuration of an internal field or, in other words, a position defined by kinship. It is from the relationship between these two movements (remarkable as much in the movement from virtual to actual as in the proximity of the Marubo mosaic to adjacent collectivities) that formations of meaning (or knowledge) and their respective regimes of control emerge.

But what happens when multiplicity and procedures of connection meet languages of closure, protection and property? How can they be reconciled with the imperative to establish mechanisms that in fact guarantee a margin of manoeuvre in the face of imminent market appropriation and the language of the State? These questions could be addressed on the basis of what I have outlined here, which should serve as a framework for a reflection on the politics of scale between the local and national levels, where the former have historically been dominated by the concepts and policies of the latter. The discussion of ontological variations does not presuppose incommensurability as an obstacle, but as a challenge for thought and dialogue.

Pedro de Niemeyer Cesarino is Associate Professor of Anthropology at the University of São Paulo and author of *Oniska: Poética do Xamanismo* *na Amazônia* (2011) and *Quando a Terra Deixou de Falar: Cantos da Mitologia Marubo* (2013).

Notes

1. *Apud* Demian (2004: 65).
2. The Marubo people was formed by a fusion of several Panoan subgroups (known as x-*nawavo, Kananawavo, Iskonawavo, Varinawavo,* 'Macaw People', 'Oropendola People' and 'Sun People', among others) scattered through the Upper Juruá and Upper Javari headwaters due to the rubber boom violence that took place in the late nineteenth and early twentieth centuries. Oral history and ethnography (see Welper 2009) attribute the invention of today's Marubo sociocosmological system to João Tuxáua, an important shaman and elder active at the beginning of the twentieth century. Although protected by a huge reservation, the Marubo population (numbering 1,705 people, according to a FUNASA census of 2010, http://pib.socioambiental.org/pt/povo/marubo/751) has suffered devastating epidemics of malaria and hepatitis at least since the beginning of 2000. These have been almost completely ignored by Brazilian public authorities. Present-day health conditions and other social conflicts (mostly produced by the influence of Brazilian local cities) justify the label 'Age of Death' (*Vei Shavá*) used by Marubo shamans in metaphysical and millenarian reflections to understand our times, as if the previous history of violence that somehow created them were still alive today.
3. The notion of owner/master is recurrent in lowland South America. Viveiros de Castro has noted its conceptual scope in various publications (e.g. 2002). Fausto (2008) offers an extensive review of the subject, also covered by various other authors in this volume.
4. Elsewhere in this volume, Santos Granero mentions a cognate Conibo term, *hibo,* and these Panoan terms are similar to others such as the Trio *entu* (Brightman and Grotti), the Kanamari *warah–* (Costa) and the Kisêndjê *kande* (Coelho de Souza).
5. Chief (*kakaya*) and shaman (*romeya* or *kēchĩtxo*) are convergent roles among the Marubo, since a good chief must also be a praying shaman. There are few *romeya* shamans, and they are not necessarily also maloca owner/chiefs. See also Ruedas (2004, 2004).
6. See Fausto (2008) and Brightman (2010) for similar arguments on the inapplicability of the notion of private property and of primitive collectivism for lowland South American societies.
7. On perspectivism, see Lima (1996) and Viveiros de Castro (2002).
8. 'Shed' refers to shed skin, a reference to entities of the sky-world, where the skins of the dead are changed.
9. Marubo thought has frequent recourse to terms that I call classifiers (such as 'shed' [*shokõ*], 'death', 'blood', 'fog' and 'sun'), used to indicate the variety of elements among the different worlds or cosmological positions (e.g. the home of the Sky-Fog is where the Fog-Malocas, the Fog-Tapir, the Fog-People etc. are found) as well as to classify items as diverse as cultigens, animals, material artefacts, body parts and forest remedies. The system has something of the distribution of the Marubo social segments (replicated through the cosmos), usually denoted 'X-*nawavo*' (X-people, e.g. blood-people, earth-people etc.), but cannot be reduced to a distribution of items within a closed series determined by social mor-

phology (e.g. there are classifiers that are not used to vary the segments, whose affinal relations determine the kinship system). Nor do they behave exactly like adjectives or qualifiers (i.e. elements classified as 'sun' need not be hot or solar). See Cesarino (2011a: 194ff.) for more details.

10. The replication of the 'owner' image (and its variations, e.g. 'body', 'master' and 'chief') on indefinite scales is also found in other Amerindian cosmologies, e.g. Costa (2007 and this volume), Bonilla (2005 and this volume) and Kohn (2002).
11. Montagner (1996: 66) states that the central maloca is the body of the pajé, from which emerges a great path-spirit (*yove vai*), decorated with the lozenge-shaped design *tao peika*. The surrounding malocas are those of spirits and are distributed on their respective levels (celestial and terrestrial layers).
12. The collection of drawings gathered during my fieldwork, mostly produced by three different shamans at my request, are made up of a common repertoire of graphic rules. The shamans did not explain these rules or patterns before they produced the drawings; their logic rests rather in a virtual connection with the general patterns of the verbal arts and its criteria for visual memorization and transmission, as I have shown elsewhere (Cesarino 2011a, 2011b, 2013b). Such rigorous structuring of the graphic narrative space is a common characteristic of other Amerindian pictographic traditions, as studied by Severi (2007).
13. Costa, in this volume and elsewhere, discusses a similar ontology in his ethnography of the Kanamari, particularly with reference to the notion of 'body-owner' (*warah*) and its relation with the mythical Jaguar.
14. *Yove-pa-se*, spirit-comparative-predicative.
15. See Melatti (1977) for a detailed study of the Marubo kinship system.
16. *Yove-vo*, spirit-plural.
17. See certain philosophical theories of the virtual (see Lévi 1998), especially Deleuze (1968), as discussed by Viveiros de Castro (2002, 2006, 2007). The Marubo themselves use the relation between the virtual and the actual when postulating the multiplicity of references characteristic of their cosmology..
18. Compare the incompatibility of the notion of identity with the regime of creativity among Nekgini speakers in Leach (2003: 138).
19. Marubo shamans are all male, although shamanism extends to both genders and women can acquire knowledge in a similar way.
20. The metaphor of the radio, which the Marubo use themselves, is also used by other native Amazonian people.
21. *yove-vo   vana-rivi,   atõ-na-rvi*
    spirit-plural speak-emphatic 3rd person demonstrative-possessive-emphatic
22. There is no space here for a detailed discussion of the problem of imitation that lies at the heart of Marubo shamanic epistemology, though it is worth noting that it should not be confused with *mimesis*, a founding problem of Western philosophical discourse. See Leach and Aragon (2008: 619) for such a discussion on the problem of imitation.
23. See Tedlock (1983) on the *Popol Vuh*.
24. See Coelho de Souza (This volume) and Brightman (2010) on the relationship between ownership and creativity in Amazonia.
25. See the recursive models identified by Strathern (1988), Mosko (2009) and Wagner (1991) for Melanesian ethnography; see also Gell (1998). The recursivity shared by these cases rules out the use of analytical tools based on fixed dichotomies such as whole/part, inside/outside, mind/world.

26. This toponym comes from "Mata pasto" (*Senna alata, Cassia alata*), an important herb associated with shamanic rituals because of the power of its double/master.
27. Ruedas (2001, 2004) and Welper (2009) offer more details of Marubo ethnogenesis.
28. Although *papa* (father, father's brother) belongs to Marubo kinship terminology and is found in mythic narratives, the term seems to have been used here in a discursive strategy of comparison.
29. I am thinking here of Kalinoe's (2004: 45–46) account of an Australian aborigine involved in a court case with the Reserve Bank of Australia over the reproduction of a traditional motif, who ended up assuming the legal position of author. From the point of view of his community, however, he was considered the holder of knowledge that came to be commercialized.
30. I refer to Strathern's distinction between gift societies and commodity societies (1988), which does not necessarily implicitly refer to a 'great divide' (*pace* Carrier 1998). The Marubo seem to have their own criteria for thinking about transactions that extend beyond the gift and its processes of replication, many of which were probably present in other moments in their history (e.g. trade for axes with the Inca [Cesarino 2013]). There are cohabitations and overlaps, even where one logic seems indeed to predominate over the other – see Fausto (this volume), who shows how the Kuikuro prioritize the results of 'relations between persons.' It is precisely the particular forms of elaboration of this mode of relationality that now mark the originality of the sociocosmologies of lowland South America, which in this respect are radically distinct from Western ones characterized by private property, profit and the separation between the producer and the means of production. The shamanic ontology analysed here gives a clear example of this in that it presupposes persons (visible or invisible owners) behind things (such as motors and jerry cans) who are always ready to attack those who would misappropriate them. Even the buying and selling of things does not extinguish the subjectivity virtually present in them, for the owners of such bodily extensions continue to be linked to them as their makers (*shovimaya*). Hence a sense of threat comes with the acquisition of goods, because the hidden person may retaliate (*kopía*, from which the term for money, *kopímati*, derives) if his or her bodily extension is misused; however, that hidden person may also bring benefits to the buyer through the transfer of knowledge/vital substance (*chiná*) such as that of white people.
31. See Aragon and Leach (2008) on Papua New Guinean art and the State, as well as Brown (2004) for North American Indians.
32. There are other possible convergences between these two forms of the virtual: the Creative Commons movement presumes a diversity of licences adaptable to the intentions of the creator or distributor. Such a diversity could provide a basis for introducing different levels of protection (see Kalinoe 2004: 54) for shamanic technology and knowledge.

References

Agamben, G. 2007. *Profanations*. New York: Zone Books.
Benveniste, E. 1974. *Le Vocabulaire des Institutions Indo-européennes Volume II*. Paris: Les Éditions de Minuit.

Bonilla, O. 2005. 'O Bom patrão e o Inimigo Voraz: Predação e Comércio na Cosmologia Paumari', *Mana: Estudos de Antropologia Social* 11(2): 41–66.
Brightman, M. 2010. 'Creativity and Control: Property in Guianese Amazonia'. *Journal de la Société des Américanistes* 96(1): 135–67.
Brown, M. 2004. 'Heritage as Property', in K. Verdery and C. Humphrey (eds), *Property in Question*. Oxford and New York: Berg, pp. 49–68.
Carneiro da Cunha, M. 1998. 'Pontos de Vista Sobre a Floresta Amazônica: Xamanismo e Tradução', *Mana: Estudos de Antropologia Social* 4(1): 7–23.
———. 2009. *Cultura com Aspas*. São Paulo: Cosac Naify.
Carrier, J. 1998. 'Property and Social Relations in Melanesian Anthropology', in C. Hann (ed.), *Property Relations: Renewing the Anthropological Tradition*. Cambridge: Cambridge University Press, pp. 85–104.
Cesarino, P. 2011a. *Oniska: Poética do Xamanismo na Amazônia*. São Paulo: Perspectiva/FAPESP.
———. 2011b. 'Entre le Verbe et l'Image: Le Système Mythopoétique Marubo', *Journal de la Société des Américanistes de Paris* 97(1): 223–57.
———. 2013a. *Quando a Terra Deixou de Falar: Cantos da Mitologia Marubo*. São Paulo: Ed. 34.
———. 2013b. 'Cartografias do cosmos: conhecimento, iconografia e artes verbais entre os Marubo', *Mana* 19(3): 437–71.
Costa, L. 2007. 'As Faces do Jaguar: Parentesco, História e Mitologia entre os Kanamari da Amazônia Ocidental', Ph.D. dissertation. Rio de Janeiro: PPGAS-Museu Nacional, Universidade Federal do Rio de Janeiro.
Déléage, P. 2006. 'Le Chamanisme Sharanahua: Enquête sur l'Apprentissage et l'Épistemologie d'un Rituel', Ph.D. dissertation. Paris: École des Hautes Études en Sciences Sociales.
Deleuze, G. 1968. *Différence et Répétition*. Paris: PUF.
Demian, M. 2004. 'Seeing, Knowing, Owing: Property Claims as Revelatory Acts', in E. Hirsch and M. Strathern (eds), *Transactions and Creations: Property Debates and the Stimulus of Melanesia*. Oxford and New York: Berghahn Books, pp. 60–85.
Detienne, M. 1967. *Les Maîtres de Vérité dans la Grèce Archaïque*. Paris: Maspero.
Fausto, C. 2012. 'Too Many Owners: Mastery and Ownership in Amazonia', in M. Brightman, V. Grotti and O. Ulturgasheva (eds), *Animism in Rainforest and Tundra: Personhood, Animals, Plants and Things in Contemporary Amazonia and Siberia*. Oxford and New York: Berghahn Books: 85–105.
Foucault, M. 2009. *O Que É Um Autor?* Lisbon: Nova Vega.
Gell, Alfred. 1998. *Art and agency*. Oxford, Oxford University Press.
Hann, C. 1998. *Property Relations: Renewing the Anthropological Tradition*. Cambridge: Cambridge University Press.
Harrison, S. 1992. 'Ritual as Intellectual Property', *Man* 27(2): 225–44.
———. 1993. 'The Commerce of Cultures in Melanesia', *Man* 28(1): 139–58.
Hobbes, T. 1996. *Leviathan*. Cambridge: Cambridge University Press.
Kalinoe, L. 2004. 'Legal Options for the Regulation of Intellectual and Cultural Property in Papua New Guinea', in E. Hirsch and M. Strathern (eds), *Transactions and Creations: Property Debates and the Stimulus of Melanesia*. Oxford and New York: Berghahn Books, pp. 40–60.
Kirsch, S. 2004. 'Property Limits: Debates on the Body, Nature and Culture', in E. Hirsch and M. Strathern (eds), *Transactions and Creations: Property Debates and the Stimulus of Melanesia*. Oxford and New York: Berghahn Books, pp. 21–40.

Kohn, E. 2002. 'Natural Engagements and Ecological Aesthetics among the Ávila Runa of Amazonian Ecuador', Ph.D. dissertation. Madison: University of Wisconsin-Madison.

Leach, J. 2003. 'Owning Creativity: Cultural Property and the Efficacy of Custom on the Rai Coast of Papua New Guinea', *Journal of Material Culture* 8(2): 123–43.

———. 2004. 'Modes of Creativity', in E. Hirsch and M. Strathern (eds), *Transactions and Creations: Property Debates and the Stimulus of Melanesia*. Oxford and New York: Berghahn Books, pp. 151–76.

Leach, J. and L. Aragon. 2008. 'Arts and Owners: Intellectual Property Law and the Politics of Scale in Indonesian Arts', *American Ethnologist* 35(4): 607–31.

Lévi, P. 1998. *Qu'est-ce Que le Virtuel?* Paris: La Découverte.

Lima, T. 1996. 'O Dois e Seu Múltiplo: Reflexões Sobre o Perspectivismo em uma Cosmologia Tupi', *Mana: Estudos de Antropologia Social* 2(2): 21–49.

Melatti, J. 1977. 'Estrutura Social Marubo: Um Sistema Australiano na Amazônia', *Anuário Antropológico* 76: 83–120.

Montagner, D. 1996. *A Morada das Almas*. Belém: Museu Paraense Emílio Goeldi.

Mosko, M. 2009. 'The Fractal Yam: Botanical Imagery and Human Agency in the Trobriands', *The Journal of the Royal Anthropological Institute* 15(4): 679–700.

Risério, A. 1993. *Textos e Tribos*. Rio de Janeiro: Imago.

Ruedas, J. 2001. 'The Marubo Political System', Ph.D. dissertation. New Orleans: Tulane University.

———. 2004. 'History, Ethnography and Politics in Amazonia: Implications of Diachronic and Synchronic Variability in Marubo Politics', *Tipití: Journal of the Society for the Anthropology of Lowland South America* 2(1): 23–65.

Severi, Carlo. 2007. *Le principe de la chimère*. Paris: Musée du quai Branly, Éditions Rue d'Ulm.

Strathern, M. 1988.. *The Gender of the Gift*. Berkeley: University of California Press.

———. 1998. 'Divisions of Interest and Languages of Ownership', in C. Hann (ed.), *Property Relations: Renewing the Anthropological Tradition*. Cambridge: Cambridge University Press, pp. 214–33.

———. 2004. 'Transactions: An Analytical Foray', in E. Hirsch and M. Strathern (eds), *Transactions and Creations: Property Debates and the Stimulus of Melanesia*. Oxford and New York: Berghahn Books, pp. 85–110.

Tedlock, D. 1983. *The Spoken Word and the Work of Interpretation*. Philadelphia: University of Pennsylvania Press.

Viveiros de Castro, E. 2002. *A Inconstância da Alma Selvagem*. São Paulo: Cosac and Naify.

———. 2006. 'A Floresta de Cristal: Notas Sobre a Ontologia dos Espíritos Amazônicos', *Cadernos de Campo* 14/15: 319–39.

———. 2007. 'Filiação Intensiva e Aliança Demoníaca', *Novos Estudos* 77: 91–126.

Wagner, Roy. 1991. "The Fractal Person". In: Marilyn Strathern e Maurice Godelier (org.). *Big Men and Great Men: Personifications of Power in Melanesia*. Cambridge: Cambridge University Press.

Welper, E. 2009. 'O Mundo de João Tuxáua: (Trans)formação do Povo Marubo', Ph.D. dissertation. PPGAS-Museu Nacional, Universidade Federal do Rio de Janeiro.

CHAPTER 8

Ownership and Well-Being among the Mebêngôkre-Xikrin
Differentiation and Ritual Crisis

Cesar Gordon

In this chapter I offer an initial reflection on the themes of ownership and well-being among the Xikrin of the Cateté, a Mebêngôkre people of Pará, in Brazilian Amazonia. The Xikrin of the Cateté are some nine hundred people who inhabit the region of the Itacaiúnas River basin in South-Western Pará, Brazil. They are one of the Mebêngôkre-speaking groups, classified in the Gê linguistic family. They share with the other Mebêngôkre an identical origin, language and set of sociocultural characteristics that are well known in the regional literature (for the Mebêngôkre-Kayapó groups see Lea 1986; Turner 1966; Verswijver 1992; for the Mebêngôkre-Xikrin see Vidal 1977; Fisher 2000). As a whole, the Mebêngôkre (Xikrin and Kayapó) number some nine thousand individuals living in various villages in the Brazilian states of Pará and Mato Grosso. Each village amounts to a relatively autonomous political universe, although there are also profound connections between them that preclude a consideration of them in isolation.[1]

Although the two major concepts tackled in this volume are ownership and nurture (see Introduction), I suggest that for the Mebêngôkre-Xikrin, notions of care, feeding and commensality, while important, are expressed mainly through the more inclusive idea of a good, beautiful and correct way life, which I subsume in the notion of 'well-being'. A beautiful and proper life is achieved at an optimum zone between the two processes that govern Mebêngôkre sociality: 'identification' and 'alteration' (Gordon 2006:, p. 399). Identification is associated with the production of identities and the constitution of a specific, common corporality and morality. Alteration is associated with symbolic mechanisms of differentiation designed to create not the 'common' but the 'uncommon', the quota of difference needed to ensure that the process of kinship and conviviality remains possible through time.

The notion of well-being is therefore what articulates the more private domain of kinship and commonness, characterized by nurture, with the encompassing collective order. In other words, it cuts through the process of identification implied in 'making kin out of others' (Vilaça 2002) and the process of alteration intended to avoid extreme identification or undifferentiation. Throughout this sophisticated indigenous social dynamics, the problem of ownership is also fundamental. Beauty and the good life depend, ultimately, on a balance between different regimes of property: one in which ownership is thought to be universal (as in the case of food), and the other in which ownership is strictly regulated and confined to individuals or families (as in the case of ceremonial wealth, also qualified as 'beautiful and good').

In the first part of this chapter, I clarify my usage of the somewhat vague notion of 'well-being' from the viewpoint of Mebêngôkre ethnography. As said above, I suggest that it can be expressed by a concept that simultaneously conveys ethical and aesthetic dimensions: the concept of the 'beautiful' and the 'good' (*mejx*), a term that other ethnographers have described (Lea 1986, 2012; Turner 1984). Although I too have analysed it elsewhere (Gordon 2011), I believe it is worthwhile to revisit this crucial concept alongside others that are likewise present in Xikrin formulations of 'well-being', such as shame or respect (*pia'àm*) and understanding (*kuma*). I will suggest that notions of well-being should be articulated to a wider Indigenous philosophical and existential problem, to wit, the matter of differentiation. In brief, I propose that one of the definitions of well-being in the Mebêngôkre world is the maintenance, at every level of social life, of a certain coefficient of differentiation – or, in what amounts to the same thing, of avoiding a state of undifferentiation.

In the chapter's second part I articulate this proposition with the idea of ownership, or of something that in the Xikrin social context retains a certain analogy to (or otherwise functions as) 'property'.[2] At the risk of grossly simplifying the problem, I suggest that in the Mebêngôkre case, the task of finding a concept analogous to 'property' is facilitated by the widely attested existence of a set of ritual prerogatives expressed by the terms *nêkrêjx* or *kukràdjà*, which constitute familial or personal archives as described by Vanessa Lea (1986, 2012), the ethnographer who first regarded these goods as a type of 'wealth' in Kayapó society. The hypothesis I will explore here is that well-being is associated with the problem of differentiation, which in turn is linked, on the sociological plane, to the question of property, particularly ceremonial property. The Xikrin ritual system can be understood as a basic mechanism for differentiation at the collective level. The establishment of a totemic-type system of dividing property is thus an important mechanism for avoiding crisis and undifferentiation, and thereby ensuring well-being. For that reason, I suggest, the Xikrin use the term *mejx* to refer to both ceremonial property (and its owners), and the good or correct Mebengôkre way of life. It is all about *mejx*.

I will conclude by suggesting that the Mebêngôkre ritual system has undergone important changes in which a type of differentiation based on an equistatutory totemism has been displaced by a type of differentiation that is more evidently hierarchical, allowing antagonistic relations to develop both within and between communities. As described and analysed by anthropologists who have studied Mebêngôkre groups, this latter type of differentiation finds expression as the native opposition between 'beautiful people' (*me mejx*) or owners of names and ritual prerogatives versus 'common people' (*me kakrit*) who lack valuable ceremonial goods (Lea 1986; Turner 1984; Verswijver 1992). I suggest that this change may have resulted in what I will call a ritual crisis, by which I mean a 'schismogenetic' process (Bateson 1958) through which the dynamics of rivalry were accelerated. This is all the more evident if we take into account the historical process of increasing interaction between the Mebêngôkre and Brazilian society. Given the Mebêngôkre's resulting inability to generate differentiation, the system has veered towards a more 'centrifugal' character (Fausto 2001) marked by an antagonistic aspect that ethnographers have described as 'factionalism'.

Well-Being and Differentiation among the Xikrin

A number of anthropologists have explored native Amazonian notions of well-being. Luisa Elvira Belaúnde (2001) has examined the centrality of notions of the *buena vida* (good life) and *vivir bien* (living well) in the communal constitution of the Airo Pai of northern Peru, speakers of western Tukano language.[3] More recently, Vanessa Grotti (2007; see also Grotti and Brightman this volume) has studied the concept of well-being among the Trio and Wayana of Suriname. She shows that the concept is situated within a set of indigenous phenomena and discourses that have been studied by several Americanist ethnologists whose analyses Eduardo Viveiros de Castro (1996) labelled 'the moral economy of intimacy'. Indeed, the notion of 'well-being' resonates with the idea of 'conviviality', as it has been formulated by Joanna Overing, most notably in a volume edited with Alan Passes (Overing and Passes 2000).

Rejecting the so-called 'grand narratives of modernist thought', Overing and Passes (2000: 1) suggest that the Amazonian indigenous world must be understood through the idiom of conviviality, which 'broadly defines an Amazonian mode of sociality' (xiii). Amazonian conviviality, they argue, consists of elements found in the Western, Thomistic, Christian tradition (friendship, freedom in personal relations, absence of coercion, egalitarianism), to which are added properly native elements (also found in the Western Romantic tradition), such as a desire for tranquillity, 'high morale and high affectivity, a metaphysics of human and non-human interconnectedness, a stress on kinship, good gifting-sharing ... a propensity for the informal and performative ... and intense ethical and aesthetic valuing of sociable sociality' (xiii–xiv).

In indigenous Amazonia, well-being would thus be related to an aesthetic and a morality in which value is attached to feelings of belonging, relations of daily care among kinspeople, familiar affects, commensality, sharing, gift-giving, emotional support, compassion and personal liberty. This aesthetic and ethic is strictly tied to the flux of daily life and to the universe of close kinship and intimate coexistence of the cognatic group.

One of Overing and Passes' central arguments consists in opposing this state of conviviality to a 'jural' or 'structural' view of the Amazonian world. Indigenous people, they argue, are hardly concerned with formal or institutional aspects of social life, and have little to say about roles, status, corporate groups or hierarchies (2000: 2). They are more inclined to seek a happy and psychologically comfortable life through daily conviviality than through 'building social structures' (ibid.). Overing and Passes' critique of 'conventional' (Enlightenment or Modern) anthropology, whether in its functionalist or structuralist guises, is clear: it is as if sociological or structuralist thought were incapable of comprehending Amerindian sociability, as it is not based on the formation of social structures, but rather on the constitution of a more or less undifferentiated social universe that is 'smooth', egalitarian, uniform and based on the aesthetic and ethic of conviviality. Overing and Passes furthermore point to a supposed incompatibility between the desire to live well and mechanisms of structuration or social differentiation.

I will not discuss the merits of all aspects of Overing and Passes' model in this chapter. For instance, I will not discuss its reliance on a tradition of Western thought that is as ancient as the 'grand narratives of modernity', despite their reconfiguration under New Age and postmodern influences; nor will I consider its inapplicability to vast tracts of Amazonia including the Upper Xingu (Franchetto and Heckenberger 2001), Central Brazil (Maybury-Lewis 1979) and North-Western Amazonia (Hugh-Jones 1993; Lasmar 2005). The model does not seem to be generalizable when we leave the small, atomized, territorially dispersed communities Overing and Passes focus on and move towards a landscape with larger, territorially stabler sociological units in large villages with upwards of a thousand people.

In the more restricted ethnographic setting of the Xikrin, however, I suggest that the concept of well-being has little do with Overing and Passes' propositions. On the contrary, an analysis of the Mebêngôkre allows us to infer that, as opposed to what those authors affirm, there is no incompatibility between the desire to live well and the sociological ('structural') mechanisms of social differentiation. Indeed, it is the latter that make the former possible (for a similar argument concerning the Trio, Wayana and Akuriyo, see Grotti and Brightman this volume).

What can we say about the ideas of living well among the Xikrin and the Mebêngôkre in general? Initially, and apparently in contradiction to what I have just said, Xikrin discourse on what is or should be the good life presents a series of elements that are common to other indigenous (and non-indigenous) peoples, recalling the figures of Amazonian sociality enumerated by Overing and Passes. Here, too, as anywhere else, harmony and peace within and between Mebêngôkre villages is emphasized as a factor in well-being. The Xikrin often say that living well is living without fighting, violence or disease, with abundant food and large festivals in which everyone participates – a state of affairs that is harmonious, balanced and structured, and that makes people happy (*me mã kinh, kam me kuni kinh*). Contemporary insularity within the Brazilian state means that living well is also related to communal autonomy and a certain juridical-institutional security, which involves the demarcation and protection of indigenous territory and a degree of control over political decision-making processes that affect village life, among other factors. These superficial traits do not exhaust the problem, however. Let us approach the matter through certain key categories of the Xikrin worldview.

Lacking a specific term to designate it, the Xikrin generally verbalize notions of well-being through the Mebêngôkre word *mejx*, as in the expressions '*kam mejx*', '*mejx o ari ba*' and '*mejx kumrenx*', which respectively have the meaning of 'to stay well', 'being well' and 'very good/very well'. The semantic field of *mejx* covers a series of attributes that we might translate as 'good, well, beautiful, correct, perfect, great'. The word is widely used in quotidian discourse, qualifying both physical things (objects and bodies) and more abstract ones (names, persons, situations), and expressing aesthetic, ethic and moral values. In sum, *mejx* designates essential values for the Xikrin. To produce or obtain things, persons, villages and, finally, a *mejx* life, seems to be the ultimate goal of Xikrin action, manifested in both the individual and collective spheres. An important point to note – one I will return to shortly – is that obtaining this *mejx* quality or state, both individually and collectively, is, on a certain level, intrinsically related to the ritual domain and depends fundamentally on property and control over certain ceremonial rights and objects, including names, ornaments, ritual roles and prerogatives.[4]

A formal element in Xikrin definitions of *mejx* is that the same principles and criteria for recognizing beauty and integrity are replicated on different planes or levels. Like a beautiful object (an ornament, for instance), a beautiful body and a beautiful festival are, equally, the harmonious result of the production of alignments, approximations and differential distancing of the elements that compose the unit in question (Gordon 2011: 221). The order and the spatio-temporal structuring of the ceremonial goods that compose a particular action or ritual phase, for example, are constitutive factors of the ceremony's beauty, as are its sequence, and the order and the space between the sets of feathers that make up the beauty and integrity of a headdress. Formal parallelism extends to the constitution of persons, since their beauty depends on the differential management of distinct social relations. In other words, the beauty of a person depends on the differential action, in each stage of that person's life cycle, of his or her relatives, parents (genitors), classificatory or putative parents, cross kin – maternal uncles or grandparents (name-givers) – and formal friends (a special relationship that some ethnographies consider to be a sort of compadrazgo relation). A certain idea of differentiation is hence intrinsic to Xikrin notions of the good and the beautiful. The beautiful, materialized on different planes, depends on differentiation, that is, on a particular structural positioning of differential elements.

Now, in order to demonstrate the connections between *mejx* and well-being, we must ask what constitutes its opposite, which is a 'bad' (*punure*) life. It is here, I believe, that the question of differentiation re-emerges. From Xikrin discourse there emerges a set of negative elements that are destructive and impose limits on well-being. Violence can be an external, unpredictable factor, as in the case of attacks perpetrated by enemies. Fortunately, this dimension is increasingly confined to the past, for relations with indigenous and non-indigenous foreigners have mostly been peaceful since permanent contact was established with Brazilian society. But there remains the possibility of another type of violence that is of great concern: internal violence, which emerges from tensions at the heart of the village.

One characteristic of Mebêngôkre groups is their pronounced 'factionalism' (Bamberger 1979). Reports issued as early as the nineteenth century reveal a high degree of internal dissent, conflicts, factional disputes, violent divisions of communities, enmities and fratricidal hatred. The Mebêngôkre lived through periods of intense rivalries that mostly began within villages, leading to fissioning, before being perpetuated in intercommunal warfare (Fisher 2000; Turner 1966; Verswijver 1992; Vidal 1977). Between the nineteenth and the twentieth centuries, up until the period just prior to 'pacification' by the organs of the Brazilian state during the 1950s, various Mebêngôkre groups were involved in blood feuds. At the start of the last century, for instance, after the Mekrãnotire Kayapó separated from the Gorotire Kayapó, both groups were involved in mutual hostilities (Verswijver 1992). Conflicts between the Xikrin and the Gorotire Kayapó started around 1910 and lasted for decades, leading to numerous deaths on both sides. Afterwards a similar process occurred, this time within the Xikrin community, resulting in the separation of the Bacajá group (Bacajá River, near the present-day municipality of Altamira) and the Cateté group (Fisher 2000; Vidal 1977). In the latter group, rivalry between a father and a son over control of the village led to fissioning in 1962. More recently, the rivalry between a chief's two eldest sons, and later between their sons (who were also in dispute over prestige and leadership of the community), resulted in a further fissioning of the Cateté village in 1993 (Gordon 2006: 163). The Mebêngôkre were also involved in 'external' warfare – that is, warfare against 'culturally different political communities', both indigenous and non-indigenous.[5]

In the past, the Mebêngôkre elaborated ritual mechanisms for resolving internal conflicts, such as the collective, formal duels known as *aben tak* ('hitting each other'), in which the defeated would recognize the superiority of the victors, terminating their complaints (Turner 1966). However, as ethnographies make abundantly clear, this instrument was not always effective and often had the opposite effect of escalating tensions and furthering conflict (ibid.; Verswijver 1992). As the growing proliferation of new villages testifies, fissions continue to occur today, though violent conflicts have decreased considerably, coming to be substituted by solutions that are more political than bellicose in character. But the spectre of internal violence continues to haunt the Mebêngôkre. It no longer affects the community as a whole, but it can be manifested in individualized and personal relations.

Traditionally, internal disputes stemmed from accusations of sorcery, extramarital affairs, theft, disputes over rights and prerogatives, or any other event that carried a strong emotional component, since these fed the desire for revenge. Even though the warrior 'ethos' and bellicosity, expressed by the term *djàkrê*, are valued among the Mebêngôkre (Verswijver 1992), their positive aspects concern relations with a social universe that is external to the domain of the village. Within the village the logic of domesticity, a symmetrical quality expressed by the term *djuabô*, should reign (Gordon n.d.).

In any case, conflicts are invariably seen to result from factors such as greed or miserliness (*õ djö*), jealousy and envy (*djàpnhin*) and rivalries (*aben o kurê, aben mã àkrê*, literally, 'mutual hate', 'to be overtaken by mutual rage'). Miserliness, jealousy and envy are phenomena that result from processes of undifferentiation, in the sense that they instate a *mimetic* type of relation (Girard 2007b) among those involved, narrowing the distance that guaranteed the complementarity of terms. Without this distance, the terms come into conflict in disputes over the same position and complementarity is replaced by rivalry, as in the narrative of the twins Sun (*myt*) and Moon (*myturwa*). In this myth, the separation of Sun and Moon ensures cosmic balance, while their encounter results in mimetic rivalries that inevitably lead to violence, struggle or murder (Lukesch 1976: 27–33). A reduction in the distance between Sun and Moon symbolizes the process of undifferentiation stemming from appropriative mimetism: one desires the things of the other, or wishes to occupy the place occupied by the other. This loss of difference leads to a sort of specular relation upon the emergence of identical doubles. This is perhaps why twins have negative connotations among the Xikrin, and are associated with animals such as the dog, the snake and insect larvae.[6]

Difference and distance are hence correlative. We must thus consider well-being in its articulation with another set of crucial categories: those that imply *distance*, such as 'shame', 'respect', 'sensibleness' and 'understanding'. In fact the Xikrin generally agree that it is impossible to live well in the absence of proper *respect* and minimum rules of social coexistence, expressed by the term *pia'àm*. This word, usually glossed as 'shame' or 'respect', is of fundamental importance to Mebêngôkre sociality, for it defines what is proper to the social relations between human beings, acting as the quintessential operator of social distance (see Coelho de Souza 2002: 497–513 for an excellent comparative analysis).

The absence of *pia'àm* is the unmistakable mark of undifferentiation, characteristic of a bestial social world where kinship relations remain nondistinct and people are mixed and confused, like a herd of peccaries or a pack of dogs. What Coelho de Souza described for other Northern Gê speakers applies to the Mebêngôkre: 'All relations characterized by a difference, be it sexual, generational or of age, are, in some degree, marked by piâm ...' (Coelho de Souza 2002: 500). Distance is hence basic to both the realm of interpersonal relations and the relations between groups or collective units, such as men's associations. As Coelho de Souza (2002: 501–2) puts it, the Kayapó explicitly refer to piààm [sic] between men's houses as a contributing factor to the peace of the community and an advantage for those villages with two men's houses (Turner 1966: 43–44). Once this peace is endangered and disputes reach the point where they may overflow into physical confrontations, piààm [sic] demands an even more drastic separation of the parties involved. 'The Kayapó say that the vanquished depart because they have too much "shame" (piaàm) to remain in the same village with those people with whom they have fought, and to whom they have lost' (Bamberger 1979: 139). When the Xikrin speak disparagingly of white people or foreigners in general (*kuben*), they tend to stress that their somewhat monstrous character derives, in large part, from a lack of shame. As Da Matta (1982: 47) trenchantly observed, 'Piâm is therefore a sociological marker indicating the necessary degree of respect that certain relationships require. That is to say, *it denotes separation*. But at the same time it reveals the disposition on the part of each person to conduct the relationship in a proper way' (my emphasis).

A lack of shame and respect is also associated with incest, a dramatic dimension of undifferentiation. As far as I was able to gather, the Xikrin do not usually speak of incest. I was unable to find many references to it in Mebêngôkre myths. Nonetheless, those mythical references that are available suggest that incest is conceived of as a return to nonhuman and bestial undifferentiation. Myths that speak of incest generally narrate how the incestuous were transformed into animals – including those animals that are considered to be pests or vehicles of death (such as the stork) and provoke cosmic cataclysms (Lukesch 1976). Some informants associate incest with the birth of twins, which makes sense in light of my observations above.

Complementarily, shame and respect are associated with the more positive notion of 'understanding', expressed by the Mebêngôkre verb *ma*. The verb *ma* denotes physical and moral or mental qualities, and may be translated as 'to listen', 'to attend to, 'to understand' or 'to remember'. The word *kuma*, which is the inflected form of the verb, designates the capacity to think rationally or reflexively, in a way that is concordant with the precepts of *pia'àm*. A lack of reflexive conscience – which is tantamount to an inability to listen, understand, remember (*kuma kêt*, where *kêt* is a particle denoting negation) – and the absence of shame (*pia'àm kêt*) are interrelated phenomena that can be equated with the problem of undifferentiation and consequently violence. The Xikrin say that a person who is excessively fierce or who is overtaken by an uncontrollable fury is incapable of listening to his kinspeople (*me inhõbikwa mari kêt*). He loses the capacity for understanding. In such cases, this person is said to be 'deaf' ('does not listen, deaf' is the translation for the expressions *amakre kêt*, which literally means 'without ear'). In this sense, it is as if his body were an inhuman body, as if the person has reached a stage of absolute corporeal undifferentiation: not feeling pain, hunger, thirst, fear, pity, compassion, unable to dodge obstacles in the forest, always walking in front, in a straight line, through vines, branches and thorns. This person is a grave danger, a killer unable to discern anything.

There is thus no incompatibility between living well and structural and differentiating mechanisms. On the contrary, differentiating structures are what guarantee the possibility of a good life. As a consequence, undifferentiation is the problem. It is the enemy of well-being. Against its effects, the Mebêngôkre expend symbolic and practical effort to sustain a series of ethical, psychological and sociological mechanisms.

The theme of undifferentiation, which I have discussed in reference to the Xikrin and the Mebêngôkre, could no doubt be analysed in broader comparative and theoretical terms. We may recall, for instance, Lévi-Strauss' discussion of twins in *The Story of Lynx*. After a brief review of the mythology of twins in different cultural traditions, Lévi-Strauss suggests that the indigenous symbolism of twins never claims an identity that is not itself unstable and provisional ('identity cannot last', he says). For Lévi-Strauss (1991), this suggests that 'Amerindian thought attributes to symmetry a negative, even malefic value' (305). Hence his famous concept of a 'dualism in perpetual disequilibrium' (311) that marks indigenous social philosophy, being reflected in 'ideology' and 'social organization'.

Lévi-Strauss limited himself to the philosophical and sociological dimensions of the problem, rather than its ethical or existential dimensions. The Xikrin material, as I have tried to show, helps illuminate this latter aspect. Symmetry is but the symbol of undifferentiation. In the Xikrin case, we may take note of Girard's (2007b) hypothesis that this mirroring, these figures of doubles and twins, are decisive representations of crises of undifferentiation – of (hypothetical or perhaps historical) epidemics and strongly destructive situations of mimetic rivalry.[7] After all, symmetry, as expressed in the mythology of twins, is the expression of the complete dissolution of differences from a more concrete than purely logical point of view, having the dimension of an existential problem. It is an infernal mirroring that can only lead to conflicts, violence, disorder and, ultimately, individual and collective death. Thus Amerindians reject the symmetry of twinship not only for theoretical or aesthetic reasons but also, and mainly, because it is a symbol for everything that prevents them from living well.

Ritual Property as a Mechanism of Differentiation

At the level of interpersonal relations, undifferentiation – which generates mimetic crises and violence – is avoided through ethical or moral mechanisms, such as the notions of shame, respect and understanding. But do the Xikrin follow procedures that seek to guarantee a differential relational structure at a wider collective or sociological level? What are they? And how are such procedures related to the Xikrin notion of property?

I suggest that such procedures fundamentally refer to the ritual domain. By ritual domain I mean the set of performances, feasts and rites that constitute ceremonial life, as well as the system of partitioning and transmitting sets of names, prerogatives, rights, regalia and objects of value (*nêkrêjx* or *kukràdjà*) that Turner (1992) describes as 'valuables' and Lea (1986) calls 'wealth'. Indeed, all Mebêngôkre groups traditionally possess sets of symbolic and ceremonial goods that function as distinctive signs of individuals and family groups. Names and *nêkrêjx* are the property or rights of certain people and families, and are transmitted intergenerationally from individual to individual as inheritance according to a fixed rule concerning the relation of specific 'cross' kin. This transmission mechanism is very well documented in the available ethnography, so I only allude to it here. A boy receives names and *nêkrêjx* from one or more kinsmen of the *ngêt* category, which includes the genealogical positions of the MB, MF, FF and so forth. A girl receives names and *nêkrêjx* from one or more kinswomen of the *kwatyj* category, which includes the FZ, MM, FM and so forth. In relation to both these sets of kin, an Ego of either sex (that is, the individual who receives the inheritance) is in the *tàbdjwö* category.

The main objective of the most important Mebêngôkre ceremonies is to publicly and collectively attribute to children the ceremonial goods they have inherited from their kin. During performances, the children thus honoured exhibit their *regalia* in the village plaza and dance with the name-givers who have transmitted the goods. In this way, the fact that these children are henceforth also the owners of these goods is made public, as is the fact that they consequently have the right to transmit them, once they become adults, to their own nephews, nieces or grandchildren. Ritual is thus the proper context in which the collectivity ascertains 'who's who' in terms of goods and items of cultural value. Feasts are the events at which the ceremonial prerogatives of children should be made to 'appear' before all and thus are displayed (*o ami rint*; *ami* is a reflexive particle, and *rint* is a verb meaning 'to appear' or 'to reveal'). At the end of the ritual, the children are seen to be more social and complete, or 'beautiful', as expressed in the indigenous category *mejx*. Precisely for this reason, the children honoured in this way are called *mereremejx*, an expression that means something like 'those to whom beauty is given' or 'those upon whom beauty is conferred'. Hence Mebêngôkre rituals always evoke the image of a social totality.

In sum, rituals supply the social framework in which ceremonial objects are visualized and made explicit before everyone in the community as emblems of certain people and families. Ritual performances are temporal and spatial orderings of different ceremonial goods (Fisher 1991, 2003). In fact, the proper distribution of sets of adornments, roles and songs during the ceremony – their appearance at the centre of the village plaza in the correct sequence, disposition or position – indicates harmony, symmetry and beauty. In a certain sense, as I have already mentioned, this makes the ceremony beautiful and, ultimately, makes the collectivity beautiful, correct and complete.

Vanessa Lea (1986) was the first ethnographer to emphasize the differentiating aspect of ceremonial goods among the Mebêngôkre. Lea carried out a detailed study of the sets of names and prerogatives and described them as the 'wealth or property' of matrilineal units that she called 'Houses' or 'Matrihouses' (e.g. Lea 2012). She drew inspiration from Lévi-Strauss' notion of the *sociétés à maison* ('house societies'), although she used the concept somewhat differently, as for Lévi-Strauss it applied to cognatic societies or societies without an exclusive principle of unilinear descent (see Gordon 1996, 2006: 369). My data collected among the Xikrin contradict Lea's emphasis on the house as a matrilineal unit and seem to suggest that perhaps we should be more faithful to Lévi-Strauss' elaboration of the concept of *maison*, in which ceremonial property is linked to cognatic families and can be transmitted along both the maternal and paternal lines. However, I concur with Lea on the fundamental importance of the differentiating dimension of the system. She writes: 'Names and *nekretx* [sic] constitute the ancestral essence ... that composes the distinctive identity of each House' (2012: 98). Furthermore, according to the women of the Metyktire village in which Lea worked, 'any specific Mebêngôkre village is a partial version of an ideal village in which the totality of matrihouses forms a single circle' (121). This means that, as in a structuralist system, the ideal prototype of a Mebêngôkre village is conceived of as a finite set of differentiated units, and is therefore a differentiating system in which units are defined through their property of certain distinctive ceremonial goods.

This system has clearly totemic features. It is perhaps useful to clarify what I mean by 'totemic', since Descola (2005) has revived the use of this classic term. For him, totemism is primarily a mode of identification between humans and nonhumans, one of the modalities of the four possible relational schemes for objectifying nature – naturalism, totemism, animism and analogism – which, according to Descola, are sustained by the perception of an ontological dimension that simultaneously posits an intentionality (or interiority) and a physicality (or corporality). Briefly, in Descola's scheme, totemism is the mode of objectification in which the same type of physicality and interiority is considered to be specific to certain sets of humans and nonhumans, which together constitute particular totemic groups. That is, totemic groups are formed by human and nonhuman beings thought to share the same physicality and the same interiority.

Though ingenious and elegant, Descola's model obliterates what I consider to be a fundamental aspect of another famous definition of totemism, put forth by Lévi-Strauss (1962) some fifty years ago. Lévi-Strauss dissolved what he called the 'totemic illusion' in formal structuralist terms, analysing the phenomenon as a logical mechanism of differentiation and classification arrived at through the projection, in the axis of human social relations, of significant differences comprehended in the domain of natural species. Totemism was basically a mental operation, a means for relating series of relations of difference. Though he considered the sociological implications of this operation – particularly its role in guaranteeing the existence of basic social units that could engage in matrimonial exchanges – Lévi-Strauss did not postulate an overarching sociopolitical function for totemism. I believe that such a function allows us to situate it within a vaster framework of interdictions that are common to nonmodern societies, as suggested by René Girard (2007c: 20). Girard seems to me to be correct in demonstrating that the function of interdictions, such as totemic interdictions and those of a sexual nature, 'is to distribute all desirable objects in advance, so as to prevent mimetic rivalries' ('c'était de repartir à l'avance tous les objets désirables, de façon de prevenir les rivalités mimetiques'). This seems to me to be a very important point. In effecting a prior partitioning of available and desirable symbolic resources, totemism does not limit itself to a mental operation or a logical and intellectual game of differentiation. On the contrary, it has an important practical goal that is intrinsically associated with the existential dimension of well-being.

If Girard is right, an institution like totemism works to prevent internal rivalries and disputes over symbolic resources by putting into effect their prior partition, conferring upon groups or the relevant social units a form of property whose distinctive character is relatively stable and more or less fixed. Totemism thus provides for a global scheme whose goal is analogous to the ethics of interpersonal relations, to wit, the avoidance of processes of undifferentiation and mimetic rivalries in the heart of the community. This totemic type of system features the possibility of the existence of differential properties capable of systematically harmonizing a whole composed of distinct and complementary parts. This seems to me to be perfectly coherent with the system of Mebêngôkre ceremonial goods described by Lea. Each group (whether matrihouse or cognatic family) ideally possesses its own set of names, goods and resources that can be exchanged or articulated with other sets through formal ritual procedures and matrimonial alliance, but should ultimately remain distinct, as a means to prevent disputes and disruptive mimetic processes.

As is to be expected, the cosmological or 'religious' basis for this system is established in myth. Some well-known Mebêngôkre origin myths narrate the emergence of this type of totemic system. For instance, the myth of the Great Predator Bird (*Àkti*) explains the emergence of the diversity of birds and of all sorts of feather ornaments (*nêkrêjx*) that make up present totemic differences. A further example is the myth of the acquisition of the great ceremonial names from the subaquatic world (see Lea 1986; Lukesch 1976; Wilbert 1978). All of these narratives attest to Lévi-Strauss's famous 'passage from the continuous to the discrete', from the undifferentiated to the differentiated. But they are also aligned with Girard's formula for sacrifice (Girard 2007b). As Girard noted in two brilliant articles (1976, 1977), the passage from the continuous to the discrete invariably occurs through a radical, violent elimination, a fact that Lévi-Strauss' structural analysis intuitively perceives, only to reject. In Mebêngôkre myths, the sacrificial theme appears for example in the destruction of the Harpy Eagle (*Àkti*) and the creation of totemic-like feather ornaments; in the raid on the society of the Fish and the capture of the great ceremonial names; and in the murder of the Jaguar Woman and the theft of fire, which marks the transition from the raw to the cooked. The differentiated, totemic cultural order is installed in the aftermath of a sort of originary act of predation, which is itself the instalment of an initial founding difference between the collectivity and the victim.

Rituals, for their part, likewise promote the re-enactment of the mythical drama that created differentiation, through the performance of the events that narrate its origin – in other words, the passage from the undifferentiated to the differentiated. Although ritual re-enacts undifferentiation and the transformational state, it also re-enacts its end and the instatement of the cultural order of totemic differences. Thus ritual metamorphosis, which we might situate in the field of undifferentiation, or of the representation of undifferentiations (hence the presence of monstrous figures, masks, bird-men, jaguar-men), ultimately serves to reaffirm differences in the stage of social processes. If ritual metamorphosis evokes undifferentiation (between men and animals, myth and history, etc.), the latter can only be temporary and circumscribed to a controlled spatiotemporal context. The final aim of ritual is precisely the reaffirmation of global differentiation between all terms, and segmentation at the heart of the community. These divisions guarantee that life does not drift dangerously close to the limiting state of undifferentiation that threatens the well-being of the whole community.

History and Crisis of the Ritual System

I have thus far described how notions of well-being among the Xikrin are tied to a particular indigenous ethic that sees undifferentiation as a symbol of danger and threat, and posits, as a therapeutic resolution, its elimination through the establishment of differentiation as a structural system. I have sought to show that in a wider sociological plane, this ethic seems to be ideally realized in the establishment of a type of totemic property that delimits the ritual domain and projects the idea of society as a totality made up of distinct and complementary units, relatively stable and discrete, so as to prevent the emergence of rivalries and mimetic disputes geared towards acquisition.

However, things are more complex, since the Mebêngôkre ritual system features a further type of differentiation, which I have called 'hierarchical', that is characteristic of its encounter with the more dynamic landscape of historical change (Gordon 2010a, 2010b). To be precise, this modality of differentiation is characterized by its acquisitive and mimetic character, contradicting the totemic type of model first described by Lea.

The best ethnographies of Mebêngôkre groups have always registered a sort of internal division of prestige and social value, often explicitly expressed in indigenous discourse, between so-called 'beautiful' people (*me mejx*) – who possess ceremonial goods and social and material standing that guarantees the performance of ritual – and so-called 'common' people (*me kakrit*), who lack beauty because they either do not possess a significant set of ceremonial goods, or they cannot afford the material costs of producing rituals.

The hierarchical dimension of Mebêngôkre sociality was studied by Turner (1984), whose approach focused less on a political economy of symbolic goods than on a 'political economy of people' (see Gordon 2006, especially chapter 2). Turner described Mebêngôkre society as a political order based on a hierarchical structure of relations of exploitation and social production. He posited the exploitation of the young by elders and of women by men, generating an asymmetrical distribution of social value (n.d.: 2). However, the notion of an asymmetry based on ceremonial goods was already contained, if incipiently, in Vanessa Lea's (1986) ethnography.

I have previously drawn attention to Lea's ambivalent conclusions (Gordon 2006: 93). Even though she did not draw the necessary implications from her own data, Lea (1986: 341) noted en passant towards the end of her ethnography that ceremonial goods were not only the emblems of Houses, but had become a source of prestige for their holders. This is precisely why her ethnography referred so much to disputes, thefts and conflicts around names and *nekrêjx*, as well as to the enormous concern on behalf of some families and individuals that they should not lose their goods. Curiously, Lea also mentioned ceremonial goods that could be devalued because of their excessive circulation, coming to be despised by their original owners (why else would someone abandon the distinctive emblem of their House?); or, in contrast, could be valued because of their rarity and exclusiveness. The resulting scenario of often antagonistic, almost obsessive disputes and acquisitions, and the complicated game of valuation and devaluation, concentration and dispersion, was already at some remove from the totemic model of the prior and harmonious partitioning of ceremonial property. We were already in the delicate realm of mimetic desire (Girard, 2007a).

Although I was not yet familiar with the conceptual tools of mimetic theory at the time of my fieldwork, I sought to extract all of the analytical consequences of this state of affairs. It seemed clear that the totemic aspects of the ritual system described by Lea were, at that time, less visible or operative among the Metyktire and, particularly, the Xikrin. I therefore tried to demonstrate the existence of the hierarchical and markedly rivalrous component of Xikrin society, expressed through their ceremonial system and also in processes of incorporating goods and objects that originate in other societies – including non-indigenous society – such as merchandise and money (Gordon 2006). The thrust of the argument was that the Xikrin sought distinction. This means of hierarchical differentiation resulted in attempts at aggrandizing certain families and political leaders or chiefs in terms of greater 'beauty' and capacity to utilize objects of value that originate in the exterior, such as merchandise and money. The quest for distinction was coupled with an acquisitive impulse – that is, the attempt to acquire and restrict symbolic, ritual and monetary resources.

Instead of partitioning the field of property into stable and fixed elements so as to avoid rivalries, the system I described enabled both its accumulation and incessant mimetic disputes, not only within each village but also between villages in a constant game of undifferentiation and new attempts at differentiation. In the case of industrial goods, the increasing consumption that resulted from this game led me to label the Xikrin's relationship with these goods as a sort of 'indigenous inflation' (Gordon 2010). I explained how goods and values from the world of the whites and the traditional ceremonial goods both functioned according to the same logic: a complex political economy and a quest for distinction whose effect was no longer to establish equistatutory differences, but instead hierarchical differences of social value, prestige and power. A comparative historical analysis of the diverse Mebêngôkre and Xikrin villages allowed me to show that this process had been operative since the Amerindians' definitive contact with whites, and that it had impelled the former to intensify relations with the latter, seeking objects capable of functioning as differentiating property.

But there was something of a paradox in this process. At first incorporated as ceremonial goods by the Xikrin, the objects that came from the world of the whites ultimately saturated the system with both their quality and their quantity. Furthermore, the increase in industrialized objects available to Xikrin society came to facilitate or democratize access to the material conditions for producing rituals. In the midst of a generalized mimesis, the effect of all this was to accelerate ritual mechanisms as more and more people became able to produce ceremonies of ritual confirmation, resulting in a sort of vulgarization of beauty that contributed to the progressive effacement of the sociological consequences of the distinction between 'beautiful' and 'common'. With this came the differential consumption (or 'luxurious' consumption) of industrial goods as a substituting mechanism capable of producing hierarchical differentiation. The difference between 'rich' and 'poor' became more salient in Xikrin discourse than that between 'beautiful' and 'common'. The former difference was no doubt a transformation of the latter. But the transformation affected the system as a whole.

Behind inflationary consumption was a process in which ritual, despite becoming increasingly regular (and precisely for this reason), proved itself less capable of creating differentiation. I suggested that the ritual system was reaching a state in which it was unable to produce differences – not only totemic differences, but also hierarchical ones. The latter had shifted from the extraritualistic field towards what might be called an 'economic' field, even if its roots were still in the ritual domain. Meanwhile, beyond the ritual domain distinctive consumption and wealth were more easily subjected to mimetic pressures, thus taking on an incremental character that, in caricatural terms, evoked a game of cat and mouse. Chiefs sought to appropriate more industrialized goods and money, and nonchiefs, pressured by communal interests, imitated them, driving chiefs to find newer niches of consumption and ever more exclusive quantities of money, and so on (see Gordon 2006, 2010b).

All the elements of a crisis of undifferentiation – a crisis of ritual – were in place. The Xikrin tried to solve this crisis with increasingly rapid absorption of wealth and resources from the exterior. The mimetic escalation and the antagonistic quest for distinction required increasingly large doses of nonritual objects: merchandise, industrialized goods and money. This seemed to me to be the reason behind the inflationary nature of Xikrin consumption.

Faced with this scenario during my fieldwork, I did not think to ask about well-being. Had this perhaps been transformed in this accelerated race of consumption, with its effect of expansion of the mimetic impulse from the interior to the exterior? Becoming increasingly similar to whites is, after all, a radical means of creating internal difference. The Xikrin did not, however, have any certain answers about what was going on. But although some considered the benefits of a life more similar to that of the whites, which sometimes served as the model to be copied, there was clearly an unavoidable malaise expressed, somewhat obliquely, in the fear of 'becoming white'. The Xikrin seem to have intuitively perceived that, at the expense of differentiating themselves from each other, they were paradoxically bound to fall into the mimetic labyrinth, placing their model of well-being at risk.

To conclude, a system geared towards differentiation became incapable of realizing itself, resulting, paradoxically, in growing undifferentiation. No totemic-ritual differentiating mechanism was operative, which meant that the hierarchical and rivalrous dimension of the system, lavished with cash and commodities, enabled the irruption of something very similar to a mimetic crisis in Xikrin and Mebêngôkre society. But what, after all, is the nature of the totemic system that we read about in Lea's ethnography and that seems so consistent with the Xikrin notions of well-being that I discussed in the first parts of this chapter? Had Lea described the system of Houses or matrihouses based on a purely normative perspective? Had the Metyktire women reported to Lea an ideal model of what should be, and not of what actually happened in real life? I cannot give a definite answer to these questions in this chapter.

It is nonetheless possible to offer a hypothesis, one with a historical bent. Perhaps the progressive crisis of undifferentiation that took hold of the Mebêngôkre and became particularly acute among the Xikrin can be explained by postulating the historical existence of a wide-ranging totemic system that collapsed at some point in the Mebêngôkre's history, resulting in the appearance of a ritual system that was, we might say, 'imperfect' because it permitted the accumulation and consequent transformation of totemic emblems into 'sources of prestige' and wealth. It is possible to suppose that this system was already in decay when the Mebêngôkre groups were first contacted in the second half of the nineteenth century, and that when anthropologists began to study these groups in the 1960s, all that remained of the system were partial fragments in the shape of sets of names and prerogatives, as reported by Lea.

It is conceivable that these sets of ceremonial goods constituted, in the past, a more general totemic system of global partitioning of all material and symbolic resources. Such a system may have been associated with matrimonial exchanges and would have been capable of sustaining larger villages with a greater population density, which accords with what the contemporary Mebêngôkre often say of the past. It is true that no anthropologist ever described such a system; Lea is the researcher who has come closest. Yet there are clues that can perhaps be followed by more intensive historical and comparative research among the many groups that compose the Gê language family. It is worth recalling Nimuendaju's (1946: 90) hypothesis about the groups of the Timbira plaza, which were ceremonial societies of the same type as some that exist among the Mebêngôkre. Nimuendaju saw these groups as corresponding to an ancient clanic organization that had lost its genealogical regularity. A further, somewhat tenuous clue is the existence of certain ancient Mebêngôkre names that, though currently restricted to naming only mythical characters, are the exact same names that designate the seasonal moieties of the Timbira.[8]

The impact of the expansion of colonial fronts into the territory historically occupied by the Mebêngôkre must also be taken into account. This process resulted in a considerable decline in population, leading to successive moves between territories, decomposition and recomposition of villages, separations, greater isolation and so on (Fisher 2000; Turner 1992; Verswijver 1992). A series of important discontinuities may have furthered the collapse of the system, insofar as the group's conditions for social reproduction may have been considerably altered. The implosion of the totemic system may have furnished the occasion for certain individuals to become repositories of knowledge, accumulating ceremonial goods that would otherwise have become lost. The divisions and dispersions of villages would have also allowed the totemic goods to be transferred from one family to another through *ad hoc* strategies and negotiations.

The new situation would have made personal aggrandizement possible through property or the control over symbolic resources and coveted materials. It would also have furthered the need for firm and brave leadership in times of crisis. Although ceremonial goods were transmitted through a fixed kinship rule, they could also be accumulated and disputed, having ultimately lost their unequivocal totemic references. Finally, these new conditions would have unleashed the mimetic and conflictual mechanisms whose effects were evident at the end of the nineteenth century in the progressive segmentation of society, the proliferation of villages and the notorious Mebêngôkre propensity for factionalism. The constant fissioning that followed – always as a result of internal rivalries, increasing sorcery accusations, disputes over women and the search for prestige – generated the mutual enmities and internal warfare so characteristic of the recent history of these groups.

This hypothesis would also explain the centrifugal aspect of Mebêngôkre social dynamics in the last hundred years in one more sense. A possible solution to the failure of a system of totemic partitioning, whose objective was to fix property over coveted objects and to prevent the irruption of appropriative mimesis, is the multiplication of the range of desirable objects so as to reduce the pernicious effects of envy in disputes. This may have been why the Mebêngôkre groups, since the nineteenth century, have launched themselves in the direction of other indigenous groups and whites, attempting to increment their fund of cultural goods. In sum, the collapse of a totemic system of differentiation explains, on the one hand, the increase of internal warfare (between Mebêngôkre groups) due to the emergence of mimetic rivalries and the crises of undifferentiation that, as already noted, produced envy, jealousy, conflict over women, accusations of sorcery and so forth; and on the other hand, the increase in external contacts, almost always bellicose, with other indigenous groups and with whites in a desperate attempt to increase the availability of desirable objects as a way to alleviate the internal mimetic dynamics.

'Pacification' seems to have attenuated conflicts, and it is no surprise that this has occurred through promises, made by the organizations that deal with indigenous issues (especially the Serviço de Proteção aos Indios – SPI and Fundação Nacional do Indio – FUNAI), of the almost miraculous multiplication of objects. Though this has temporarily resolved the problem of external conflicts, it is not enough to completely placate internal rivalries, which persist, even if in a less violent key. The Mebêngôkre would quickly perceive that there are other, more efficient means for intervening in the world of the whites, such as through politics and economics. But that is another story. Regardless of whether an effective totemic system existed in history or only in the moral imagination of the Mebêngôkre, the fact is that its absence seems to have stifled the Mebêngôkre ideal of well-being. Meanwhile it remains for the Mebêngôkre to find new ways of living a good and beautiful life.

Cesar Gordon is Associate Professor at the Institute of Philosophy and Social Sciences, Federal University of Rio de Janeiro, and Fellow of National Council for the Development of Science and Technology (CNPq). He is the author of *Economia Selvagem: Ritual e Mercadoria entre os Xikrin-Mebêngôkre* (2006) and the coeditor of *Xikrin: Uma Coleção Etnográfica* (2011).

Notes

1. Although the terms 'Mebêngôkre' and 'Kayapó' are often synonymous in the literature, I use them in the following way: the first term generically indicates the groups that speak the same language and compose the wider Mebêngôkre sociocultural universe, including the Xikrin and all other Kayapó subgroups; the latter denotes all non-Xikrin Mebêngôkre groups, such as the Kayapó-Gorotire, Kubenkrãkenh, Mekrãnoti or Metyktire. There is a further convention: since the mid 1920s the Xikrin have been divided into two blocs, the Xikrin of the Cateté and the Xikrin of the Bacajá, in reference to the rivers next to which they built their villages. For the sake of economy I use 'Xikrin' to mean 'the Xikrin of the Cateté', which is where I carried out fieldwork, unless otherwise stated in the text. See Fisher (1991, 2000), for a historical and ethnographical description of the Bacajá Xikrin group.
2. I use 'property' and 'ownership' roughly as synonyms in this chapter. Furthermore, I do not provide a theoretical anthropological examination of these concepts or discuss their transcultural applicability (on this topic see Brightman, Fausto and Grotti this volume; Hann 1998, 2007; von Benda-Beckman, von Benda Beckmann and Wiber (2006). Rather, I use them in their lexically trivial sense to mean the right of possession, use, transfer or disposal of something. See Gordon (2006: chap. 10) for a more detailed analysis of the equivalences and differences between the Mebêngôkre categories *nekrêjx* and *kukràdjà* and the notion of property.
3. On of the concept of well-being in anthropology, see Jimenez (2007) and Matthews and Izquierdo (2009).

4. Elsewhere I analyse in detail the concept of *mejx* among the Xikrin, seeking to discern its attributes in the aspects of its application to objects and persons, as well as in its immaterial component, stressing its tie to the sociological and cosmological domains (Gordon 2011).
5. Gustaaf Verswijver shows how internal and external warfare are conceived as different modalities involving distinct objectives and methods. For a more detailed study of Mebêngôkre bellicosity, see Verswijver (1992) and Gordon (2006).
6. The Mebêngôkre phrase I recorded was *krabipo ne kam mejx kêt*. *Kabipo* means 'twins', *ne* is a stative particle and *kam* is a preposition. *Mejx* means 'good' and *kêt* is a negative particle. On the association with animals, some Xikrin claim that a pregnant woman should not look at the sexual acts of dogs, since this increases the chance she will give birth to twins. Some of the Mebêngôkre myths of the origin of whites and of the Juruna (Yudjá) Amerindians describe them as the multiple twins of a woman who copulated with a serpent, lizard or caterpillar, depending on different variants of the narrative (Turner 1988: 205; Wilbert 1978: 152–54).
7. See e.g. René Girard's discussion of symmetry, undifferentiation and the specular relationship of characters in Greek tragedy (2007b: 349–56).
8. For instance: the Mebêngôkre names Wakme (no longer in use and only mentioned in mythical narratives) and Kàtàm (still in use, but rare) faithfully correspond to the Timbira seasonal moieties *Wakmejê* and *Katamjê*. The name categories Bep, Katám, Wakme and Tàkàk could, perhaps, be totemic names in the manner of Australian systems, seeing as they are subdivided in accordance with the corresponding animal parts (see Lea [1986] for a detailed description of Mebêngôkre names). Some Xikrin say that the person named after a part of an animal possessed, in the past, rights over the part of the animal or plant indicated in the name.

References

Bamberger, J. 1979. 'Exit and Voice in Central Brazil: The Politics of Fight in Kayapó Society', in D. Maybury-Lewis (ed.), *Dialectical Societies: The Gê and Bororo of Central Brazil*. Cambridge, MA: Harvard University Press, pp. 130–46.

Bateson, G. 1958. *Naven*. Stanford: Stanford University Press.

Belaúnde, L. 2001. *Viviendo Bien: Género y Fertilidad Entre los Airo-Pai de la Amazônia Peruana*. Lima: Centro Amazônico de Antropologia y Aplicación Práctica/BCRP.

Coelho de Souza, M. 2002. 'O Traço e o Círculo: O Conceito de Parentesco Entre os Jê e Seus Antropólogos', Ph.D. dissertation. Rio de Janeiro: PPGAS-Museu Nacional, Universidade Federal do Rio de Janeiro.

Da Matta, R. 1982. *A Divided World: Apinaye Social Structure*. Cambridge/London: Harvard University Press

Descola, P. 2005. *Par-delà Nature et Culture*. Paris: Gallimard.

Fausto, C. 2001. *Inimigos Fiéis: História, Guerra e Xamanismo na Amazônia*. São Paulo: EDUSP.

Fisher, W. 1991. 'Dualism and Its Discontents: Social Process and Village Fissioning. Among the Xikrin-Kayapo of Central Brazil', Ph.D. dissertation. Ithaca: Cornell University.

———. 2000. *Rainforest Exchanges: Industry and Community on an Amazonian Frontier.* Washington, DC: Smithsonian Institution Press.
———. 2003. 'Name Rituals and Acts of Feeling among the Kayapo (Mebengokre)', *Journal of the Royal Anthropological Institute* 9(1): 117–35.
Franchetto, B. and M. Heckenberger (eds). 2001. *Os Povos do Alto Xingu: História e Cultura.* Rio de Janeiro: Editora UFRJ.
Girard, R. 1976. 'Differentiation and Undifferentiation in Lévi-Strauss and Current Critical Theory', *Contemporary Literature* 17(3): 404–29.
———. 1977. 'Violence and Representation in the Mythical Text', *MLN: Modern Language Notes* 92(5): 922–44.
———. 2007a [1961]. *Mensonge Romantique et Vérité Romanesque.* Paris: Éditions Grasset.
———. 2007b [1972]. *La Violence et le Sacré.* Paris: Éditions Grasset.
———. 2007c. *De la Violence à la Divinité.* Paris: Éditions Grasset.
Gordon, C. 1996. 'Resenha de J. Carsten and S. Hugh-Jones (eds) *About the House: Lévi-Strauss and Beyond* (1995)', *Mana: Estudos de Antropologia Social* 2(2): 192–95.
———. 2006. *Economia Selvagem: Ritual e Mercadoria Entre os Índios Xikrin (Mebêngôkre).* Rio de Janeiro: EDUNESP.
———. 2010a. 'L'Inflation à la Mode Kayapo: Rituel, Marchandise et Monnaie chez les Xikrin de l'Amazonie Brésilienne', *Journal de la Société des Américanistes de Paris* 96(2): 205–28.
———. 2010b. 'The Objects of the Whites: Commodities and Consumerism Among the Xikrin-Kayapo (Mebengokre) of Amazonia', *Tipití: Journal of the Society for the Anthropology of Lowland South America* 8(2): 1–22.
———. 2011. 'Em Nome do Belo: O Valor das Coisas Xikrin-Mebêngôkre', in C. Gordon and F. Silva (eds), *Xikrin: Uma Coleção Etnográfica.* São Paulo: EDUSP, pp. 207–62.
———. n.d. 'Ferocidade e Domesticidade: Fundamentos da Violência Entre os Índios Kayapó-Mebêngokre', unpublished manuscript.
Grotti, V. 2007. 'Nurturing the Other: Wellbeing, Social Body and Transformability in Northeastern Amazonia', Ph.D. dissertation. Cambridge: University of Cambridge.
Hann, C. 1998. *Property Relations: Renewing the Anthropological Tradition.* Cambridge: Cambridge University Press.
———. 2007. 'A New Double Movement? Anthropological Perspectives on Property in the Age of Neoliberalism', *Socio-Economic Review* 5: 287–318.
Hugh-Jones, S. 1993. 'Clear Descent or Ambiguous Houses: A Re-examination of Tukanoan Social Organisation', *L'Homme* 33(126–28): 95–120.
Jimenez, A. 2007. *Culture and Well-being: Anthropological Approaches to Freedom and Political Ethics.* London: Pluto Press.
Lasmar, C. 2005. *De Volta Ao Lago de Leite: Gênero e Transformação no Alto Rio Negro.* São Paulo: EDUNESP/ISA/NuTI.
Lea, V. 1986. 'Nomes e Nekrets Kayapó: Uma Concepção de Riqueza', Ph.D. dissertation. Rio de Janeiro: PPGAS-Museu Nacional, Universidade Federal do Rio de Janeiro.
———. 2012. *Riquezas Intangíveis de Pessoas Partíveis.* São Paulo: EDUSP.
Lévi-Strauss, C. 1962. *Le Totémisme Aujourd'hui.* Paris: PUF.
———. 1991. *Histoire de Lynx.* Paris: Plon.

Lukesch, A. 1976 [1968]. *Mito e Vida dos Índios Caiapós*. São Paulo: Pioneira/EDUSP.
Matthews, G. and C. Izquierdo. 2009. *Pursuits of Happiness: Well-Being in Anthropological Perspective*. Oxford and New York: Berghahn Books.
Maybury-Lewis, D. (ed.). 1979. *Dialectical Societies: The Gê and Bororo of Central Brazil*. Cambridge, MA: Harvard University Press.
Nimuendaju, C. 1946. *The Eastern Timbira*. Berkeley: University of California Press.
Overing, J. and A. Passes. 2000. 'Introduction: Conviviality and the Opening of Amazonian Anthropology', in J. Overing and A. Passes (eds), *The Anthropology of Love and Anger: The Aesthetics of Conviviality in Native Amazonia*. London and New York: Routledge, pp. 1–30.
Turner, T. 1966. 'Social Structure and Political Organization Among the Northern Kayapó', Ph.D. dissertation. Cambridge, MA: Harvard University.
———. 1984. 'Dual Opposition, Hierarchy and Value: Moiety Structure and Symbolic Polarity in Central Brazil and Elsewhere', in J. Galey (ed.), *Différences, Valeurs, Hiérarchies: Textes Offerts à Louis Dumont*. Paris: Éditions de l'École des Hautes Études en Sciences Sociales, pp. 335–70.
———. 1988. 'History, Myth, and Social Consciousness among the Kayapó of Central Brazil', in J. Hill (ed.), *Rethinking History and Myth: Indigenous South American Perspectives on the Past*. Urbana: University of Illinois Press, pp. 195–213.
———. 1992. 'Os Mebengokre Kayapó: História e Mudança Social de Comunidades Autônomas Para a Coexistência Interétnica', in M. Carneiro Da Cunha (ed.), *História dos Índios no Brasil*. São Paulo: Cia das Letras/FAPESP, pp. 311–38.
———. n.d. 'The Mebengokre Kayapo: Hierarchy, Social Consciousness and Social Change from Autonomous Communities to Inter-ethnic Systems', unpublished manuscript.
Verswijver, G. 1992. *The Club-Fighters of the Amazon: Warfare among the Kayapo Indians of Central Brazil*. Ghent: Rijksuniversiteit te Gent.
Vidal, L. 1977. *Morte e Vida de Uma Sociedade Indígena Brasileira*. São Paulo: HUCITEC/EDUSP.
Vilaça, A. 2002. 'Making Kin out of Others in Amazonia', *Journal of the Royal Anthropological Institute* 8(2): 347–65.
Viveiros de Castro, E. 1996. 'Images of Nature and Society in Amazonian Ethnology', *Annual Review of Anthropology* 25: 179–200.
Von Benda Beckmann, F., K. von Benda Beckmann and M. Wiber. 2006. *Changing Properties of Property*. Oxford: Berghahn Books.
Wilbert, J. (ed.). 1978. *Folk Literature of the Gê Indians*. Los Angeles: UCLA Latin America Center Publications.

CHAPTER 9

Temporalities of Ownership
Land Possession and Its Transformations among the Tupinambá (Bahia, Brazil)

Susana de Matos Viegas

> Land is generally conceived by Indians as something inalienable; any report of their selling and buying it under aboriginal conditions is suspect.
> —Robert Lowie, 'Property among the Tropical Forest and Marginal Tribes'

> But all property necessarily originated in prescription, or, as the Latins say, in *usucapion*, that is, by continuous possession. I ask in the first place, then, how possession can become property by the lapse of time [only]? Continue possession as long as you wish, keep it for years and for centuries, but you can never give duration, which by itself creates nothing, changes nothing, and modifies nothing, the power to transform the usufructuary into a proprietor.
> —Pierre Joseph Proudhon, 'What Is Property?'

The epigraphs to this chapter refer to two debates that normally do not enter into mutual dialogue. On the one hand, Robert Lowie (1949: 351), writing about property in the *Handbook of South American Indians* in the 1940s, describes ownership in lowland South America, arguing that 'under aboriginal conditions', land would be an inalienable space. Reflecting on various sources, ranging from observations by naturalist Wied-Neuwied on the Botocudos living in the south of Bahia in the nineteenth century, Manizer on the Kaingang in southern Brazil at the beginning of the twentieth century or the Yecuana in Amazonia, Lowie argues that for indigenous peoples of lowland South America, various factors elicit an 'impermanence of ownership' particularly concerning the land. Very occasional exceptions occur: for instance, among the Cubeo, who predominantly engage in fishing, 'each Cubeo clan jealously guards its fishing rights along the river frontages' (355). However, a more frequent situation in the lives of indigenous peoples in lowland South America, Lowie argues, is possession of certain areas of cultivated land for only short periods of time, due either to ecological circumstances resulting from slash-and-burn agriculture, or to dislocations associated with death (355). Dwelling places burned down in the wake of their inhabitant's death are thus among the relevant aspects that on occasion 'force' displacement and cyclical abandonment of these places. On the other hand, Pierre Joseph Proudhon (1809–1865) – a key figure of the opposition to liberal conceptions of property – argued in the first half of the nineteenth century that not even 'continued possession' would justify property of land: 'Who is entitled to the rent of the land? The producer of the land, no doubt. But who made the land? God. Therefore, proprietor, retire!' (Proudhon 1994: 71). Thereby, an analytical window is opened to consider how time, or specific temporalities of possession, can intervene in the historical diversity of land ownership in Lowland South America.

In this chapter I approach experiences of land possession and their transformations, integrating anthropological traditions arising out of Lowie's preoccupations and those inserted in the philosophy of social life in which property was immersed by authors such as Proudhon. I address and re-evaluate continued occupation of land as a criterion for determining ownership, but my analytical path clearly diverges from Proudhon's comparative political philosophy, aiming instead to seek out concepts 'that might correspond to what is understood in other traditions as property' (Brightman 2010: 136). I deal here specifically with experiences of land possession among the Tupinambá of Olivença, a population regarded as 'mixed blood' in multiple different respects that resides in an area of the Atlantic Forest in the south of Bahia, where they first settled in a Jesuit-controlled indigenous village in the early period of Brazil's colonization.[1] Their long-term experience of dealing with colonizers, the land privatization in the region and their inhabitation of the Atlantic coast rather than the Amazon region distinguish their case from Amazonian situations discussed in other chapters of this book.

Based on ethnographic descriptions of the different historical instances and meanings of possession developed by the Tupinambá, I will discuss temporalities illuminated by the contrast between the Gê and the Tupi, as framed long ago by Manuela Carneiro da Cunha and Eduardo Viveiros de Castro (1985). In a well-known text, the authors enunciate a Tupi-like philosophy of time that does not have recourse to a 'return to an Origin', but inversely configures an 'order of creation and production' in which time is 'institutive, not instituted or re-constituent', 'an openness to the other, places distant and the beyond: towards death as a necessary positivity. It is, in sum, *a way of fabricating the future*'[2] (205). In this text the debate around Tupi temporalities emerges as an alternative reinterpretation of functionalist perspectives of cannibalism and revenge among the Tupinambá in the sixteenth and seventeenth centuries, proposing that 'revenge', as it appears associated with cannibalism, should not be seen as a function of another ordering of the social (i.e. war, or the need to restore order through retaliation), but rather as an indicator of the very type of Tupi meanings of historicity: 'Tupinambá revenge is mostly a way of speaking about the past and the future'; it is a temporality 'which does not point to the beginning of times but rather to their end', in the form of a longing for future immortality (Carneiro da Cunha and Viveiros de Castro 1985: 198, 200).

My intention, in bringing this debate about the sixteenth-century Tupinambá into an ethnographic understanding of the Tupinambá's sense of possession of land in the present day, is not in any way to reify their history. Instead I invoke this as a theoretical device that sheds light on temporalities of land ownership among the Tupinambá of Olivença. I will argue that among these Tupinambá, resettling – abandoning a house site and opening a new one by cutting the forest – is entangled with aspects of life that can be illuminated by what Carneiro da Cunha and Viveiros de Castro (1985: 203) call a Tupi-like temporality, where 'memory is in the service of a destination, not of an origin; of a future and not of a past'. These temporal parameters are also present in the analysis of ownership among the Trio living in Suriname (Brightman 2010). In contrast, a Gê-like temporality is spatialized, in the sense that space mirrors the past, the present and the future 'within the circumscribed limits of the village', where 'everything has its place' – or even further, 'everything *is* place; immutable place exorcises time' (Carneiro da Cunha and Viveiros de Castro 1985: 201–2). A third contrast of temporalities could be envisaged through socialities of exchange like the ones described by Bonilla, Gordon and Fausto (each in this volume), where distribution is constitutive of cycles of renewed duration.

Rather than searching for a tupinization of the Tupinambá of Olivença's sense of land possession, my argument in this chapter suggests that those temporal parameters are not only an integral part of the Tupinambá's living in the world – in the sense discussed by Toren (1999) – but also part of the understanding of their articulation with the historical process of land privatization in the region. As I have discussed in detail elsewhere (Viegas 2007, 2011a), in the period from the mid-1930s until 1970, when demand for land in Olivença was peaking due to the rise of cacao prices on the international market, among other factors, the Tupinambá sustained exchanges with non-indigeneous people, based on equivocations about the meaning of plots of land. These exchanges, which resulted in 'equivocal compatibilities' between the parties concerned and those who acted as intermediaries in the register of land titles (Pina-Cabral 2002; Viegas 2007, 2011b),[3] implied the Tupinambá's surrender of swidden areas and even dwelling spaces that were destined to be abandoned anyway and therefore had relatively low value for the Tupinambá (Viegas 2007: 237–34, 2011b). This, then, set in motion a process of transformational historicity of land possession. In fact, as Peter Gow (2001) and Fausto and Heckenberger (2007) argued, a 'transformational model' of historicity reveals mutual implications of continuity and change, 'without resorting to romantic motifs ... which suppose self-similarity across time' (Fausto and Heckenberger 2007: 10; Viegas 2012). Applied to the theme of land possession, this approach contains a reflection on different facets of the same motor of history. It implies considering relationships between different agents in multiple political encounters while also regarding the environment as a lived place.

Personalized, Transitory Possessions

The territory the Tupinambá currently occupy includes numerous different socio-ecological zones across an area of five hundred square kilometres. Exploration of the lived experience of the Tupinambá reveals that the more circumspect, small, kin-based dwelling places dispersed in this area, which they call *lugares,* are core aspects of their sociality (Viegas 2011b). These dwellings incorporate a set of places, namely, *casas* (houses) encompassing dwelling buildings, *quintais* (vegetable gardens) situated in the backyards of houses, *córregos* (water ponds), *roças* (swiddens) for cultivating root crops, and *casas de farinha* (flour houses) – buildings where manioc flour is processed. Pathways interconnect each of these elements with others. Each Tupinamba dwelling places is small in area, with an average size of only two hectares. Despite its small size, each *lugar* may have three, four, or occasionally five or six houses, each household tending a swidden cultivated exclusively by its members. Manioc is the most common crop in the swiddens, although beans, pumpkin, maize and yams are also found.

For the Tupinambá, the dynamics of affects and the process of growing up are heavily concentrated in these small-scale, kin-based dwellings. In their everyday life, children who live in the same *lugar* move freely between houses as they play and bathe together in the water ponds, prepare manioc roots, compete to get an adult's attention and experience the affective dynamics between relatives, mostly sustained in feeding practices (Viegas 2003, 2007, 2012; see also Brightman and Grotti this volume; Costa this volume). As soon as they learn to walk, they move between houses to play. From the baby's viewpoint, growing up involves wriggling free of one's mother's arms and joining siblings, who live in the same house, and cousins, who live in other houses in the same dwelling place. It is rare for small children to visit other *lugares*; this occurs only on special occasions. Children begin to move about more freely and go further afield when they are between nine and eleven (Viegas 2003, 2011b).

People who reside in these dwellings or *lugares* may move to other sites several times in their lives for many different reasons, including conjugal separations, the development cycle of domestic groups, and most certainly when a close relative who lives in the same *lugar* actually dies. Conjugal ruptures outline a social imaginary of moving women and fixed men. Thus, regardless of how a husband and wife began their courtship, when conjugal ties break down it is most frequently heard (and surprising to people from other regions) that it is the woman who has left (*largam*) her partner. In fact, women and men easily seem able to argue that women have a natural tendency to flee their husbands, even to the extent of abandoning their children. As I have demonstrated elsewhere, such formulations configure gender dynamics with a heavy emphasis on the intimacy developed around the kin-based dwellings and therefore tend to describe affine relationships through experiences of movement (Viegas 2007: 164–67, 2008, 2011b).

The pathways running across the dwelling places offer a suggestive image of shared and individualized possession of different spaces. Thus, there is generally a single pathway to access the water ponds, which are shared by the set of houses, while individual pathways connect each house to its own swidden; yet other pathways link the backyards of each house (Figure 9.1)

Sentiments of possession vary along those different spaces. For example, the sense of possession of one swidden by the members of only one household is explicit, particularly when manioc flour processing occurs. Grinding manioc to make flour is a cooperative effort by people from several houses, but the final processed manioc flour always returns to the household that owns the swidden where the manioc was grown. Within a dwelling, each house's possession of its own swidden is a core feature of sociality among the Tupinambá. Sharing the raw products of a swidden is thus hardly imaginable for them.

This house-based possession of swiddens contrasts with the image of communal property that is frequently deployed in projects for producing food via collective swiddens (*roças colectivas*) run by NGOs and Catholic Church organizations in rural and indigenous areas in Brazil.[4] These projects promote collective labour to cultivate the *roça*. As such this is not problematic, but the projects also presume communal sharing of the cultivated crops, which is indeed most problematic for the Tupinambá. In projects previously implemented in the region, each individual would go independently to the swidden and harvest what he or she had grown, instead of sharing the total collected crops. Episodes of this sort were con-

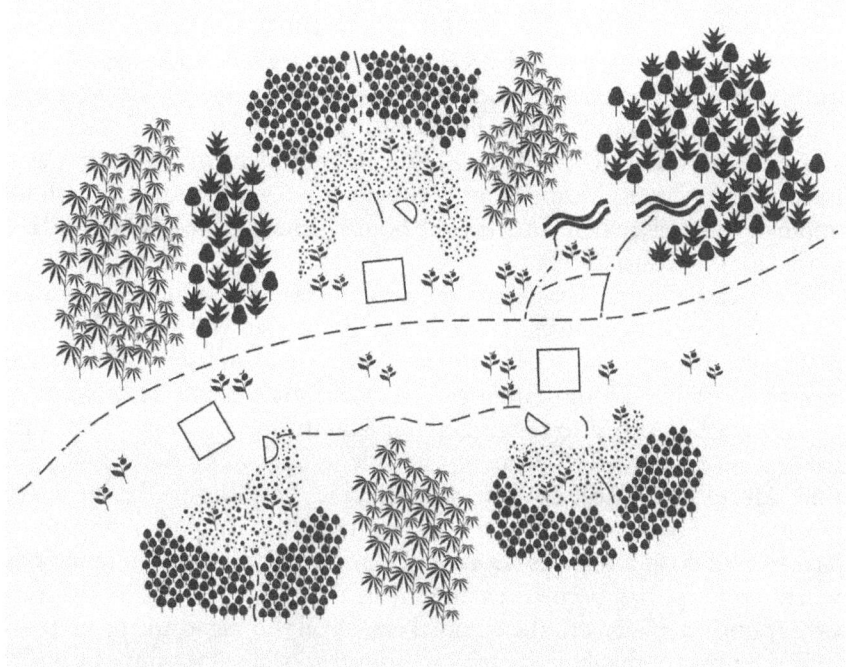

Figure 9.1 *A dwelling place. Diagram by Susana de Matos Viegas*

veyed to me time and again by both Tupinambás and project promoters. In fact, the project promoters had initially expected the Tupinambá to accept collective swidden cultivations in the same way other rural peoples had elsewhere in Brazil. Their references are genuine and can easily be identified in the anthropological literature. Among riverine peasants, for instance, communal harvesting has been observed and constitutes a 'moral sense of community' (Harris 2000: 74–75; Lima 2004). In those contexts we may even find a traditional model of land tenure based on a notion of 'collective ownership'. Nevertheless, the idea may persist that *roças* are owned by those who tend them, or more specifically 'those who have cleared the forest to plant *roças*' (Lima 2004: 13).

The more personalized, individualized sense of possession that prevails among the Tupinambá ultimately dooms these collectively based projects. This has also been the case with many other projects of the same nature implemented in other regions, which similarly presumed communal possession and usually failed when the crop or object resulting from communal work was supposed to be shared. Among the Kaxinawá in the 1980s, Cecilia McCallum observed the failure of one such project that involved sharing a motor boat, noting that in the first phase, as long as the motor was used individually by people who paid for its fuel, the project was unproblematic for the Kaxinawá (McCallum 2001: 123). Only when the motor boat broke down and it became necessary to decide who should carry the burden of its repair did problems arise. The underlying idea that it belonged to all implied that no individual was in charge of its control and care (McCallum 2001: 92, 123). The sentiment of possession as a form of control/responsibility over others is relevant here, approaching findings from elsewhere in lowland South America (Brightman 2010; Costa 2010; Fausto 2008).

In the case of land possession, it is broadly recognized throughout Brazil that the right to harvest crops is held by those who have cultivated them – even in areas owned by someone else. The ownership of cultivated crops falls within a long-standing legal tradition of *usucapion*, based specifically on the 'acquisition of rights over land through its cultivation', that has prevailed in Brazilian property rights legislation since the colonial period (Motta 2009: 16). Diverse ethnographies have shown the incidence of variants of these rights of ownership through the cultivation of plots of land very often identified as *benfeitorias* ('improvements'). Even in regions where the land has been concentrated in the hands of owners of great estates since the outset of the colonial era, as on the sugarcane plantations in Pernambuco, smallholders acquired rights to the ownership of land by cultivating and harvesting its fruits. For this reason, as anthropologists working in the region of Pernambuco have shown, the cultivation of swiddens by resident paid labourers (*moradores*) on large estates was frequently banned by some landowners to keep the cultivators from gaining effective rights of ownership over that land (Herédia 1979).[5]

In actuality, the recognition of property rights over cultivated crops as a *benfeitoria* is a key element of Brazilian land law. When a piece of land is recognized as 'land occupied traditionally by Indians', all non-indigenous occupants must leave the area, and previously issued titles to that land are declared null and void, though the former owners of these titles are compensated for their *benfeitorias* ('improvements'). These are the so-called compensation rights (*direitos de indenização*) (Constitution, section 231, 6 in Constitution 2010: 152–153). In these cases the land is declared traditionally owned by the Indians, so the valuation of this compensation takes into consideration not the extent of the area previously owned by non-indigenous occupants, which is neglected as such, but rather the existing number of fruit trees (or rubber trees, or cacao trees etc.) that are considered *benfeitorias* of previous non-indigenous occupants.

The Tupinambá clearly perceive an overlap between this generalized right of possession to whatever is cultivated on a particular piece of land and their own sense of personalized possession, mostly of cultivated products. In 1998, I witnessed concrete situations in which people changed their residence to another location and thus abandoned cultivated land but then, when the manioc was expected to be fully mature, returned to the *roça* to harvest its last manioc. Seldom do third parties usurp these crops, as it would also be unusual for the individuals who cultivated the *roça* not to harvest them, exemplifying a sense of possession that is simultaneously exclusively possessed, and personalized.

The personalized sense of possession among the Tupinambá is even more prevalent in the case of the *quintal* (garden). Located close to one of the building's entranceways, the garden is usually planted with herbs for seasoning food (especially annatto, *Bixa orellana*), herbs for healing purposes, fruit trees and flowers. Unlike the swiddens, which are perceived as the joint possession of all the home's occupants, each garden is associated with one particular person. This is normally the woman who most often cooks at the house's fireplace. She tends the garden and bears the main responsibility for everything inherent to its maintenance. In a very literal sense, a garden projects the person who tends it – to the point that it may perish with the gardener, as I heard in the explicit formulation 'when the person dies, the garden dies with her'.

The possession of a garden is personalized to the point that it ceases to exist when the life of the person who tends it ends. It is not expected to remain as an asset to be inherited by the next generation. I built up an understanding of this sense of a finite, transitory possession in various different ways, one of which became particularly revealing. This occurred when I served as a messenger in a request to exchange plants between a non-indigenous woman who was my friend and lived in an urban house in a town far from the Tupinambá, and a Tupinambá woman who was my host in the inland rural area. My friend in town requested cuttings to complete a herb garden in her own backyard, as she was already advanced in age and felt she was approaching the end of her life. Confessing her great desire to complete her own *quintal* with different plants that were missing, so that her nephews would inherit as complete a garden as possible – a situation that was common in town – she asked me to obtain those plants from my host in the Tupinambá area. I transmitted the message in these exact terms to my host, who happened to be a distant relative of my town friend. Her reaction was very illuminating: she immediately sharply accused the elderly woman from town of a certain degree of ignorance. First, she neither had nor could ever have had those herbs in her garden, as the requested type of plant grew well only near the coastline (where the town actually lies), not inland in the forest-rural region. In addition, she considered it absurd to presume that a garden could survive the death of the one who cared for it and concluded: 'I don't know what [she] means by this; but a 'herb-garden' (*jardim de quintal*) … Well, when the person dies, the garden goes with her.'

Possession of a garden is thus associated with looking after, or having the responsibility for, a given thing. In the case of *quintais*, this entails an extreme personalization. Not only does the garden perish when its gardener dies, but any disease afflicting a plant or even the sudden death of a plant extends to whoever tends it. People may explain the death of a common rue bush as the result of an evil eye cast (*mau-olhado*) on the herbs by someone who is jealous of the woman who tends that garden and her home. To attack plants in a garden is therefore a way of attacking the person who looks after it.[6] This extension of personhood to the garden can be understood as a principle linking creativity and ownership, similar to that by which some sort of vital substance is passed from the maker to the made object (Santos-Granero this volume).

Among the Tupinambá of Olivença, the temporal finitude of possession (implying a sense of transitory possession) applies to gardens as well as to swiddens. Gardens are perishable because they do not survive the death of their tender. Swiddens are perishable because they have a limited life cycle. They are attached to households, which, as I will detail in the next section, shift cyclically. Neither gardens nor swiddens are plots of land conceived as items with heritability or alienability – two elements of possession that are equivalent to each other and exogenous to the Tupinambá. As we shall see, this idea of a temporality grounded more in finite cycles than in cycles of continuity that bear marks of sites inhabited in the past, is replicated in several other dimensions in the lives of the Tupinambá of Olivença.

Personalized possession of *quintais* and its strong identification with the world of women have been observed in other Brazilian contexts, both peasant and indigenous. Recent ethnographic works emphasizing a feminine perspective and based on ethnography of daily life are particularly sensitive to these dimensions of possession. For instance, Juliana de Machado (2012) presented an ethnographic view of how women in Caviana in the Amazon basin have a personalized sense of possession regarding the plants they cultivate in *canteiros* (a kind of backyard garden). Possession of *canteiros* by Caviana women has two meanings that are close to what I described above for the Tupinambás' *quintais*. The first concerns the differentiated senses of possession between *canteiros* and swiddens (*roças*): 'a plant can either belong exclusively to a woman, if it grows in a *canteiro*, or be shared with men, when it is located in *terreiros, sitios* or *roças*' (Machado 2012: 173). The second is more about the personalized identification of one woman with the canteiro/*quintal* that belongs to her, insofar as tending and exchanging plants are acts that simultaneously guarantee possession and enhance the value of female personhood (178, 184, 211). As Machado shows, women elders who are no longer capable of tending their garden, and no longer managing to exchange plants with female neighbours and relatives, fall into self-deprecation of their moral personhood, to the point of claiming they have become useless (*não presto mais*) (173–83).

The practices Machado observed in Caviana are distinguished from those I describe here for the Tupinambá of Olivença by the aspect of temporality. Machado's ethnography shows the centrality of continuity more than of finite cycles of possession of land, implying a sense of transitory possession. The identification between *canteiros* and women in Caviana seems to be inscribed in a matrix of continuing transmission over generations – at least with daughters, who learn from their mothers how to tend their plants, which they also receive from elders (Machado 2012: 182). Later I will return to this significant comparative element.

Cycles of Abandonment and Re-opening of New Places

Observation over a longer time period demonstrates that at least until the 1970s Tupinambá undertook cyclical displacement, heading up the branches of rivers and streams. As I mentioned at the beginning of this essay and have developed elsewhere, this means that from the 1930s, during the period of land privatization in the region, cycles of abandonment and foundation of new kinship settlements were able to continue (Viegas 2007: 237–74, 2011a). Thus, privatization did not immediately wipe out a particular way of life. In many cases, the Tupinambá entered directly into relationships of 'exchange', sometimes based upon debt bondage with parties interested in the acquisition of land. Those who served as intermediaries for landowners affirm that the 'caboclos' (Tupinambá) would hand over their areas of residence in exchange for items of little value, such as *cachaça* (sugarcane spirit) or equivalent assets like mirrors and kerosene that nowadays they tend to regard as much less valuable than land. For the Tupinambá, the plots of land exchanged in this way in the past were devalued because they were temporary residential spaces destined to be eventually abandoned – thus, transitory possessions (Viegas 2007: 265–68).

The compatibility between the Tupinambá's meanings of transitory possession and capitalist landowners' estates diminished in the 1970s, when the Tupinambá began running out of space to continue carrying out these displacements, due certainly to the increased price of cacao internationally and the subsequent expansion of the landed ownership interests behind the estates in the region.[7] Before the 1970s, exchanges of plots of land and displacements of kin-based dwellings were intertwined. The Tupinambá repeat life narratives of their past displacements every five to eight years, telling of places of habitation they then left behind. These narratives show that such displacements always involved short distances covered in one hour on foot, on average. I heard several stories of how in the past people would plant 'a little there and a little here', living in a certain place only for a while (five, six, eight years) and then moving: 'He'd head off into the jungle and open up a clearing and go and live there.' Genealogical diagrams of close kin exemplify the effects of displacement on the dispersion of members across the scope of their kin network (Figure 9.2).

The Tupinambá do not perceive this dispersion solely as a result of pressure from estate owners. The absence of new areas to move to is instead felt to result from a complex history. The movement once associated with abandoning inhabited sites and opening new ones is now mirrored in the movement of the houses on the same site of inhabited *lugares*. Nowadays, after a time of absence from a kin-based dwelling site (as I observed when I returned after more than a year) changes in the number of houses there are clearly apparent. 'Dismantled' houses are slowly absorbed back into the forest. The land returns to forest, and the reordering of houses and reconfiguration of space in the new houses all make it difficult to know just where somebody lived or who was living in each settlement at a particular point in time. This is connected to the cyclical process of abandoning houses that then merge back into the forest. The Tupinambá use a very descriptive expression in reference to abandoned homes and their reconstitution: an abandoned house is said to have been 'left isolated' (*deixada isolada*), because it becomes disconnected from daily human care and reverts to forest.

A house that stops being inhabited is no longer cared for. The daily brushing of the mud floor in front of each house ends, weeds are not kept

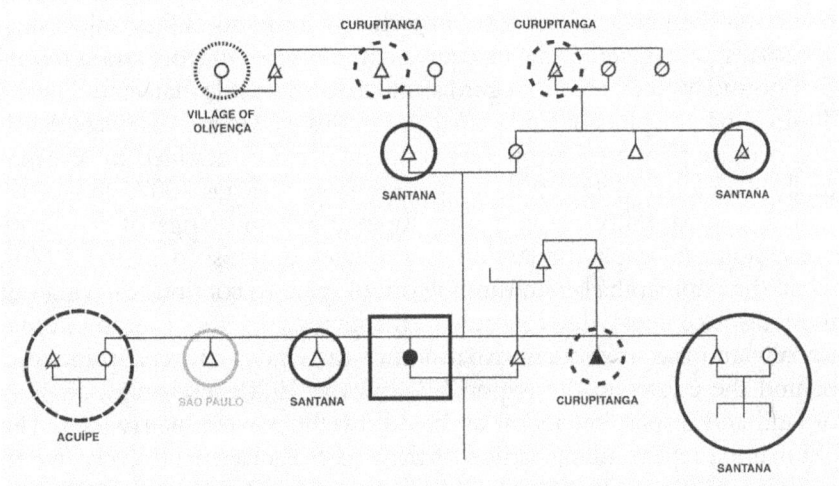

Figure 9.2 *Genealogical diagram showing distant places of residence in the territory. Diagram by Susana de Matos Viegas*

at bay and, in a terrain that has to be trodden to be deemed living and inhabited, the pathways connecting the house with other houses begin to fade.[8] Houses are ephemeral clay buildings, called *casas de sopapo* (Figure 9.3). Despite knowing techniques enabling greater clay durability (e.g. 'working' the clay well and taking it from the subsoil – 'from the nests of biting ants', as they say – to better withstand the rain and the heat, or treading it firmly), the Tupinambá do not necessarily apply them. One of the typical sounds of a clay house, when there is otherwise total silence, is the sound of small grains of dried clay dropping downwards inside the walls. The greater the level of structural 'degradation', the louder this noise becomes.[9]

Faced with the slow but no less inevitable process of the building's destruction, its inhabitants' most frequent attitude is to cover the biggest breaches using a range of materials, very often the remains of cloth or plastic. On certain walls of the home, especially the wall nearest the fireplace and garden, these cracks in the clay become ideal niches for storing utilitarian objects. The walls of a *sopapo* house thus have the appearance of stick structures dotted with objects of diverse origin – knives, pieces of cloth and very commonly newspapers and bits of black plastic – stuck in amidst clay filling.

This attitude towards buildings has been described in other indigenous and rural contexts in Brazil. Patrick Menget gave an accurate description in his monograph on the Txicão in the Xingu (2001: 145). Highlighting

Figure 9.3 *A nonplastered* casa de sopapo *or* casa de taipa de mão. *Bahia, Brazil, 1998. Photo: Susana de Matos Viegas*

that the Txicão have no great sense of durability in houses, which last on average between two and five years, Menget (ibid.) describes how the Txicão do not consider the house a building whose preservation is worth great care; in fact, they 'easily rip up bunches of herbs at the bottom of the wall to throw onto the fire and any accidental burning down of a house represents an incident of little importance as they only need a few weeks of work to build themselves a new place of habitation'.

According to the Tupinambá, when a house's clay begins to break up, the building is said to be 'falling apart'. The performance of the clays in the support pole framework varies, but they all inevitably dry out, break up and turn to dust. In the same area of residence, it is therefore common to find new buildings going up at another location chosen within the same *lugar* as the '*envaramento*' (structural construction) of vines and soil begins. On completion of this phase, inhabitants move in, often bringing with them the roofing of their former house as they now often have resistant fibrocement roofs that are able to outlast more than one clay structure.

The effects of the processes of 'isolating' buildings (*casas isoladas*) are observable within the scope of the currently inhabited terrains. In some areas, the current house might be just half a dozen paces away from that the one undergoing abandonment. However, moving the building leaves a physical trace in the abandoned site in the form of holes up to two metres deep, dug in order to extract the clay used for each building (Figure 9.4).

Figure 9.4 *The hole from which clay was extracted for a home in a kin-based dwelling. Acuípe, Bahia, Brazil, 2004. Photo: Susana de Matos Viegas*

The terrain surrounding kin-based settlements may thus be transformed into a complex grid of fruit trees, gardens, clay buildings and holes in the ground, which all contribute to the circulatory character and effects of the residential dynamic.

Land Possession and Its Transformations

One outcome of the land privatization from the 1930s to the 1970s was an effective restriction of the space available for the Tupinambá to open new kin-based settlements.[10] In this section, I will further detail how abandonments and rebuildings occurring through displacement – which in the past meant movement of kin-based dwellings – have steadily been transformed into movement of houses within the same dwelling place. This is particularly clear in attitudes towards death and the extension of people and places through life and death.

Among the Tupinambá, the death of a person is reflected in the 'death', degradation or destruction of the individual's home. The death of somebody in a home may contribute to the degradation of the building and may likewise impinge upon the health of its members. The dead may disturb living relatives with visits to the house where they lived, normally preannounced by noises (e.g. footsteps next to the house) or names called out by doorways or open windows. Some Tupinambá deny this occurs but simultaneously insist that many people believe in 'ghosts and apparitions'. The ideas that the house remembers the dead, and that the dead can meet the living through the house's intermediation, meet with greater consensus. In fact, contact between the dead and the living is recurrently described in reference to the place of residence. The closest relatives of the deceased refer to their dead kin as consubstantiated in the sensation of 'an air' that passes through the house and enters through doorways. At dusk, the time most propitious to such sensations, they lock the house's door.[11]

The son of a man who had passed away told me that he avoided going past his father's house, particularly at dusk. He felt 'shivers' but insisted that I should not consider this to be out of fear as he did not believe that his father would 'haunt' (*assombrasse*) him – the sensation was uniquely about 'remembrance' (*lembrança*). The term remembrance was also insistently used by the mother of a young man who was only 28 years old when he died in 1998. At that time, she and I were living in the same kin-based dwelling. She very vividly described to me how she sensed her son's death through the intermediation of the house environment. The son had passed away in her house after having been released from hospital. After he died, his presence was felt not only in her own house, but also in the house where he had lived with his wife and two children in another dwelling place about ten kilometres away. As we sat inside his mother's house, where the death had occurred, the mother began talking about her dead son, saying that on a certain occasion after he had died, at dusk – 'in the mouth of night' – she and her mother and daughter were at home when they felt a strong wind and, simultaneously, his presence. She said that she had not seen him, explaining that this was not a vision but something that she had felt (like shivers). The sister of the deceased, who was by the window, heard the sound of flip-flops on the floor and the dead man calling her by her name. He called but once. Afterwards, she turned to listen to the wind blowing in the direction of the house where he lived with his wife. Days later, she continued, the wife of the deceased told her that on that same night, a strong wind had brought her dead husband to pass by there at her home. Seeing my concern, the mother assured me that this would only happen in the six months after someone's death and would then stop. The dead only reappear because people 'go on remembering'. And here lies a dilemma: though it is necessary to forget, she said, we end up 'always remembering'. 'Remembrance' is, after all, among the affective ties that define kinship and that need overcoming, at least partially, when faced with death. This dilemma has received particularly incisive treatment in Amerindian ethnology, in particular in the wake of Anne Christine Taylor's essay (1993) on the Jívaro Achuar.

Among the Tupinambá, people sometimes do continue to live in the house after the death of a relative there, despite the possibility of 'remembering' the departed is greater. Failing to abandon a building carries risks, as illustrated by the case of a widow who remained throughout an entire year in the house where her husband had died. She was stubborn and wanted to remain there even in the face of reprimands and criticism from her children. Eventually her children dismantled the house, that is to say, 'isolated' it. They afterwards explained to me that they had done so because the widow was 'practically dead'; they had saved her by giving her homemade herbal medicines and taking her to a medical doctor, but also by taking her out of the house where her husband had passed away and bringing her to one of her children's homes.

I heard many reports about abandoning a space or a house, and ideally destroying it, as a means of continuing with life after the death of somebody close. In some cases the house is destroyed and rebuilt nearby; in others people depart for periods of variable length, especially when the deceased person was a particular close kin or elder – thus leaving longer memories in his kin.[12] Abandoning the place of habitation is a way of breaking with connections of life, that is, the 'remembrance' bound up with the body as a bundle of affections that provoke shivers, headaches and other sensations. From the perspective of the living, the places where the dead lived return to the forest, just as the sites of these abandoned houses revert to secondary forest growth. This reversion of abandoned environments to the forest allows the jettisoning of the social and affective and even human ballast bound up with the departed person.

The same sense behind the abandonment of habitation spaces following a family member's death is found in various indigenous contexts across lowland South America.[13] For example, among the Piro, 'the site once inhabited is densely overgrown with new forest, and people must search about for paths leading to new houses' (Gow 1991: 189). In his study of 'acculturated' indigenous people in the Atlantic north-east, Eduardo Galvão (1979) attributes dislocations to the limitations of swidden horticulture. However, he mentions in a footnote that 'death and belief in the supernatural' do in some cases definitively influence dislocation and movements of villages and kinship settlements (1979: 233). In other Amerindian indigenous contexts, it is rare to return to a previous place of residence, though the Yaminawa represent one example (Calavia Sáez 2005: 112). Among the Tupi Waiãpi, Dominique Gallois affirms that they do not return to the sites of former settlements: Waiãpi leaders maintain that '[i]n past times, when somebody died, people would move place immediately and leave the village of the dead to turn into a cemetery' (2002: 101), as indeed also happened with the Nahua in Peru, who in the past 'would abandon an entire village, including its gardens, when an adult died' (Feather 2009: 79) and the Trio in Suriname (Brightman 2010: 146).[14] Among the Tupinambá of Olivença, the physical abandonment of the house is accompanied by an explicit action of making it revert to forest, that is, 'isolating' it from human contact to revert to the wild, while people move, sometimes only a few steps from the old building, to build a new house.

It is thus important to notice that it is not only the displacement that retains meaning but also this prospective movement. Allowing the jungle to invade the immediate vicinity of the home in the present, can thus be envisaged as a transformation comparable to allowing the jungle to invade former places of residence in the past. This type of transformation bears resemblances to that detailed by Waud Kracke (1978) for the Tupi Parintintin. According to Kracke, following pacification, the Parintintin gave up moving their units of residence in five- or ten-year cycles but still perpetuated the mobility of the houses themselves, which 'are easily taken apart'. A settlement might therefore end up moving only in the event of the death of several of its members (1978: 9). More recently, and from an analytical perspective closer to the transformational process described here, Marc Brightman sets out just how abandonment and the founding of new sections of Trio villages might be seen as replicating the displacement processes and founding of new villages in the past (2010: 146).

As is the case among the Trio, the reasons for abandoning homes among the Tupinambá and their past cyclical displacements do not derive only from death and are integrated into many other aspects of social life, incorporating dynamics of kinship and the resolution of existing tensions (2003, 2007). In fact, as I have argued elsewhere, the debate triggered by Rivière about the segmentation of Trio villages and the value placed on ways of conflict-free living may equally be mentioned for the case of the Tupinambá (Rivière 2000; Viegas 2007: 170–73). I focus here on death because it is one of the most explicit means of understanding the transformation processes bound up in the displacement and possession of land.

In the Tupinambá case, cycles of abandonment of dwelling places accompanied the process of land privatization that took place after 1930, which entailed both the surrender of dwelling places destined to be abandoned, and the Tupinambá's occupation of new spaces to inhabit. As I mentioned in the previous section, this process became unviable in the 1970s after four decades of progressive land privatization and a surge in the demand for land throughout the 'cacao area' (*região cacueira*) due to rising prices of that commodity on international markets. Thereafter it became virtually impossible to find new free spaces in which to settle and establish dwelling places.

The process of indigenous land claims initiated in this region in the 1980s has to be understood in this historical perspective. In formal terms, the claiming of indigenous territory by the Tupinambá started in 2001, but it had antecedents, most notably an encounter with FUNAI in the early 1980s. At the beginning of the twenty-first century, the Tupinambá were in a subservient situation in the management and control of their own territory, despite having developed close ties over the years with non-indigenous inhabitants, including cross-marriages. They at last managed to organize themselves and muster the strength to face the challenges involved in claiming indigenous land in an adverse regional conjuncture in which landowners' influence over the political and juridical systems could be interpreted as a remnant of the old *coronelista* arrangements.

Brazilian legislation's highly original, anthropologically fruitful way of recognizing 'indigenous land' includes indigenous senses of space and temporality, attending not only to the meaningfulness of specific pieces of land for present livelihoods but also those required for their future reproduction as well.[15] The demarcation of the Indigenous Land of the Tupinambá of Olivença, comprising 47,000 hectares, was recognized by the state in 2009 – but it has not yet been implemented. Since then the Tupinambá have continued to reside in the same dwelling places, or else in areas where they build '*aldeias*' (villages), a demographic structure closer to the one that the state normally organizes for Indians. The legal demarcation of indigenous land implies that the Tupinambá hold the land in usufruct though it remains Federal Brazilian state property. Given that the management of that territory is granted to the Indians, they will be able to reproduce various senses of land possession there along a historical route that must necessarily introduce modifications into our own understanding of land ownership issues.

Conclusion

The description of transformations in land possession set out in this article would not have been possible just a few decades ago, as a fine 1982 article by Philippe Descola illustrates. Descola describes the collapse of the 'traditional' conditions of life among the Jívaro Achuar following the introduction of cattle breeding by missionaries in the 1970s. Interested in raising cattle and lacking 'any previous experience of private land ownership', the Achuar, assisted by the missionaries, undertook a division of the land in which they adopted the trails heading into the forest as the borders of their plots: 'Each personal hunting trail, leading to a distant portion of the forest, tends increasingly to be considered as a kind of exclusive property, and the use of someone else's hunting trail may cause bitter resentment' (Descola 1982: 306, 316). In a Marxist tone, Descola argued that the Achuar were undergoing a reorganization of land rights that was moving on from the previous system of 'short-term appropriation of resources, justified by labour, to an exclusive and transmissible appropriation of parcelled land' (316). Furthermore, he perceived such changes as a sign of fixed settlement in concentrated areas of habitation that 'seems now irreversible' in rendering the Achuar nondifferentiated as 'members of the Third-World Peasantry' (314, 319). As we know from the important subsequent work by the same scholar (Descola 1996), this process of irreversible change from an indigenous to a peasant society did not take place. In fact, the growing ethnographic and comparative knowledge developed among lowland South American Indians over the last twenty years points to a very different picture.

The ethnography developed in this chapter has aimed to show the diversity of land possession forms through senses of temporalities, following transformations of meanings and values ascribed by the Tupinambá to land possession. I have argued that among the Tupinambá a sense of *personalized possession* is constituted through the relationship of women to their gardens and household members to their swiddens, as far as they are associated with the foundation of a new residential compound. The latter can be approximated to the situation of the Kanamari, where the chief, as Costa (this volume) shows, becomes the 'garden body-owner'.

Among the Tupinambá, however, personalized possession of a residential compound is only temporary. Bonds between people and places are thus necessarily provisional, and their eventual abandonment generates a condition of historicity: that of *transitory possession*. Responsibility of a named subject (also underlined for other Amerindian contexts, e.g. Brightman 2010; Costa 2010; Fausto 2008) such as a woman to her garden, or a named home, is a second relevant sense of ownership revealed in the Tupinambá's transformational processes of land possession. In both cases (personalization and responsibility) possession is effective only for a determined period of time, thus articulating specific temporalities of transitory possession. These temporalities intertwine land dynamics with kinship dynamics, creating meaningful comparative axes that can even be further developed.

In rural agricultural contexts in North-East Brazil, ownership of land implies continuity via a family-based succession (Woortman 1995: 248–49), sometimes invoking founding ancestors, denominated the 'old trunk' (Godoi 1998: 97). In the dry inland region of 'sertão' in Piauí (North-East Brazil), the meaning of the land is connected to a value of inheritance and to preserving the original terrain of an extended family that people call 'the floor' (*o chão*) with reference to a shared ancestry that shapes 'a social memory in close relationship with its spatial support' (ibid.). Transmission of the land through the family line is such a key factor here that the areas of residence where an extended family live are entitled either 'land of kin' (*terra de parente*) or 'land of inheritance' (*terra de herança*) 'in which what legitimated the right to the land is descendent in conjunction with residence' (Godoi 1998: 109). In these peasantry-like contexts, land possession is based on the principle of heritage by family lines: 'The land, as the individuals, is conceived as owned by the "old Vitorino trunk", that is, those descended from Vitorino and, therefore, the principle of shared ancestry converges with the principle of rights over the land' (Godoi 1998: 104, 111). In some contexts of riverine Amazonia, such as the Caviana mentioned above because of its echoes of the Tupinambá's personalized sense of possession of gardens, the value of continuation of a household/family house also prevails, as 'land is regarded as a family asset. Ideally indivisible, people strive to keep it united through generations. With the death of parents, land passes on to their children ... and is shared among them, but not divided' (Machado 2012: 126). Inheritance is also substantiated in other Amerindian contexts, as in the case of the transmission of ceremonial goods through children among the Gê-speaking Xikrin as described by Cesar Gordon (this volume).

Regarding the articulation between the diversity of temporalities and the processes of land privatization (the second analytical perspective followed in this essay), José Glebson Vieira (2012) has done some especially relevant work on the Tupi Potiguara, who inhabit in the state of Paraíba, in a area of Atlantic Forest located in the north-east of Brazil and who, like the Tupinambá, went through the experience of settling in a missionary village during the colonial period. Vieira demonstrates how the Potiguara developed different senses of possession of the land in the wake of differentiated processes of legal recognition of land ownership rights. After Paraíba state legislation recognized the Potiguara right to land ownership at the end of the nineteenth century (though in a different way from Bahia state's absence of recognition of indigenous land rights in that period), it proceeded to divide up plots in a village in one area, known as Aldeamento da Preguiça, and grant them to the Potiguara families who lived on them. In another area – São Miguel – the state granted 'collective ownership of the land' to the Potiguara inhabiting in that area (Vieira 2012: 28). Vieira's ethnography contributes to understanding of how different histories of land privatization (between the recognition of family plots in the village and collective areas in São Miguel) had repercussions in subsequent meanings of land possession among the Potiguara. In the village, Aldeamento da Preguiça – the area divided into plots – 'land is conceived of as property transferrable through means of inheritance', that is, through family lines; whereas in the settling of São Miguel, where the land is legally common, personalized ownership seems to be sustained and articulated to successive displacements along rivers and streams 'following a tendency to dispersion' (Vieira 2012: 39–49, 120). The settlements following this latter pattern of digression through the territory are launched when a family opens a *roça*, where the area of residence of each family is referred to as *pertenção* ('belonging') and deemed the personal site of so-and-so, who is the founder of that area and considered its 'owner' (*dono*) (Vieira 2012: 54). However, ownership of land is a transitory possession in the latter case.

To sum up, the analysis presented here contributes to thinking about possession of the land at the crossroads of a wide-reaching comparative spectrum. In the case of the Tupinambá of Olivença, meaningful experiences of dwelling are a key factor in transforming the past by abandoning a place and leaving it to the forest, not to be inherited. Instead of handing land down, it is heading forth to open up new spaces for cultivation, building new homes and thereby establishing a new house that informs these practices of possession, which imply on the one hand personalized, temporary possessions sustained in the owner's responsibility for the owned object/subject, and on the other hand cutting ties with former places of origin. As I argued, these relevant senses of ownership of the land are not only present in the lives of the Tupinambá in the present, but were also constituted in processes of transformation of land possession during the period of increasing capitalistic land ownership in the region. Temporalities of ownership here reveal short-term possessions that are meant to be transitory and finite, but replicable in the future in other places, in prospective movements in which new kin-based settlements are founded and the memory of a death is left behind. Nowadays, the Tupinambá have made this feasible by struggling for the conquest of a large territory via claims to an indigenous land.

As this chapter has argued, the historicity of this territory has been constituted through processes of ownership marked by temporalities of finite cycles, where 'memory is in the service of a destination, not of an origin' (Carneiro da Cunha and Viveiros de Castro 1985: 203). This is why temporary possessions have played such a key role in the historical transformation of land ownership. The major contribution of this ethnographic analysis to a broader anthropological discussion on ownership is thus sustained in the idea that temporalities should be considered a key perspective in the understanding of the lived experience of possession, namely, in the history of entanglements in the possession of land.

Susana de Matos Viegas is Associate Professor and Research Fellow in Anthropology at the Institute of Social Sciences, University of Lisbon. She is the author of *Terra Calada: os Tupinambá na Mata Atlântica do Sul da Bahia* (2007), and co-editor of *Nomes: Género, Etnicidade e Família* (2007).

Notes

1. My field research among the Tupinambá began in 1997 and has since been continued with a diverse range of funding from the Foundation for Science and Technology (Ministry of Science/Portugal), currently under the research project Ref. PTDC/CS-ANT/118150/2010, and previously funding Ref. PTDC/CS-ANT/102957/2008. Seminars promoted by our research team, namely on territoriality and ownership, have been vitally important to the development of the argument presented in this chapter. I thank Rui Feijó for the reading and translation of the article and Carlos Fausto for the thoughtful reading and comments, subsequently complemented by those of the other editors.
2. My emphasis.
3. On equivocations of meanings see also Coelho de Souza (this volume).
4. For a discussion of the problem of indigenous collective ownership and the need for change in the concept of the subject of ownership as such see Coelho de Souza (this volume).
5. In the words of the anthropologist Afrânio Garcia Júnior, who did fieldwork in the region in 1970: 'Coffee bushes that are planted by a labourer, who afterwards then tends them, are thereby considered his *benfeitorias* and, as such, eligible for compensation should the labourer be dismissed and expelled from the estate' (Garcia 1983: 57). I would like to thank Ana Luísa Micaelo for these references, which are also confirmed by her own field research in the region (cf. Micaelo 2014).
6. In this sense, the personal dimension of the gardens is similar in nature to that described by Descola in the case of the Achuar to show how this connection is 'practically physical' and actually becomes 'a public projection of the personalities

and qualities of those tending to them', to the point at which '[w]hen a woman dies, her quintal (*garden*) also disappears in her wake' (Descola 1996: 175).

7. In the 'cacao area' next to Olivença, cacao cultivation developed under a monoculture type of system (less devastating than sugarcane plantations, given that its agrarian techniques are reputed to be sustainable). Known in the region as *cabruca*, this system consists of alternating cacao plants and shade trees (normally from the Atlantic Forest). The cacao economy developed historically through a social regime of great promiscuity between the social and the political spheres, known as *coronelismo* (see Carvalho 1997: 230). Although Olivença does not belong properly to the 'cacao area', proximity to it had particularly important effects at key moments of its history, such as the cycle of land privatization in the early twentieth century (Viegas 2007, 2011a). In the 1970s the boom in international cacao prices caused cacao cultivation to expand to surrounding regions where it had not existed previously, including Olivença.

8. Peter Gow highlights the same regeneration process among the Piro: 'The house and the garden establish the human space of settlement. Both are transformed forest, and both must be constantly maintained in the face of forest regeneration' (1991: 121).

9. In the region, *casas de sopapo* ('sharp slap houses') or *casas de taipa de mão* ('rammed earth houses') are clay and mud constructions built around a structure of wooden poles tied with vines that are then covered with clay, normally thrown at the wooden structure. The expression *sopapo* derives from this gesture of throwing the clay. Such clay structures are common throughout the entire north-east of Brazil and have been classified by some authors as 'neo-Brazilian'. One of the characteristics that differentiates *casas de sopapo* from the more generic category of *casas de taipa* is that the former are not plastered.

10. To put this in perspective, the average size of a kin-based dwelling corresponds to just 0.1% of what is considered a smallholding in the region (Viegas 2007: 77).

11. In fact, the stories I have heard about strange apparitions, e.g. werewolves and winds carrying evil intent, are always set at dusk. In the Xinguano context, Gregor (1982: 55) mentions that the Mehinakú also lock their doors at nightfall 'as a precaution against mosquitoes and the witches – that they believe, roam the darkness'.

12. When a death occurs in a Tupinambá family, the relatives of the deceased who have other relatives residing in distant places tend to go and visit them, staying there for several months, in order to avoid living in the same place where the death took place.

13. See Descola (1996: 117); Feather (2009: 79–83); Gallois (1981); Gow (1991: 189); C. Hugh-Jones (1988: 45); S. Hugh-Jones (1993: 107); McCallum (1999); Rivière (1984: 26); Viveiros de Castro (1992), especially a comparative study of the Tupi (Viveiros de Castro 1992: 51), and Lowie (1949: 354) for indigenous Guiana.

14. As Peter Rivière has shown, the displacements and abandonments of dwelling places are explained in diverse ways across lowland South America: they may take place following the death of a leader, the deterioration of the house, a search for an area with better hunting, aggravation caused by the increasing distance between the village and the *roça*, attacks by enemies, a desire to be farther from or closer to migrant communities, divisions in a settlement or, alternatively, a search for a location likely to generate future exchanges (1984: 26, 75, 81–82).

15. Brazilian legislation established not only the right but also the urgency of indigenous land demarcation. As I have discussed elsewhere (Viegas 2010), Article 231 of the Federal Constitution is the critical element stipulating a set of criteria for demarcation of indigenous territory based on four main principles, two of which provide for, first, a diversity of relations with the land, and second, the amount of land required to guarantee the perpetuation of an indigenous way of life. These aspects are contemplated in recognition of areas that are 'essential to the preservation of environmental resources necessary to their wellbeing ... and necessary to their physical and cultural reproduction in line with their traditions and manners' (cf. Constitution 2010: 153).

References

Brightman, M. 2010. 'Creativity and Control: Property in Guianese Amazonia', *Journal de la Societé des Américanistes de Paris* 96(1): 135–58.

Calavia Sáez, O. 2005. 'Kin Paths in an Alien World: Yaminawa Territory and Society', in A. Surralés and P. Hierro (eds), *The Land Within: Indigenous Territory and the Perception of Environment*. Copenhagen: IWGIA, pp. 110–124.

Carneiro da Cunha, M. and E. Viveiros de Castro. 1985. 'Vingança e Temporalidade: Os Tupinamba', *Journal de la Société des Américanistes* 71: 191–208.

Carvalho, J. 1997. 'Mandonismo, Coronelismo, Clientelismo: Uma Discussão Conceitual', *Dados: Revista de Ciências Sociais* 40(2): 229–50.

Constitution of the Federative Republic of Brazil. Biblioteca Digital da Câmara dos Deputados. Centro de Documentação e Informação. Coordenação de Bibliotecas. 2010. Acess: http://bd.camara.gov.br/bd/handle/bdcamara/1344

Costa, L. 2010. 'The Kanamari Body-Owner: Predation and Feeding in Western Amazonia', *Journal de la Société des Américanistes de Paris* 96(1): 169–92.

Descola, P. 1982. 'Territorial Adjustments among the Achuar of Ecuador', *Social Science Information* 21(2): 301–20.

———. 1996. *In the Society of Nature: A Native Ecology in Amazonia*. Cambridge: Cambridge University Press.

Fausto, C. 2008. 'Donos Demais: Maestria e Domínio na Amazônia', *Mana: Estudos de Antropologia Social* 14(2): 329–66.

Fausto, C. and M. Heckenberger. 2007. 'Introduction: Indigenous History and the History of the "Indians"', in C. Fausto and M. Heckenberger (eds), *Time and Memory in Indigenous Amazonia: Anthropological Perspectives*. Gainesville: University Press of Florida, pp. 1–43.

Feather, C. 2009. 'The Restless Life of the Nahua: Shaping People and Places in the Peruvian Amazon', in M. Alexiades (ed.), *Mobility and Migration in Indigenous Amazonia: Contemporary Ethnoecological Perspectives*. New York and Oxford: Berghahn Books, pp. 69–85.

Gallois, D. 1981. 'Os Waiãpi e Seu Território', *Boletim do Museu Paraense Emílio Goeldi* (série Antropologia) 80: 1–38.

———. 2002. 'Vigilância e Controle Territorial Entre os Wajãpi: Os Desafios para Superar uma Transição na Gestão do Coletivo', in M. Gramkow (ed.), *Demarcando Terras Indígenas II: Experiências e Desafios de Um Projeto de Parceria*. Brasília: FUNAI/PPTAL/GTZ, pp. 95–112.

Galvão, E. 1979. *Índios e Brancos no Brasil: Encontro de Sociedades*. Rio de Janeiro: Paz e Terra.
Garcia, A. 1983. *Terra de Trabalho*. Rio de Janeiro: Paz e Terra.
Godoi, E. 1998. 'O Sistema do Lugar: História, Território e Memoria no Sertão', in E. Godoi and A. Niemeyer (eds), *Além dos Territórios: Para um Diálogo Entre a Etnologia Indígena, os Estudos Rurais e os Estudos Urbanos*. Campinas: Mercado de Letras, pp. 97–131.
Gow, P. 1991. *Of Mixed Blood: Kinship and History in Peruvian Amazonia*. Oxford: Clarendon Press.
———. 2001. *An Amazonian Myth and Its History*. Oxford and New York: Oxford University Press.
Gregor, T. 1982. *Mehináku: O Drama da Vida Diária em uma Aldeia do Alto Xingu*. São Paulo: Brasiliana.
Harris, M. 2000. *Life in the Amazon: The Anthropology of a Brazilian Peasant Village*. Oxford and New York: Oxford University Press.
Herédia, B. 1979. *A Morada da Vida: Trabalho Familiar de Pequenos Produtores do Nordeste do Brasil*. Rio de Janeiro: Paz e Terra.
Hugh-Jones, C. 1988. *From the Milk River: Spatial and Temporal Processes*. Cambridge: Cambridge University Press.
Hugh-Jones, S. 1993. 'Clear Descent or Ambiguous Houses? A Re-examination of Tukanoan Social Organisation', *L'Homme* 33(126–28): 95–120.
Kracke, W. 1978. *Force and Persuasion: Leadership in an Amazonian Society*. Chicago: University of Chicago Press.
Lima, D. 2004. 'The Roça Legacy: Land Use and Kinship Dynamics in Nogueira, an Amazonian Community of the Middle Solimões Region', in M. Harris and S. Nugent (eds), *Some Other Amazonians: Perspectives on Modern Amazonia*. London: Institute for the Study of Americas, pp. 12–36.
Lowie, R. 1949. 'Property Among the Tropical Forest and Marginal Tribes', in J. Steward (eds), *Handbook of the South American Indians: The Comparative Ethnology of South American Indians*. Washington, DC: US Government Printing Office, pp. 351–67.
Machado, J. 2012. 'Lugares de Gente: Mulheres, Plantas e Redes de Troca no Delta Amazónico', Ph.D. dissertation. Rio de Janeiro: Universidade Federal do Rio de Janeiro.
McCallum, C. 1999. 'Consuming Pity: The Production of Death Among the Cashinahua', *Cultural Anthropology* 14(4): 443–71.
———. 2001. *Gender and Sociality in Amazonia: How Real People are Made*. Oxford and New York: Berg.
Menget, P. 2001. *Em Nome dos Outros: Classificação das Relações Sociais Entre os Txicáo do Alto Xingu*. Lisbon: Assírio e Alvim.
Micaelo, A.L. 2014. 'Essa terra que tomo de conta: parentesco e territorialidade na Zona da Mata de Pernambuco', Ph.D. dissertation. Lisbon: Universidade de Lisboa.
Motta, M. 2009. *Direito à Terra no Brasil: A Gestão de um Conflito 1795–1824*. São Paulo: Alameda.
Pina-Cabral, J. 2002. 'Equivocal Compatibilities: Person, Culture and Emotion', in *Between China and Europe: Person, Culture and Emotion in Macao*. London: Continuum, pp. 105–25.

Proudhon, P. 1994 [1840]. 'What Is Property?' in D. Kelley and B. Smith (eds), *Cambridge Texts in the History of Political Thought*. Cambridge: Cambridge University Press.

Rivière, P. 1984. *Individual and Society in Guiana: A Comparative Study of Amerindian Social Organization*. Cambridge: Cambridge University Press.

———. 2000. 'The More We Are Together ...', in J. Overing and A. Passes (eds), *The Anthropology of Love and Anger: The Aesthetics of Conviviality in Native Amazonia*. London: Routledge, pp. 252–67.

Taylor, A.-C. 1993. 'Remembering to Forget: Identity, Mourning and Memory Among the Jivaro', *Man* 28(4): 653–78.

Toren, C. 1999. *Mind, Materiality and History: Explorations in Fijian Ethnography*. London and New York: Routledge.

Viegas, S.M. 2003. 'Eating With Your Favourite Mother: Time and Sociality in a South Amerindian Community (South of Bahia/Brazil)', *Journal of the Royal Anthropological Institute* 9(1): 21–37.

———. 2007. *Terra Calada: Os Tupinambá na Mata Atlântica do Sul da Bahia*. Rio de Janeiro and Coimbra: 7Letras, Almedina.

———. 2008. 'Mulheres Transitivas: Hegemonias de Género em Processos de Mudança Entre os Tupinambá de Olivença (Brasil)', in M.V. Cabral, K. Wall, S. Aboim and F.C. da Silva (eds), *Itinerários: A Investigação Nos 25 Anos do ICS*. Lisbon: Imprensa das Ciências Sociais, pp. 623–40.

———. 2010. 'Ethnography and Public Categories: The Making of Compatible Agendas in Contemporary Anthropological Practices', *Etnográfica* 14(1): 135–58.

———. 2011a. 'Transforming Values of Land Among the Tupinambá of Olivença (Bahia, Brazil)', *International Symposium on The Value of Land, Lisbon, September 2011*.

———. 2011b. 'Can Anthropology Make Valid Generalizations? Feelings of Belonging in the Brazilian Atlantic Forest', in C. Toren and J. Pina-Cabral (eds), *The Challenge of Epistemology: Anthropological Perspectives*. New York and Oxford: Berghahn Books, pp. 147–62.

———. 2012. 'Pleasures that Differentiate: Transformational Bodies among the Tupinambá of Olivença (Atlantic Coast, Brazil)', *Journal of the Royal Anthropological Institute* 18(3): 536–53.

Vieira, J. 2012. *Amigos e Competidores: Política Faccional e Feitiçaria nos Potiguara da Paraíba*. São Paulo: Humanitas.

Viveiros de Castro, E. 1992. *From the Enemy's Point of View: Humanity and Divinity in an Amazonian Society*. Chicago: University of Chicago Press.

Woortman, E. 1995. *Herdeiros, Parentes e Compadres: Colonos do Sul e Sitiantes do Nordeste*. São Paulo: HUCITEC, EDUNB.

Index

adoption, 16, 39, 46–7, 51, 54, 56, 67, 73, 120–1, 123, 128n20
adoptive filiation, 12, 14, 56
affinal
    adoption, 121
    amnesia, 52
    categories/terms, 12, 68
    consanguinity, 56
    relation, 70, 76, 205n9
affine, 68, 70–1, 142, 150n1
    forest, 52
    kin and, 23, 48, 54, 150n3, 152n24, 202
    potential, 75, 121, 123
    relationships, 236
affinity, 68, 70–1, 76–7, 121
    and consanguinity, 123
    potential, 128n16, 128n18
    slavery and, 68
    subordination and, 69
agency, xii, 11, 15, 18, 26n7, 39, 46, 66, 88–9, 95, 102n3, 103n12, 182–3
    productive, 38, 44, 47–8, 55
Agha, A., 103 n12
Airo Pai, 51, 211
Akuriyo, 17–8, 63–79, 213
alterity, 12–3, 16, 20–1, 39, 41, 54, 56, 76–7, 104n17, 126
altership, 20
Amahuaca, 41
Amish, J., 43, 49
anaconda, 23–4, 102n4, 189, 199
Andrello, G., 24
animal, ix, 12, 15, 20, 28n25, 41, 85–8, 101, 102n7, 115, 118, 122–3, 187, 192, 197, 204n9, 216–7, 222, 229 n6, n8
    as person, 188
    as pets, 102n4, 122
    captured, 14
    domestic/familiar, 46–7, 104n16
    doubles, 189
    familiarization of, 121, 123
    game, 23, 46, 96, 102n5, 168
    human for of, 116
    procreative, 92
    quasi-, 46
    wild, 45, 85, 103n13
    young, 86
animality, 15, 40
animism, 11, 220
Århem, K., 52
Ashaninka, 41
asymmetrical relation/bond, 1, 14, 16, 18, 20, 28n5, 69, 70–1, 82, 84, 88–90, 94, 102n1, 103n13, 105n22
    and symmetrical orientations, 98
    origins in, 100
    distribution of social value, 223
asymmetry, 74, 85, 88–9, 102n3, 223
    consanguineal and affinal, 67, 71
    dynamic, 15
    and inequality, 17
    of the feeding bond, 86
    of the relationship, 63, 68
    ownership, 81
    reversible, 74
Augustat, C., 22, 27n21

authorship, 4, 19, 21–2, 153n32, 187, 193–7, 200
Aweti, 135–6, 150n5, n7

Baier, A., 18
Barasana, 40, 102n6
Barcelo Neto, A., 11, 148
beauty, 16, 82, 96, 158, 168, 184n7, 210, 214, 219, 223–4
becoming
    brother-, 28n24
    jaguar-, 98, 100–1, 104n18, 105n23
    -kin, 14, 70, 77
    -property, 2
    state of, 66
    white, 225
beer, 50, 65, 72, 79n11, 98
Belaunde, L.E., 15, 51, 82, 126, 211
Biocca, E., 48–9, 52
birds, 119, 123–4, 129, 169–70, 187, 190, 221
    as pets, 86, 102n4
birth, 45, 54, 73, 92, 104n15, 142, 229n6
    of twins, 217, 229n6
Blackfoot, 8
blood, 204n9
    flesh and, ix
    mixed, 41, 233
body, ix, 9, 28n27, 44, 88, 78n3, 152n20, 177, 188, 214, 217
    as a bundle of affections, 246
    beautiful, 184n7, 214
    -carcass, 189, 192, 196
    chiefs, 200
    decoration, 158, 168
    inhuman, 217
    ornaments/adornment, 11–2, 197
    owner's, 48
    -owner, 88–93, 95–7, 99–100, 103n11, n12, n13, 104n15, 205n13, 249
    painting/designs, 28n26, 134, 154, 160, 162–3, 167, 169, 173–5
    -person, 199
    -people, 201
    shaman's, 198, 205n11
    -strengthening techniques, 72

Bonilla, O., 15, 18, 95, 104n15, 111–2, 114–6, 118–26, 128n10, n11, n15, n16, 129n23, n24, 205, 234
Bororo, 27n17, 51
breastfeeding, 84, 90
bride service and bride price, 11, 17, 71, 76, 78n6, 79n7, 92, 114, 142
Brightman, M., 10, 17, 36, 38, 48, 123, 145, 201, 204n4–6, 205n24, 211, 213, 228n2, 234–5, 238, 247, 250
Brown, M., 3, 7, 23, 25n5, 27n15, 206n31
Butt Colson, A., 22

cannibal, 17, 26n7, 129n21, 182
cannibalism, 14, 17, 26n8, 41–3, 66, 99, 233–4
Capanahua, 41
capitalism, 2, 4, 7, 10
captives, 16, 17, 65, 68, 70, 75–6, 122
    adoption of, 39, 46–7, 51, 54, 56
    as concubines, 49–50, 52
    as less-than-human beings, 38–9, 54
    as potential affines,
    as property, 37–9, 42, 44, 46–8, 51, 53–6
    domestication (taming) of, 12, 46–7, 102n7
    execution of, 49, 51
    incorporation (integration, assimilation) of, 39, 42, 46, 51–4, 55–6
    marriage with, 39, 51–4, 157
    native terms for, 46–7
    singularization of, 55
    treatment of, 18, 46, 50
    war, 37–8, 44–7, 50, 52–3, 55, 76
capture, ix, 26n8, 42–3, 45, 47, 64–5, 71, 120, 127, 128n20, 129n.20, n.22, 222
    and appropriation of persons, 75
    and enslavement, 38
    and mastery, 15
    and the rituals of enslavement, 54–5
    and subordination, 69
    (counter-) of foreigners, 124
    of agentive capacities, 27n20
    of a boss, 120
    of wild Others, 75

Index 259

regimes of, 37
warfare and, 17, 67
capturing societies, 17, 36, 39, 42, 45, 55–6
care, xii, 1, 13–4, 16–8, 24, 25n1, 71, 73, 75–6, 81, 93, 117, 120, 142, 168, 209, 238, 242
Carib, 17, 63, 68–70, 76, 104n16, 135
Carneiro da Cunha, M., 1, 7, 25n2, 127n1, 181, 194–5, 203, 233–4, 252
Carvalho, M.R., 83
Cashinahua (Kaxinawá), 51, 102n3, 104n14, 186, 237–8
Cesarino, P., 4, 8, 10, 21, 23–4, 93, 116, 153n32, 188–9, 192, 194, 196–8, 200, 203, 205n9, 205n12, 206n30
Chané, 18, 41, 44, 50, 53–4
Chernela, J., 40
Chiriguaná, 37, 41–4, 47, 50, 52–5
Christianity, 16–7, 27n24, 73–4, 77, 140
civilized, becoming
  captives, 51
  ways of, 68, 115
  status, 52, 54
  world, 128n8
civilizing
  project, 46
  the Other, 56
Clastres, P., 9–10, 36, 181
Coelho de Souza, M., 2, 9, 22, 104n17, 145, 184n13, 194, 202–3, 204n4, 205n24, 216, 252n3
coercion, 36, 56, 212
Cohen, G., 18
Collier, J., 27n21
Combès, I., 41, 50
commensality, 1, 13–4, 16, 39, 51, 70, 82, 84, 92–101, 121, 123–4, 209, 212
commodities, 22, 27n18, 110–5, 121, 148, 171, 183, 195, 201, 203, 206n30, 226, 248
compensation, 9, 26n11, 134, 141–2, 153n28, 179–80, 238, 252n5
Comrie, B., 83, 94
Conibo, 37, 40–3, 46–7, 49–50, 52–3, 55, 186, 204n4
conquest, 1, 75
  European, 16–8
  of the Americas, 4, 26n11

consanguinity, 67, 75
  affinal, 56
  and affinity, 70
  idiom of, 73, 76
  meta-, 14,
consubstantiality, 38–9, 51, 54
consumption, 93, 96–8, 104n17, 195, 224–5
Convention for Biological Diversity, 7
conversion
  to Christianity, 73–4, 77
  of relations into things, 148
  systems, 28n24
conviviality, x, 51–2, 54–5, 70, 82, 126, 210–2
copyright, 8–9, 23, 27n15, 147, 194, 200
coresidence, 39, 51–2, 66–7, 69, 82, 97, 158
Cormier, L., 56, 85, 104n16
cosmology, 99, 118, 188–9, 192, 205n10, 206n30
Costa, L., 10, 14–5, 79n9, 82, 88, 96, 98, 102n2, 111, 121, 127n2, 200, 204n4, 205n10, n13, 235, 238, 249–50
counterprestation, 141, 150n2
Course, M., 92
creativity, 3, 4, 11, 16, 17, 20, 21, 22, 44, 48, 160, 170, 194
  appropriative, 182, 200
  distributed, 180, 182
  human, 92
  individual, 198, 201
  modes of, 157, 171, 196, 201
  natives acts of, 14
  ownership and, 205n24, 240
Crocker, C., 45, 51
Crocker, W., 64, 71, 184n9
Cubeo, 40, 52, 232
culture, 2, 6–7, 72, 133, 145, 160, 172, 198, 201
  acquisition of, 182
  commerce of, 201
  loss, 145
  material, 12, 21–2, 158
  nature/, 13
  ownership and, 203
  preservation of, 180

reified, 194
cultural fundamentalism, 160

Da Matta, R., 92, 217
death, 44, 120–1, 144, 182, 184, 215, 218, 239–40, 245–51, 253n12, 253n14
   age of, 204n2
   as a necessary positivity, 233
   compensations for, 142
   of a pet, 87
   power of life and, 50
   Sky-, 200
   substitute for, 42
   vehicles of, 217
DeBoer, W., 40, 49
debt, 113, 117, 120, 144
   between affines, 142
   bondage, 241
   -peonage, 15, 110, 114, 127n1
   relation, 44, 125
deception, 143, 154n36
Déléage, P., 28n29, 86, 100, 198
Deleuze, G., 125–6
DeMallie, R., 81
dependence (dependency), x, 12, 38, 81, 83, 86–91, 94–5, 103n8, 124
   declarations of, 18
   idioms of, 14
   relations of, 13, 15–7, 27n24, 93
Desana, 40, 52
Descola, P., 28n25, 56, 220, 249, 252n6, 253n6
design, 22, 28n26, 156–7, 160, 162–3, 166–72, 174–5, 178–9, 180, 183, 184n7, n15, 190, 202, 205n11
desire, 239, 253n9
   for commodities/goods, 111, 138
   for difference, 16
   mimetic, 223
   mutual, 101n1
   parasitic, 126
   to cut bonds, 64
   to engage with alterity, 13, 77
   to live well, 212–3
   to preserve, 22
   to share, 95
   to trade, 137
Dienst, S., 102n7

difference, 3, 218, 222
   affinal, 77
   banishing, 126
   desire for, 16
   equistatutory and hierarchical, 224
   linguistic, 135
   loss of, 216
   meaningful, 148
   of perspectives, 171
   quota of, 209–10
   relations of, 220
   totemic, 221, 225
differentiation, 16, 27n20, 182, 209–14, 220–1, 223–5, 227
   undifferentiation, 215–8, 221–2, 225–6
disease, epidemics, 65, 73, 112, 115, 124, 213, 218
displacement, 233, 241–2, 245, 247–8, 251, 253n14
dogs, 46, 105n19, 184n8, 191, 216, 229n6
domestication, 12, 66–8, 70–1
double, 152n17, 187–93, 197, 199–200, 206n26
   identical, 216, 218
Dumont, L., 18, 44
Dutfield, G., 7

egalitarian societies, 16–8, 36–7
egalitarianism, 16, 36, 212
enemies, 20, 37–8, 40–5, 50, 55–6, 66, 72, 75, 78n5, 112, 122, 126, 253n14
   adoption of, 16
   as less than human, 38–9, 54
   as potential slaves, 38–40, 47, 55
   dreamt, 20–1
   enslavement of, 42
   equation with prey, 46–7
   transformation into potential father-in-law, 123
Engle, K., 7
ensoulment, 38, 44–5, 48
equivocation, 171, 234, 252n3
   equivocal compatibility, 17, 234
Erikson, P., 12, 28n25, 37, 44–5, 85–6, 102n7, 103n9
exchange, 21–2, 24, 27n18, 72, 75–6, 110–3, 134, 150n3, 151n7, 180, 182

against contract, 183
commercial, 116
commodity, 203
gift, 44
marriage, 52, 171, 221, 226
model, 157
of captives, 49–51, 55
of children and wives, 48, 79n10
of goods, 120, 124, 133, 136
of land, 241
of plants, 239–40
of people for things, 12
of pets, 88, 103n8, 104n18
of perspectives, 171
relationship of, 77
ritual, 137, 139
socialities of, 234
value, 68

familiarization, 11, 38, 46, 54, 56, 65–8, 121, 124, 201
Fausto, C., 9, 19, 23, 36, 38, 46, 67, 71, 73, 81, 85, 88, 92, 99, 102n7, 103n11, n13, 111, 116, 121, 123, 127n6, 143, 145, 148, 152n21, 190–1, 204n3, n6, 206n30, 211, 228n2, 234–5, 238, 250.
feeding, 1, 13–4, 40, 71, 82–95, 98–101, 102n6, 103n12, 104n5, 105n18, n22, 209, 235
Ferguson, B., 17
Ferguson, J., 18
Fisher, W., 209, 214–5, 219, 227, 228n1
Fleck, D., 102n7
food, ix, 45, 70, 82–7, 90, 92, 94–5, 97–8, 102n6, 104n17, 113–4, 121, 123, 126, 138, 142, 153n29, 210, 213, 236, 239
as a return for collective work, 150n2
cooked, 45, 134
exchange of, 79n10
giving, 14
humanizing, 67, 71
manufactured, 114
real, 51, 65
sharing, 51, 150n3, 186
soul-bodies of, 118
-spirit, 120, 128n12

foreigners, 40, 50, 54–5, 124, 127n6, 173, 214, 216
Foucault, M., 195–6
fractal/fractality, 10, 19
Franchetto, B., 21, 134, 141, 143, 148, 212
friend(ship), 12, 46–7, 64, 68, 78n2, 212, 214
formal, 12, 214
FUNAI, 2, 25n3, 77, 84, 114, 150n1, 159, 184n3, n4, 228, 248

Gallois, D., 247, 253n13
Galvão, E., 45, 247
gardens, 11, 23–4, 38, 42, 44–5, 49, 65, 67, 73–4, 78n6, 94, 96, 98, 101, 168, 186, 235, 239–40, 243, 245, 247, 249–50, 252–3n6, 253n8
Geisler, C., 5, 26n12
Geismar, H., 25n4
Gell, A., 89, 205n25
gender, 41, 51, 205n19
dynamics, 236
hierarchy, 105n22
relations, 102n3
studies, 13
Giacone, A., 40, 46, 48, 52
gift, 27n18, 51, 55, 124, 133, 182–3, 193, 201, 212
and commodity, 206n30
exchange, 44
free, 134
giving, 124, 133, 148, 212
logic, 203
of life, 42
regime, 193, 202
Girard, R., 215, 218, 221, 223, 229n7
glass beads, 135, 139, 162, 171–3
Global Coalition for Bio-Cultural Diversity, 7
Godelier, M., 9
Goldman, I., 43, 49, 52
goods, 3, 74, 110, 114, 121, 134, 138–40, 143–4, 151n3, 152n25, 195, 206n30, 210
alien, 160
ceremonial, 211, 214, 218–21, 223, 226–7, 250
circulation of, 120

European, 12
exchange of, 124, 133, 136
industrial, 49, 137, 141, 145, 224–5
intangible, 2, 196
logic of, 202
luxury, 135, 141–2
manufactured, 115, 126, 150n1
movable, 26n14
prestige, 49, 55
symbolic, 115, 223
totemic, 227
trade, 44
white people's, 113
Gordon, C., 13, 15, 93, 210, 214–5, 220, 223–5, 229n4, 229n5, 234, 250
Goulard, J.-P., 86
Gow, P., 1, 13–5, 23–4, 25n3, 51, 90–1, 97–8, 101n1, 121, 123, 127n2, 128n8, 129n21, 235, 247, 253n8
Gregor, T., 153n26
Grotti, V., 12–7, 38, 64, 98, 104n17, 105n22, 123, 127n2, 145, 204n4, 211, 213, 228n2, 235
Guerreiro, A., 97, 105n22, 152n21

Halbmayer, E., 56
Handbook of South American Indians, 8, 9, 232
Hann, C., 5, 8, 228n2, 189, 228n2
Harrison, S., 2, 25n4, 193, 202–3
Heckenberger, M., 2, 97, 148, 212, 235
heritage, 3, 7, 48, 180
    cultural, 6
    historical, 48
    intangible, 2, 22, 25n5
Hirsch, E., xiin1, 6, 25n4
Howard, C., 16, 64, 66, 71, 104n16
Hugh-Jones, C., 40, 44, 253n3
Hugh-Jones, S., 9, 11, 12, 27n18, 45, 102n6, 111, 148, 212, 253n3
human, ix, 15, 19, 20, 24, 67, 73, 81, 85, 91–5, 105n19, 125, 189, 191–2
    and nonhuman, 4, 5, 11, 15, 19, 21–2, 24, 212, 217, 220
    appropriation of, 17
    beings/persons, x, 7, 17, 126, 216
    condition, 26n8
    culture, 182

definition of, 90–2
fabrication of, 95
-form, 115–9, 121, 128n12, n16
less than, 38, 54, 56
-like, 188
modes of being, xi–ii
others, 17
owner, 86
ownership of, 39
perspective, 70
quasi-/semi-, 46, 63
real/true, 39, 51, 158
status, 4
humanity, 4, 40, 42, 46, 54, 75, 91
humanness, 38, 40
hunter-gatherers, 17, 63–5, 67, 73
hunting, 22, 40, 45–7, 65, 74, 78n6, 92, 96, 98, 187, 253n14

identity, 45, 51, 65–6, 76, 148, 170, 173, 182, 193, 201, 205n18, 218, 220
    and alterity, 16
    and kinship, 1, 15
    claims to, 2, 218
    marker, 112
    production of, 14
    protection of, 202
    self-, 16, 26n7, 76
    vector of, 99
identification, 209–10, 220, 240–1
incest, 16, 217
inequality, xi, 5, 17–8, 36–7

Jackson, J., 40, 44, 52
jaguar, 12, 46, 70, 99–100, 135, 161, 178, 182, 205n13, 222
    -becoming, 98, 101, 104n18, 105n23
    -songs, 20–1, 98

Kalapalo, 105n22, 150n4, n5, 151n8, 152n26
Kamayurá, 135, 156–7
Kanamari, 14, 81–105, 200, 204n4, 205n13, 249
Karadimas, D., 12, 27n23, 128n13
Kayapó, 15, 157–8, 209–10, 215–6, 228n1

Index

Kensinger, K., 92, 102n3
kinship, 1, 5, 13–4, 18–9, 78n6, 82, 92–3, 97–9, 105n22, 120, 123, 128n8, 189, 192, 194, 199, 227, 246
   as mutuality of being, 89
   commenslity and, 94, 99–101
   concepts, 10, 81
   conviviality of, 15, 210, 212
   dynamics, 248, 250
   fabrication of, 81
   fictive, 51, 115
   morality of, x
   network, 9, 75, 202
   and ownership, 103n14
   practices/processes, 71, 104n17, 203
   relations, 70, 121, 144, 216
   settlements, 241, 247
   slavery to, 39, 54
   system, 205n9, 206n28
   terms, 66, 68, 85, 104n15
Kĩsêdjê, 20–2, 140, 145, 156–60, 162–3, 166–75, 178–84, 202
knowledge, ix, 2, 45, 69, 128n8, 149, 183, 195–6, 202–3, 205n19, 206n29, 227, 249
   Christian, 67, 72–3
   musical, 139, 144–6, 153n36
   network of, 197
   payment for, 147
   practices, 157
   regimes of, 180, 193
   rights, 22, 181
   ritual, 98
   shamanic, 79n12, 187, 201
   source of, 198–200
   traditional, 7, 27n15, 153n32
   transmission of, 13, 73, 79n12, 143
   white people's, 67, 160
Koch-Grünberg, T., 43, 46, 48–9, 52
Kockelman, P., 103n12
Kopytoff, I., 39, 54–5
Korowai (West Papua), 92
Kuikuro, 134–41, 143–6, 149, 150n3, n5, n7, 151n14, 152n19, 153n28, 153n30, 153n36, 206n30

Lagrou, E., 11, 45, 103n13
Lima, D., 237
Lima, T., 14, 116, 128n10, 204n7
land, x, 2–5, 22–4, 26n7, 26n11, 45, 121, 186, 197, 238, 240–2, 254n15
   cultivated, 232, 239
   indigenous, 3, 114, 157
   knowing the, 82, 94, 96, 100
   no-man's, 187
   ownership of, 5, 233–4, 249, 251–2
   possession, 235, 245, 248
   privatization, 233–4, 241, 245, 248, 250–1, 253n7
   tenure, 237
law, 6, 20, 125–6
   ancient, 186
   international, 7, 22
   land, 238
   property, 4, 25n5
   Roman, 37
   rule of, 5
Lea, V., 11, 27n17, 209–11, 219–21, 223–4, 226, 229n8
Leach, J., 6, 25n4, 157, 182–3, 200, 202, 205n18, 205n22, 206n31
Lepri, I., 82
Lévi, P., 205n17
Lévi-Strauss, C., 25n1, 28n26, 70, 218, 220–2
Locke, J., ix, xi, 4–5, 9, 19, 26n7, 182
Lorrain, C., 102n3, 105n22
love, 14, 47, 56, 82, 86–7, 90–4, 100, 102n1
Lowie, R., 8–9, 10, 19, 22, 232–3, 253n13
Lowrey, K., 41

Machado, J., 240–1, 250
MacLeod, W.C., 41
MacPherson, C.B., 4, 25n6
Maine, H., 3, 8, 186
Marcoy, P., 50, 55
Makú, 18, 40, 42–3, 46, 48–9, 52, 79n7
Makuna, 40, 52
Malinowski, B., 9
manioc, 64, 67, 71–2, 101, 112, 168, 239
   beer, 65, 72
   bread, 65, 73
   drink, 79n11, 86
   flour, 235–6

porridge, 135, 150n6
processing, 74, 158, 182
market 5, 51, 74, 113–4, 137–8, 203
  anti-, 148
  -based consumerism, 111
  economy, 26n10, 26n14
  international, 234, 248
  place, 139
  society, 5
  super, 115, 173, 179
Maroons, 72
marriage, 69, 72, 78n6, 92, 142, 148, 152n24, 168, 171, 248
  payment/compensation, 9, 134, 141
  with captors, 39, 51–4, 67–8, 70–1, 74, 78n7
Marubo, 21, 187–206
Marxism, 9–10
master, 14, 75, 77, 81, 100, 116, 125, 127n6, 143–5, 189, 191, 202, 204n3, 206
  and chiefs, 48, 95–8, 190
  and hunting, 46
  and mistress, 45, 48–50
  and pet, 12, 15, 28n25, 85, 87
  and shamanism, 139, 197–8, 201
  and slaves/captives, 37–9, 42–3, 47, 49–53, 70, 125
  as adoptive fathers, 12
  as fictive grandparents, 54
  as owners, 20, 24, 48–9, 54, 67, 88, 93, 123, 186, 205n10
  of animals, 67, 187–8
mastery, 15, 18, 20, 28n25, 48
  relations, 1, 10, 14, 17, 21
  and ownership, 2, 11, 67, 71, 81, 93, 111
  property and, 38, 48
Mayoruna, 41
McCallum, C., 13–4, 44–5, 51, 97, 104n14, 121, 237–8, 253n13
Mebêngôkre-Xikrin, 13, 15–6, 209–11, 213–4, 226–8, 228n1, 228n2, 229n5, 229n6, 229n8
Mehinaku, 153n26, 253n11
Melanesia (New Guinea), x, 6, 10, 22, 25n4, 185n17, 186, 202
Menezes Bastos, R., 21

Menget, P., 56, 243–4
metal tools, 77, 135–6
Métraux, A., 54
Miller, J., 12, 19–20
mimesis, 205n22, 224, 227
mimetic, 223, 225
  crisis, 226
  disputes, 222, 224
  rivalry, 216, 218, 221, 227
  theory, 224
missionary, 17, 63–7, 69, 71–4, 76–7, 124, 133
mission, 113
  era, 114
  Unevangelized Fields Mission, 64
monetization, 150n3
money, 110, 115, 137–8, 140–1, 145, 149, 150n3, 152n22, 179–80, 206n30, 224–5
Montoya, R. de, 41, 47
Morgan, H., 8
multiplicity, x, 19, 100, 189, 192–4, 198, 203, 205n17
Munn, N., 144
Murphy, R., 44
music, 20–1, 143, 162, 169–70, 143, 153n35, 160, 162, 170
  forró, 128n12
myth, 70, 99–100, 102n7, 172, 182, 217, 221–2, 229n6
  and jaguar, 70
  feeding in, 82
  of primitive collectivism, 187
  of origin of Whites, 229
  -songs, 197–8
  of Sun and Moon, 216
mythic
  acquisition of culture, 182
  characters, 102n7, 226
  jaguar, 205n13
  narrative, 24, 79n10, 118, 124, 203, 206n28, 216n28, 229n8
  position of the boss, 128n16
  post-, 99, 116
  times, 197–8
  world, 99
mythology, 158, 191
  of twins, 218
mythopoiesis, 197–8

Index 265

names, 23, 45, 90
   and chiefs, 96, 103n11, 144–5
   as a form of address, 68
   as valuables, 11, 213, 218–23, 226, 229n8
   and ownership, 8, 45
   avoidance, 152n24, 168
   Christian, 115
   for pets, 85–6, 102n7
   foreign origin of, 21, 172, 182, 193, 221
   -givers, 214, 219
   of mythical characters, 102n7
   ritual, 166–8, 184n7, 211, 222
   sur, 114
   transmission, 166–8
nature, ix, xi–ii, 13, 220
   state of, 4
Needham, R., 13
Nimuendaju, C., 184n9, 226
North-West Amazonia, 9, 11, 24, 212
nurture, 74, 77, 210
   and interethnic contact, 105
   as control and appropriation, 15–6, 98
   care and, 17, 24
   and familiarization, 11, 38, 67
   maternal, 71, 73, 91
   of animals, 104n16
   of distant others, x
   of kin, ix
   metaphysical, 13
   ownership and, xi, 1, 3, 14, 209

objects, 12, 19, 22, 134, 151–2, 163, 171–2, 174, 177, 213, 229n4, 240, 243
   and value, 135–6, 142, 218, 224
   beautiful/desirable, 214, 221, 227
   cultural, 170
   ensouled, 45
   inanimate, ix, 115
   of payment, 150n6
   ownership of, 145, 175, 180
   persons as property, 56, 76
   -oriented regime, 148
   -rich and -poor, 9, 11
   ritual, 21, 24, 49
   subject/, xi–ii, 6, 11, 181–3, 251
   tangible and intangible, 2, 4
   trade, 77, 138–9, 225
objectification, 22, 88, 185n16, 220
ontology, 192–3, 205n13, 206n30
orphan, 45, 73, 124
Ortner, S., 2, 27n21, 88
otherness, 75–6
other, ix, 77, 84, 89, 93, 100, 115, 124, 127, 190, 195
   appropriation of human, 17
   as client, 113
   as different from us, 54
   avenged by, 122
   connection/relations to, xii, 76, 90, 92, 110
   control of, 126, 238
   distant, x, 70
   domesticate, 16
   enemy, 56
   enslavable, 75
   familiarized by, 123
   knowledge of, 201
   living with, 19
   slave of, 40
   making kin out of, 15, 56, 210
   making into kin, 56
   mastery over, 92
   orientation towards, 82
   words of, 196
Overing (Kaplan), J., 14–7, 19, 82, 97, 126
owner, 8–9, 11–2, 27n16, 54, 76, 115–6, 123, 150n2, 186–7, 219, 223
   absolute, 19, 51
   and chiefs, 48–9, 67, 193, 197, 200, 204n5
   and pet, 20, 85–8
   and source, 28n29
   and music, 145, 149
   as boss, 23, 125, 127n6, 127n7
   as a maker, 197
   author as, 195
   body-, 88–90, 92–3, 95–7, 99–100, 103–4, 205n13, 249
   -controller, 20–1
   double-, 199
   estate, 238, 242
   excess of, 193

house, 46, 142, 150n1, 190–1, 199–200
  of ceremonial properties, 211–3
  of place, 23, 153n30, 251
  of knowledge, 171, 181
  ritual, 150n6, 151n14, 153n29, 175
  rubber states, 113
  trade store, 115
  visible and invisible, 206
  without, 45
ownership, ix–xii, 1–16, 18–24, 26n9–11, 26n14, 27n16, 17, 18, 36, 38–9, 44–5, 48, 56, 64, 67, 71, 73, 75–7, 81–2, 88–93, 95, 99–100, 103n11, 104n14, n15, 111, 123, 145, 148–9, 209–11, 228n2
  self-, 18–9, 26n7

Parakanã, 9, 17–8, 20–1, 134
patrimony, 178
payments, 22, 134, 136, 139–48, 150, 152–3, 154n36, 168, 178–80, 184n14,
parasitism, 15, 111, 119–120, 124–7, 128n.13
peccaries, 23, 102n4, 103n13, 186–9, 216
personhood, x, 11–2, 21, 27n16, 39, 104n16, 240–1
perspectivism, 11, 115, 124, 127, 204n7, 226
  and perspective, 15, 21, 70, 73, 116, 122, 124, 171, 246
pet, 12, 14–6, 20, 23, 67, 70, 84–90, 92–5, 100–1, 102n4, n5, n6, 103n8, n9, n11, 104n17, 111, 122, 124, 127n3
  adopted, 120, 129n20
  artefacts as,
  auxiliary spirits as,
  captives as, 46–7, 75
  employee, 119, 125
  vocatives, 102n7
  wild pet, 12, 28n25, 71, 73, 148
pet-keeping, 14, 85, 87, 89, 92, 100, 104n16
Pina-Cabral, J., 17
pinta (*Treponema carateum*), 112

Piro (see Yine), 23, 90, 127n8
pito, pëito, poito, 68–71, 75–6
Posey, D., 7
possession, 3, 104n14, 145, 187, 195, 228n2
  as a mysterious quality, 197
  intangible, 24, 145
  of territory/land, 2, 26n11
power, xii, 27n16, 36, 89, 121, 183, 224
  aversion to, 2
  centralized, 10
  low thematization of, 16
  of the boss, 114, 125
  of words, 195
  over persons, xi, 37–8, 49, 50–1
  transformational, 122–3
predation, 10, 27n20, 56, 82, 222
  and capture, 38, 120, 129n20
  and commensality, 101
  as a relational structure, 15
  cynegetic, 93
  familiarizing, 18, 28n24, 67–71, 73, 76, 85, 92, 148
  generalized, 99–100
  ideologies of, 38
  idiom of, 14
  micro-, 125–6, 128n19
  ontological, 111, 125
  viewpoint of, 123
pretium doloris, 135
prey, 15, 73, 110, 116, 119, 122–3, 127n3, n4
  -client, 124–6
  enemies as, 45–7
  captives as, 45–7, 75
  familiarizable, 129n20
  position of, 15, 111
  women as,
Proudhon, P., 37, 232–3
project, 2, 16, 145–7, 149, 153n34, n35
property, ix, 2–8, 11, 22, 26n10, 27n19, 36–7, 39, 42, 51, 129n20, 175, 189, 193, 195–6, 202–3, 210, 213, 219, 221, 227, 228n2, 232, 248
  absence of, 3, 9
  absolute and coalescent, 48, 51, 54
  and political theory, 3–10
  as category, 6, 27n16

authorship and, 187
ceremonial, 210–1, 220, 223
corporeal vs. incorporeal, 9
common/communal, x, 236
cultural, 2, 8, 21, 24, 26n14
differentiating, 224
exclusive, 249
history of, 3
individual, 4, 5
in Amazonia, 8–13
in persons and things, xii
corporeal and incorporeal, 9
intangible, 8, 21, 24
intellectual property law/rights, 3, 7, 26n15, 194, 201
of land, 4, 5, 7, 22–24, 233, 251
movable, 12
private, x–xii, 3, 5, 6, 9, 26n10, 36, 187, 192, 200, 204n6, 206n30
property of the warriors/masters/captors, 47, 53, 55, 64, 76
rationality of, xi
real, 5
regimes, 5–6, 24, 210
rights, 6, 10, 23, 25n6, 26n7, 26n12, 48, 171, 180, 238
ritual, 218
totemic, 222
transformation of captives into, 44, 46, 56
Western (Euro-American) definition of, 38, 182
Proudhon, P.J., 36

Reesink, E., 83
Reichel-Dolmatoff, G., 40, 52
Renard-Casevitz, F-M., 148
resistance, 37, 76
revenge (vengeance), 42, 78n5, 99, 122–3, 215, 233–4
ritual, 20–1, 67, 118–9, 120, 122, 125, 128n9, 129n24, 139, 141, 145, 150n6, 153n29, 153n36, 163, 219, 222–5
cannibalistic, 42
crisis, 209, 211
intertribal, 135, 137, 141, 144
Jaguar-becoming, 98, 100–1, 104n18, 105n23

objects, 24
of enslavement, 45, 55
of excess, 13
positions/roles, 152n23, 166, 213
production, 17
prerrogatives, 8, 210–1
property, 218
puberty, 122
time, 27n21
trophy, 44
Rival, L., 15, 92, 102, 127n4
Rivière, P., 10–1, 19, 25n1, 44–5, 68–70, 79n10, 97, 248, 253n13, 253n14
Rodgers, D., 103n13
rubber, 113–4
boom, 2, 110, 204
economy, 111
trees, 99, 238

Sahlins, M., 81, 89
salt, 135–6, 148, 150n5, 150n7, 187
sameness, 16, 75–6
Santos-Granero, F., 12, 17–8, 70, 75, 91–2, 98, 100, 104n17, 105n18, 127n2, 128n9, 129n20, 148, 240
seclusion, 182
killers', 178
post-menarche, 141, 158, 184n7
Seeger, A., 20, 27n15, 92, 157–8, 167, 174, 184n8, 184n11
Serres, M., 110, 125–6
servant, 40, 42, 46, 50, 55, 69, 74, 76, 79n7
groups, 37, 41–4, 47–9, 52, 66–8, 70
Setebo, 41
Silverwood-Cope, P., 40, 52, 79n7
shaman, 115–6, 118, 120–4, 134, 139–40, 143, 145, 151n15, 151n17, 152n18, 152n20, 152n22, 153n27, 175, 188–90, 192, 196–8, 204n2, 205n12
anaconda-, 194, 199
and apprentice, 84
and auxiliary spirits, 12, 84, 92, 129n23, 153n31
and chief, 186, 195, 199, 204n5
and gender, 205n19

initiation, 152n20
  -paediatricians, 141
  praying, 200, 202
  and warriors, 71
shame, 142, 152n26, 153n28, 210, 216–8
shell belts and necklaces, 135–7, 141–3, 150n5, 151n9
Shipibo, 41, 186
slave, 41, 54–6, 69, 125
  and affinity/marriage, 68, 70, 79
  as domestic animal/pet, 46–7
  captive, 36–7, 39, 42–3, 46–55
  domestic, 43
  holding societies, 38, 55–6
  markets, 51, 55
  (master and) dialectic, 28n25
  natural, 4, 72
  raids, 42, 47, 49–50
  potential, 38, 40, 47, 55
  trade, 17, 49–51, 55
slavery, xiin2, 38–9, 42, 47, 54, 75–6
  and husbandry, 28n25
  and kinship, 39, 54, 68
  as process, 39, 46–7, 54–6
  conquest and, 17, 26n8
  indigenous forms of, 37–8, 46, 56, 70
  time of, 2
  Western, 18, 38
songs, 112, 128n11, 144–9, 153n29, 153n36, 158, 169
  and authorship, 194–6
  and ownership, 8, 139, 146–7
  as culture, 172
  design and, 167, 171, 201–2
  joking, 153n32
  master/owner of, 145, 149
  myth-, 197
  ritual, 98, 100, 104n18, 143, 162
  rights over, 181
  sacred, 44, 144, 147
  shamanic, 122–3, 190, 192–6, 198
  source of, 20–1, 174, 182, 199
soul, 26n8, 45, 48, 103n13, 139, 148, 151n17, 169–70, 188
  -body, 117–8, 120–1, 128n10
  -doll, 151n15

spirit, 21, 121, 140, 144, 151n14, 197–8
  and double, 189–90, 192–3
  and ownership, xii
  attacks, 72, 78n5, 151n15, 151n17
  auxiliary/familiar, 12, 44–5, 84, 92, 129n23, 139, 152n20, 153n31, 201
  Christian, 28n27
  food-, 120, 128n12
  human, 20
  masters, 67, 188
  -soul, 103n13
  speech of, 196
standard(ization) of value/measure, 134, 137–9, 143–4, 147–9, 153n35
Stasch, R., 92
state, xi, 5–7, 10, 18, 26n11, 26n12, 27n19, 36–7, 180–1, 203, 206n31, 248
  of nature, 4
  real, 8, 22
Sterpin, A., 103n13
Stradelli, E., 49, 52
Strathern, M., xii, 6, 13, 25n4, 88–9, 94, 103n12, 103n14, 183, 185n16, 185n17, 200–2, 205n25, 206n30
stratification, 37–8
Sztutman, R., 81, 93, 183
subject, 22, 76, 125
  alien, 85
  and object, ix, xi–ii, 6, 11–2, 181–3, 251
  as prey, 111, 122
  composite, 19
  conversion of objetct into, 148
  individual creative, 193
  position, 116
  of a boss, 120
  of property/ownership, 56, 252
  responsibility of, 250
  subjected, 15
subjection, 17–8, 47, 72, 111, 116, 120, 124–5
subordination, 38, 56, 69–70

tapir, 23, 102n4, 119, 125, 186, 188, 204n9

Index

Taylor, A-C., 14, 23, 25n3, 43, 56, 85, 92, 123, 126, 127n2, 129n20, 129n22, 246
territory, 2, 22–3, 26n9, 145, 157, 159, 187, 213, 226, 235, 248, 251–2, 254n15
things, 136, 146, 151n9, 151n15, 202, 213
   as property, 3, 189, 200–1
      attachment to, 151n13
      conversion of relation into, 148
      exchange of, 134
      extraordinary, 44
      obedient, 12
      people and, xi–ii, 1, 6, 8–13, 22, 142, 171, 182–3, 185n16
      persons behind, 206n30
tick, 119–20, 125
trade, 12, 77, 112–5, 127n.7
   international, 26n14
   intravillage, 137–8
   river, 112–5, 127n7
   slave, 17, 50–1, 55
   trading networks, 12, 26n14, 49, 51, 137–8
   war and trade, 64–5, 68–9
trading partner, 12, 64, 72, 74, 78n2
   whites as, 170–1, 173, 180, 183
traditional resource rights (TRR), 7
tributary populations, 37, 41, 70
Trio, 17, 28n29, 63–79, 98, 104n17, 145, 204n4, 211, 213, 234, 247–8
trophies, 42–4, 56, 148
Tukano, 37, 40, 42–3, 46, 48–50, 52, 54–5, 148
Tully, J., 4, 26n7
Tupi-Guarani, 41, 47, 53, 104n16, 127
Tupinambá, 76, 232–53
Turner, T., 11, 19, 209–11, 214–6, 218, 223, 227, 229n6

Ulturgasheva, O., 104n6
Uni (Cashibo), 41, 47
Upper Xingu, 9, 21, 27n17, 105n22, 133, 135, 144, 148, 152n26, 158, 173–4, 212

Valeri, V., 105n19

Van Velthem, L., 11
Vander Velden, F., 85, 104n16
Verswijver, G., 209, 211, 214–5, 227, 229n5
Viegas, S., 4, 10, 23–4, 26n9, 45, 234–8, 241, 248, 253n7, 253n10, 254n15
Vilaça, A., 1, 13, 14, 16, 28n27, 76, 81, 91, 122, 129n20, 210
Viveiros de Castro, E., 11, 13–4, 19, 25n2, 76, 99, 116, 122–3, 125, 127, 128n18, 129n22, 171, 183, 184n12, 188–90, 196, 200, 203, 204n3, 204n7, 205n17, 211, 233–4, 252, 253n13
Von Benda-Beckmann and Wiber, 5, 26n10, 27n19, 228n2

Waiwai, 64, 71–2, 78n4, 79n11, 79n12, 104n16
Walker, H., 15, 27n22, 92, 127n5
war(fare), 17, 37, 41, 44, 47–8, 50, 52, 65, 72, 75, 78n5, 112, 123, 214, 234
   and trade, 65, 68
   external/internal, 215, 227, 229n5
   shamanism and, 18, 182
Wauja, 9, 135–6, 153n26, 174
Wayana, 63–6, 68–9, 72, 75, 78n1, 79n10, 79n11, 211, 213
wealth, 11–2, 27n16, 218, 220, 225–6
   bride-, 142
   ceremonial, 210
well-being, 15–6, 18, 26n11, 38, 73, 82, 86, 91, 209–14, 216–7, 221–2, 225–6, 228, 254n15
Welper, E., 204n2, 206n27
Whitehead, N., 17, 25n2, 26n8, 68–9
whites (non-indians), 112–5, 117, 124, 127n6, 128n9, 137, 141, 160, 168, 171–4, 184n13, 200, 224, 228
   as enemies, 110, 123, 216
   as trade partners, 49, 55, 87, 134, 170
   as source of wealth, 227
   becoming, 77, 225
   cities of, 189–90
   knowledge, 67, 206n30
   myths of the origin of, 229n6

Wilbert, J., 44, 221, 229n6
wildness, 42, 72–5

Xinguano, 133, 137, 141, 148, 150n3, 152n22, 156–8, 160, 162, 173–4, 181–2, 184n7, 184n13

Yine (Piro), 23, 41, 51, 90, 127n8, 247, 253n8

Zo'é, 77

www.ingramcontent.com/pod-product-compliance
Lightning Source LLC
Chambersburg PA
CBHW070914030426
42336CB00014BA/2405